Romancing the Gullah

SERIES EDITOR

Riché Richardson, Cornell University

FOUNDING EDITOR

Jon Smith, Simon Fraser University

ADVISORY BOARD

Houston A. Baker Jr., Vanderbilt University

Leigh Anne Duck, The University of Mississippi

Jennifer Greeson, The University of Virginia

Trudier Harris, The University of Alabama

John T. Matthews, Boston University

Tara McPherson, The University of Southern California

Claudia Milian, Duke University

Romancing the Gullah in the Age of *Porgy and Bess*

Kendra Y. Hamilton

The University of
Georgia Press
ATHENS

© 2024 by the University of Georgia Press
Athens, Georgia 30602
www.ugapress.org
All rights reserved
Set in 10/13 Warnock Pro Regular by Kaelin Chappell Broaddus

Most University of Georgia Press titles are
available from popular e-book vendors.

Printed digitally

Library of Congress Cataloging-in-Publication Data

Names: Hamilton, Kendra Y., author.
Title: Romancing the Gullah in the age of Porgy and Bess /
    Kendra Y. Hamilton.
Identifiers: LCCN 2023053864 (print) | LCCN 2023053865 (ebook)
    | ISBN 9780820362892 (hardback) | ISBN 9780820362885
    (paperback) | ISBN 9780820362908 (epub) | ISBN
    9780820363615 (pdf)
Subjects: LCSH: Gullahs—History. | Gullahs—Social life and
    customs. | Gullahs—Influence. | American literature—
    Southern States—History and criticism. | American
    literature—Southern States—20th century. | African
    Americans—Social life and customs. | Language and
    culture—Southern States.
Classification: LCC E185 .H27 2024 (print) | LCC E185 (ebook) |
    DDC 973.0496073—dc23/eng/20240122
LC record available at https://lccn.loc.gov/2023053864
LC ebook record available at https://lccn.loc.gov/2023053865

To Anna Hall Hamilton

CONTENTS

ACKNOWLEDGMENTS ix

FOREWORD Of Myth, Memory, and Romancing the Gullah xiii

Part I. Contexts The Carolina Lowcountry, Reconceived

CHAPTER ONE Mother Tongues and the King's English:
Language and the Gullah Geechee Coast 3

CHAPTER TWO Toward a Triangular Topos:
Landscape and Lineage on the
Gullah Geechee Coast 18

Part II. Texts Cartographies of Struggle and the Canon

CHAPTER THREE Pastoral Scenes of the Gallant South:
"Beautiful, Historic" Charleston 39

CHAPTER FOUR "I Can Peep through Muddy Waters":
Seeking the Black Authentic in Georgia 63

CHAPTER FIVE What Miss Ann Saw:
The Imperial Eyes of Charleston
Renaissance Painting 87

CHAPTER SIX All God's Chillen Got Traveling Shoes:
Modern Subjects, Florida Roots,
Diasporic Routes 108

CHAPTER SEVEN Plenty o' Nothin:
Spectacular Blackness and
Global Miscegenation in *Porgy and Bess* 137

AFTERWORD South of Tomorrow 179

NOTES 185

WORKS CITED 207

INDEX 229

ACKNOWLEDGMENTS

This project began with a gift—a first edition of *Porgy*. That gift turned into another: the opportunity to talk to my father, my grandmother, and friends affiliated with the Jenkins Orphanage Band about the city of my birth, to see myself and my neighborhood, and my Geechee identity, with new eyes. Many thanks are due for the many gifts that have continued to shower on me since that first Christmas during my first year in graduate school.

In the city of Charleston, thanks are owed to my family as well as a group of passionate local historians: in particular, a debt is owed to the late Sarah Dowling, the late Virginia Mixson Geraty, Alphonso Brown, and Alada Shinault for their insights on Gullah culture and to Walter Boags, Harlan Greene, the late and much loved Ted Ashton Phillips and his wife, Janet Hopkins, for their knowledge of Charleston and Charleston Renaissance lore. All were generous with time and research materials and shared permissions for the use of photos and rare manuscript materials before I even asked. U.S. Park Service ranger Michael Allen, who led the research team that produced the "Low Country Special Resource Survey and Environmental Impact Statement" for the National Park Service, shared the process and described the role his team played both in the National Trust nomination and in the legislative feat of creating the four-state Gullah Geechee Cultural Heritage Corridor. Thanks are also due to Dr. Carlie Towne and Halim Gullahbemi of the Gullah Geechee People Nation, who provided critical insights during the "All-Star Gullah Geechee Reunion Tour" that I co-curated under the auspices of the Spoleto Festival U.S.A. as well as to our partners and hosts during that tour. These included, in Charleston, the men and women of the East Cooper sweetgrass basket communities, especially the Phillips community's Rev. Harry Palmer, Elijah Smalls, and Richard Habersham as well as the sweetgrass basket historian, Joyce Coakley of Six Mile. In Georgia, Wilson and Ernestine Moran of Harris Neck, Ga., shared a Mende song handed down in their family since enslavement, and Dr. Carolyn Dowse made possible our visit to Sapelo Island. In Florida, then-Spelman College president Johnetta B. Cole provided the contacts that led us to the American Beach, Fla., preservation project launched by her sister, MaVynee O. Betsch, and to Carolyn Alexander of Jacksonville's Ritz Theater / LaVilla Museum and N. Y. Nathiri of the Association to Preserve the Eatonville Community / Zora! Festival.

Research for this volume was undertaken with funding from the Woodrow Wilson National Fellowship Foundation and with key logistical and funding support from the Evoking History Artist's Collective/Places with a Future Artists Collaborative, sponsored by the Spoleto Festival U.S.A.'s visual art program under the leadership of the visionary curator Mary Jane Jacob of the Art Institute of Chicago. Contacts, conversations, and research leads gained through my work with Spoleto from 2001 to 2008 were critical in giving me the tools to deepen my inquiries and broaden my project's scope, and I am especially grateful for the opportunity to discuss the clash between colonial land use and contemporary zoning practice with designer Walter Hood of the University of California, Berkeley; the role of grasses and especially rice in human evolution and Atlantic World history with ethnobotanist John Rashford of the College of Charleston; monumental architecture and race with Rob Miller of the Clemson University Architecture Center; and the shifting landscape of fill and marsh that has created the built environment of the coast with preservationist and landscape architect Jim Ward. Both practical and personal support were offered at key moments, in addition, by Jack Bass and Nathalie Dupree, Robert and Holly Behre, Hope Derrick, Lis Gambino, and M. Eliza Hamilton Abegunde—not to mention the organizational and community leaders, Nigel Redden, artistic director of Spoleto, Charleston mayor Joe Riley, and Rep. James E. Clyburn III (D-S.C.). But the person whose impact on my project cannot be overstated is the conceptual artist and photographer Ernesto Pujol, for his ability to see with his heart and speak truth to power with passion and eloquence, for his facility in crafting metaphors that became central to the work of the team, and for his generosity in sharing his extraordinary photographs of Charleston's "mortuary landscape."

In Virginia, art historian Maurie McInnis, literary critics Charles Rowell, Anna Brickhouse, and Jennifer Greeson, and ecologist Manuel Lerdau brought key insights from their fields, while Clare Kinney helped me keep alive the flame of my first true love: the English Renaissance. More important are the three men without whose help this project never would have been realized. The first is the late Charles Perdue, whose commonsense advice and whose folklore archive were always a refuge and a rich resource. The second was Alan Howard, my first advisor, who helped me to navigate a particularly difficult passage and who helped keep hope alive. And finally, there was Eric Lott, who took me on after Alan's retirement. He gave me lots of rope, was swift to redirect my footsteps whenever I hit a brick wall, and always, always came through with a rescue mission, practical support, or a reason to celebrate when I needed them. Additionally, Susan V. Donaldson's editorial insights were key to shaping the version of chapter 1 that appeared in *Mississippi Quarterly*'s special issue on Roots and Routes (vol. 65.1, Winter 2012).

I should not neglect to note the critical support received at various periods from several foundations and institutions, including the Huntington Library under the aegis of a Mellon Foundation seminar grant and the Rockefeller Foundation's research and conference center in Bellagio, Italy. I also enjoyed fruitful research stints courtesy of Virginia's Skinner Foundation and the University of South Carolina's Institute for Southern Studies. Thanks also to the librarians and research staff at the Getty Institute in Los Angeles, Kentucky's Berea College, Tulane University's libraries, as well as the South Carolina Historical Society and the Charleston County Library's South Carolina room.

Helping me to hold all the threads together were my friends—in Charlottesville and out of it, in academia and everywhere else. You were always interested, curious—and helpful in the most unexpected ways. Thanks from the bottom of my heart to Anjana Mebane-Cruz, Drake Patten, Toni Barskile, Kevin Barnard, Colette Dabney, Leni Sorensen, and Marcia Pentz. I also want to remember friends of my heart, no longer with us, who started out on this path with me—Ayla Turki, Reetika Vazirani, and Clive Papayanis: you are missed; memories of you are sweet to me.

Finally, I'd like to acknowledge the people who kept the home fires burning during this long and complicated birth. First, my parents, Lonnie and Clarissa Hamilton, from whom I inherited this passion to know and to understand. And last but certainly not least, my husband, Marc McVicker. Without what you do, I could never do what I do. Thank you for your sacrifices and your love.

FOREWORD

Of Myth, Memory, and Romancing the Gullah

Interstate 26 from Columbia to Charleston, South Carolina, traverses a flat, semitropical swath of terrain studded with live oaks and pines, where slow rivers meander and deep forests, wetlands, and salt marshes teem with wildlife. This is the Carolina Low Country—usually written "lowcountry"—a geographical formation that stretches roughly from Cape Fear, North Carolina, to the mouth of the John River outside Jacksonville, Florida. This low demesne of swamps and pine barrens with few large towns and many wild open spaces has since 2006 had a second name. In the culmination of a process involving scholars, artists, activists, and a multiyear bipartisan political effort, the region was given the preservation designation of Gullah Geechee Cultural Heritage Corridor, a mouthful of a moniker that also plainly states the region's most salient and, until quite recently, least recognized characteristic: as the physical and spiritual home of Gullah Geechee heritage and culture. Indeed, the lowcountry is one of only a handful places in North America of which it can be truthfully said that this was where African American identity was born.[1]

I-26 leaving Columbia is one of the northern gateways to this corridor—I-95 being the other—and this roughly hundred-mile stretch connects sprawling suburbs, tiny towns, massive "dirty" industrial sites, and the odd multimillion-dollar resort development in a headlong march toward the sea. Before 2015, it was possible to drive the route thinking of nothing more momentous than the subtle beauty of the pine barrens. Then came June 17, the day of the slaughter of innocents at Charleston's Emanuel African Methodist Episcopal Church, and forever and for all time students of American history will have occasion to reflect on the spectral presence haunting this road: that of Dylann Storm Roof's rickety black Hyundai, prowling interstates and back roads, bolstering his resolve as he hunted his chosen prey, the Black flesh he deemed suitable to sacrifice to his angry white god.

Most are familiar with the bare facts of the Emanuel AME tragedy, but they do bear repeating: On a sultry night in June 2015, a young Caucasian man with a bowl haircut and the ill-fitting clothes of the down-and-out walked into an African American church in Charleston's historic district, joined the Wednesday evening Bible study for nearly an hour of fellowship, then opened fire. Killed in the spray from a Glock purchased with birthday money from his father were the Reverend Clementa Pinckney and eight members of the flock: Cynthia Hurd, Sharonda Coleman-Singleton, Tywanza Sanders, Ethel Lance, Susie Jackson, DePayne Middleton Doctor, Daniel Simmons, and Myra Thompson.

Just as shocking as the violence was the justification for his action. Roof, a waif discarded by his family, sleeping mostly in his car or at times on a friendly couch, claimed he sought to ignite a race war. "Somebody had to do something," he told the FBI after his capture, "because, you know, black people are killing white people every day on the street, and they're raping white women."[2] Through an act of symbolic vengeance against people he didn't know, innocents who'd never harmed him, Roof proclaimed what Rachel Kaadzi Ghansah was to call "his proper lineage": "the long line of white men who thought the letting loose of black blood, the finding and maiming of random black lives, could somehow reprieve and rescue a white woman's honor while securing a white man's position." Many have been eager to dismiss Roof as a madman, his murders as acts of random, chaotic violence. But we would do better to consider him a man on a mission and to consider further the nature of that mission, for it is the reverse image of our own in this book. Dylan Roof rained death and murder in Charleston on June 17, 2015. But before that came a very personal—twisted, obsessive—quest. A quest for the Gullah.

What transpired in the immediate wake of the killings has obscured this particular reading of the evidence. Recalling to memory the chaos that reigned in those days suggests why. The state's political leaders, jostling and elbowing in their haste to denounce the murderer—"pure evil . . . pure hate," said then-governor Nikki Haley; "sick and twisted" said U.S. senator Lindsey Graham[3]—had a singular determination to declare the killer an outlaw, his act incomprehensible, and the white community, by extension, innocent. Haley's call a mere seven days later to "remove the flag from our capitol grounds" testified to the exigency, and the furious cries of "keep it flying" that countered her shifted the battleground even as it moved the focus from the killer.[4] Beside a series of spectacular images unfolding in the immediate aftermath of the crime—the astounding grace extended by the families of the slain at Roof's arraignment, President Obama's eulogy and rendition of "Amazing Grace" at the first of the funerals, the Sunday spectacle of grieving, chanting, defiant throngs stretching in a human chain across the two-and-a-half-mile length of the Arthur Ravenel Bridge over the Cooper River—Roof's crime shrunk to the status of mere backdrop for a dramatic narrative of racial reconciliation.

Viewing the electric display of chanting, hugging, hand-holding defiance at the bridge, Casey Huff, twenty-two, of Charleston, told a *Washington Post* reporter, "To be honest, it's surprising how many more white people are here. But it's amazing. Because people say Charleston is so racist and I don't see that at all."[5] One should not discount the power of Miss Huff's narrative. The men and women who fought "the battle of the Confederate flag" on the streets of Charleston and in the ornate, marbled halls of the Statehouse in Columbia remember their part in those stirring events in 2015 with a pride that is well deserved. Not in a hundred fifty years had the myth of the Lost Cause met so forceful a defeat at the hands of the real: a multicultural, multiethnic state population refusing to accommodate itself to ideals both outmoded and destructive to their existence. Even more astonishing to residents of the "Holy City" was the sequel five years later: the decision by a unanimous Charleston City Council to remove the statue of John C. Calhoun from a place of honor it had occupied—less than two blocks from the location of the massacre, we should note—since 1896.

But this story of progress and change is only part of what transpired: We must also acknowledge Roof's victory. For on the day the Confederate flag vanished into the state archives, smaller versions of it popped up on homes and businesses, hat brims, and truck tailgates all across the state. Indeed, the cycle of scapegoating and violent retribution reanimated at Emanuel AME on that terrible June night has continued to claim victims—at Charlottesville, Québec City, Christchurch, El Paso, and many more—and shows no sign of slackening in its pace. Here we return to the idea of the quest. A man charges forth, seeking to know and understand the people he's decided to claim as his enemies, if only to better target them. To put matters in the simplest terms, *Dylann Roof went in search of Black people*. Systematically, the killer researched historic sites, punctiliously, he visited them, and in a series of sixty self-portraits posted on his provocatively styled website, lastrhodesian-dot-com, he documented his compulsion.

Roof went to Sullivan's Island, the sleepy beach community where, over a period of centuries, enslaved Africans were brought for "seasoning" before being sold on the mainland—brought in such numbers that Sullivan's could be considered the South's Ellis Island, if Ellis were also a place where immigrants were beaten and raped and allowed to expire of starvation and disease. Roof looked at the historic marker there, strolled to the beach and wrote "1488" in the sand—the first two numbers referring to David Lane's "fourteen words" ("We must secure the existence of our people and a future for white children"); the second signifying "heil Hitler" ("H" being the eighth letter of the alphabet). The self-portrait he snapped there shows Roof squatting on his heels as the sun set over his shoulder and the water lapped at his shoes.

Roof went to Boone Hall Plantation, which has a serpentine wall like the one at Thomas Jefferson's Academical Village and a "big house" that's a fair-to-middling imitation of "Tara" (though not original—built in 1936 by a Canadian enamored of the *Gone with the Wind* lifestyle). Boone's oak allée is impressive, its slave cabins original (and brick, a testimony to erstwhile wealth). But like the house, it's an ersatz kind of place, a jumble of everything—butterfly garden, a creek-side wedding venue, a "Geechee Theatre"—that could possibly make a buck in the fiercely competitive market for historic tourism dollars in Charleston.

Our quest knight went to Magnolia and McLeod plantations as well, sites where the historic mission and commerce are in better balance. At Magnolia, named for its magnificent gardens, enslaved gardeners and their descendants are given coequal credit for creating and maintaining the attractions of the site; meanwhile, at McLeod, the owners themselves are an afterthought, while the lives of the workers, enslaved and free, take center stage. Roof snapped photographs here, too, but not satisfied, the restless quest continued.

This is the image of Roof that haunts me: traveling so frequently and so obsessively to African American *lieux des memoires* during the planning of his atrocity that one observer likened a map of his GPS movements, tracked by the FBI, to "a cat's cradle strung out by evil."[6] This meandering progress back and forth from Columbia to Charleston would continue for more than six months as, methodically, he began to zero in on his target: churches, selected for their vulnerability and the low odds of meeting armed resistance. Roof drew up a handwritten list of historic African American churches in Charleston—including my family's, a historic Episcopal church founded in 1847.[7] Roof seems to have zeroed in on Emanuel for its size, its historical connections (to the Black revolutionary, Denmark Vesey, and his failed 1822 rebellion), and its pastor's political activism (Sen. Pinckney figured in the headlines as a fierce advocate of body cameras in the wake of the unprovoked slaying of Walter Scott by a North Charleston police officer earlier in 2015). After making his choice, Roof visited the site no fewer than eight times in the period leading up to the murders.[8]

And one has to marvel—marvel at the time, the attention, the single-minded focus given to a quest that was so misguided. Dylann Roof went looking for Black people and found them: real African Americans and a reality-based community of sites and institutions presenting the Gullah Geechee past, everywhere he went. But Roof ultimately saw only what the preexisting narrative he had digested before and during his period of radicalization allowed him to see: "Somebody had to do something, because, you know, Black people are killing white people every day on the street, and they're raping white women."

Such is the power of the Lost Cause narrative, which political and cultural leaders from the lowcountry, past and present, have done so much to propagate.[9] While contested, discredited, and abandoned by large swaths of even the southern white population, this narrative was powerful enough to give an alienated young man sanction to seek vengeance for his diminished social power through the sacrifice of scapegoats. Similarly, it gave the gossip and rumor mills percolating after the crime a readily available framework to explain and contain the shame of Roof's act. Rather than beginning with the obvious—that Roof had trained himself in hate, immersed himself in the works and the virtual world of white supremacists online while he screwed his courage to the sticking place of violent direct action—apologists offered a set of lurid counter-conjectures:[10] that his heart had been broken by a school crush who *picked a n— over him*; that *some woman in that boy's family* had been raped, or even gang-raped, by a *n—* or *n—s*.

Ugly talk, uglier thoughts, aimed, quixotically enough, at absolving Roof of his self-proclaimed racism—it wasn't that "the boy" had hate in his heart; he had been *wronged*—while also placing him in a recognizable framework of violated honor and redemptive revenge more reminiscent of 1915 than 2015. Invoking the concept of "proper lineage," Ghansah places Roof in the framework of justified/justifiable violence by which the "hegemonic masculinity" he embraced—a masculinity that "affirm[ed] the hierarchy of men over women . . . assert[ed] the dominance of white masculinity . . . over . . . racial and sexual minorities"—could be made manifest.[11]

Five years after his crimes, Roof's empty-eyed countenance haunts American memory even as he continues to inspire assassins in what appears to be morphing into a globalized war of the disconnected and disaffected heirs of a fallen master class, grieving the loss of their dominion. Similarly, he dogs our footsteps here, for Roof—however "sick" and "twisted" he may have been—was not aberrant. He is indeed emblematic of the white South's insistence on maintaining what in the psychiatric literature is called the "false memory" of slavery. Allowing his violent act of narratorial zeugma, yoking a rich and complicated history, culture, and identity to a self-justifying and prefabricated narrative of white supremacy, to go unanswered, in effect, allows the underlying ideology to "flourish unchecked."[12]

But if Roof's quest shows us the destructive power of hegemonic narratives—the central, if often invisible, role they play in upholding structures of racial, political, and cultural dominance—*Romancing the Gullah* is, by contrast, inspired by the paradigm shift that has occurred over the past half century in documenting the history and memory of African America. An inquiry into the deep structures of African American origins/identity and the art that differing cultural understandings of those matters inspired, *Romancing the Gullah* seeks to reveal the tangled relationships between *darkness* in the Morrisonian sense, as it relates to American literary production, and the nation's secret heart of darkness that stands as a sort of Foucauldian *heterotopia*,[13] a space of subversion and contrast to the utopic Lost Cause impositions white supremacy places upon the American memory of race.

Thus, three concerns shape this inquiry, constituting effectively a *triangular topos* of exploration, with language, landscape, and lineage composing the legs of the triangle. Language matters because Gullah Geechee culture and identity are inextricable from the form of the English language that evolved in the lowcountry—a language form stigmatized as "ignorant baby talk," but that is neither abnormal nor unique in the New World and that furthermore evinces the U.S. South's connections via the Anglophone Caribbean to a global history of imperial settlement. We concern ourselves with landscape—the geography at the intersection of Space and Place—in order to make visible the social lives that have so often been rendered invisible or characterized as "vanishing" by neoclassical accumulations of marble, brick, and bronze and narratives that highlight the so-called southern "sense of place." Finally, we focus on the creole lineages and interconnections between the populations of this region in order to engage and complicate post-Reconstruction myths of southern identity that emphasize racial separation and, especially, racial "purity." This triangular analytical topos, established in part I, "Contexts," allows us to illuminate the cracks and fissures in the origin stories of the lowcountry's historic political elites, pointing up, contextualizing, and eventually refuting a set of tropes that has historically highlighted the African American presence in order, effectively, to erase it.

But the story of the Gullah Geechee is a lengthy one, stretching back to the arrival of the first ships from Barbados landing on the West Bank of the Etiwan (now Ashley) River in 1670, and evolving and dynamically changing up through the transformation of the colonial landscape by rice culture up to the present moment. Thus, in part II of *Romancing the Gullah*, which adds *textual* analysis to our discussion of contexts, we impose one final organizational framework upon the narrative: that of time. Specifically, the volume focuses on the period from roughly 1919 to 1940, as the "nadir" of African American life gives way to the Jazz Age, the Great Depression, and the great European war. This period treats Harlem Renaissance writers and artists such as W. E. B. Du Bois, Jean Toomer, Zora Neale Hurston, and Edwin Augustus Harleston, whose explorations of the forms and meaning of African American cultural expression drew them inexorably to the "authentically" African life ways of the Gullah Geechee Coast. But *Romancing the Gullah* goes beyond this, placing this familiar grouping, for the first time, in conversation with artists from the so-called Charleston Renaissance: men and women like

DuBose Heyward, Herbert Ravenel Sass, Alice Ravenel Huger Smith, and Elizabeth O'Neill Verner, among others, who saw with alarm their hitherto exclusive claim "to know"—and speak for—"the Negro" challenged by African American artists quite capable of speaking for and representing themselves.

This productive tension—between Black artists and white; between forms of primitivism that seek to liberate or, ultimately, oppress; between Black speech, music, and expressive arts as innovation or savagery; between Black lives as dynamically growing and changing or as "leftovers of history," in August Wilson's memorable phrase,[14] who soon would die out and vanish utterly from the earth—is what makes *Romancing the Gullah* such an important and necessary addition to the literary and cultural history of the lowcountry and, by extension, to the American studies classroom, for it is only in revealing such connections that we will be able to understand, rather than just romance, the Gullah and fully account for them in our understanding of America.

It would, of course, be the height of naïveté to imagine that this project has a snowball's chance in Savannah of removing Scarlett O'Hara from her throne. But through this volume I hope to demonstrate that the lowcountry offers the literary critic a set of texts and countertexts, narratives and counternarratives, that greatly enrich our understanding as scholars and teachers of the world through which our students move and the paradigms they may one day crack. An exciting path forward through the literature and history of the South more broadly is being offered by a group of African American, American, and southern studies scholars in cross-disciplinary work that is deeply informed by postcolonial studies, especially of the Caribbean, transatlantic studies, especially of the Black Atlantic, and by new work on globalization. These scholars are exploring new transnational narratives and paradigms that offer provocative directions for reconceptualizing and revitalizing African American and southern studies. I hope to enter this conversation and enrich it with this study of the land, the people, and the literature of the lowcountry.

Romancing the Gullah

PART I

Contexts

THE CAROLINA LOWCOUNTRY,
RECONCEIVED

CHAPTER 1

Mother Tongues and the King's English
Language and the Gullah Geechee Coast

> Every colonized people . . .—every people in whose soul an inferiority complex has been created by the death and burial of its local cultural originality—finds itself face to face with the language of the civilizing nation . . . with the culture of the mother country. The colonized is elevated above his jungle status in proportion to his adoption of the mother country's cultural standards. He becomes whiter as he renounces his blackness, his jungle.
> —FRANTZ FANON, *Black Skin, White Masks*

In the Charleston of my childhood, the language that was spoken had vigor and color and—not least—music. The pitches and tones of my grandmother's voice rose and fell like song. The words were dense thickets of metaphor and proverb—"crack ee teet'" meant "smile," "dayclean" meant "dawn." And when she spoke to her friends, to her sisters and cousins and nieces and nephews—my "aunties" and "uncles"—the laughter and allusions piled on so thick and fast that I couldn't understand one word in three. Later I came to know this was intentional: the elders retreating behind the curtain of their "secret language" to discuss those matters not fit for curious little ears.

Linguists speak of the rules of "universal grammar"—by which they appear to mean that a child placed in the environment of spoken language, any spoken language, learns that language without the slightest need to be taught. She learns because she cannot help learning. So it was that I learned the speech of my environment—Gullah, as I've learned the linguists call it though, to be sure, we thought we were speaking English[1]—and learned as well that, however natural it felt to speak that way, that that speech was somehow inadequate, that it was *wrong*.

"Don't say 'be.' Say 'is,'"—my mother's daily refrain. An English teacher who had conquered one nonstandard tongue already—the hillbilly twang of her home in South Carolina's red clay country—would not be defeated by another. "What kind of talk is that? Don't say, 'e ain go do'"—'e being the all-purpose third-person pronoun substituted for he, she, or it—"say 'she isn't going to do.'" "Don't say 'um'"—the all-purpose objective case pronoun—"say 'him!'" Don't say . . . Don't say . . . she'd repeat, not always patiently, day after day.

When I ironed out my speech—enunciated my Gs, flattened out my diphthongs, used he, she, or it rather than the ubiquitous 'e or um—I won the praise of my parents, who were teachers, and their friends, who were also teachers, but felt the subtle exclusion of peers, the sting of my cousins' mockery: "Listen to her. Think she cute! Talkin' proper!" When I spoke as I wished to, as felt natural to me, it was with the full knowledge that I was being willful, disobedient, and defiant: a "bad girl" who was "like to break her mama's heart." It was a terrible struggle, this becoming a "good girl," a struggle against nature. I was being offered a choice: between my grandmother, the warmth of her lap and her kitchen, where there was always something good to eat and some beloved someone with whom to share it, and the World, which resembled nothing so much as my school: Immaculate Conception, a Catholic school for Negro children, with its heart pine floors, soaring ceilings, and acoustics perfect for songs sung in Latin; with its hard Gs and Rs, rulers stinging knuckles, and love offered only on condition of one's ability to "uplift" the Negro race—an uplift we were assured could never be achieved if we remained burdened by what Paul Laurence Dunbar called "a jingle in a broken tongue."[2]

In offering these personal reminiscences I have chosen the stance of the "vulnerable observer," Ruth Behar's 1996 coinage for an approach to ethnography that interrogates and rejects the hierarchies implicit in the observer and even participant-observer modes of inquiry. Vulnerable observation reveals the observer's subjectivity and positionality, even as the observer becomes not just visible but vulnerable to the subjects of study. This particular term is no longer new, but it should be pointed out that vulnerable observation has a venerable history in Black feminist writing: a matrilineage linking early "race women" such as Anna Julia Cooper in the 1890s, with "New Negroes" such as Zora Neale Hurston in the early to mid-twentieth century, with the "womanists" of the seventies, eighties, nineties, and beyond. I choose this stance not just because I happen to agree with Behar when she writes, "Call it sentimental, call it nineteenth century and Victorian, but I say that anthropology that doesn't break your heart just isn't worth doing,"[3] but also because, as one whose ancestry and origins are from *within* the Gullah Geechee community, any other stance seems less than honest.

Then, too, vulnerable observation offers distinct advantages. While much of the research and, indeed, the vast majority of the recent literary and tourist narratives focused on the Gullah Geechee coastal region have been trapped in a binary of competing discourses—discourses of cultural "celebration" contrasted with discourses of "vanishing" Gullahs—vulnerable observation brings us face to face with a third term, the *abject* status—in Julia Kristeva's sense of matter that is both despised and desired, that produces both fear and fascination—of Gullah Geechee language and people. The assertion may be difficult to credit, given the culture's remarkable staying power as popular entertainment and object of scholarly inquiry over many generations. But as Gayatri Spivak has argued, even a vivid and popular presence at the margins may ultimately serve only to reinscribe the power of the center.[4]

I offer one example. While metaphors of migration, movement, circulation, and recirculation have become dominant in the critical discourse surrounding African American literature and culture, Gullah Geechee identity has remained a marker for . . . stasis. Island-dwelling Gullahs and mainland Geechees—the product of a vast and violent Atlantic World encounter that created a common culture of the languages, ethnicities, and lifeways of three continents—have been understood as the exact polar opposite of what James Clifford referred to as a "traveling culture."[5] The rest of the world gets around—Gullahs and Geechees stay in place.

And *in* their place. Yes, the word "Gullah" carries romantic resonances: Gullah sweetgrass baskets and iron-working traditions have entered the realm of art, winning pride of place at museums and selling for thousands of dollars at auction, while at the popular level, wearing kente, adopting African names and alternative religious practices, performing at fairs and festivals have become staples of life in the lowcountry. Yet "you ain't nothing but a rice-eatin' Geechee," a favorite insult since at least the time of the Great Migration, still marks the folks who "talk that Geechee talk" as backward and ignorant. It matters little that today this language supports a small cottage industry among scholars, particularly in anthropology and linguistics, when actual speakers of the language—those one encounters outside the pages of books—face discrimination in school and employment settings and remain incarcerated in an identity that is synonymous with lack of education, lack of opportunity, lack of means.

We must be careful of narratives of celebration, especially when offered by the tourist industry, for several reasons. On the one hand, the fact that goes unexamined is that very few activities of cultural "celebration" have had the slightest influence in tempering the vicious linguistic and racial prejudice Gullah Geechee people face or in easing the poverty and powerlessness of far too many Gullah Geechee lives. On the other, the power of the binary is that implicit in the celebrating is its opposite: *mourning* for a vanished and vanishing way of life. This pose of nostalgia may, as anthropologist Renato Rosado has written, be implicated within and infected by cultural imperialism. Rosaldo describes this "imperialist nostalgia" thus: "A person kills somebody, and then mourns the victim. In a more attenuated form, someone deliberately alters a form of life, and then regrets that things have not remained as they were prior to the intervention. At one more remove, people destroy their environment, and then they worship nature. In any of its versions, imperialist nostalgia uses a pose of 'innocent yearning' both to capture people's imaginations and to conceal its complicity with often brutal domination."[6] Indeed, applied to the example of the lowcountry, we must consider the possibility that celebratory gestures that mask the abject status of Gullah Geechee language and culture may, in fact, exacerbate the pressures that have driven the language to the brink of an extinction that, in turn, our dominant culture takes such apparent pleasure in mourning. In these chapters, we shall thus examine the ways in which framing the Gullah Geechee experience as isolated and immobile has masked both its birth amid a vast, forcible, global migration and its contemporary reality as what American poet, playwright, and critic Amiri Baraka has called, in the context of African American music, a dynamically "changing same" characteristic of all living cultures.[7]

But first, a bit of context. We have for some time now been speaking of Gullah and Geechee without precisely defining our terms. Let us consider a bit more closely this language of apparent stasis and further probe a few of the discourses in which it has been entrapped. First of all, rather than asking "what" is Gullah Geechee, we should recognize that a more pertinent question might be "where," for Gullah and Geechee are geographically determined terms, derived from West African tribal names to refer to people—generally but not exclusively African American—and language communities—on both sides of the color line—in coastal South Carolina and Georgia and portions of southern North Carolina and northern Florida. This definition, we must note, flatly contradicts dominant narratives that stress Gullah's remoteness, its unintelligibility, its imminent demise—but, as we have seen, it is a reading of Gullah culture that is supported by comparative readings in scholarship across multiple disciplines and also by the 2005 "Low Country Gullah Culture Special Resource Study and Environmental Impact Statement" compiled by the National Park Service in support of the region's nomination as a U.S. cultural heritage corridor.

The language that is called Gullah on the South Carolina Sea islands and Geechee in the city of Charleston and throughout Georgia is currently defined as a creole (and sometimes as a post-creole) language arising from conditions of First Contact between European and African migrants to the coastal plain of the southeastern United States. Sufficiently isolated by geography and demography from the main currents of American linguistic development, it has remained distinct—though not statically so—for nearly four centuries. As late as the 1970s, the language took this form:

> Dear Massa Jesus, we all uns bid Ooner ... come make us a call dis yere day. We is nutting but poor Ethiopian women and people ain't tink much 'bout we. We ain't trust any of dem, great Massa, great too much dan Massa Linkum, you ain't shame to care for we African people.
>
> Come to we, dear Massa Jesus. De sun, he hot too much, de road am dat long and boggy and we ain't got no buggy for send and fetch up Ooner. But Massa, you 'member how you walked dat hard walk up Calvary and ain't weary but tink about we all de way. We know you ain't too weary for to come to we. We pick out the t'orns, de prickles, de briar, de back-slidin' and de quarrel and de sin out of your path so dey shan't hurt Ooner or pierce feet no more.[8]

This is "Aunt Jane's Prayer," analyzed in Harold Carter's 1976 volume on the prayer tradition of African Americans. The creole syntax may be unfamiliar, owing little to the forms of Black English that are more available to us through music videos and television comedy, but its meaning is intelligible, and the language itself is obviously patterned and rule-governed, in the sense referred to by Walt Wolfram, the William C. Friday Professor of Linguistics at North Carolina State University and a past president of both the Linguistics Society of America and the American Dialect Society, when he states, "The most fundamental principle of language is that all language is patterned and rule governed, which you can apply to African American English, Appalachian English, every other dialect."[9] One might go so far as to say that the snippet of prayer is musical to anyone familiar with the tones and cadences of lowcountry speech, and even, in the immediacy and intimacy of the rural imagery, poetic.

Of course, it requires a linguist to do justice to the distinctions among ASE (American Standard English), Gullah, and AAVE (African American Vernacular English)—which lie in conventions for handling pronouns, naming, gender, and number, not to mention verb tenses that did not exist in English until they sneaked in through the back door of the speech of southern whites. But while we shall not attempt an extended analysis here, there are a few points that are important for the layman to grasp. For a language purist in the William Safire mold, for example, "he gone" might simply sound like an ungrammatical way of saying "he has gone." And for some speakers—an educated WASP from Vermont, let's say—that would be so. But for speakers from other regions and other cultural backgrounds, there's a difference in what is meant, and that difference is embedded in the differences between English and the Niger-Congo languages it encountered during the era of enslavement.

That is to say, in English, we *inflect* verbs: add suffixes or change the base to indicate changes in tense and mood. But African American speakers of English—and some southerners—have an additional linguistic inheritance: the Niger-Congo region, where the languages use less inflection because they have more ways of expressing *pastness*: from simple past, near past, and remote past to tense markers that distinguish between continuing or habitual action and completed action. So "he gone" and "he been gone," while typically interpreted as "bad English" or "broken English"—Dunbar's "jingle in a broken tongue"—in fact, express concepts of "near past" versus "remote past." A phrase like "he done gone" could well be symptomatic of the speaker's lack of formal education, but it also expresses completeness of action, while "he be going" informs us that the subject is still in the process of performing or has a habit of performing the action.[10]

Gullah has shown a steady erosion of African vocabulary over time, but while this fact could be seen as evidence supporting a discourse of "cultural vanishing," it must also be noted that the degree of African content has been notoriously difficult to pin down with any precision. Lorenzo Dow Turner's groundbreaking 1949 study *Africanisms in the Gullah Dialect* describes the extreme secrecy of Gullah-speaking communities, where informants told him they had "fared so badly at the hands of strangers that they are suspicious of anyone whom they do not know very well" and also that the "curiosity" and "lack of understanding" of outsiders was "a source of great annoyance to them and increase[d] their reticence." Turner added, "A few years ago I invited the late Dr. Guy S. Lowman, Jr., principal field investigator for the Linguistic Atlas of the United States and Canada, to accompany me on one of my field trips to the Sea Islands. . . . [D]uring an interview with one of my informants, Dr. Lowman unintentionally used a tone of voice which the informant resented. Instantly the interview ended. Apologies were of no avail. The informant refused to utter another word. . . . On my return to the Sea Islands several years later, I was confronted on every hand with this question, mɛk uno fo brIn dI bAkro? meaning, 'Why did you bring the white man?'"[11]

Moving forward in time to Carter's contribution, except for the use of "ooner"—a second person pronoun rendered as "oona" and "unna" in other sources—the African content lies in the syntactical pattern not the vocabulary, a phenomenon that might have indicated erosion . . . and that might have simply reflected the speaker's desire to be understood. Further back, in sources from a generation before, one finds African words and phrases aplenty, though of course the interlocutors had specifically asked their informants for such material. Turner's estimate of "four thousand" words and phrases from West Africa is probably a bit overdone as, it has been noted with disapprobation, he included proper names in his analysis, but other sources support the general outlines of his conclusions.[12]

Drums and Shadows: Survival Studies among the Georgia Coastal Ne-

groes (1940), produced by the Savannah Unit of the Georgia Writer's Project, interviewed more than a hundred men and women, most of them in their eighties, with vivid memories of elders from Africa. Katie Brown, a wizened woman from Sapelo Island with "enormous work-hardened hands," could recite bits of the Muslim prayers passed down in her family as well as things she'd learned from her "gran," who'd come to Georgia by way of the Bahamas speaking "funny wuds we didn't know." "She say 'mesojo' and sometime 'sojo' when she mean pot. Fuh watuh she say 'deloe' and fuh fyah she say 'diffy.' She tell us, 'Tak sojo off diffy.' Wen sumpm done she say, 'Bim-boga-rum.' Yuh tell uh sumpm wut is a suhprise lack somebody die, den she say, 'Mah-foo-bey, ma-foo-bey.'"[13] In 1983, Liz Young, an "SOB" from Charleston's elite white South of Broad neighborhood, admirably demonstrated in one of a series of taped "Interviews with Charlestonians" a once-common bilingualism. "I speak Gullah," she explained,

> because I was raised on a plantation called Brick House Plantation on Edisto Island. It's forty miles from Charleston and there were a great many colored persons on that plantation and, of course, this is the language of the Sea Islands—not to be confused with any other type of language because it is absolutely native to the lowcountry of South Carolina. And it's a very musical and very fascinating language, but it almost needs now to be translated. . . .
>
> Of the Gullah *that is spoken today* [emphasis added], you cannot understand it if you were not someone born on one of these plantations. For instance, if I were to say to you, "I'se got a shut secka yourn." . . . "Shut" means shirt, "secka" means like, and "yourn" means yours. So, what I said was, "I have a shirt like yours." There's an interesting heading in *Charleston Receipts*, a cookbook [produced by the Junior League of Charleston in 1950 and reprinted several times since] we've had the most marvelous success with. At the head of the sections, there's a little bit of Gullah and this section was beverages. "If you tekka heap uh ha'd liquor, you gwine t'ink deep and talk strong." That means if you drink too much, you talk too much.
>
> And they have a very interesting way of saying each particular thing. "I made it here" means "I found it here." "Shroud ain't got no pocket"—that means, "You can't take it with you."

Young concludes, "I find it is not only fascinating, but it's a language that's disappearing. Very few people can speak it—my own children cannot understand what I'm saying." Noting with puzzlement that "the Negroes are really getting ashamed of Gullah," she adds, "And so . . . [it] is disappearing because the colored people now think it's a language that shouldn't be spoken except among themselves. And it is absolutely nothing to be shamed of because it's a fabulous bit of lowcountry. To me it will be a great sadness when it disappears from our scene."[14]

Young provides us with a fascinating moment: a member of the former slaveholding class in the twilight of her own years, interviewed on the piazza of her historic Charleston mansion as the church bells tolled marking Confederate Memorial Day, singing the swan song of a disappearing culture. "[Y]ou cannot understand it unless you were someone born on one of these plantations," she says, emphasizing her own membership in an exclusive society, highlighting the African content of Gullah speech even as she strikes a pose of imperialist nostalgia, expressing her opinion that it will be a "great sadness when it disappears from our scene." Young's is a powerful evocation of the trope of the "vanishing Gullah," this dominant, if relatively uninterrogated, narrative against which we have seen it is possible to juxtapose ample counterevidence of Gullah's multiplicity, adaptability, and mobility. But while Gullah fluency is a source of pride for her, establishing her impeccable lineage as a Charleston blueblood, she seems quite clueless as to why it might be a source of abjection and a badge of shame for someone of a different class or a darker hue . . . someone such as the youthful Clarence Thomas.

Let us return, for the moment, to the historical period of my personal reminiscences, about 1968, a year infamous in South Carolina for the massacre of Black students at South Carolina State University in Orangeburg then further marred by the King and Kennedy assassinations.[15] This was also a year in which, amid the loftier struggles over the Bill of Rights and the Constitution, many lowcountry Blacks were, like me, dueling with dilemmas of speech and social mobility, of color, consciousness, and double consciousness. Among that teeming number was someone whose bootstrap story of individual success is hardly ever mentioned in this context: the youthful Clarence Thomas, born in 1947 to poverty-stricken parents in the Gullah Geechee settlement of Pin Point, off Shipyard Creek, near Georgia's celebrated Moon River.[16]

As described in *Supreme Discomfort* (2007), the search by *Washington Post* reporters Kevin Merida and Michael A. Fletcher for the controversial Supreme Court justice's "divided soul," Thomas was a Catholic schoolboy, too, in 1968: first at Savannah's St. Pius X High School, a segregated Catholic academy I imagine to have been much like Immaculate Conception, and then at St. John Vianney Minor seminary on Isle of Hope, Georgia. Here, Thomas sought to pursue the dream of his grandfather, Myers Anderson: that the boy would become the first Black Catholic priest in the family. But while only six miles removed from Savannah geographically, the Isle of Hope was worlds removed socially and culturally. And for Thomas, speech was a critical marker of that difference.

Recall that even at St. Pius, among African American peers, Thomas had endured teasing as "a jet-black boy with a bow-legged gait who spoke with a Gullah Geechee accent. One nickname—though no one in his family or peer group will admit to using it—was particularly cruel: ABC, 'America's Blackest

Child!'" The pressure at St. John was different in intensity but not in kind. Told by Father William Coleman, the rector and dean of studies, that "his spoken English was [so] poor, [u]nless he got rid of his Gullah Geechee dialect . . . , he wouldn't make it at the school and wouldn't reach his goals when he left," the authors say, Thomas was "shattered."[17]

It's doubtful that Thomas ever encountered the words of Ambrose Gonzales, the Redeemer-era newspaper editor and amateur folklore collector who expressed history's judgment of Gullah Geechee language in 1922: "Slovenly and careless of speech, these Gullahs seized upon the peasant English used by some of the early colonists and by the white servants of the wealthier colonists, wrapped their clumsy tongues about it as well as they could, and enriched with certain expressive African words, it issued through their flat noses, and thick lips as so workable a form of speech that it was gradually adopted by the other slaves and became in time the accepted Negro speech of the lower districts of South Carolina and Georgia."[18] But Thomas, like every other denizen of the Gullah Geechee Coast, would have felt their force, not in the library, but in his life, in everyday interactions in a region warped by a legacy of slavery and Civil War and clinging stubbornly to the embattled remnants of Jim Crow.

Yes, voices had been raised to challenge Gonzales and his ilk. In 1939, an African American linguist named Lorenzo Dow Turner had written the following to his friend, the anthropologist Melville Herskovits: "Up to the present time, I have found in the vocabulary of the Negroes in coastal South Carolina and Georgia approximately four thousand West African words, besides many survivals in syntax, inflections, sounds, and intonation. . . . I have recorded in Georgia a few songs which are entirely African. . . . Sometimes whole African phrases appear in Gullah without change either of meaning or of pronunciation. Frequently African phrases have been translated into English."[19]

But while these insights would certainly have been important to the work of a rising generation of linguists, anthropologists, and historians,[20] on the polyglot streets of Charleston and Savannah—where little was known of Africa in 1968 beyond "lord of the jungle" stereotypes and virtually nothing would be known of "Black Power" until James Brown's "Say It Loud" began climbing the charts in August of that year—few would have found Turner's claims relevant. It was a crucible of color consciousness, linguistic pride/prejudice, and family expectation that shaped Gullah Geechee youth like Thomas and myself. For him, social mobility, in the form of "a priest in the family," was the prize the family early set its sights on; and failure came with a cruel consequence. When Thomas stumbled off the path of the family dream—withdrawing from a lily-white Ohio seminary after one excruciatingly painful and lonely year—his grandfather threw him out of the house, and the rift between them never fully healed, even as Thomas graduated from College of the Holy Cross, then Yale University, and began to move through Republican circles of power. The old man died in 1983, never knowing that his grandson would rise from Pin Point to the highest court in the land.[21]

A somewhat gentler calculus shaped my own life—no one, for example, would have cast me out for failure—but the hierarchies were so clearly demarcated that they could be grasped intuitively, without conscious thought. And what was plain as pound cake to me was the fact that Gramma—who talked Geechee and only Geechee—was a domestic, while Daddy—who had a master's and could talk "that Geechee talk" but usually used, and seemed to prefer, "the King's English"—was a teacher and a trained musician whose life was full of possibility. When my parents looked at me and dreamed of the future I could have, the exact dimensions of that glorious apotheosis might have been vague, but it was clear that my will was no more than dandelion fluff in the wind of all that concentrated longing.

No trace of the Gullah tongue is apparent today in Clarence Thomas's public speech (or, indeed, in mine), though as recently as the last decade he was citing lingering embarrassment over his long-vanished accent to explain his reluctance to engage in oral argument at the high court. To extend the metaphor of the Fanon epigraph that introduces this chapter, Thomas—among many thousands of Gullah speakers over many decades—rejected his "mother tongue" in favor of the language of a "civilizing" power, not just renouncing his so-called interior jungle but, indeed, paving it over to put up a strip mall for the exchange of cultural capital. Thomas, in fact, succumbed, as the sociolinguists might describe it, to the pressures of "the classic three-generation shift": a process of language death by which a minority tongue is overwhelmed by that of an economic elite.[22]

The three-generation shift is a transnational and transcultural phenomenon in which a parental generation—speaking, say, Yiddish on the Lower East Side of New York in the last century or Tlingit in Canada today—is monolingual in a tongue that has a powerful economic rival. The second generation, facing the lure of economic betterment, the lash of persecution (the anti-Irish laws of Great Britain in the last century; the sanctions faced by Kurds in Syria, Turkey, and Iran today), or both at the same time, becomes bilingual. With continued or intensified pressure, subsequent generations abandon the parental tongue entirely, becoming monolingual in the rival language. Without the counterforces of population (whites were, at times, a tiny minority on the Gullah Geechee Coast) or popularization (the revitalization movements that "saved" Cajun French and Hawai'i Creole English), a language may simply . . . die.

"Every dialect is a way of thinking," said Fanon. "And the . . . [adoption of] a language different from that of the group into which [one] was born is evidence of a dislocation, a separation."²³ Yet there are many ways to experience that separation, a continuum stretching from outright rejection to nostalgic, but frustrated longing to reclaiming and reimmersion. My own response has been complicated. Sometimes at night when it's very still, I recall my grandmother's voice and hear its echoes distantly ringing in the silence. Sometimes when I'm talking to someone from the Bahamas, Jamaica, or Barbados—where the accents and cadences are so similar to those I knew as a child²⁴—I'll feel myself relaxing and my whole body starting to sing with pleasure. Once in a very great while, when I'm home and talking to someone very familiar and very dear, I'll fall into the songlike rhythms of my native speech. I've previously written that sociolinguists call this "accommodation"—the act of unconsciously picking up the accent of the person we're addressing—and say it's something we all do, for "social bonding and peer acceptance."²⁵ But most of the time when I open my mouth to speak, what issues forth is plain old American Standard English: effective in the professional realms in which I travel, but often without color and, most regrettably, without song. In moments of bitterness, I think I traded my birthright for a mess of pottage.

It is here, in the area of language, that the power dynamics of the center-margin dichotomy are most vividly seen. Here is where it becomes most abundantly clear that, to paraphrase Arnold Krupat, there is no post- to the colonial condition in the United States.²⁶ For nowhere within discourses of Gullah celebration and the social practices of Gullah exclusion has there been a suggestion that one could inhabit what Homi Bhabha has called a "third space" beyond both otherness and assimilation: satisfy the desire to speak the (abject) language of kin *to* kin and *simultaneously* acquire and exercise the language skills that would allow one to navigate those necessary "other worlds" of economic and educational opportunity. It is indeed true that, nearly a century after Gonzales, the Gullah language has given its name to a congressionally designated heritage corridor, but it has yet to gain a presence in what the linguist David Crystal has called the "serious side of life."²⁷

In other parts of the Atlantic World and the Pacific Rim, creole languages such as Krio in Sierra Leone, Papiamentu in the Netherlands Antilles, and Bislama in Vanuatu—to name just a few—are used in politics, the news media, churches, and even, in some contexts, in educational settings. In the Caribbean, the poet-scholar Edward Kamau Brathwaite's "nation languages" have been a proud vehicle for poets from Louise Bennett-Coverley to Mikey Smith and have informed and enriched the imaginative and linguistic worlds of fiction writers from Paule Marshall to Nalo Hopkinson. In the United States, by contrast, Gullah Geechee remains a cultural curiosity—whose presence in literature and art is taken for granted while remaining virtually untheorized, with no presence or power in schools or institutions of governance and, most markedly, no ability to influence American, or even African American, habits regarding what is surely one of the last remaining socially acceptable forms of prejudice: linguistic prejudice.

Indeed, Gonzales may well have been relegated to the dustier shelves in the depths of the stacks, but his spirit is alive and well in the twenty-first century and, as recently as 2004, it was speaking in the voice of . . . Bill Cosby.

> Just forget telling your child to go to the Peace Corps. It's right around the corner [laughter]. It's standing on the corner. It can't speak English. It doesn't want to speak English.
>
> I can't even talk the way these people talk: "Why you ain't?" "Where you is?" . . . I don't know who these people are. And I blamed the kid until I heard the mother talk [laughter]. And then I heard the father talk.
>
> This is all in the house! You used to talk a certain way on the corner and you got into the house and switched to English. Everybody knows it's important to speak English except these knuckleheads. You can't land a plane with "Why you ain't." You can't be a doctor with that kind of crap coming out of your mouth! There is no Bible that has that kind of language.
>
> Where did these people get the idea that they're moving ahead on this? Well, they know they're not. They're just hanging out in the same place, five or six generations sitting in the projects when you're just supposed to stay there long enough to get a job and move out.[28]

This reference to "ebonics" comes from a speech delivered at Constitution Hall on May 22, 2004, in commemoration of the fiftieth anniversary of the landmark *Brown v. Board of Education of Topeka* Supreme Court decision. But there's little doubt given Cosby's previous history of hostile commentary on Black dialects—e.g., his "Elements of Igno-Ebonics" piece published in the *Wall Street Journal* on January 10, 1997—that the analysis would extend to Gullah. We may ponder the ironies of the fact that the man launching this jeremiad is the very man who gave the world Fat Albert, Mushmouth, and Weird Harold. But we cannot help but pause to examine the radical and open expression of linguistic prejudice on display by the man who was once America's beloved, avuncular comedian. "*It's* on the corner," Cosby says, speaking of Black youth who speak in dialect: "*It* doesn't want to speak English." "I don't know who *these people* are," he continues. "Where did *these people* get the idea that they're *moving ahead* on this?" he adds, making explicit the connection between language and social mobility that was elsewhere implied in his remarks (all emphases added).

For Americans generally, language has ever been a frontier to cross, not a border to inhabit. Cosby's view of this frontier appears a particularly stark one. On one side of the line he seems to see a hopeful, progressive vision in which "mastery" of standard English leads in linear fashion to success in desirable professions, those most associated, literally, with progress: airline pilot, doctor. On the other, he associates dialect speakers with a brutish and barely human existence characterized by immobility, indeed entrapment, in a carceral geographic wasteland, "the projects," even as Cosby's own voice is, without apparently intentional irony, bidialectal: the full text of his remarks show him code-switching rapidly and fluently among vernacular and standard forms of speech. American ethnicity, for Cosby, appears to resemble nothing so much as that gumbo pot of cliché, into which, with enough simmering, all flavors may be reconciled into one. One cannot help but note, however, that the Black poor linger in the corners of this figuration, an undigested and perhaps indigestible ingredient he hesitates even to add to the pot.

While African Americans routinely dismiss Clarence Thomas's critiques of Black people and culture—his 2007 opinion using the language of Justice John Marshall Harlan's historic dissent in *Plessy v. Ferguson* to strike down school integration plans in Seattle and Louisville stung African American court observers, while his vote in the 2013 *Shelby County v. Holder* decision, eviscerating the 1965 Voting Rights Act, further established him as a figure of anathema—Cosby's crusade, coming a full decade before the drugging and rape allegations that were to prove the entertainer's downfall, appeared to trouble and thus to resonate more broadly in Black America. Cosby may have been roundly critiqued in a special 2004 issue of the *Black Scholar*, but the preeminent Langston Hughes scholar Arnold Rampersad was among those who defended him. "Common speech is indeed vigorous and creative, but typically only someone who is educated can see the degree of creativity in such speech, and then romanticize what is essentially monolingualism," Rampersad said in a press interview about a month after the entertainer's initial remarks, adding, "people who romanticize monolingualism of the type attacked by Bill Cosby (the type founded on ignorance and the active disdaining of books) need to have a monolingual social class in order to satisfy their romanticism. Mr. Cosby is absolutely correct that monolingualism of this type is a guarantee of economic and other forms of poverty—including intellectual and spiritual poverty."[29]

Rampersad's was a nuanced reaction, recognizing the vital distinction between mono- and multilingualism. It was also quite rare. Overwhelmingly, such debates as the Cosby one in 2004—not to mention subsequent national "moral panics" centered on Spanish speakers and immigration—have revealed a middle-class America concerned with enforcing hierarchies of class and language that it also steadfastly refuses to examine. One could argue that, in all these debates, language is made to figure as "frontier": a zone of conflict where an Othered minority is, in fabular terms and in fact, in the process of being forcibly subdued and assimilated. The phrase "resistance is futile" did not, of course, appear in Frederick Jackson Turner's landmark 1893 essay "The Significance of the Frontier in American History," but it has not gone unnoticed by recent generations of critics that figurative "frontiers" such as this enact "strateg[ies] of empire and alien-making" that are fundamentally at odds with democratic claims of the inalienable rights of individuals.³⁰

While individuals in modernity, particularly minorities, frequently inhabit Bhabha's "third space" of multiple, sometimes conflicting, identities, arguments about language diversity in the United States overwhelmingly fall into simplistic binaries of pro versus con. U.S. white supremacists (both conscious and unconscious) and assimilationists tend to show up on the anti-diversity end of the continuum, while arguments for language tolerance tend to originate with the "celebratory" discourses of primitivists and Afrocentrists—Rampersad's "romantics." But it is well to keep in mind that whenever and wherever these arguments originate, whether their impulse is condemnatory or celebratory, they are at their marrow essentialist—a response that, in the hands of colonialist power, reinforces hierarchies of class, race, and power and that, even when deployed strategically, in the Spivakian sense, as a form of resistance to colonialist domination, carries the danger of trapping one in an oppositional stance that only reifies the colonialist center.

As illustration I offer this thought experiment: Imagine standing in an airport bookshop in Charleston or Savannah thumbing through a copy of *The Charleston Renaissance* (1998) or *A DuBose Heyward Reader* (2003)—something I myself have done a time or two and a souvenir purchase that a visitor to a coastal hub might contemplate. In such texts, one most definitely encounters a culture and a people frozen in time, trapped like flies in an evil honey, to paraphrase Alice Walker,³¹ that purports to celebrate them. Now imagine another airport bookstore at an Atlantic World hub a bit farther afield—say, in Kingston, Jamaica, or Bridgetown, Barbados—where one would find, by contrast, vitality and vigorous innovation among the speakers and writers of Gullah's Caribbean cousins.

In Kingston, you'd certainly find works by Louise Bennett-Coverley, the beloved Jamaican poet and folklorist whom the *Times* of London eulogized upon her death in 2006 as "a cultural icon" who turned patois from a "shamed and disowned" dialect to "a proud vehicle for poetry" inspiring the likes of Bob Marley, who claimed that it was "Miss Lou" who gave him the courage to write songs in his own voice; the internationally acclaimed Jamaican performance poet and musician Michael "Mikey" Smith; and the contemporary fantasist Nalo Hopkinson, whose novels and short fiction have been showered with awards and honors in the United States and Canada. In Bridgetown, national pride would likely center around Edward Kamau Brathwaite, considered, along with Derek Walcott, as one of the "twin peaks" of Caribbean poetry and widely acknowledged as the "father of dub," a performance poetry form that melds words and the drumbeat.

Brathwaite, as fine a critic as he is a poet, is fierce in his rejection of the word "dialect," noting its origins in representations of the plantation among the conquering Portuguese, Spanish, English, French, and Dutch who imposed their own languages of "obedience [and] command" upon the conquered. In its place, he offers the term "nation languages"—adapted from Edouard Glissant[32]—as well as a beautifully evocative and nuanced description of what he means:

> Nation language is language which is influenced very strongly by the African model, the African aspect of our New World/Caribbean heritage. English it may be in terms of some of its lexical features. But in its contours, its rhythm and timbre, its sound explosions, [it is far more]. . . . [I]t is an English which is not of the standard, imported, educated [variety], but that of the submerged, surrealist experience and sensibility, which has always been here and which is now increasingly coming to the surface and influencing the perception of contemporary . . . people. . . . It may be . . . English: but often it is . . . an English which is like a howl or a shout or a machine-gun or the wind or a wave. It is also like the blues. And sometimes it is English and African at the same time.[33]

The exuberance of the Caribbean artist's embrace of "nation language" has few peers in American literature, but few does not mean none.[34] And so, in our exploration of this perhaps unexpectedly complicated terrain, we shall confront powerful evidence that third cultural spaces are not the recent invention of theorists but have been present from the earliest moments of the Atlantic World encounter. Likewise, we shall see that the contexts for the texts we shall examine are so intertwined with a shadow narrative of American unfreedom as to stretch neatly linear "official" paradigms of migration-to-emancipation and even immigration-to-assimilation to their limits. And we shall learn that the texts that will be our objects of study are so deeply implicated with shadow desires expressed literally and figuratively in the form of mimicry, minstrelsy, and miscegenation as to hopelessly complicate both the official ideology and informal practices of social apartheid and racial purity to which the lowcountry region is heir.

Before we proceed to specific texts, however, we must fully elaborate our triangular conceptual model, adding to our new understanding of language the other two legs of the foundation. On the one hand, we will consider the *location* of Gullah Geechee culture in a shifting landscape ruled by water and the force of the hurricanes. On the other, we'll examine its embodiment as a creole rather than pure *lineage*, with all the contradictory meanings, histories, and processes the use of that term implies.

CHAPTER 2

Toward a Triangular Topos
Landscape and Lineage on the Gullah Geechee Coast

> [I]nvestigating the Black Atlantic diaspora means that you have to reckon with a founding moment, a point in time when new relations, cultures, and conflicts were brought into being.
> —PAUL GILROY, *Small Acts*

> We are all contaminated by each other.
> —KWAME ANTHONY APPIAH, *In My Father's House*

Let us imagine for a moment the beach communities surrounding the major population hubs of the southeastern Atlantic Coast. Cities like Myrtle Beach, Charleston, and Beaufort in South Carolina; Savannah and the "Golden Isles" in Georgia; Jacksonville in Florida are noted for their hustle-and-bustle, for their restaurants and retail attractions, their crowded and vibrant night life. But the casual visitor making a foray into the interior, let's say to the ACE Basin of South Carolina, would gain quite the opposite impression: of a land surprisingly and hauntingly remote, even empty. The ACE, named for the riverine estuary formed by the convergence of the Ashepoo, Combahee, and Edisto rivers, is a latticework of blackwater rivers, abandoned farmlands, and alluvial swamps; it is also, in historical terms, the beating heart of the nation-state of rice. It was here, on this coastal plain, on the prison farms known euphemistically as plantations, that "Carolina Gold" rice was cultivated with trafficked human labor and technology expropriated from the Senegambia of West Africa. It was this region that fueled the "staggering" scale of colonial and antebellum prosperity in the capitals that rice built.[1]

The historical connections between the countryside and the capitals in the region most accurately called the Gullah Geechee Coast are obscured in our time. Indeed, it requires a heroic act of rememory in the Morrisonian sense to connect this landscape of scattered gated communities, linked by interstate highways traversing creeks and depthless forests to a vanished past of large plantations growing rice—and sometimes indigo or luxury-grade cotton—and no less to the smaller communities of yeoman farmers and tradesman who lived at their flanks and served their needs. The challenge is helped, however, by recalling that roads are secondary in the evolution of the coastal plain, that it is indeed *water* that was the life-blood of community, the vital liquid providing oxygen to the beating heart of the nation of rice.

One does well to recall Keith Cartwright's lyrical framing in *Sacral Grooves, Limbo Gateways: Travels in Deep Southern Time*: "The lowcountry is a gateway of terrestrial, riverine, and marine flows," he writes.[2] Water connected this countryside not just to cities like Charleston and Savannah, but also to the Caribbean and a broader global empire of trade. It was water that swept indigenous populations up into a global Indian slave trade and that repopulated the landscape denuded by war, disease, and enslavement with peoples of African descent. It was the Afro-creole's mastery of the ways of water that invested both the food source (rice) they grew and the culture that grew alongside it with an authority that was recognized, if only unofficially and in ways denied even up to the present,[3] by those who claimed the right to extract life, liberty, and happiness from those expropriated goods.

Of course, the casual visitor to this region is as unlikely to recognize the hidden histories of these locales as the exiled native is likely to extol them. Franklin Burroughs's "Low Country Legacy," a 2014 feature in *National Geographic* magazine, is representative of a genre in which a poetics of Place depends on an idealized definition of Space.[4] "When I was growing up in South Carolina, the oldest places I knew were also the wildest places," he begins. "History and natural history cohabited in the antebellum rice-field country and the barrier islands, which began 35 miles south of Conway, where we lived, and stretched past Georgetown and Charleston and on to the Georgia line. History had populated these places, then depopulated them. Their sense of vanished human presence and their teeming life—fish, flesh, and fowl, to say nothing of snakes, sea turtles, and alligators—gave rise to two rumors. One was that cougars still lurked in the deepest swamps. The other was that ghosts hung around particular plantations. Reliable people saw unaccountable things. That is what other reliable people told you, and what you secretly wished to believe."

Burroughs's essay is an homage to "wildness": a paean to white-tailed deer, loggerhead sea turtles, and migrating waterfowl that is a worthy heir to a tradition of southern sublime stretching back to the travels of William Bartram. But like the broader tradition of American sublime to which it is related, works in this vein purify the landscape of an inconvenient human presence in order to map upon it a preferred set of moral values.[5] That is not to say that the characterization is incorrect: a remarkable 20 percent of the ACE ecozone—about 200,000 of its 1.1 million acres—is completely undeveloped.[6]

However, it is well to recall the agendas—and possible hidden agendas—of the agents of this region's conservation: an unusual partnership of federal, state, local, and private stakeholders, including not just "usual suspect" actors such as the U.S. Fish and Wildlife Service, the state Department of Natural Resources, the Nature Conservancy, and Ducks Unlimited but also charismatic high-wealth individuals. On the charismatic end of the scale is news mogul Ted Turner—his Hope Plantation was the site of the first conservation easement granted in the region 1980.[7] On the high-wealth end are the descendants of conservationist and Chicago printing magnate Gaylord Donnelly, whose Ashepoo Plantation has been donated and rebranded as the Donnelly Wildlife Management area.

Few artifacts of planter opulence remain in the built environment. As the palatial country houses that survived Sherman's march fell to the vicissitudes of time and fortune, conservation overtook preservation as a local priority. "Outmigration," a term more precise than Burroughs's "depopulation," also has been a feature of the region's twentieth-century history, as the collapse of the rice economy combined with the atrocities of the Redeemer and Jim Crow eras to push some African American populations out of the region while the rise of manufacturing, so-called good jobs, in regional hubs pulled others to the cities—or outside the region entirely. Nonetheless, rice has left its mark, and that mark lingers on the landscape.

Amid meandering waters, a cane-straight creek edge glimpsed from a bridge offers mute testimony of an erstwhile rice canal. At ground level, these and other traces of the past are visible—more precisely legible—only to a native or an educated eye, but from the air, the massive hydrological systems constructed to support the cultivation of the crop are not just legible but unmistakable. The imprint of this hand- and mule-built system of dams, dikes, and floodgates (or "trunks")—pathways that partitioned the swamps into regular rectangular fields that then could be flooded and drained with the movement of the moon and the tides—is quite literally carved upon the earth. The straight lines on satellite images constitute traces of a history not so much vanished as hiding in plain sight. And just like these traces on the landscape, Gullah Geechee people also remain—a presence not so much absent as elided from narratives that should center their presence. It might seem curious, for example, that the words "Gullah," "Geechee," and "Cultural Heritage Corridor" should appear nowhere in Burroughs's piece, that the luminous photographs illustrating the story should include images of horseshoe crabs, cypress swamps, duck hunters (white), and their bird dogs but no African Americans—indeed, the Gullah Geechee presence is limited to "subscriber-only" content on the *National Geographic* website—but I shall argue that these artistic choices are in fact conventions of a genre: a genre that links ante- and postbellum Plantation School literature with elite painting and fiction with the sporting, tourism, and "home and garden" narratives presented in glossy lifestyle magazines of our own time.

Using such materials, we shall test the two remaining legs of our triangular conceptual model as we theorize the particular historical experiences and interrogate the mythos developed to explain—and explain away—the Gullah Geechee presence. Just as I argued in chapter 1 that the "Geechee talk" of my childhood exists and persists within a linguistic third space between and beyond "otheredness" and assimilation, in this chapter I shall turn to a deeper analysis of the location of Gullah Geechee culture. Probing historical, cultural, anthropological, ecological, and literary contexts for third spaces/places "between," we shall examine not just the crucible of the landscape of the coastal plain and the human lineages forged therein, but also, critically, the ways in which the connections among them have been rendered illegible.

I quoted Keith Cartwright's *Sacral Grooves, Limbo Gateways* a bit earlier. The passage continues with a critical insight: "Any effort to *territorialize this space within a strictly national narrative* can account for only part of the Sea Islands' cultural history. Indeed the creole cultures surrounding Charleston, Savannah and Jacksonville *test the waters* separating the plantation South from the West Indies, and the Americas from Africa" (emphases added).[8] Narratives of the region's landscape have done exactly what Cartwright warned against: territorialized the landscape in terms of region and nation, in part, by eliding or excluding the Gullah Geechee presence from both figurations. Given the fact that Gullah Geechee communities constituted upward of 80 percent of the population in the rice-growing counties of a three-state region, this disassociation of African Americans from Gullah Geechee identities both displaces Afro-creole cultural authority on the meaning and use of the lands in which they were planted and which they planted and also, effectively, disinherits Gullah Geechee persons from their vital ancestral connections to those lands. So, to begin, let us consider more deeply the languaging of landscape: the fact that "that Geechee talk" developed in a physical third space, an inland-to-island environment that was literally littoral. This is a deceptive geography, both between the shores of bodies of water—whether of the great Atlantic herself or of rivers, lakes, creeks, marshes, and so on—and yet also within marshes and dense swamps, locales that are neither solid earth nor water, but a shifting landscape of both.

The terrain itself stretches the implications of "betweenness" in a variety of conceptually provocative ways. For example, it lies between legal definitions for, in the English Common Law tradition from which early South Carolina jurisprudence derived, land was conceived as private property yet water had been historically considered a public resource, needful to and thus to be shared with all.[9] Pitched battles are fought to this day over the principle,[10] and ample testimony to these tensions can be found in the legal record of disputes between Gullah Geechee and indigenous Indian communities, conservation and development interests, and states. In addition to the legal, these landscapes lie between racial definitions, for the Europeans, while styling themselves "lords proprietors" and "masters" able to command the labor of the Othered, were nonetheless far less able to navigate these lands than their so-called inferiors, the Amerindians and the enslaved.[11] To a certain degree, these distinctions were classed as well as raced. For whites, too great an ease in traversing the wilderness was itself dangerous, evidence of "trashiness," a nineteenth-century-vintage slur that called one's claim to "civilization," and thereby to whiteness itself, into question.[12]

Finally, and perhaps most critically, these landscapes lie between cultural definitions. For the European settler-colonists whose concern was to conquer and wring profit from them, they could be fearful sites of the abject: the source of deadly, disease-causing "miasmas," the haunt of devils and wicked spirits.[13] For the marginalized others—the Amerindians from whom the land was violently seized, and the enslaved, whose bodies were expropriated in a cruel regime of forced labor—these lands were, by contrast, fecund and, if not always actually home, then at least familiar. The palmetto as well as a landscape of extensive wetlands alternating with savannas and dense forests would have been reminiscent of western and west-central Africa—as would have fauna such as alligators, big cats, and venomous snakes.[14] Most importantly, for the enslaved, the cultural meanings of the forest would not have changed; it would have remained in their eyes the *nfinda*, a KiKongo word still in use in the lowcountry during the period of our study: a site where food and medicines could be found; where manhood testing rituals and contacts with the invisible realms of spirit and ancestors could be enacted; where respites from toil and even escapes from enslavement could be stolen.[15]

These countercultural meanings, which Cartwright characterizes as sources of "Afro-creole authority" and which other times and other discourses have christened "cultural authenticity," are the heart of a lowcountry lacuna; they represent the missing pages of a manuscript wherein the story of the African presence was once to be found. Instead, inserted in its place are variations on a Lost Cause theme, in which a backward exceptionalism has been contorted to become a point of pride. To restore them, we shall turn our attention to the terrestrial, riverine, and marine flows characterizing the landscape of the swamp—a word whose very origin, the *Oxford English Dictionary* reminds us, is not European at all but North American. The movements of these waters cannot be contained within the neat, linear dikes of U.S. national and southern regional myths of origin constructed to control them. The immigration-to-assimilation and migration-to-freedom narratives, even the Lost Cause narratives, we shall see, are hopelessly inadequate to the task of coping with the reality of the lowcountry spaces and Gullah Geechee places.

And so, in the beginning was the word, and the word for lowcountry was "swamp." The Great Dismal Swamp, along the Virginia-North Carolina border. The great lowcountry swamp that once covered the whole of the Atlantic coastal plain from Cape Fear, North Carolina, to the southern tip of Florida. The word applies broadly, connecting locales transatlantic, Black Atlantic, circum-Atlantic, and archipelagic. In all these, explorations of the swamp offer compelling evidence of a geographical "third space" whose history and memory are part of what one may think of as a "shadow canon": narratives of nation, race, and region that hopelessly complicate the neat, linear territorialized narratives that U.S. children learn in school and that are iterated in Thanksgiving Day, July Fourth, African American History Month, and Lee-Jackson-King Day commemorations. The swamp represents the shadow side of a Transcendentalist sublime—a place where light, air, and democratic vistas are eclipsed by a sullen curtain of green. Within the swamp, identities may shift and mutate; traditional hierarchies be overthrown; social verities proven lies. Historian David Noble's formulation is useful here in recalling that notions of the sublime became internalized and eventually institutionalized within U.S. national culture in the form of binary oppositions "between the pure spaces of New World freedom and their contamination by despised and demonized groups overseas or abroad marked as 'other.'" These binaries pose difficulties for settler-colonist subject formation, as Anthony Wilson's *Shadow and Shelter: The Swamp in Southern Culture* (2006) instructed us: "The swamp can be seen as the essence of nature, . . . *distinct from and unassimilable into* the literary and cultural construct of Southern civilization. It, like the animal self always battled and denied by the cavalier,[16] was in many ways the essence of the Southern problem: it had no place in the myth of self-creation that constituted the ideal South, and yet it remained utterly inalienable from the South itself and therefore ingrained into Southern identity from the very beginning" (emphasis added).[17]

In other words, the lowcountry was quintessentially a swamp, and yet the logic of colonization occurred in a Christo-capitalist context of conquest, of dominion: draining and denying the swamp, imposing human will upon it—in stark contrast, by the way, to the ways of African and indigenous Others, for whom nonhuman nature was sacred and ensouled, and whose technologies worked *within* natural rhythms. We shall continue to explore this dynamic function of landscape within the lowcountry: its oscillation between poles from heaven to hell, graveyard to homeland, proving ground to resting place. But here, we must turn to the final topos in our conceptual triangle: the set of concepts, imported from ethnography, history, and cultural theory, which speak to the formation of creole lineages, creole selves. Fascination with criollo/creole figures and contexts has a four-hundred-year history in Hispanophone and Francophone accounts of settlement of the Americas.

The notion that Old Word populations *changed*, especially for the worse, in the encounter with the New has occupied observers from the very earliest period of colonial settlement to the present, as priests, soldiers, political figures, and, much later, anthropologists, linguists, and historians have analyzed and sought to understand the challenges of First Contact and its contemporary legacies.[18] José Antonio Mazzotti and Ralph Bauer offer a detailed account of a vast literature, including the questions ("acculturation" versus "retention"), the models ("transculturation" versus "creolization" versus "inculturation"), and the emphases ("creative adaptation," cultural "syncretism," and "bricolage") that have animated the twentieth-century debate.[19] But we should be careful to note that this discourse of creolization has historically been much more submerged in the United States and, indeed, in all the Anglophone former colonies of the Americas for reasons that appear tangled both with the root meanings of the word and with questions of the self-landscape binary that so unsettled the discussion of the meaning of the swamp.

What precisely *is* "creole"? What is implied by the condition of "*creolité*"? The word has a lengthy and complicated history, but at its heart, it denotes the offspring of "Old World progenitors in the New World," whether animal, vegetable, or human.[20] That is, while we commonly think of creoles as a class (or heritage, lineage) of persons, it's important to note that domestic plants and animals may be creolized—*hybridized* is the more familiar term—to create breeds that are better adapted to the environment and more useful to humans. The landscape, too, may be so modified: the swamp disciplined and forced to yield up orderly (rice)fields, magnificent formal gardens, even villages and towns. Of course, it's the application of these concepts to human populations amid schemes of power making and resistance to power that has most vexed historical accounts of circum-Atlantic migration and settlement. Thus, we shall offer a brief account of views of the creole condition during the period of early modern settler colonialism before turning to the intersection of this history with the peoples and culture of the Gullah Geechee Coast.

It is no exaggeration to say that creoles and creolization have occasioned anxiety virtually from the moment of colonial expansion. One of the earliest examples of this anxiety—in the account of Bernardino de Sahagún (1590), the Franciscan friar, missionary, and early ethnographer—makes reference to the "great defects and imbecility of those who are born in these lands." De Sahagún continues, "Those who are born here become like the Indians, and although they look like Spaniards, in their constitution they are not; those who are born in Spain, if they do not take care, *change within a few years* after they arrive in these parts; and this I think is due to the climate or the constellations in these parts" (emphasis added).[21] Two centuries later, stereotypes of "defects and imbecility" were staples of early Anglophone accounts as well, particularly that of J. Hector St. Jean de Crèvecoeur. In Letter IX of his *Letters from an American Farmer* (1782)—posted from a Charleston that he never, in fact, visited[22]—Crèvecoeur was careful to draw a distinction between himself, a French émigré to New France who became a naturalized citizen of New York—and southern/Caribbean creoles whom he invariably depicted as swaggering home laden with riches got by almost certainly unsavory means or staggering home as invalids, wasted by tropical disease or by unnamed dissipations among the darker races.

"Here," he writes of his supposed sojourn in Charleston, "are always to be seen a great number of valetudinarians from the West-Indies, seeking for the renovation of health, *exhausted by the debilitating nature of their sun, air, and modes of living.*" He continues, "Many of these West-Indians have I seen at thirty, *loaded with the infirmities of old age*; for nothing is more common in those countries of wealth, than for persons to lose the abilities of enjoying the comforts of life, at a time when we *northern* men just begin to taste *the fruits of our labour and prudence*" (emphases added).[23] In contrast to de Sahagún, who sought with Galen and Aristotle in the stars for the causes, Crèvecoeur deploys tropes of the "environmental determinism" common to Enlightenment thought. This theory, which attributed the dominance of so-called northern nations over more southerly ones to the active, industrious character of peoples of northern climes in contrast to the "laziness and torpor" that was a product of the tropical environment,[24] was accepted fact among the Enlightenment's "natural scientists," *philosophes*, and men of reason. Colonists to the New World were always in danger of being "infected" by their environment and subsequently stigmatized as lazy, disease ridden, promiscuous: as if the shock of relocation to a different climate or hemisphere could actually make one "physically denatured and morally degenerate."[25]

Stereotype threat related to this stigma appears to have resonated with particular strength among Anglophone colonists of the Americas, especially in the thirteen "American" colonies, where they conjoined a simplistic and phenotypic notion of race with the need to justify seizure and control inheritance of land. A provocative text in this regard is Thomas Jefferson's *Notes on the State of Virginia*. Written in part to refute the Comte de Buffon's theories on the degeneracy of New World life forms,[26] the book vigorously defends the American climate and the American people from all charges—though in such a fashion that its ironic legacy in the nineteenth and twentieth centuries was its contribution to polygenist theories of human origin that later became central planks of the eugenics movement.[27] In Jefferson's own time, of course, *Notes* served as the founding father's (successful) bid to join the ranks of the *philosophes*, but one cannot help but note how different was the treatment meted out to the creole cousins of those Frenchmen he so admired once they were in the New World. Crèvecoeur's scorn and suspicion are echoed three-quarters of a century later by Washington Irving, whose *Astoria; or, An-*

ecdotes of an Enterprise beyond the Rocky Mountains (1836) excoriated the French creoles of an Oregon Country that he, in a curious echo of Crèvecoeur, likewise never visited. "Haphazard wights of Gallic origin," was Irving's dismissive characterization, "who abound upon our frontier, living among the Indians like one of their own race."[28] The Irving quote gets straight to heart of the Anglophone's problem with the concept of creolization: its uncomfortable emotional resonances with ideas of miscegenation.

The creole is, as Chris Bongie has argued, a *"contaminated* usage, in which race partially gives way to place," and exclusionary meanings denoting racial purity slide without warning into inclusionary meanings in which race and even racial mixture are accepted and at times even celebrated.[29] The way linguists use the term is a good example of the slipperiness of the signifier. Linguists name as creole those languages that are the result of mixture. That is to say, creole languages are native to the places in which they emerged, but they emerged from conditions in which native speakers of other tongues were forced by trade or other exigency (e.g., modern slavery) to create a common tongue.[30] The creole is, thus, both native and Other.

Anglophone culture, of course, could and did embrace certain notions of American mixture. Crèvecoeur's Letter III, "What Is an American?" is paradigmatic in that regard. Asking, "[W]hence came all these people?" he answers the question in language that prefigures the imagery of the melting pot: "[T]hey are mixture of English, Scotch, Irish, French, Dutch, Germans, and Swedes. From this promiscuous breed, that race now called Americans have arisen. What then is . . . this new man? He is either an European, or the descendant of an European, hence that strange mixture of blood, which you will find in no other country. I could point out to you a family whose grandfather was an Englishman, whose wife was Dutch, whose son married a French woman, and whose present four sons have now four wives of different nations. *He* is an American, who leaving behind him all his ancient prejudices and manners, receives new ones from the new mode of life he has embraced, the new government he obeys, and the new rank he holds. He becomes an American by being received in the broad lap of our great *Alma Mater.* Here individuals of all nations are melted into a new race of men, whose labours and posterity will one day cause great changes in the world."

Crèvecoeur offers a vision of an acceptable mixture: of European stocks renewing themselves through intermarriage and producing, through the hybrid vigor thereby achieved, "fair cities, substantial villages, extensive fields, an immense country filled with decent houses, good roads, orchards, meadows, and bridges, where an hundred years ago all was wild, woody and uncultivated!"[31] Creole status was the opposite of this ideal. Creoles were bordercrossers whose ease among Indians and amid the untamed wilderness outside the "fair cities" hinted too strongly that the Anglo's much-vaunted purity of descent might, in fact, be a "contaminated" lineage. His ease in navigating the alien topographies of the New World, an ease that was, significantly, a birthright, was the embodiment of the danger posed by the new environment: that one might become *too* much a part of the landscape, lose oneself, become *too* native. As that landscape consisted not only of plants and animals but also of Amerindians and Africans, there was the ever-present fact—and the accompanying need to deny it—of mixture: living among and moving like the Others, the creolized European might yield to the temptation to form families and have offspring, endangering the unfree labor source on which the economic system depended by muddying the categories that had to be maintained for it to function. For a people clinging to the concept that one could maintain "inviolate boundaries between people living in proximity to each other"[32]—indeed, Jefferson's *Notes* go so far as to suggest that whites, Blacks, and Indians might represent separate species of humanity—the threat represented by creolization was immediate and directly felt.

Southern colonists had received a graphic illustration of the dangers of social "mixing" as early as 1676, when Bacon's Rebellion in Virginia pitted a loose coalition of lower-class whites, runaway slaves/servants, and "unruly" women against settled communities devoted to agriculture, commerce, and slavery along European models. The Black Codes passed in the wake of Bacon's death and the failure of his rebellion were explicitly aimed at preventing such a coalition from ever forming again.[33] A century later, colonies from Pennsylvania south to Georgia were similarly exercised over the threat of "white Indians"—bands of whites who went scantily clad (at least by European standards), while depending mostly on hunting for subsistence, mingling freely (and, one imagines, reproducing without shame) across racial lines, and occasionally devolving into violent bands of robbers. So great a threat was this unacceptable mixture perceived to be that it gave rise to anti-vagrancy statutes in North Carolina in 1745 and Georgia in 1764, before igniting the yearlong war of South Carolina "Regulators" (1768–69) determined to make these "Vagrants—Idlers—Gamblers, and the Outcasts of Virginia and North Carolina" settle down to the respectable trade of farming, or else.[34] Many studies of race and the American mind—more, in fact, than can be readily numbered—have deconstructed the array of legal, social, and psychological barriers that had to be erected to "regulate" the white settler's encounter with the American wilderness, whether that wilderness was the lowcountry swamp or the interior jungle of the psyche. Specifically, this literature has revealed what Paul Gilroy called the "founding absurdity" of racial purity as a principle of "power, differentiation, and classification."[35] There is not time or space to rehearse this history here, but in the case of the South Carolina, it's important to offer just a few demographic facts that undermine persistent attempts to characterize the populations of the Gullah Geechee Coast—whether white or Black—as "pure."

Here, we should pause again to consider the historic marker erected to commemorate the Middle Passage at Fort Moultrie, the port of quarantine and entry on South Carolina's Sullivan's Island for the Atlantic slave trade that was one of the locations targeted by domestic terrorist Dylann Roof in 2015. According to the language of the plaque, the African captives brought to the site numbered in the "tens of thousands . . . from 1700 to 1775." Now, those numbers may sound small in the context of the cumulative total of over 10 million Africans imported to the New World in chains from 1500 to 1900 and the more than 1.5 million estimated to have lost their lives in the Middle Passage.[36] They certainly are no more than a drop in the bucket of the projected 2020 African American population of 44.6 million.[37] But in historical terms, "tens of thousands" was, in fact, a tremendous tide of humanity. The city of Charleston may have been one of the largest in early America, but its population numbered a mere 10,863 in 1990, more than half whom—5,833—were Black.[38] "Tens of thousands" was a number to swamp not just colonial Charleston but the entire region. One Swiss newcomer to Carolina described the colony in 1737 as "more like a negro country than a land settled by white people."[39] A European tourist in 1772 wrote to the *South Carolina Gazette* that, arriving in Charleston, one might be forgiven for thinking one had arrived in "Africa, or *Lucifer's court.*"[40] Indeed, so many enslaved Africans passed through Charleston and neighboring smaller ports that it's been estimated that the number encompasses one out of every four ancestors of the native Black population of the United States.[41]

Lowcountry population ratios were strongly skewed by the size of rice plantations, which, unlike tobacco or even cotton lands, required literally hundreds of slaves to work. Lowcountry whites, thus, faced both a literal swamp and the constant threat of being *swamped*. The menace was physical, with sources in mosquito-borne diseases, to which Africans and Amerindians had at least some resistance, and the very real danger of insurrection, among both the enslaved population and the maroons who escaped to Florida to join what was to become an increasingly well-organized and militarized Seminole nation—a history that we shall examine in more depth in chapter 6. And, too, the menace was genetic, with sources in the massive population of Africans and the embattled and dwindling populations of enslaved and free Amerindians among whom this tiny white minority lived.

"We are all contaminated by each other" is the epigraph from Kwame Anthony Appiah that begins this chapter, in recognition of the fact that race mixing was the rule rather than the exception in the making of the Americas, particularly in the colonial period. Because of the long history of trade and subjugation of Spain by north African Muslims, at least some of the Spanish conquistadors were themselves of mixed ancestry, and the first documented Africans in the Americas, north and south, were not slaves.[42] Indeed, the first documented nonnative settlers of Carolina were not Europeans but Africans abandoned in the Port Royal Sound region by Spaniards whose colonial dreams were smashed by disease, hostile Indians, and what may have been the first slave insurrection in North America.[43] Presumably, the Africans blended with the local Indian population, and such blending was to continue. As AfraAmerIndian specialist A. Anjana Mebane-Cruz says, "On the ground, people mix no matter what arbitrary borders or boundaries are placed between them, through mutual consent or force. In fact the very idea of mixing is a cultural one, not a biological one."[44]

Given the twin imperatives to control land and secure an ever-larger unfree labor force to work it, the historical record of the lowcountry offers few examples of men or women who can be brought to admit these realities. But few does not mean none. There are, of course, the notable antebellum examples of Sarah and Angelina Grimke—the elite Charleston belles who broke with their heritage over the treatment of their family's African American slaves and their brother's biracial children in order to join Quaker communities in the North, writing prolifically in the service of the abolitionist cause.[45] Similarly, the British actress Fanny Kemble's marriage to slaveholder Pierce Butler of Georgia produced years of misery for the couple as well as the remarkable *Journal of a Residence on a Georgian Plantation, 1838–39* (1863), in which the demise of her marriage is clearly linked to her inability to cease viewing the enslaved as human beings. But, arguably, the most notable departure from the privileged narrative of the ideal South may have come courtesy of George Dionysius Tillman, the older brother of South Carolina's legendary race-baiting governor and U.S. senator, "Pitchfork" Ben Tillman. The elder Tillman's remarks—delivered to state lawmakers debating the adoption of a "one drop" racial integrity standard for the 1895 state constitution and recorded by a reporter for an African American newspaper, the Columbia *Daily Register*—offer a picture sharply at odds with the one we shall find predominant in part II of this study: "George Tillman, with rare realism, opposed reducing the quota below one-eighth [Negro ancestry, the equivalent of a single Black grandparent], pointing out that he was acquainted with several families in his Congressional District which had a small degree of Negro ancestry, yet had furnished able soldiers to the Confederacy and were now accepted by white society. He did not want to see such families needlessly embarrassed. In addition he made the astounding claim that there was not one pure-blooded Caucasian on the floor of the convention. He maintained that all had ancestors from at least one of the colored races, though not necessarily the Negro race. Therefore he called for a provision that would define 'Negro' as a person with one-fourth or more Negro ancestry."[46]

It helps in contextualizing this passage to understand that the 1890 census showed only three counties in the entire state of South Carolina with Black populations below 30 percent. Twenty-three of the thirty-five counties had populations between 50 and 80 percent, while another three had populations greater than 80 percent. It's worth noting also that another forty years would pass before the Great Migration would allow whites to achieve majority status in the state.[47] As late as the mid-1940s, bi- and triracial population enclaves—called by such colorful pejoratives as Brass Ankles, Red Bones, Red Legs, Croatans, Turks, and Marlboro Blues, among others—were the rule not the exception in almost every county of the state.[48] As for Tillman's spasm of "racial realism," it certainly attests to the pressing need to recruit troops for the white race, but it didn't persuade his fellow delegates to the constitutional convention to adopt the one-quarter standard. Still, his gesture remains provocative. By invoking "honorable service" in the Civil War as a memory framework and myth structure, Tillman offered the protection of law to the informal practices of "whitening" that were occurring in towns and small communities across South Carolina.[49] Though one might be tempted to see this as "generous" in the context of the time, perhaps even progressive, it's ultimately a strategy of white supremacy, a thin plank shoring up a white identity that is actually built on a shifting landscape of water and sand.

Similarly, discourses of "Gullah purity" serve the same purpose. In chapter 1 we explored the "abject Geechee" stereotype that has so long bedeviled African Americans dwelling along the southeastern Atlantic coast. But this figure has a foil: the "good Gullah," usually a grandmother or grandfather figure, untrammeled by modern life, free, "pure," the embodiment of both pastoral and spiritual ideals. So, what are we to make of the strategy of celebrating and praising "good" Gullahs while oppressing and rejecting "bad" Geechees? When the Gullah is imagined as pure and its presence is mapped onto distant, romanticized islands, while the Geechee is mapped onto mainland urban spaces that offer disturbing opportunities for economic competition and social miscegenation, then I think we can safely conclude that this, too, is a strategy of white supremacy. A pure Black population, after all, implies that the white population is also pure. Invoked as a memory frame and myth structure, these categories justify the maintenance of social and legal structures that keep Gullahs isolated upon their islands and leave them prey to forces of late capitalism bent on acquiring their lands and preventing their access to goods and meaningful labor. Meanwhile, on the mainland, Geechees and more assimilated African Americans of Gullah Geechee descent may remain detached from, perhaps even unaware of, their historic and cultural links to Gullahs (not to mention entrenched in prejudices against them) and thus unable to partner meaningfully with rural populations in the political and economic realms.

It's an irony well worth noting that I myself, as a researcher, was first drawn to the study of Gullahs by the fact that I had been born and raised in Charleston—yet had never heard of the word or the mysterious people and language so celebrated by scholars. Quite literally—until I heard my first Gullah recording in 1998 and recognized it as the speech of my grandmother and all my paternal relations—I was a woman "without a past": disinherited from a rich and complex history and heritage. My experience is not a singular one, according to the National Park Service's "Special Resource Study," the process that resulted in designation of the Gullah Geechee Cultural Heritage Corridor in 2006. People who participated in the stakeholder focus groups at the extreme northern and southern boundaries of the study area in Little River, South Carolina, and Jacksonville, Florida, ended up *thanking* the researchers for, in effect, "telling them who they were."[50]

I'm well aware that I'm arguing a controversial point in arguing *against* Gullah Geechee purity. The Gullah Geechee enclaves in South Carolina and Georgia are renowned for the stability of their populations. But stability is not the same thing as purity, nor is the foundation of that stability as secure as we may imagine. Just as Gullah Geechee speech is creole speech, both native and the product of mixture, so may the same be said of Gullah Geechee as a lineage. The official slave trade may well have ended in the United States proper in 1807, but slave ships continued to ply the Atlantic Coast to Florida until 1821, the year the state entered the Union. And even then, illegal smuggling continued to the Gullah Geechee Coast, the New Orleans region, and even Galveston, Texas, up until the eve of the Civil War.[51] *The Wanderer*, designed as a fast pleasure sloop but operated as a slaver, was captured after landing nearly five hundred "salt-water Africans" (that is to say, imported directly from Africa without "seasoning" in the Caribbean) on Jekyll Island, Georgia, in 1858. The schooner *Clothilde*, believed to be the last ship to smuggle enslaved Africans to the United States, slipped into Mobile Bay in 1860.[52] While historians can only guess at the scale of illegal smuggling operations, their overall result was a continued steady infusion of African peoples, cultures, and languages, particularly along the Gullah Geechee Coast—an infusion that was to make this region ethnically and culturally the most Africanized of any region on the Eastern Seaboard.[53]

But again, "most Africanized" need not imply "pure." When a scholar such as William Pollitzer, for example, notes the presence of "relatively *unmixed* blacks on the coast of South Carolina and Georgia" (emphasis added)[54]—ironically, just before launching into a detailed explanation of ethnicity among victims of the slave trade—he's using a rhetorical flourish that's almost ubiquitous and yet, at essence, fallacious. Edward Said may have said it best: "Partly because of empire, all cultures are involved in one another: none is single and pure, all are hybrid, heterogeneous, extraordinarily differentiated, and unmonolithic."[55] The very words "Gullah" and "Geechee" are themselves creolizations, with African tribal names (Ngola, Gola, Kissi, Giggi), American place names (Ogeechee River), and Europeanized spellings just a few of the ingredients in the multicultural brew. As for the people and the culture all these elements created, they are no less vigorously hybrid, a mixture of West African, American Indian, and European gene pools, languages, and lifeways.

Even if we concentrate solely on the African side of the equation, one may assert that there was nothing ethnically or certainly culturally "pure" about the population. Science has long noted that genetic diversity in Africa, even between closely related groups, is high—much higher than in any other human population.[56] European slave ships, meanwhile, plied their trade along a stretch of African coastline that was roughly equivalent to the length of the U.S.-Mexico border, around nineteen hundred miles. The slave traders and the raiders on whom they relied, moreover, drew their captives from deep in the interior, with some coming from as far east as Madagascar, in the Indian Ocean—as distant from the Western Sudan as Buenos Aires is from North Carolina.[57] Recent advances in slave trade historiography have made it possible to determine the ethnic mix of the enslaved, at least between 1716 and 1807, with great accuracy, and the results of those studies are fascinating: 19.7 percent of captives came from the Senegambia (present-day Senegal and Gambia); 6 percent from today's Guinea-Bissau and Sierra Leone; 17.3 percent from the Windward Coast (Liberia and the Ivory Coast). These, it should be noted, are the chief rice-growing regions of the western Sudan, giving force to Judith Carney's contention that particular West African groups were targeted for capture due to their mastery of a superior rice-growing technology. Continuing our progress down the African coast, 13.4 percent of captives came from the Gold Coast (Ghana), 1.5 percent from the Bight of Benin (Togo, Benin, and western Nigeria), and 2.5 percent from the Bight of Biafra (western Nigeria, Cameroon, and Gabon); fully 39 percent had their origin in Angola (including southern Gabon, Congo, Cabinda, Angola, and northwest Namibia); while a sprinkling, 0.5 percent, originated in present-day Mozambique and Madagascar, on the Indian Ocean.[58] This is the population—drawn from the most ethnically diverse continent on the planet—that we have been taught to think of as "pure."

The process of creolization that made these multitudes recognizable as a single people—Gullah Geechee African Americans—was not a gentle one. Indeed, it is helpful to recall that it occurred amid a great dying. I'm speaking not just of slave mortality during the Middle Passage itself—though that has been estimated at roughly 15 percent per voyage, and high death rates persisted during "seasoning," the period of quarantine the captives endured in places like Sullivan's Island.[59] Even after seasoning, life chances along the rice coast continued to be particularly precarious, as the rice planting regime—with its snake-, alligator-, and mosquito-infested swamps and extremes of heat and humidity—proved to be the deadliest in North America.

Only 5 percent of U.S. slaves were associated with rice cultivation in 1850—the period during which rice ruled the coasts of South Carolina and Georgia, just as short-staple cotton, worked by 73 percent of the total enslaved population, ruled the interior and the Deep South—but rice was consistently associated with the highest probability of death.[60] Among infants, the probability of death was 41 percent higher than the combined probabilities for cotton, hemp, tobacco, or sugar; among children ages one to four, the figure fell to 26 percent; but among those aged five to fourteen, death probabilities rose tenfold, to 287 percent.[61] Slave mortality rates were even higher in the overcrowded conditions of cities like Charleston, Savannah, and New Orleans.[62] Indeed, the seasonal cycle of epidemics—from malaria to yellow fever to smallpox and half a dozen others—led a doctor visiting Charleston in the 1780s to give this postmortem: "Carolina was in the spring a paradise, in the summer a hell, and in the autumn a hospital."[63]

Sobering as this picture is, we must not forget the subtler yet no less devastating dying that was not physical but spiritual: the massive commingling of cultures and extinction of languages that occurred as slave sellers and buyers forced together people of different backgrounds in the vain hope that they'd be less likely to make common cause to revolt or run away. Let us try to imagine it, to imagine the African captives not just as the collection of nations listed above but as rural, rice-growing villagers and as wealthy, urbanized metropole dwellers; as Mandinkans remarkable for their height and beauty; as short-statured Ibos shunned by Carolina planters for their alleged propensities to rebellion and suicide; as slaves, kings, warriors, priests, skilled craftsmen, peasant farmers, Muslims, and "pagans" from hundreds of distinct tribal groupings—all swept up in the wars of religion, ivory, and gold that wracked West Africa from the arrival of the Portuguese in the fifteenth century through the "scramble for Africa" among European empire builders in the late nineteenth century.[64] Let us imagine one final fact: that these many hundreds of thousands of men and women spoke hundreds of languages: Songhai, Wolof, Fulani, Temne, Kissi, Gola, Mende, Kru, Ewe, Twi, Yoruba, Igbo, Bantu, Kongo, to name just a few. And let us take just a moment to reflect on the fact that not a single one of those languages survived intact.[65]

A great dying indeed.

And that is the question that asserts itself yet again as we set out on this journey into the linguistic, cultural, and literary heritage of the Gullah Geechee coast: Is Gullah culture dying? Has it perhaps already died?

There are many who have answered that question with a resounding yes: Gullah, they say, is in the final stages of language death, and the culture is itself no longer distinct. Of course, it should be noted that "they" have been saying so for over a century. The pessimists include historians of the late nineteenth and early twentieth centuries who thought the language would soon be extinct along with the entire Negro race, unable to cope with the "rigors" of freedom.[66] They include eminent folklorists such as Bruce Jackson, who declared in his introduction to a 1965 reissue of Lydia Parrish's *Slave Songs of the Georgia Sea Islands*, "There is yet much old Negro folklore on the Sea Islands, but not very much."[67] We'll recall that Liz Young lamented the imminent death of the Gullah language in 1983, while in 1987 the most admired Gullah ethnography of the decade—the one that, along with Charles Joyner's *Down by the Riverside* (1984), put Gullah studies in its current iteration on the map—was titled *When Roots Die*.

Others dispute this idea. Linguist Salikoko Mufwene has argued, "Gullah is pretty much alive, probably as lively as it was in its beginnings, despite what outsiders may think,"[68] and his view is echoed by those working at the grassroots. "People speak my language all day long," said Marquetta Goodwine, the "art-ivist" crowned "Queen Quet" of the Gullah Geechee People Nation in a widely reported conceptual art performance in 2000. As Goodwine argued in the newspaper profile that accompanied her "enstooling," "Someone will write me and say, 'I was doing research there [in the lowcountry], and I didn't hear [Gullah] spoken.' But then I ask them if they went to the people, or did they just read a book. Why did they think they were getting to the people if all you did was go and read a book? See, they missed the whole point. They didn't go to the people themselves."[69]

Mufwene's is, it must be admitted, a minority view. Measured against the certainties of so many other powerful cultural forces, Goodwine's words and those of the members of the cultural revitalization and preservation groups scattered up and down the Gullah Geechee coast may seem as distant and lonely echoes of voices in the wilderness. Discourses of "the vanishing Gullah" are far more numerous, louder, with far greater access to amplification in official media. But even if arguments for language death have been exaggerated, we should at least consider the possibility that discourses of "the changing same"—especially those articulated by various activist and preservationist Gullah Geechee coalitions—are an excursion into romantic, antimodern fantasy: a way of elevating and freezing in time a "pure" African essence that does not in fact exist.

Contemporary scholarship offers us tools for deeper analysis of these issues that must not be scorned. Examining Gullah Geechee contexts—and the texts they inspire—from a transnational perspective, using postcolonial, psychoanalytic, performance, and border studies as well as traditional analytical tools such as the close textual reading, we can begin to answer questions that have yet to be asked about the role Gullah Geechee figures and culture play in the artistic and literary imaginary of the region and nation. We can begin, for example, configuring a canon of texts that responds not just to temporal categories and the somewhat artificially constructed "schools" and "movements" we have inherited from previous generations of scholars but instead to Gullah Geechee coastal contexts. Such a canon would place familiar figures from the so-called Charleston Renaissance, including DuBose Heyward and Julia Peterkin, into conversation with figures firmly associated with Harlem Renaissance contexts, such as W. E. B. Du Bois, James Weldon Johnson, Claude McKay, Jean Toomer, and Zora Neale Hurston.[70] With this new configuration of familiar figures, we can also begin to ask new questions: questions, for example, about the deployment of tropes of hybridity and purity in their work; about representation of frozen mortuary landscapes versus vividly alive "third spaces," whether cultural or geographic. We can inquire into the tension between incarceration in abjected identities versus the circulation and recirculation of tropes and texts across lines of color in a circum-Atlantic formation we now know to be paradigmatic of modernity.

Most critically, we can explore the ways in which Gullah Geechee contexts nourished a notion of Black authenticity intended to form an explicit contrast with minstrelsy's "darky act." Indeed, I will argue that this notion has been foundational in serious literary work by African American artists—and that it lingers, as a vivid caricature, in popular genres by white southerners. All these questions and many others will serve to engage our attention, as we move from the contexts of language, landscape, and lineage to the texts of a critically important period, the interwar years from roughly 1915 to the outbreak of the Great War, and the well- and lesser-known artists associated with it: the artists of the Harlem Renaissance and the newly minted Charleston Renaissance.

PART II

Texts

CARTOGRAPHIES OF STRUGGLE
AND THE CANON

CHAPTER 3

Pastoral Scenes of the Gallant South
"Beautiful, Historic" Charleston

> We found the place as pleasant as possible, for it was covered with mighty oaks and infinite store of cedars, and with . . . [Myrtle] growing underneath them, smelling so sweetly, that the very fragrant odor made the land seem exceedingly pleasant. On every side were to be seen palm trees and other sorts of trees bearing blossoms of very rare shape and very good smell.
>
> —RENÉ GOULAINE DE LAUDONNIÈRE, *History of the First Attempt of the French (the Huguenots) to Colonize the Newly Discovered Country of Florida* (1592)[1]

What if there never was a Charleston Renaissance?

It has become the fashion among literary and art critics to attach the label "renaissance" to the activities of the preservationists, writers, visual artists, and others who lived in or were drawn to Charleston between the world wars and who joined forces to refashion the city's story, in part for tourist consumption and in part for their own, into a pastoral dream of the gallant South. It will even be productive for our purposes to accept that nomenclature in this study, if only for the sake of convenience. But in adopting the term "renaissance" to discuss the productions of Charleston's art and preservation community, we should be clear about what we mean.

When canon-makers refer to "renaissance" moments, they generally mean to suggest a furious flowering of new thought and new forms. In the twentieth century, for example, we're familiar with not one but two historically conscious modernist literary movements that emerged from the South: the New Negro Renaissance, a product of migration adopting the symbolic home of Harlem, its artists delving deeply into the creole folk cultures of the South while also seeking for their African roots; and the Southern Literary Renaissance, with multiple centers from Nashville to New Orleans, and artists producing work at the intersection of race, class, and questions about their own personal legitimacy as heirs of a grand but tattered plantation tradition. Both movements emerged from "crossroads needs to reassess the past," as literary critic Keith Cartwright framed the matter, and from that wrestling a mighty art was born.[2]

There was much less wrestling in Charleston. The city's art-loving coterie was willing to entertain modernity—and that's meant quite literally. Carl Sandburg and Gertrude Stein were warmly feted guests of the Poetry Society of South Carolina in the 1920s, and there was a grand reception when the Gibbes Art Museum took the daring step of exhibiting Sol Guggenheim's collection of nonobjective paintings during the period.[3] But apart from these excursions into the bold, the radical, the new, Renaissance institutions like the Poetry Society of South Carolina, the Society for the Preservation of Spirituals, the Society for the Preservation of Old Dwellings, and the Carolina Art League, among others, tended to produce works that, looking backward through a haze of romance, were proudly, profoundly antimodern. And that was just as their audience of down-at-heels southern gentility and monied northerners—the Doubledays, DuPonts, Huttons, Whitneys, Guggenheims, and Vanderbilts, who all purchased prime plantation lands as hunting preserves and second homes in the interwar years—preferred it.[4] Charleston's ruling caste eagerly embraced a narrative that amounted to the invention of a "usable past," celebrating their ancestors, their grand houses, their storied way of life as a way of reasserting their own cultural and political significance in the present.[5]

The much-celebrated results of their literary and artistic efforts have been adjudged lovely, lyrical, and worthy of recovery and reexamination, but we must not forget that they constitute a "violent mis-remembering" of the facts of the case.[6] Renaissance writers tended to imagine slavery on a narrow spectrum that ranged from John C. Calhoun's "positive good" to something on the order of a "slight blemish" on an otherwise dazzling portrait. But such terms are entirely inadequate to the task of imagining Charleston's past, in which slavery functions more like, as Fred Moten argues, a "durational field" embracing both Enlightenment and Darkness—one whose nature and indeed whose very materiality the artists of the Charleston Renaissance were determined to obscure.[7]

Thus, in this chapter, we shall meet some of the patriarchs of the Charleston Renaissance, a mostly male group of masters of its written word, a group that is led by DuBose Heyward, the slight and affable author of the best known of the works of the Renaissance, the novel *Porgy*, which was to transform over time into that beloved staple of the operatic repertory, *Porgy and Bess*. Alongside Heyward stand lesser known men, men who, in never leaving Charleston to venture into the miscegenated spaces along Broadway's Great White Way, are in fact more representative of its ethos. The group includes Herbert Ravenel Sass, "Hobo" to his friends, a self-taught naturalist and nature writer who turned his considerable literary gifts not just to the glories of creation but also to the writing of lyrical historical novels on the passing of the "Red man" and vitriolic screeds against racial mixing. Rounding out the patriarchs were Archibald Rutledge, the passionate huntsman and South Carolina poet laureate from 1934 to 1973; Thomas R. Waring Sr., newspaper editor and father of the newspaper editor who was to become the leading journalistic voice defending segregation in the South;[8] and Alfred Huger, a maritime lawyer and raconteur. These, and a few others, were the combined talents that produced what was arguably the most important literary document of the Charleston Renaissance: *The Carolina Low-Country*, published in 1931.

Collecting poetry, visual art, and essays from the various culture-making clubs of the Renaissance, along with a carefully curated selection of Negro spirituals, this anthology stood in deliberate counterpoint to *The New Negro* (1925) and other volumes from the emergent New Negro Renaissance tradition as an overt celebration of "the old Negro" that also engaged in a critique, indeed a rebuke, of the headlong American embrace of progress and modernity. The anthology had quite a bit in common with *I'll Take My Stand: The South and the Agrarian Tradition*, published by the Nashville "Fugitives" the year before—chiefly, the fact that both celebrations of the so-called agrarian tradition glibly ignored the fact that plantations were themselves scenes of production: what Donna Haraway has called the very "model and motor for the carbon-greedy machine-based factory system" that was the target of both groups' collective wrath.[9]

In this chapter, we shall focus on *The Carolina Low-Country* as a manifesto of the worldview of the Charleston Renaissance operating in much the same way as *I'll Take My Stand* served the Southern Literary Renaissance and *The New Negro*, the "Harlem: Mecca of the New Negro" issue of *Survey Graphic*, and *FIRE!! Devoted to Younger Negro Artists* had served the Harlem Renaissance. This act—placing two groups of artists and place- and culture-makers who were never intended to mingle in an intentional conversation—is a deliberate attempt to consider the possibilities for canon formation our adjusted cartographies of the Gullah Geechee Coast create. Over the course of four chapters alternating in focus on "old Charlestonians" versus "new Negroes," we shall consider the forces set in motion by the Great Migration, contrasting the perspectives and the art produced by both groups.

On the one hand, we have those left behind: though still in possession of the field, their means are diminished and their longings, resentments, and mystification appear to intensify as the plantation districts empty out and the descendants of slaves, now become a modern, "uppity" generation, flock to Charleston and Savannah, Washington, New York, and all points beyond and between in search of education, better wages, and, yes, art. On the other hand, we behold the "new Negroes" themselves—some, like Edwin Augustus "Teddy" Harleston, are homegrown Charlestonians, or, as with James Weldon Johnson (Jacksonville) and Zora Neale Hurston (Eatonville, Florida), native to points further south along the Gullah Geechee Coast. Others—for example, W. E. B. Du Bois and Jean Toomer—were educated urbanites thrilled by the encounter, in an Afro-creole South that was both familiar and oh-so-very Other, with a "authentic" Black Self. Between these groups and occupying a central place that is yet a marginalized (third?) space are the folk communities we have learned to name Gullah Geechee: inheritors and cocreators of a creole tradition that their interpreters experienced as counterbalanced between an Enlightenment-era ideal of whiteness and the abjected Darkness of those Hurston called "the Negro farthest down."[10]

Both artist groups had legitimate claims to "know" and therefore speak for this folk community. Both had firsthand knowledge of its music and of their vernacular tongue, which was not of the minstrel stage, being infinitely older and far more capable of depth and even poetry. Both artist groups struggled with stereotype threat in encountering this folk community: that is to say, the community's abjected status threatened to tar them with its brush and they needed to develop strategies to combat the threat. At the same time, each artist group faced challenges in positioning themselves in a culture-making marketplace dominated by northern technology titans and the need to cater to national even more so than in-group tastes. But at the very marrow of this emergent literary tradition, the Charleston-Harlem convergence reveals complex issues of inheritance and disinheritance, fought over the landscape of General Sherman's Field Order No. 15, as well as in newspaper column inches and New York publishing contracts, over a period of decades.

For the white artist, this convergence constituted a crisis of legitimacy, the first challenge to the unassailable social position their caste had assumed since the period of Redemption. Trapped by personal loyalties and the Jim Crow code of silence on matters regarding race, Charleston artists in particular were to prove incurious about or incapable of questioning the South's unjust patrimony except indirectly, all the while remaining conscious, to greater and lesser degrees, of an undertow: a maternal inheritance from a "dark mother" who must be denied even as they drew upon the inheritance she left them[11]: the mother wit of three continents grafted onto the "singing tree" of a trifold creole heritage that was at once indigenous and African and European.[12] Unable either to wrestle with or work through these challenges to Lost Cause subjectivity, Charleston Renaissance artists retreated into sentimentality, creating a pastoral landscape, territorialized in terms of region and nation, in which this Gullah presence that was so omnipresent, so inescapable, could be centered and yet also excluded. Such unpredictable energies for art and nation making as their threefold inheritance represented could not in fact be contained by these means, as we shall see in our exploration of the bitter contestation over the meaning of the spirituals the Gullah Geechee sang—but it certainly was not for want of trying.

The Charleston group has somewhat belatedly achieved acceptance from the literary critical and artistic establishment, but while the standard of artistic merit they achieved is arguable, the durability of the pastoral dream of the gallant South they wove is absolutely indisputable. Its power to comfort the South's—and the nation's—comfortable allowed it to rise to a dominant and decades-long grip on the American popular imagination. We shall digress for a moment for a discussion of this pastoral dream, before delving into the specifics of *The Carolina Low-Country*'s investment in the pastoral as a mode for conveying it.

A Place with a Past: Charleston and the Pastoral Dream

"Porgy lived in the Golden Age. Not the Golden Age of a remote and legendary past; nor yet the chimerical era treasured by every man past middle life, that never existed except in the heart of youth; but an age when men, not yet old, were boys in an ancient, beautiful city that time had forgotten before it destroyed."[13]

So begins the novel that has had the most enduring legacy as a text of the Gullah Geechee Coast. The novel is, of course, DuBose Heyward's *Porgy*, whose distinct phases of existence—as a book birthed at the MacDowell Colony and respectably reviewed in the national press; as a Broadway hit; as the first truly "American" opera in the repertory; and finally, as a globe-trotting cultural ambassador for Cold War–era U.S. values—we shall explore in depth in our final chapter. But the road that ends with *Porgy* also begins there, as in Heyward we find the high-water mark of a tradition of southern pastoral nearly a century in the making.

Pastoral is usually a mode in which the vices of the city are contrasted with the innocence of the country. But the southern pastorals of the Charleston Renaissance make less distinction as to place. It is *time*—the sense of a glorious past contrasted with a fallen present—that serves as the productive site of creative tension. This manipulation of chronotope emerges especially in Heyward's descriptions of his city's faded glories. While theatrical productions usually emphasize Catfish Row's crepitude, Heyward's prose is more precise: the setting is, in fact, one of the city's more magnificent mansions, abandoned by its former owners and fallen on hard times. The entry to Catfish Row is described as a "massive grill of Italian wrought iron, [with a] . . . battered capital of marble surmount[ing] each of the gateposts." The wayward, seductive Bess swans across flagstones "which even beneath the accumulated grime of a century, glimmered with faint and varying pastel shades in direct sunlight"

(21). The longing for a vanished past is encoded into the very landscape, while the presence of the Gullah cast of characters as the unworthy heirs of this tarnished splendor seems at times ponderously symbolic.

Also symbolic are the spaces of the harbor—circling the neighborhoods of the lower Charleston peninsula—and especially the sea, which Heyward captures in all their many moods in passages of startling lyric intensity. At moments of calm, the harbor is a "dazzling" blue, "between its tawny islands like a sapphire upon a sailor's weathered hand." Just before the devastating hurricane that drowns the men of Catfish Row's "Mosquito Fleet," though, it is "black, and strangely lifeless," with "[t]hin, intensely white crests [riding] the low, pointed waves" (49). Images of modern rot and decay, moments of pulsating "Negro" passion, alternate with picture perfect descriptions of leisured "[l]adies on the deep piazzas" (141), houses draped with rose trellises and framed by broad drives that serve as an ironic backdrop for a novel of struggling primitives baffled by and hopelessly inadequate to their encounter with the modern world.

Critics of the time were admiring, struck by Heyward's ability to chronicle what the *New York Times* called the "strange, various, primitive and passionate world" of the Negro. But though the characters in *Porgy*—the star-crossed lovers and the vicious, conscienceless killer who destroys their idyll—are vivid, it is "beautiful, historic Charleston" that looms largest over them all as *locus amoenus*, the legendary "pleasant place" of the pastoral mode where "men, not yet old, were boys" in a "an ancient and beautiful city that time had forgot before it destroyed." *Porgy* shares with a long and still lively tradition in southern literature this pose of longing for an absent presence. Figured simultaneously as an Edenic paradise lost and as a romantically haunted homeplace, images of a lost "Golden Age" Charleston both fascinate within and reverberate throughout the narrative.

Serious inquiry into the pastoral is something that for a time fell on hard times among Americanists. As Sara Blair put the matter in *American Literary History* some years back, "Traditional categories of U.S. space and place—nature, region, landscape, pastoral, the frontier—had until recently been so discredited that literary scholars had virtually abandoned them."[14] Indeed, witness the previous chapter, where our discussion of landscape and creole lineage as critical frameworks for reconsidering the Gullah Geechee Coast owed more to history, anthropology, and cultural geography than to purely literary categories of analysis. But while the ecocritical lens brings into focus nuances of culture and environment that are of central importance, I would agree with Blair that something important is lost when we too quickly discard the traditional categories, which are in her view "crucial to the writing of American material and experiential histories" because "they continue powerfully to mediate contemporary social relations."[15] Thus, our task in this chapter will be to reclaim the pastoral as a relevant category of study and to consider the ways in which it reverberates through the social relations of the time as well as its critical interrelationships with other "southern" modes.

Simply stated, the pastoral is a literary or artistic mode characterized by nostalgia for a largely hypothetical state of lost love, plenitude, and/or innocence: a "Golden Age," as since Hesiod the matter has been framed.[16] The pastoral and the sentimental are related modes[17]—indeed, they are often confused with one another, for each seeks to make its audience weep: the sentimental, for the sake of affect as an end in and of itself; the pastoral, to mediate a painful, some would argue potentially fatal, loss.[18] Both literary modes, as well, are associated generically with a certain range of conflicts that the text seeks to resolve. Typically, in each, a dream of plenitude/innocence/love falls under threat from an outside force. What separates the two is subtle, but closer examination reveals the pastoral's roots to be of a more ancient, more pagan Western tradition.[19] Both, for example, may invoke the "innocent" pleasures of country games and amusements, but only the pastoral pairs these amusements with orgies and seductions, ritual combats and ritual murders; both contemplate the possibility of loss, but only the pastoral dares look upon that possibility without the ameliorative cushion of a happy ending; indeed, only the pastoral is fully involved with and invested in the notion of tragedy in general and a tragic landscape in particular.

I am invoking the "tragic landscape" here in a specific Americanist context: as a complex set of memory frames and myth structures in which the utopic promise of the United States is undermined or actively threatened by a dystopic devolution, familiarly expressed in the binaries "civilization" and "savagery," though there are, of course, others. "Tragic landscape" has points in common with other critical figurations, for example, Richard Slotkin's "fatal environment." But even though both terms describe spaces "defined less by maps and surveys than by myths and illusions, projective fantasies, wild anticipations, extravagant expectations,"[20] there is an important difference in emphasis—as "fatal" suggests the distant grinding of the mills of God, slow but "exceeding small,"[21] while "tragic" implies the human dimension of hubris, the excessive pride or defiance of the gods that leads to the confrontation with nemesis, the implacable agent of one's own downfall.

Of course, even in drawing distinctions, what separates the two ultimately may not be as significant as what binds them, for both of these readings of the American landscape occur within specific, racialized contexts. Slotkin's notions of "fatality" are explicated in his epic three-volume examination of the myth of the West in the national psyche,[22] while the "tragic" myths and cultural memories of the plantation South are inextricable from nearly a century of Lost Cause inspired historiography/hagiography, but in both cases, what the myth seeks to mystify is a reality of racialized violence: histories of human trafficking, forced labor, war, pestilence, even genocide that still torment the national imagination, that must be hidden because they cannot be faced. Black-white conflicts have traditionally been framed as the originary clash informing the history and culture of the American South, but it is well to keep Slotkin's ideas close, for he reminds us to look for traces of Indian War in our own southern landscape and especially in our literatures; indeed, his work invites a reimagining of the centuries of bloody conflict among Amerindians, Africans, citizens of every warring European power, and all their various Creole offspring before the first shot was fired in Charleston Harbor.[23]

Pastoral, on the other hand, invites the reader to look away. Whenever the mode is invoked—whether in a novel, an interior design "style" book, or a docent's spiel for a historic home tour—its effect is to mystify and mask the existence and the effects of violence: the violence of personal loss, yes, but also and especially the ways the personal can be interwoven with what we rather antiseptically call the violence of imperialist contestation. Wendell Berry's *The Hidden Wound* (1970) gives a devastating account of the uses of this sentimental, idealizing language in helping to avert the southerner's gaze from the inherent violence of the plantation system and the mark it left on both humans and the land:

> The language . . . involves a sort of schizophrenia, a curious ability to confront the most horrible acts and then to look away from them, as if they did not exist, into a medieval fantasy [of knights and fair maidens]. And the medieval fantasy is sometimes ornamented with Napoleonic fantasy. . . . [Men of violence were] not an anomaly within that society; [they] served one of its designated functions, and [their] mentality and behavior were therefore characteristic. [Their] fellow citizens had to contend with [them] as a reflection of something in themselves, and short of attempting to change the society, they had to try to live as painlessly as possible with the harsh truth that [they] represented. Their solution was to romanticize [them]. . . . Once this mythology was accepted, the moral ground could be safely preempted by rhetoric.[24]

Through the romanticizing operations of an "innocent" yearning for a glorious, yet vanished past, pastoral nostalgia gains the ability to become a source of pleasure in and of itself. In the poetics of repetition—specifically, repetitive invocation of certain landscapes, certain associations—the pastoral tale masks both the actual social relations the narrative claims to relate and effects a cathartic transformation in the emotions of the audience. Loss may be the reality hiding behind the rhetoric; but the repetition of the pastoral refrain—in our case, "beautiful, historic Charleston"—somehow serves to mitigate that loss.

And what are the losses? In the case of our artists' community in Charleston, the losses—of land and plantations, of the power of life and death over everyone under one's sway, of the charmed status as the "pink" of the lowcountry's wealthy, cultured *bon ton*—were significant, even catastrophic. But a militant refusal to give an inch in the war of representations of slavery and the Lost Cause gives away the game, betraying that the pose of "innocent" yearning is implicated, as anthropologist Renato Rosaldo has described, in southern cultures of imperialism and "imperialist nostalgia," using "a pose of 'innocent yearning' both to capture people's imaginations and to conceal its complicity with often brutal domination."[25]

Rosaldo's critique asks profound questions about the causes and nature of loss, and there are profound reflections on such matters to be found in the memoirs and letters of the generation that fought the Civil War. These are men and women, plain folk and haughty, grappling with questions of life and death, fatality and tragedy, in their recollections of slavery and war, not to mention the night riders and election riots, the general unrest of the years between the end of Reconstruction and the pacification of the Black population that was the goal of "Redemption." As we have said, however, wrestling has never been Charleston's strong suit; romance has always been the city's stock in trade. The choice to counter criticisms of the city's dependence on slavery and the violent means by which whites were restored to power by inventing a myth was no doubt an instinctive one, but it was anything but an innocent one. Charleston—and the lowcountry landscape—are beautiful and historic, but as Tressie McMillan Cottom has reminded us, "beauty isn't actually what [things] look like; beauty is the preferences that reproduce the existing social order."[26] And in this instance, the social order is also fatal and tragic, making the beauty of Charleston thereby a *guilty beauty* that is complicit with a horror and a lie.

This notion of "guilty beauty" was propounded by Atlantic World conceptual artist and social choreographer Ernesto Pujol in the exhibition notes for *WALK*, a photographic essay that uses Magnolia Cemetery, chief resting place for the city's Confederate dead, as the setting for a meditation on the remembrance of war, the end of empire, and the relationship between white identity politics and mourning.[27] For *WALK*, the Buddhist artist donned black robes that recalled his former life in a monastic order at Mepkin Abbey, forty miles north of the city, in order to subtly critique Magnolia's role as a staging ground for costumed remembrances of the Confederacy, in which veiled female reenactors gowned in nineteenth-century dress annually perform a walk of mourning in honor of their never-to-be-forgotten dead. Noting that the series was inspired by dreams, site visits, and the Civil War poetry and letters of Walt Whitman, Pujol writes that his images invite the audience to ponder what, amid all the stone and marble plinths, broken obelisks, and carved sarcophagi, amid the iterated and reiterated gestures of mourning and remembrance, the visitor is being invited to forget.

> The calm, seductive, and seemingly transcendent neoclassical beauty of Charleston is ... a guilty beauty created through slavery, white columns constructed on black backs. It is a terrible beauty of workers in chains and gardens watered with blood. The low country landscape is a grave; the city boasts as many ghost tours as garden tours. ... It is a painful beauty where elegance and good taste betray us publicly. It is an ultimately disturbing environment whose sweetness leaves a bitter taste, whose perfume becomes foul the minute one seeks consciousness. It is, finally, ... [a] place that can only elicit gestures of deconstruction, of exposure, of reclamation and healing among the culturally aware.[28]

Note that Pujol suggests the consciousness of guilty beauty can come only to the "culturally aware." His artist's note serves as a cogent reminder that an artistic praxis can be attuned to eliciting such awareness and can be equally capable of putting the audience back to sleep. As the signature work and indeed the manifesto of the artists of the Charleston Renaissance, *The Carolina Low-Country* offers a primer on Katherine McKittrick's assertion that cartographies "organize human hierarchies in place and reify uneven geographies in even, seemingly natural ways."[29] The collaborators use the project to erect a wall of personal legitimacy around the Gullah spirituals that are the object of their "guilt-less" yearning; at the same time the text works actively to suppress any readings other than its own of the meaning of the spirituals or the culture from which they emerged. The volume conjures a vision of the past that is just right for dreaming, but even though the essays framing the spirituals are steeped in Lost Cause ideology, they also offer a glimpse of a terrain through which an oppositional reading allows a new story, a creole story, to emerge.

The Spirituals Society and the Invention of Tradition

In a dramatic scene-setting passage in *A Golden Haze of Memory: The Making of Historic Charleston*, Stephanie Yuhl describes the benefit performance at a private mansion that constituted the official launch of the Society for the Preservation of [Negro] Spirituals. So striking is it that it is worthy of quoting at length: "During the performance a thirty-six-year-year old white woman named Panchita Heyward Grimball stepped forward from her fellow chorus members and explained her organization's main purpose: to collect and preserve African American spirituals ... [and] not ... just any spirituals, only those identified with a specific time and place—spirituals 'that were sung in slavery days and the 25 years immediately following in the Carolina coast country'. . . [Spirituals that possessed] 'as much as possible of the pure African wildness and beauty of tone, only touched by the religion of the Anglo-Saxon, not as the negro of today sings the Baptist, Methodist and Episcopal hymns, merely varied by the African love of syncopation.'"[30] The words hint at deep waters. Officially, when Charleston's spirituals society took up the cudgels in defense of their vision of Gullah Negroes and their music, the debate over the origins and nature of Black "jubilee" songs, later called "spirituals," had raged for nearly sixty years. The songs emerged into the national consciousness in a trickle starting in 1861 with the publication of "Oh Let My People Go," a song of "contrabands" that thrilled northern soldiers and civilians at Virginia's Fortress Monroe,[31] followed by the first definitive collection, *Slave Songs of the United States*, edited by William Francis Allen, Charles Pickard Ware, and Lucy McKim Garrison, in 1867.

Unofficially, however, the musical elements that characterized African American song and performance—polyrhythmic percussive accompaniment, communal singing in a call-and-response pattern, vocal glides, runs, and sometimes free-floating arrhythmic vocalizing in the manner of an extended meditation or improvisation, among many others—had been recognized for centuries, and the spirituals themselves had been "sung widely and . . . discussed in letters, diaries, and the periodical press" of the South since the time of the Great Awakening.[32] These formed a key part of the southerner's claim that only someone *from* the South could really "know the Negro." So yes, for elite Charlestonian culture-makers, the spirituals were, indeed, the songs of their youth, but Grimball's testimony reveals they were more than that: they constituted, as had their African American captives, a species of, let's call it, spiritual property, one that, given the loss of the Black bodies that had constituted their economic wealth, Grimball's class was particularly loath to relinquish. Indeed, the artistic and literary production of the Charleston Renaissance period in general testifies to a preoccupation, verging on obsession, among elites with the language and culture of their former slaves. The notion that lowcountry Blacks were "the strongest remaining vestige of a vanishing civilization" was a veritable idée fixe among Charleston Renaissance literati,[33] and they vied fiercely, even with each other, for supremacy in collecting, appropriating, and finding channels for disseminating local Black folklore and linguistic traditions.

Newspaper editor Ambrose Gonzales styled himself an expert on the Gullah after publishing four collections of tales "from the black border" in quick succession between 1922 and 1924, but, in terms of authenticity, his books vied, and not always to their benefit, with earlier collections—for example, Charles Colcock Jones Jr.'s *Negro Myths from the Georgia Coast* (1888)—as well as with works by contemporaries John Bennett, cofounder along with DuBose Heyward of the Poetry Society of South Carolina, and the lower Richland County physician and author E. C. L. Adams.[34] Alongside the folk tale collections, "rice plantation memoirs," of which Duncan Clinch Heyward's *Seed from Madagascar* (1936) serves as one of the preeminent examples, also flourished as a mini-genre in the interwar period. So widespread was the cultural fixation that even ladies could participate without damage to reputation. Elizabeth Allston Pringle's pseudonymously published *A Woman Rice Planter* literally saved the family farm when it became a bestseller in 1914—so her second memoir, *Chronicles of Chicora Wood*, was published (if posthumously) under her own name in 1922. Even performance was permitted to the female gender when such performances served the purposes of solidifying class and racial authority. Facing a decline into a not-so-genteel poverty after early widowhood left her with two young mouths to feed, DuBose Heyward's mother, Janie Screven Heyward, became a published author—of *Songs of the Charleston Darky* in 1912—and also a much-admired Gullah "dialect recitalist" whose performances earned her a handsome wage even in times of economic depression. The cultural authority of white Charlestonians over the representation of African Americans was so absolute that when Columbia University researchers went looking for "authentic" examples of Gullah dialect for their library archives, their gaze didn't land on Hell's Kitchen, the destination only blocks from the school's Morningside Heights campus where so many migrants from the Sea Islands and lowcountry plantation districts had washed ashore. Instead, they called on the "quintessential Charlestonian," preservationist Samuel Gaillard Stoney, coauthor of *Black Genesis* (1930) along with multiple books on Charleston architecture.[35]

This carceral authority over Black cultural production might have seemed unassailable, but Grimball's declaration also demonstrates that, by the 1920s, Charleston's elites perceived there to be cracks in the façade. There was, for example, a new assertiveness on the part of African Americans to contend with. W. E. B. Du Bois's *The Souls of Black Folk* (1901) had given to the spirituals a new name, one to which the Charleston culture-makers must have experienced an instinctual revulsion: "the sorrow songs," Du Bois called them, in direct repudiation of the happy darky archetype so beloved of minstrelsy and the elite white southerner. Du Bois opened each chapter of *The Souls* with a musical phrase in "a haunting echo of these weird old songs in which the soul of the black slave spoke to men"; he celebrated the discovery of this music in the Sea Islands of the Carolinas "not simply as the sole American music, but as the most beautiful expression of human experience born this side of the seas." And completing his genealogy of the spirituals, a genealogy, by the way, that explicitly excludes southern white agency, Du Bois credits the Fisk Jubilee Singers as the instruments who "sang the slave songs so deeply into the world's heart that it can never wholly forget them again."[36]

So it was that, by the time Charleston's spirituals society had moved from informal meetings to their first performance for the benefit of St. Philips

Church (the final resting place of John C. Calhoun, among other icons of the Confederacy), the claimants for cultural authority over African American musical production constituted a crowded field, none of whom looked to sources like the elites of the Charleston Renaissance to give force to their arguments. The need to reassert cultural dominance might well have seemed increasingly urgent. The Fisk Jubilee Singers and the Hampton Singers were just the most prominent of the touring groups from historic African American schools in the South that had published spirituals collections. And yes, these were singers who had undergone vocal training, singing spirituals in arrangements modified in response to exposure to white and European models—but while this has often been read as an act of rejection or dilution of the originals, as an act of conformity with "the Baptist, the Methodist and the Episcopal hymns, merely varied by the African love of syncopation," in Grimball's phrasing—we may also view these performance choices as part of that "changing same" of which Baraka spoke: the nearly invisible previous centuries of constant innovation from a common root language suddenly made visible by changing technologies of the dissemination of sound.

The African American songbooks, to be crystal clear, focused not on Protestant hymnals but on African American interpretations and reinterpretations of the original source material—material to which the writers had ready and privileged access either through personal or family connections with the period of enslavement. Championed by the likes of Antonín Dvořák, whose 1891 Symphony No. 9 in E Minor "From the New World" drew directly upon African American themes, elevated by scholarly tomes such as H. E. Krehbiel's *Afro-American Folk Songs: A Study in Racial and National Music* (1914), Negro spirituals had become by the time of the First World War the center of a robust national debate on the origins and meaning of African American identity. In this debate, *The Book of American Negro Spirituals* (1925), cowritten by the brothers from Jacksonville—James Weldon Johnson, the Harlem Renaissance novelist and poet, and his brother, J. Rosamond Johnson, the successful Tin Pan Alley and Broadway arranger-composer—was so popular that they rushed out a second volume in 1926. Suffice it to say that, from the standpoint of the members of the spirituals society, dressed in crinolines and tuxedoes as they channeled the sounds of their youth for elite white audiences, a debate in which the coauthors of "Lift Ev'ry Voice and Sing," the "Negro National Anthem," were their primary competitors challenged the memory and myth structures of the South they cherished and were determined to promote in ways that demanded a response. That response was to be *The Carolina Low-Country* (1931).

Published somewhat late in the publication boom surrounding spirituals (though not so late as Lydia Parrish's 1942 *Slave Songs of the Georgia Sea Islands*), *The Carolina Low-Country* is today considered a foundational text of the Charleston Renaissance. Collecting in one-volume essays, poems, paintings, and etchings by the movement's most significant figures in celebration of its vision of "beautiful historic Charleston," the volume holds great interest for the scholar and the casual reader, allowing one to inhabit the plantation landscape from an intimate, personal level and to "hear" the Gullah spirituals (despite the wretched Ambrose Gonzales spelling conventions adopted to "standardize" the text) as the members of the Spirituals Society claimed to have heard them.

Despite the text's many obfuscations, the spirituals emerge as a "mother tongue" in *The Carolina Low-Country*, imbibed quite literally for these white subjects with a Black foster mother's milk. But while in Faulkner's Mississippi forbidden knowledge such as this was to produce an *Absalom, Absalom*, in the Charleston of the "little Renaissance," whose demanding social code required absolute social obedience on the political matter of the Negro's relationship to his betters, it was to produce 168 pages of prose—essays by Herbert Ravenel Sass, Alfred Huger, Thomas R. Waring, and Archibald Rutledge plus assorted poems and artwork—before the reader gets the first hint—with DuBose Heyward's "The Negro in the Low-Country," Robert W. Gordon's "The Negro Spiritual," and the forty-odd spirituals themselves—that African Americans are in any way connected to the story. For a society devoted to preserving spirituals, the text comes off as singularly focused on building a wall around its members' claims of their legitimacy to tell their story, and the bricks of the wall are made from mud from the swamps of the ACE Basin.

The ACE Basin, you'll recall, is the riverine estuary at the convergence of the Ashepoo, Combahee, and Edisto rivers that we named "the beating heart of the nation-state of rice" in chapter 2. The source of "staggering" levels of wealth in their parents' time, a wealth "lost" in their own time to business failures and to a northern elite snapping up second homes and hunting preserves for a song, the plantations of the ACE take center stage for the spirituals society collaborative from the text's opening pages.[37] The title essay—"The Low-Country"—was written by "Hobo"—an affectionate nickname for Herbert Ravenel Sass, a lean redhead with a shy manner, an intimate familiarity with the ACE countryside, and family connections linking him to the most storied names in Charleston's "vast cousinage." The son of the "poet of the Confederacy," "Barton Grey" (the pen name of George Herbert Sass), Sass inherited the fire-eating family politics as well as the family facility with prose, and by the 1930s he was on his way to a national reputation as a nature writer and historical novelist.[38]

Hobo's introductory essay, "The Low-Country," takes the form of a nature walk—literally, a ramble to a long-defunct rice plantation hidden deep in lowcountry backwoods. On this walk, Sass is the all-seeing guide whose privileged insider knowledge takes the reader deep into the heart of the mysteries of a landscape that is not so much vanished as illegible—and he makes no pretense as to objectivity. He begins by declaring the lowcountry's "enchantment" to be "peculiar and irresistible." He then continues,

> [E]ven the most searching critic of the too-romantic plantation tradition admits that Lower South Carolina was one district where an order of life existed which really approximated the glowing picture painted by the story-writers. The old plantation houses, the old parish churches deep in the woods, the old gardens, the stately avenues of hoary live oaks, the wide rice fields abandoned now to rushes and waterlilies and yellow lotus—all these whisper tales of great days that once were lived here. All these are memorials, monuments, of that Golden Age which ended more than three score years ago but which somehow still lives on because the spell of it, the tradition it has left, lies like an invisible mist over this whole region and invests it with a charm that takes stronger and stronger hold upon one's consciousness.

It's all evoked so vividly, right down to the details of house and garden, with the exception, interestingly, of anything to do with the enslaved or the labor required to extract wealth from the rice. As "Hobo" moves deeper into the forest, Sass's technique of folding the chronotope, layering past over present, intensifies as he walks. "[T]he present fades like a dull colorless dream and the past comes vividly back,"[39] he writes. "Roaming on through the swamp, following some winding narrow trail made by the deer, one passes quickly in fancy out of the world of today into an infinitely wilder world of long ago. It is, one feels, a world where man was never known, except those red hunters who were as truly children of the forest as the deer themselves" (20).

Sass scholarship has noted his romantic attachment to South Carolina's Native American tribes. And indeed, he approaches the landscape's signs like a literary "red hunter," translating what he finds into a time-traveling pastoral romance that erases the brutality of the plantation regime even as it domesticates the encounter with the untamed lowcountry swamp. In Sass's "The Low-Country," we find no realistic details—no encounters with the occasional bear or the endemic water moccasins, rattlesnakes, and alligators. As for *Anopheles gambiae*, the voracious lowcountry mosquito, there's no mention of that ubiquitous (and at this period, dangerous) presence at all. Instead Sass invokes the sense impression of the "velvet paws" of a panther stealing noiselessly through cypress swamps, of eyes that watch the human intruder and move uninterested and unseen on. He invites his readers to revel in fantasies of spring—to imagine great floral drifts of yellow jessamine, Cherokee rose, wild bay, purple iris nodding on the "scented" breeze—and of summer—when the blossoms give way to a gold-green sun dappling a fern-covered forest floor. He plays the music of long-forgotten place names: Hobcaw, Seewee, Chantilly, Sea Cloud, Rose Hill, and more than seventy others. And at the same time, by exercise of a type of metonymy, Sass manages to connect these impressions to the rolling titles of the lowcountry aristocrats who claimed a vast (and populated) "virgin land" for posterity: the barons, with twelve-thousand-acre land grants from England's King Charles II; the cassiques, who were allowed two baronies; the margraves, who held four; and, second only to the king himself, the lords proprietors who held tracts of unimaginable vastness called seigneuries.

The text, it goes almost without saying, has little interest in the mechanics of how that land was claimed, or whose hands did the taming. Instead, Sass's method is to invite the reader to imagine standing, at least metaphorically, in a wilderness of swamp bay and broom grass and, by an act of will, willing away the present in order to conjure up a "memory." Under the force of that rememory, the physical reality of the wilderness and the ruins fades while the fantasy plantations take on something like human, at times superhuman, agency. In Sass's phrasing the plantations "shaped the very face of the land itself," "changed the marshes into rice fields" and "swamps into lagoons," indeed, turned forest into groves and the groves into gardens for rest and repose of the spirit . . . without apparent human assistance.

It would be difficult to find a neater fit with Raymond Williams's contention that the pastoral mode is invoked when there is a need to erase the role of labor.[40] Sass's method has the practical effect of alternately minimizing and obliterating human agency, especially that of the African Americans whose songs were, after, the raison d'être for the volume. It is a veritable aside when Sass admits the plantations were formed "from the sweat of [the Negro's] brow," but quickly his language shifts to allow the plantation houses themselves to assume agency. Plantations, of course, don't make gardens; people do. But in plantation pastorals, nostalgia itself has imperial aims, chief among them the reinscription of existing hierarchies through the erasure of labor. Sometimes the erasure of lots of labor. For example, as an amateur plantation history buff, Sass would have been well aware of the story behind Middleton Place Plantation's magnificent seventeenth-century gardens—forty-odd acres of grassy terraces, butterfly lakes, allés, groves, and canals that required the labor of one hundred slaves toiling for nearly a decade to complete.[41] And yet Sass blandly assures his readers that Africans enslaved under such conditions were "the happiest of mortals . . . to be found anywhere on earth."[42]

It's a dazzling performance that masks the fact that the activity is itself a creative act: invoking for the reader states to which we are invited to imagine we are returning. Such acts of memory and rememory, as Toni Morrison called them in another context, have been part and parcel of the "invention" of pastoral landscapes such as "beautiful, historic" Charleston from the beginnings of the endeavor, and they linger with us in many forms today.[43]

The Charleston Convention and Visitors Bureau, for example, transforms the mortuary landscape of the city—as littered with monuments, plaques, and remembrances of the vanished centuries as a graveyard—into a place "Where History *Lives*." Institutions such as the South Carolina Historical Society and the Historic Charleston Foundation speak on their websites of the project of giving, and receiving through one's gifts to the organizations, "the gift of history." But Slavoj Žižek is among those who remind us that, "in the act of returning to tradition, [we] are inventing it. As every historian knows, Scottish kilts were invented in the nineteenth century."[44]

And what tradition is Sass's text weaving from whole cloth? That of an Ideal Order, the beau ideal of an apparently almost faultless civilization. The centerpiece of Sass's narrative is an imagined encounter between the representatives of that Ideal Order: a woman with "a clean-cut, perfectly modelled face, exquisite, sensitive, proud" and a man "wide-shouldered and slim-waisted in tight-fitting broadcloth." The couple appears in bright moonlight only to disappear into deep shadows that give way rudely to a vision of the Real: "Only the old ruined house is there, its pillars shattered, its walls half-levelled, silent and lonely amid its grey-bearded oaks."[45]

In classically Lacanian terms, Sass dramatizes an originary "lack": the primordial loss that Sass mourns is that of a symbolic castration that has failed with the utter destruction of the ancien régime and the Ideal's apparent inability to withstand the encounter with the Real. But Sass ameliorates his loss of place—of cultural stature and geographic emplacement—in the classic language and imagery of the pastoral. "Although their Golden Age has ended, [the plantations] are still . . . real," he asserts, as if repetition might make it so, and indeed he succeeds in his professed aim of recreating the past (21). The narrative superimposes upon the reader's sense of the Real, that is, the "broken pillars of the fine old house," Sass's own vision of the pastoral Ideal, and it's the Ideal that lingers in memory. This may be the textual equivalent of a haunting, but it is not a signal that the romantic yearning of the pastoral is devolving into something more ominous: for example, that other staple of the southern literary tradition, the gothic. Quite simply, the desires Sass invokes *can* be satiated—through the pleasures of pastoral he offers a promise that the reader can indeed go home again, to a happy plantation home at that. And the vehicle for that trip to the Golden Age is, a bit unexpectedly given the slight role he has played in his narrative, the Gullah Negro, bearing a message for a discontented modern age. "Out of the life that was lived on the plantations came the Negro as we know him now in lower Carolina—one of the happiest of mortals, take him all in all, to be found anywhere on earth. Out of that life came the fine and significant fact that here there is no race problem, no ill feelings between white and Black but, on the contrary, much warm affection and mutual respect. Out of that life came the beautiful songs, the spirituals, which belong to neither race but to both races and which are recognized now as so important a part of American folk lore," he writes (14–15).

Sass's shift in tense is suggestive. Out of the plantations, in the past tense, came the Negro and the songs. But in the present tense, he asserts their existence is proof that "there is no race problem." Here we learn the source of the archetypal plenitude associated with the plantation as symbol: and it is the comfort, for the embattled imperial Self, of a psychic space *free of racial conflict*. In Charleston, according to Sass, no one was ever confused as to the where the top rail belonged, and everyone was happy, even the enslaved, who are depicted exchanging "warm affection" and songs with their former masters. These are songs, we should note, whose provenance Sass muddies in terms surgically tailored to diminish the role of Black creators while insinuating a white claim to ownership. Emerging from *the life* lived on the plantation—these songs belong, in a spiritual sense, to the plantation itself. Existing in a nether space that belongs "to neither race but to both races," the songs, framed by Sass's plantation idyll, take on archetypal significance as "*American folklore.*"

In the end, Sass allows no images of devastation to persist. Any holes in the narrative are neatly sutured up in the conclusion and patched over with images of hope, of resurrection: "What remained and still remains is a region beautiful despite its patches of ugliness—beautiful and deeply loved not only for what it was but also for what it is. The lowcountry—and Charleston—will always be lovely with an uncommon and memorable loveliness; a loveliness partly of the land and partly of the life that was lived in it when life had a dignity and a grace which the modern world has declared, in the main, unnecessary and therefore obsolete. A principle—the aristocratic principle of government—an ideal, a manner of living, in short a civilization which has gone forever has left its imprint here. That civilization had its faults, but it had also, among many other virtues, the shining virtue of beauty . . . and something of this survives" (29).

Pastoral is, by its very nature, a channeling of loss into socially acceptable postures of longing for an "impossible dream," and in the passages we have just examined, the intrusions of the modern figure as the enemy of the dream. But there is more to it than that. The "patches of ugliness" and "faults" to which Sass obliquely refers may have been sufficient to divert his early and midcentury readers from impolite questions about the reality of white social relations with their Gullah Geechee cousins. But however deft his use of pastoral codes, they are insufficient to bear the burden of the modern audience's precise and detailed knowledge of the "guilty beauty" of the plantations: that "terrible beauty of workers in chains and gardens watered with blood," as Pujol says. And so the remaining essays in the volume must be called upon to minimize, explain away, and otherwise contain its disruptive Africanist content.

For example, Alfred Huger is sixty pages into the next essay, his ninety-page "The Story of the Low-Country," before there is a direct mention of slavery—and this, ironically, comes in the form of a description of the ecstatic reception accorded to a returning Revolutionary War general during an unexpected visit to his plantation. When, a few pages later, Huger is moved to describe the monumental task of conquering the lowcountry wilderness, he enthuses, "Nothing but an ocular inspection of the area can give an adequate idea of the skillful engineering and patient, intelligent supervision that went to the successful result.... It was an achievement no less skillful than that which excites our wonder in viewing the works of ancient Egypt. The task of reclaiming a swamp delta such as that between the Waccamaw and Pee Dee rivers involved an engineering skill no less that the construction of a pyramid, yet no one knows how many decades went into the last and the first was performed in comparatively few years" (103–4). It goes without saying that the enslaved African, whose rice-growing technology was expropriated and raised to industrial scale to serve this profit-making machine, receives no recognition of his contributions to the task. Indeed, Huger laments that "the only labour at the disposal of *the settler who accomplished the feat* was of the most unskilled character, African savages fresh from the Guinea coast" (emphasis added).

Huger is not alone. Thomas R. Waring's essay is so dismissive of the Negro's contributions to "Charleston, the Capital of the Plantations" as to be almost comical. "It was an English civilization and it developed an English culture," he asserted, before rattling off a list of the categories of persons who had given the colony its air of romance: "The Indian roamed through all the region about and his tepees were pitched where the city rests. The Spaniard had been here and his trail may still be found. Pirates made free of the place and levied tribute until they were hunted down and hanged. French Huguenots, thwarted in their earlier endeavor to make footing at Port Royal, came to join the young colony, Germans and Irish and Italians, French Catholics from Hayti and Martinique, Spanish and German and Polish Jews, Quakers, all have contributed in important ways to the making of the city. And the Negro" (133). The Negro's demographic presence in the city and the plantation districts is so ubiquitous that his presence needs must be acknowledged. But there is apparently nothing further to say about him after that.

The reader expects more of DuBose Heyward, author of *Porgy*, which got complimentary reviews even from some Harlem Renaissance figures, but his contribution to the volume, "The Negro in the Low-Country," is a decidedly mixed bag. Heyward boldly declares, "The Negro has ceased to be a human entity and has become a symbol" in his introduction and confidently states his determination "to submit his emotions to the stern and unbiased discipline of his art" in order to create "a convincing and realistic portrait" (171–72), but matters get off to a rocky start. In a section asserting the fact of ethnic diversity among a population whom southern whites in particular tended to regard as monolithic, Heyward describes the Gullah-Gola-Angola dispute we explored in chapter 1 and even attempts a taxonomy of African cultural groups: this to be sure is a short list—study of these matters being in its infancy among American whites—but it does include "Gambia Negroes" of the heavily Islamic Senegambia region, "Corromantees" of the Gold Coast states of Ghana, Nigeria, and Benin, and "Congoes." But science quickly slides into stereotyping: Angola Negroes, or Gullahs, were "gentle and affectionate . . . and faithful to a trust" but also, "of rather low mentality, . . . gullible and easily swayed by others," which Heyward opined "possibly accounted for his proclivity to run away" (173–74). He goes on, describing, "Senegaleses, with their decided Arabic strain, their sensitive intelligent faces; Mandangoes reputed gentle in demeanor but prone to theft; Whydahs, Nagoes, and Pow Pows, all industrious and sturdy of body; Congoes, Gaboons, and finally Eboes, malarial yellow of complexion, despondent, and so apt to commit suicide on the middle passage that they were considered unprofitable by traders" (175).

Heyward's lists read as part factual, mostly fanciful with propositions that seem headed toward a grapple with difficult questions but that ultimately cancel each other out. Heyward's "Good Gullahs" are faithful, affectionate—but constantly running away. Rather than face the implications of those facts, Heyward looks away, into a pastoral dream of the gallant South. In that dream, all the suicides are safely offshore, somewhere in the mists of the Middle Passage. This, despite the fact the most famous instance of mass suicide in the Americas occurred right on the Gullah Geechee Coast, on St. Simons Island, Georgia. According to the legend, African captives seized the ship transporting them as it sailed up Duncan Creek to their final destination, and they murdered the crew and ran it aground at a place ever after known by the name "Igbo Landing."[46] Praying, dancing, singing, a group of them walked into the waters, weighting themselves with their chains, choosing death and a spiritual journey back to Africa over a life of slavery.

It could well be that Heyward, despite being a famously avid collector of curios and ghost stories, had never heard the tale—it could also be that his pastoral reflexes were simply more powerful than his commitment to truth. In either case, the tone of his essay swings wildly between warring impulses. Heyward satisfies the "stern and unbiased principles of his art" with a daring portrait in which Denmark Vesey figures not as a madman but as tragic hero. More typical, though, are passages in which Gullahs figure as "an enormous, ignorant, pauper population" whom it would have been cruelty at slavery's end to release into the wild "to fend for itself" (176). For Heyward, seeing Gullahs as a helpless race whose care he considers a personal obligation given all the "benefits" his family and caste historically derived from slavery is a matter of aristocratic identity, of noblesse oblige.

Of course, this is yet another case of pastoral reflexes erasing the contestation over labor and land. The freedmen who are the objects of Heyward's charity, in fact, pursued property ownership with single-minded intensity and had legal claim to the sea islands and the coastal plain from Charleston to Florida's St. John River—both by virtue of abandonment during the Civil War and by way of reparations as articulated in Gen. William Tecumseh Sherman's General Field Order No. 15. Heyward's stance of innocent yearning for the songs of youth hides naked economic contestation behind a gauzy golden curtain of charitable intent. In Heyward's logic, the task of "salvaging the spirituals of the Negro from a mutual past becomes not an unwarranted audacity, not a gesture of patronizing superiority, but a natural and harmonious collaboration wrought in affection and with a deep sense of reverence" (185). Even so, Heyward seems wide awake to the possibility that his project's flank is exposed to criticism. Was the Society for the Preservation of Spirituals' flirtation with minstrelsy's "darky act" an act of love or of mercenary mimicry? Was *The Carolina Low-Country*, the prestige project the SPS conceived to redeem their performances' troubling Blackness, an act of charity—or one of theft?

Or was it an act of silencing?

Robert Winslow Gordon's "The Negro Spiritual" is the last essay in the volume, and, as Gordon was the first head of the Library of Congress's Archive of American Folksong, it is still considered by some to be an important treatment of the topic. The essay reflects Gordon's folklore collecting trips to Darien in Coastal Georgia in 1927 and 1928 as well as his close collaboration with the spirituals society members.[46] As such, we see Gordon making sensitive use of his informants in describing the ways in which song permeated the life of the plantation district, for the enslaved and the free. Spirituals were sung at prayer meetings, he writes, but also "to time the oars of the boatman, to calm and encourage them to greater efforts in time of danger, or as a triumphal chant when the danger had passed. . . . It lightened the labor of the field worker; it was crooned by the women as they went about their household tasks, whether in cabin or at the big house; nurses used it to sing the children, white and colored to sleep" (191).

Gordon is able to describe how songs were composed, the ways in which they were used to create cohesion at social gatherings, the possible combinations and composite forms, the times and places for spirituals and the difference between spirituals and shouts. At the same time, he doesn't so much as deny any African origins to the songs, as simply omit the idea from serious consideration, bogging down into a speculative and ultimately fruitless discussion of the extent of borrowings from white song cultures.

More seriously, however, Gordon reveals his bias with the pains he takes to deny any possible political content to the spirituals. Arguing that they reflect a concern with spiritual rather than physical slavery, he makes the baffling call to cite as evidence the fact that only a handful of spirituals—"No More Auction Block for Me," "No Driver Lash in Heaven"—protest slavery directly. The fact that the spirituals society by its own account laid a heavy hand on the selection process is not mentioned. The fact, moreover, that there were consequences for protesting slavery too directly that might land one at the Charleston Workhouse or worse never even seems to occur to Gordon, most likely because it directly contradicts the myth of warm affection and kindly treatment upon which "beautiful historic" Charleston's myth is founded. At any rate, no overt protest songs found their way into *The Carolina Low-Country*, and the songs that were included were stripped of all but literal meanings.

References to Egypt and Ol' Pharaoh were read as strictly religious or spiritual and not as allusions to individual masters or, heavens forfend, the slave regime as a whole. In the context of slave accounts of starvation rations, "Chillun Ob Duh Wilduhness Moan Fuh Bread" certainly sounds like a plaint about stingy masters—except it can't be read that way under Gordon's rules. The same goes for a song such as "Eb'rybody Who Is Libin' Got tuh Die," which could have been interpreted as a grim warning to the high and mighty to humble their pride—except it was not. Despite ample evidence of the songs' multivocality, Gordon flatly asserts that the Negro "*did not himself create any body of song on his enslaved condition*" (217, emphasis added)—a bold and, indeed, utterly mad declaration.

Gordon's essay supplies a convincingly final answer to the questions we asked about the spirituals society's darky act. All charitable intentions notwithstanding, what is transpiring is a looting: the Charleston Renaissance captured in the act of robbing the Gullah Geechee of their inheritance. *The Carolina Low-Country*, a "celebration" of the spirituals, nonetheless winds up becoming a 327-page argument not just for denying Gullah Geechee claims to the lands that their creative labor transformed, and their stewardship maintained for four centuries, but also for denying their claims to the very songs by which they poured out their souls onto the sultry southern breeze.

We have explored in this chapter the call issued by Gullah Geechee culture-makers and the distinctive responses of white artists of the Charleston Renaissance to that call. Though "natives" by birth, "insiders" by virtue of location, that is, by virtue of imbibing with the Black wet nurse's milk the "mother wit" of the Afro-indigenous creole formation, the social practices of whiteness to which they had also pledged allegiance demanded fidelity to a code that rigorously policed the terms of the interracial and intercultural encounter.

We can clearly see the forms the struggle takes in works like *The Carolina Low-Country*, in which Charleston Renaissance culture-makers busy themselves with the project, in literature, visual arts, and music, of freezing Gullah Geechee culture in time, immobilizing and incarcerating it in a self-flattering amber of mystification and myth. Their endeavor was from its inception foredoomed to eventual irrelevance by a profound and partly unconscious, partly deliberate misapprehension of the evidence. The spirituals, even in the "pure" "essential" form the members of the Society for the Preservation of Spirituals and their sister cultural groups valorized, were not archetypes of cultural stasis they insisted them to be but, on the contrary, emblematic of adaptation and change, as Africans of many languages and tribal origins gradually accepted and, in accepting, transformed in a remarkable act of spiritual *reassemblage* the worship of a Christian god into patterns and practices meaningful to them.

The Renaissance group would have had to be aware that their sainted antebellum elders had reviled the songs they loved, dismissing them, in the very moment of their innovation and creation, as so much barbaric noise distracting from the sober contemplation of the "slaves-obey-your-masters" Gospel that was the sum and substance of their faith. The Reverend Charles Colcock Jones, Presbyterian minister father of the folklore collector and Lost Cause historian we encountered at the beginning of this chapter, expressed views typical of his time in his *The Religious Instruction of the Negroes in the United States* (1842), in which he adjured enslaved Christians to "lay aside their extravagant and nonsensical chants, and [the] catches and hallelujah songs of their own composing" in order to sing psalms in four-four time like sensible Anglo-Christians.[47] One can only imagine the good divine's dismay had he had foreknowledge that these disturbing Afro-creole revels would have so permeated the gestalt of his son's generation that the collecting and even the performance of African American mother wit would become incorporated within and indispensable to their identity.

The irony that this group—these elite lowcountry whites of the former slave holding class, the ones most loudly proclaiming the "purity" of their own racial bona fides—is also the group most eager to immerse themselves in performances that allowed their fascination with Blackness to be exercised (and perhaps even, as Ralph Ellison prompts us to ponder, "exorcized")[48] does not escape notice. And granted, these performances had a purpose, that of violently distorting the memory of slavery, intentionally misreading the meaning of the spirituals to uphold Lost Cause dogma. But not even the most impassioned outpourings of prose or paint produced by this homegrown renaissance movement could entirely erase the guilt from the lowcountry's beauty. It could only—and that only temporarily—throw up a bulwark against a dimly felt yet still outrageous assault by artists from "that other renaissance up North" on the heretofore unquestioned authority and authenticity of white elites as spokespersons for their erstwhile property.

CHAPTER 4

"I Can Peep through Muddy Waters"
Seeking the Black Authentic in Georgia

> A cultural studies approach would insist that terms like "folk," "authentic," and "traditional" are socially constructed categories that have something to do with the reproduction of race, class, and gender hierarchies and the policing of the boundaries of modernism. "Folk and "modern" are both mutually dependent concepts embedded in unstable historically and socially constituted systems of classification. In other words, "folk" has no meaning without "modern."
> —ROBIN D. G. KELLEY, "Notes on Deconstructing the Folk"

In the previous chapter, *excursion* claimed our attention. Through an extended perambulation through the urban landscape of Charleston and the guilty beauty of the plantation districts surrounding it, we journeyed some distance into the heart of a specifically southern, yet also American, darkness. In this chapter, we shall track a parallel movement, that of *incursion*: a raid by rebel forces into the hotly contested terrain of racial definition. For while the contexts of the Charleston Renaissance—both the period and the personalities associated with it—have just claims upon our attention, we must be clear that the earliest twentieth-century texts to consider seriously the character of African American lives and culture in our region of study were not written by natives to the Gullah Geechee Coast, nor, significantly, were they written by whites.

The guerrillas leading the raid are men who will be quite familiar to students of African American literature and the Harlem Renaissance: William Edward Burghardt Du Bois, a towering figure who, more than a century after the publication of *The Souls of Black Folk* (1903), stands as the intellectual and creative architect of the modern racial protest tradition as well as of Black cultural nationalism and Pan-Africanism; and Nathan Pinchback

"Jean" Toomer, who, two decades after *The Souls of Black Folk*, was to take up the theme of a South that was "beautiful and violent, earthy and mystical" as well as the task of "authentically" reproducing the "song" of the Black folk who inhabited it.[1]

Because both Du Bois and Toomer were inveterate travelers and border crossers, critics have had comparatively little to say about the Georgia settings of their work.[2] Or rather to be more precise, while the Georgia settings of their work have drawn attention for various reasons, only occasionally has either man's creative work been considered in the context of the Gullah Geechee Coast.[3] We cannot entirely blame the urban thrust of much of twentieth-century African American studies criticism—nor its recent concern with migration and movement of human populations at the expense of rootedness—but neither should we simply dismiss the question by noting that "Gullah Geechee Coast" is coinage of quite recent vintage. To previous generations, this region had an identity—it was variously known as the "Black belt," "the Low Country," "the Sea Islands," and, in those identities, it inspired folklore collections,[4] economic analyses, political handwringing, and more than a few of the sociological studies of the Negro undertaken during Du Bois's tenure at Atlanta University. In other words, Du Bois's high-flown philosophical speculations have always been grounded in a physical actuality: the specific geography and the distinctive culture of a region that was clearly within the zone of influence of that which we now call the Gullah Geechee Coast. That makes the region the apparent, unacknowledged source for four chapters of Du Bois's *Souls*—"Of the Black Belt," "Of the Quest of the Golden Fleece," "Of the Coming of John," and "The Sorrow Songs"—as well as a ghost haunting the swamp settings of his first novel, *The Quest of the Silver Fleece* (1911).[5] As for Toomer, the first and final sections of *Cane* (1923) are inextricably linked to a physical geography as well: Hancock County between the Oconee and Ogeechee rivers, where Toomer served in 1921 as the substitute principal of a school on the Tuskegee model, the Sparta Industrial and Agricultural Institute. Sparta is located in a lumber-producing section of middle Georgia that borders, and shares complex cultural and historical resonances with, the coastal plain. It is also near the cities of Perry, Augusta, and Macon—all places where Nathan Toomer, the father Jean Toomer had barely known, had lived.[6]

Allow me to be clear: these facts don't tempt me to argue that Du Bois and Toomer recognized Gullah Geechee culture as such and attempted to translate or reproduce it. As stated at length elsewhere, "the Gullah Geechee Coast" is itself a new coinage for an old formation—it is a consensus formation reached only after nearly a century of often-bitter contestation among scholars, practitioners, and their human objects of study. As for Du Bois and Toomer, there's no knowing whether either man ever even so much as heard the words "Gullah" or "Geechee" spoken—though clearly each found something in the region, some racial "essence," that resonated with their experience and compelled articulation. What I do seek to argue is this: If Du Bois and Toomer both have been foundational in the development of U.S. and African American discourses of racial essences and, thus, of racial *authenticity*—and these are discourses, we must be clear, that are still under contestation today—then there is value in exploring the degrees to which and the ways in which those discourses draw on even hazily perceived or actively misidentified Gullah Geechee sources. And there is further value in probing how and why the connection to the original source was severed.

The source of Du Bois's and later Toomer's drive to locate and elucidate their cultural and ethnic roots is not difficult to identify. As Gilroy has written, each man's project may be thought of as a "simple and direct response to the varieties of racism which have denied the historical character of black experience and the integrity of black cultures." The urgency of the drive, particularly with Du Bois at the dawn of the twentieth century, originates in the urgency of the need "to construct a political agenda in which the ideal of rootedness [could be] identified as a prerequisite for the forms of cultural integrity that could guarantee the nationhood and statehood to which [diaspora Blacks] aspired."[7] In other words, for Du Bois, "roots" were to be a "route" to full citizenship for African Americans in the United States—and eventually for people of color across the globe. But before we proceed even a step further, we must express our gratitude to Robin D. G. Kelley for the reminder that terms like "folk," "authentic," "roots," and so forth are categories constructed socially for the purposes of policing the boundaries of the "modern" and the racial, class, and gender hierarchies upon which that modernity depends.[8] Du Bois's ambitious efforts to replace dominant notions derived from minstrel shows, cakewalks, coon songs, and spectacle lynchings with an identity whose genealogy is historically derived are themselves complicated by his own troubled relationship to the authenticity he was so concerned to define. One might even call this an anxiety of authenticity, "rooted" in the details of Du Bois's—and later Toomer's—personal autobiography.

As for those personal biographies, the lives of Du Bois and Toomer offer neatly contrasting parables for the construction of racial identity. Let us consider first the case of Du Bois, who was born three years after the close of the Civil War in Great Barrington, Massachusetts, and descended from free men and women who had been among the earliest inhabitants of the region. Du Bois graduated with honors from predominantly white schools and appeared at Fisk University in 1885, a "quite thoroughly New England youth" for whom the sudden immersion into the culture and codes of the Black South was a joyful voyage of self-discovery.

Here is Du Bois's account of learning that he was to attend Fisk University rather than Harvard, the dream of his boyhood:

> [H]ere and immediately was adventure. I was going into the South; the South of slavery, rebellion and black folk; and above all I was going to meet colored people of my own age and education, of my own ambitions. Once or twice already I had had swift glimpses of the colored world: at Rocky Point on Narragansett Bay, I had attended an annual picnic beside the sea, and had seen in open-mouthed astonishment the *whole gorgeous color gamut* [emphasis added] of the American Negro world; the swaggering men, the beautiful girls, the laughter and gaiety, the unhampered self-expression. I was astonished and inspired. I became aware . . . of the spiritual isolation in which I was living. I heard too in these days for the first time the Negro folk songs. . . . I was thrilled and moved to tears and seemed to recognize something inherently and deeply my own. I was glad to go to Fisk.⁹

This awakening as racial subject was not static—the young Du Bois's ideas on race, codes of racial behavior, the proper limits of uplift, the sociopolitical obligations of the various classes of African Americans, their relationship to global communities of color, and so on were to evolve throughout his career—from his studies at Harvard University and the University of Berlin; his teaching assignments at Wilberforce University, where he met and married his wife; his arrival at Atlanta University, where he was to embark on his foundational series of sociological studies on the Black church, Black landowners, the Black family, and many others; through his editorial work at *The Crisis*; and back to academia at Atlanta University among other institutions. Du Bois's earliest insights were to be frequently complicated by later travels and refined by the continued development of his own critical intelligence—but what in the nineteenth century was quaintly termed "the genius of the black" was to remain the central preoccupation of his life and work. He never ceased to recognize "something inherently and deeply my own" in the cultural expressions of African American people.

On the other hand, we have Jean Toomer, born a generation later, in 1897, to a Louisiana Creole family whose members lived ambiguously—some might say opportunistically—raced lives on both sides of the color line in Washington, D.C. Confronted forcefully with demands that he claim a racial self-definition at M Street High School and at a series of colleges where he began but never completed studies—the University of Wisconsin, the American College of Physical Training in Chicago, and City College of New York—Toomer was to resist those demands till the end of his life, articulating that resistance particularly in "The Crock of Problems," a 1928 essay explaining his "seven blood mixtures" theory of racial origins. Indeed, Toomer was to give concentrated attention to his "Negro blood" for one and only one book,

Cane—which despite glowing reviews would be "lost" for decades before its reclamation as an exemplary text of the Harlem Renaissance in 1967.[10]

"I do not expect to be told what I should consider myself to be. I must insist that you never use such a word [the word "Negro"], such a thought, again" was Toomer's peremptory response when publisher Lawrence Liveright, concerned about the marketing of *Cane*, accused him of denying his race. Of course, Toomer may simply have been a man far ahead of his time—as in nearly a century—when it came to matters of race: "I am at once not one of the races and I am all of them. I belong to no one of them, I belong to all," he wrote in "The Crock of Problems," in words that sound suspiciously like . . . Tiger Woods describing himself as a "Cablinasian."[11] Meanwhile, a letter to Waldo Frank that's like something ripped from the contemporary press reads, in part, "the most and the least that can be said of any of us with accuracy . . . [is that we] all belong to the one pure race, . . . the human race."[12]

The contrasts between the men are pretty irresistible: the one a man with a firmly anchored if ever-evolving notion of race and identity, the other as steadfastly embracing multiplicity; the one working toward an ambitious fusion of the personal, the political, the artistic, and the scholarly that would allow him to disrupt current, rigid, academic categories of history and memory to insert "other[ed] ways of knowing" into the story of the Negro, the other with the as-ambitious aim of developing a modernist idiom for telling an American story; the one committed to transformationalist politics, the other committed to the perfection of individual self and soul.[13] But their similarities, as suggested by my reading of Kelley, are equally compelling—both are "moderns" standing at a far remove from a "folk," though with a passionate, often ambivalent relationship to that folk. The metaphors Du Bois introduces in *Souls*—metaphors of the Color Line, the Veil, Double Consciousness, and the "Damnation" of Women, among others—are extended in *Cane*, transmuted into poetry.[14] In the conversation between these texts, we gain a close-up view of the mechanisms of the invention and reinvention of an early twentieth-century tradition that has yet to die: the tradition of the Black authentic.

Souls of Black Folk and the Invention of the Authentic

Since every tradition must, by definition, have a genealogy, we turn to *The Souls of Black Folk* for the outlines of the one crafted by Du Bois. The passage that is most apropos for our purposes comes from "The Sorrow Songs," the final essay in the volume and the peroration toward which all the essays that preceded it had been building. The passage is quite dense, and worth examining at some length. Du Bois begins with an articulation of a theory of national and racial "gifts" that's remarkably reminiscent of the German idealism of Herder: "Little of beauty has America given the world save the rude grandeur God himself stamped on her bosom; the human spirit in this new world has expressed itself in vigor and ingenuity rather than in beauty. And so by fateful chance the negro folksong—the rhythmic cry of the slave—stands today not simply as the sole American music, but as the most beautiful expression of human experience born this side [sic] the seas. It has been neglected, it has been, and is, half despised, and above all it has been persistently mistaken and misunderstood; but notwithstanding, it still remains as the singular spiritual heritage of the nation and the greatest gift of the Negro people."[15]

This is a point Du Bois had argued before in *The Conservation of Races*, published in 1897 as one of the American Negro Academy's series of "occasional papers." At this stage in Du Bois's thinking, race appears as a sociohistorical concept with a mystic, quasi-religious rather than a scientific or pseudo-scientific character. Races, that is to say, exist in time and carry "gifts." And like the English with their gifts of "constitutional liberty and commercial freedom," the Germans with their gifts of "science and philosophy," the Romance nations with their gifts of "literature and art," the Negro, Du Bois says, had a gift for the world, too: a "particular message ... particular ideal, which shall help to guide the world nearer and nearer that perfection of human life for which we all long."[16] The passage in "The Sorrow Songs" continues,

> Away back in the thirties the melody of the slave songs stirred the nation, but the songs were soon half forgotten. Some, like "Near the lake where drooped the willow," passed into current airs and their source was forgotten; others were caricatured on the "minstrel" stage and their memory died away. Then in war-time came the singular Port Royal experiment after the capture of Hilton Head, and perhaps for the first time the North met the Southern slave *face to face and heart to heart with no third witness* [emphasis added]. The Sea Islands of the Carolinas, where they met, were filled with a black folk of primitive type, touched and moulded less by the world about them than any others outside the black belt. Their appearance was uncouth, their language funny, but their hearts were human and their singing stirred men with a mighty power. Thomas Wentworth Higginson hastened to tell of these songs, and Miss McKim and others urged upon the world their rare beauty. But the world listened only half credulously until the Fisk Jubilee Singers sang the slave songs so deeply into the world's heart that it can never wholly forget them again.[17]

The emphasis is intended to draw our attention to a moment of fateful encounter. The presumed subject here is Higginson's paradigm-forming chapter in *Army Life in a Black Regiment* (1900), in which he describes hearing for the first time the music of the freedmen of the Port Royal area. But the implied subject, I would argue, is in fact Du Bois himself, reversing the South-to-

North movement of the slave narratives to encounter the expressive culture of the formerly enslaved—their "sorrow songs"—"face to face and heart to heart with no third witness." Du Bois had by this time traveled the length and breadth of Georgia—had encountered this distinctive expressive culture in Darien, on the Altamaha, a fabled rice river near Sapelo Island that is the center of the Gullah Geechee culture in Georgia. Higginson's encounter with the Gullahs of Port Royal (near Beaufort)—"their appearance uncouth, their language funny"—is a mirror for Du Bois's own dis-ease at the border of a Black identity that was not "gorgeous," "swaggering," laughing, and gay—as had been the party at Narragansett Bay or his fellow students at Fisk—but of an alien, "primitive type." They are redeemed, in Du Bois's formulation, because "their hearts were human, and their songs stirred men with a mighty power."

Many have written of Du Bois's fascination with the sorrow songs—their central role in establishing in his thought a sociohistorical link to an African past, their legacy both as a "cultural immersion ritual" for those seeking this link and as the Negro race's "gift" to the world.[18] Most of this writing has sought to document Du Bois's achievement, though there are those, such as K. Anthony Appiah, who have censured this formulation, pointing out—quite correctly—the irony that Du Bois, following in the footsteps of his mentor, Alexander Crummell, was guilty of endorsing racialist theories even as his entire program of uplift was aimed at bringing succor to the victims of racism.[19] Appiah's argument is not new—though perhaps such an argument had never before been applied to someone of Du Bois's stature. Much the same has been argued of various types of primitivist celebration: that primitivism merely reverses the poles, rather than undermining the superstructure, of the moral universe of racism.[20]

For my part, I don't think Du Bois's so-called intrinsic racism can be fully understood without reference to its context: the *extrinsic* racism of the period of the "nadir," those years between the end of Reconstruction and the infamous Red Summer of 1919, when Lost Cause discourses created a contagion of racial terror that eventually infected the nation. In *Souls*, Du Bois was unusually reticent on the subject: "Of the Black Belt" makes only the briefest reference to the Georgia county where "Sam Hose was crucified" (92). *Dusk of Dawn* offers a fuller account, but that passage, too, is just two paragraphs long. The reason for the restraint seems rather obvious: the death of Sam Hose—like that of his son Burghardt that very year, 1899—was still a raw red wound to Du Bois's psyche in 1903, the year he published *Souls*. The scar still throbbed as late as 1940, the year Du Bois published *Dusk of Dawn*. To understand why, we need to review the full details of the case.

They can be described only as nauseating. On April 22, 1899, for killing a wealthy landowner in self-defense, Hose had his ears, fingers, and genitals severed and his face partially flayed; what was left of his still-breathing body,

Ida B. Wells reported, was burned alive. According to the local press, an estimated two thousand people—among them two trainloads of sightseers from Atlanta—gathered around the stake to watch the torture, the mutilation, and their grim denouement. When Hose finally died, his liver was cut out, cut up, cooked, and sold at ten cents a strip—his limbs were dismembered and some in the crowd fought for pieces of bone and tissue as souvenirs. Even worse—if anything could imaginably be worse—was the fact, reported by Ida B. Wells, that "the burning of Samuel Hose . . . gave to the United States the distinction of having burned alive seven human beings during the past ten years." That is to say, not only was this "a deed of unspeakable barbarism [that] shocked the civilized world,"[21] it was one of *seven such deeds* committed in a decade.[22] One could equate Du Bois's reaction to Crèvecoeur's encounter with the blinded slave in the cage recounted two centuries earlier in *Letters from an American Farmer*—except that encounter was fabular and Crèvecoeur was forced by a furious southern reading public eventually to disavow it. Du Bois's encounter with a primal scene of originary horror was all too Real.

In *Dusk of Dawn*, Du Bois describes his reaction upon hearing that Hose had been captured and was awaiting execution in Newnan, approximately forty miles west of Atlanta. "I wrote out a careful and reasoned statement . . . and started down to the Atlanta *Constitution* office, carrying in my pocket a letter of introduction to Joel Chandler Harris," associate editor of the paper and author of the beloved Uncle Remus tales. So far, this is classic Du Bois: one can just imagine him, in Homburg and vested suit, hurrying to his errand along the streets of Atlanta. But "I did not get there," he adds. "On the way news met me: Sam Hose had been lynched, and . . . his knuckles were on exhibition at a grocery store farther down on Mitchell Street, along which I was walking." The next sentences offer a glimpse into the existential crisis that ensued. "I turned back to the University. I began to turn aside from my work. I did not meet Joel Chandler Harris nor the editor of the *Constitution*" (*Dusk* 67).

Richard Rorty has described a human being as one who can both suffer and narrate pain. For a time, it appears, Du Bois experiences the former without being able to find comfort in the latter. Between the lines of the fleeting passage in *Dusk of Dawn*, we glimpse a man who has lost the pleasure of his research, who has lost his zest for the field of ideological battle because, in the burning of Sam Hose, he is forced to confront the capital-T Truth of his existence—and it is like "a red ray which cannot be ignored" (67) lancing across his path. Spectacle lynching represents a threat of castration that is neither abstract nor experienced at a generational remove—as was the case with Sass's loss of place in the previous chapter—but direct, immediate, inexorable. A lynch mob cannot be reasoned with, not even by an intellect as powerful as Du Bois's—it cannot be bargained with, certainly not after being actively incited over a period of days by the press. A lynch mob represents, almost by definition, the eruption into the normatively placid waters of existence of a Lacanian Real, a site of tragic recognition that one's bargain with a Big Other—with society, or perhaps even mortality—is illusory. As Slavoj Žižek has described it, "[T]he Real is not impossible in the sense that it [is something that] can never happen—a traumatic kernel which forever eludes our grasp. No, the problem with the Real is that it happens and *that's* the trauma. The point is not that the Real is impossible but rather that the impossible is Real."[23]

The direct references in Du Bois's published oeuvre tell part of the story of his reaction to learning that "the impossible is Real"—but only part. In his 1903 text, he can gesture toward the scene of the crime, utter a brief complaint that prejudice makes no distinction between a Phillis Wheatley and a Sam Hose—but no more than that (92, 152). *Dusk of Dawn* gives a bit more, allows Du Bois, in muted fashion, to narrate his rage, to state that he cannot continue to be a "cool, calm, detached scientist while Negroes [are] being lynched, murdered, and starved" (67) all around him. More critically, he has to admit to himself that his work is failing—that, without funding, his sociological studies cannot continue and that, as long as his feud with the Tuskegee "machine" continues, he'll have limited access to funding (68–71). These are bitter self-reflections, but it is not these fleeting passages that are most revealing to us of what is at stake for Du Bois—nor even the confession in 1944 that "[s]omething died in me" the day that Sam Hose met his fate.[24] It is rather in Du Bois's retreat to the pastoral that we are able to see his psyche's strategy for mediating the trauma.

We explored in the previous chapter the ways in which the pastoral is invoked in texts of the Charleston Renaissance in order to mystify and mask the existence and the effects of imperialist violence. Perhaps it surprises us to find that this is no less true of the great precursor text of the Harlem Renaissance, but perhaps it should not. The pastoral is simply the means, while the cultural work with which it is implicated appears to be vast—and not dependent on ideological orientation. We have spoken before of the saurian voraciousness of ideology—Žižek's rereadings of Lacan lay the processes bare. According to Žižek, ideology restages the encounter with the Real in order to explain—*away*—the impossibility of the contract the individual makes with society. That is, rather than face the failure of society, its inability or refusal to deliver on the images of fulfillment that it dangles before us, ideology transforms the impossibility into a theft that may be blamed on some handy social Other—as southern whites came to blame northerners and freedmen or Nazis to blame Jews. Impossibility actually *structures* reality, according to Žižek, by setting the limits of what is possible and regulating one's psychic distance from the object of desire.[25] Considered using these terms, Du Bois's act in creating from the "sorrow songs" and the "primitive"—but still recognizably human—Sea Islanders an ideal, originary "racial authentic" seems at once immensely creative and somewhat, well, inevitable. In order to live without succumbing to despair, in order to remain human, he would have had to find a way to give his pain form, to narrate it. The transcendent pastoral moments in *Souls* were to prove a useful vehicle.

Let us consider just for a moment the Negro's positionality in a regime of organized race-based terror. Such a regime depended on the moral unintelligibility of the figure of the Negro as constructed by society—the figure's oscillation between the poles of criminality, hypersexuality, bestiality on the one hand and the comic grotesques of minstrelsy on the other. Du Bois would have been aware of the function served by the blackface mask, the fact that it reduced the complex social reality and indeed the very humanity of African Americans to what Ralph Ellison three-quarters of a century later was to describe as a "sign" evoking an atmosphere in which comic face of Blackness might be enjoyed or its sinister face might be assailed.[26] In neither case would the white audience's moral identification be triggered. Laughter in the former instance and atavistic terror in the second would both prevent the recognition of the human ambiguities submerged beneath the mask and conceal or justify the racist aggression inherent in the pleasure taken or pain inflicted. Intuiting accurately that reason played little role in this process, Du Bois sought instead to disturb and disrupt a cultural archetype that was part of the foundation of the American republic, one of the cornerstones of the American psyche, by replacing it with another one: the image of the Negro as culture hero, one who laid a gift of beauty on the table the United States had set for the world. This was surely an attempt to make the Negro morally intelligible to an audience of whites that was to varying degrees hostile—it may also have served defensively to make his destiny as a man raced as Negro intelligible to himself.

In our discussion of the pastoral mode in the previous chapter, we noted the linkage between "innocent" pleasures of country games and amusements, on the one hand, and orgies and seductions, ritual combat, and ritual murder, on the other. There are vivid moments of both the pastoral and anti-pastoral scattered throughout *The Souls of Black Folk*—an idyllic portrait of the country schoolhouse in "Of the Meaning of Progress," a devastating portrait of the "tragic landscape" of Georgia—its ruined plantations and the blasted hopes of the African American survivors struggling amid the wreckage against starvation and racist violence—offered in "Of the Black Belt," for example. But it's the one fictional piece in the book—"Of the Coming of John"—that resonates most strongly with the received tradition of the southern pastoral. Briefly, "The Coming of John" is a fable about metaphorical twins, "sons," as it were, "of Master and Man": a poor Black John from a small seacoast Georgia town and a wealthy white John whose father is the judge and leading man of the same town. The boys are the same age, and they venture into the wide world at the same time to obtain education. Black John goes to the Black college in "Johnstown," white John to Princeton. And while the return of each is eagerly anticipated, the whites have one prediction for white John—"[education will] make a man of him"—and another for his Black twin—"it'll spoil him,—ruin him" (187–88).

It turns out that education "spoils" both boys. Black John must relinquish his folk identity to obtain academic success and returns home with a head so stuffed with ideas that he forgets how to talk to his family, forgets the community's religious and social standards, and unwittingly ruins the grand homecoming planned for him. White John, meanwhile, rejects out of hand the one-horse town his father wants to hand to him on a silver platter. Longing for the bright lights and sophisticated ladies of the city, he seeks to express his manhood in a way he'd never have had to leave home to discover: with Black John's innocent sister, Jennie. When the dark brother stumbles upon the primal scene—the white brother raping his dark sister—Black John takes up the nearest handy phallus—a tree limb—and beats his white twin to death. Stupefied by his action and unable to flee, he lingers near the crime scene, transported back to the one supremely transcendent moment of his life, in a New York opera house watching *Lohengrin*. Humming the "Song of the Bride" (that is to say, "The Wedding March") he waits for the lynch mob and the rope that will end his own life.

A commonplace of the pastoral tradition is that it is what happens in the "pastoral moment"—the moment of supreme lyricism that breaks through and rises above the confines of the literal narrative—that reveals what is really at stake for the author of the pastoral text. In "Of the Coming of John," there are many passages of lyricism but three important pastoral moments, each with the sea—rather than the southern landscape—as its centerpiece. This substitution should not completely surprise us. Du Bois is certainly capable of passages of exquisite beauty in describing the southern landscape—but it is the sea's "soul" that is his concern. That soul is disembedded from its place in the world, disembodied from a landscape that it fears and yet longs for. Set to wandering the world, from Wells Institute, a small southern college that sounds suspiciously like Fisk, to New York City, this soul finds its rest in an unlikely place: inside a New York opera house.

Black John has fled to the city for a summer to postpone his inevitable, yet dreaded, return to Altamaha. He stumbles, completely by accident, into a music hall where, ironically, white John is present as well. Indeed, the two nearly collide when, confused by the lights and the movement of the crowds, Black John stops in his tracks. White John's date offers a "roguish," if prescient, comment: "[Y]ou must not lynch the colored gentleman simply because he's in your way." White John, meanwhile, argues for the tender social relations between southern whites and Blacks, but stops short and "flushe[s] to the roots of his hair" when he realizes that the Negro from the foyer has purchased a seat next to his. Black John neither hears this by-play nor is conscious of what follows—white John's attempts to have him removed from the opera house—so transported is he by "the delicate beauty of the hall, the faint perfume, the moving myriad of men, the rich clothing and low hum of talking" which spoke so eloquently of a "world so different from his, so strangely more beautiful than anything he had known, that he sat in dreamland" (192).

So deprived has Black John been of beauty that his soul is depicted as being almost preternaturally sensitive to its manifestation in Wagner's music. He wonders briefly why the other concertgoers appear "so listless," why they whisper among themselves instead of listening to the music, for the music makes *him* feel "the movement of power" within himself and makes him long for a vocation in which he can exercise this power—a vocation that however "bitter hard" allows him to throw off the "cringing and sickening servility, . . . the cruel hurt" of his former life in the South. And then he has a moment of ecstatic union with the transpersonal and transhistorical: "When at last a soft sorrow crept across the violins, there came to him the vision of a far-off home,—the great eyes of his sister, and the dark drawn face of his mother. And his heart sank below the waters, even as the sea-sand sinks by the shores of Altamaha, only to be lifted aloft again with that last ethereal wail of [Lohengrin's] swan that quivered and faded away into the sky" (193).

The moment crystallizes John's determination to return south even as the sequence as a whole clarifies the stakes in Du Bois's version of the pastoral encounter. Du Bois gives the reader a confrontation of brothers—each unaware of the other's identity—in a bower of ideal love and peace, in this instance, the site where Lohengrin woos and wins his Elsa. But given the fact that this love's bright promise almost immediately sours over a question of recognition—Elsa's questioning of her groom and savior's identity—surely we are meant to associate this bower with the South, her soured promises to white men and freedmen. Strengthening this link is the fact that between the brothers stands the body of the white woman and the verbalized threat of lynching. What is at stake is the exercise of power—a power metonymically linked to the sea and to the "drawn face" of Black John's mother and the "great eyes" of his sister. In short, the white man's imperative to protect his woman sets him sharply at odds with the Black man, for whom the stakes are even higher because it's not Woman in the abstract that is his concern, but his own mother and sister. The end of the encounter in the garden—with Black John transported into "dreamland" while his white twin is working tirelessly to have him symbolically lynched, that is, thrust into the cold New York night—foreshadows what is to be the end of the tale in Altamaha.

The second pastoral moment occurs after Black John's return. His personal coldness has ruined the welcome planned for him; his speech on "scientific" principles has provoked angry snarls from the church's amen corner and a vigorous rebuttal from the preacherly elect. Amazed that he has offended, wounded at the attacks he has provoked, our noble John deigns no reply. "He arose silently, and passed out into the night. Down toward the sea he went, in the fitful starlight, half conscious of the girl [his sister, Jennie] who followed timidly after him." John's grief transports him beyond himself once again as he stands on a bluff looking out to sea. After some time passes, he recalls his sister's presence and, almost as an afterthought, embraces young Jennie, who seems to understand only that her brother is unhappy. They share a moment of mystical union "peering at the gray unresting water" while John allows Jennie's "passion of tears [to] spend itself upon his shoulder" (197).

With Black John figuring his sister in such overtly—if primly—sexual language, it is a short step indeed for white John to do the same. The "trim little body" of the "little brown kitchen-maid" stirs the bored youth as nothing has since his return to his father's house. He tries to wheedle a kiss, and when Jennie flees like a bronze Daphne into the Georgia pines, he pursues her. Black John, meanwhile, has endured a sharp dressing-down from the judge and been dismissed from his teaching post. Dazed, he is wandering the woods, intending to meet Jennie and walk her home from work, when the text bursts again into pastoral lyricism: "The great brown sea lay silent. The air scarce breathed. The dying day bathed the twisted oaks and mighty pines in black and gold. There came from the wind no warning, not a whisper from the cloudless sky. There was only a black man hurrying on with an ache in his heart, seeing neither sun nor sea, but starting as from a dream at the frightened cry that woke the pines, to see his dark sister struggling in the arms of a tall and fair-haired man. He said not a word, but, seizing a fallen limb, struck him with all the pent-up hatred of his great black arm; and the body lay white and still beneath the pines, all bathed in sunshine and in blood" (201–2).

It is fascinating to note that, after John wields the tree limb, Jennie drops entirely from the text. The reader is left with the image of the bloody and apparently nude body of John's twin, underlining the viciousness of the homosocial/homoerotic competition between the two men. John returns home briefly to tell his mother that he is "going away,—I'm going to be free," but he makes no preparations for what his mother "dimly" imagines to be a flight north. He returns, instead, to the scene of the crime, from which the body has been apparently removed and falls into a dreamlike trance. Lost in nostalgia for that moment of communion with Wagner's music, John stares vacantly out to sea, softly humming the strains of Lohengrin's "Wedding March" until the gathering storm of the lynch mob bursts around him. At the sight of the judge riding at the head of the mob, John closes his eyes and turns to face the sea: "And the world whistled in his ears" (202–3) is the final sentence—an ambiguous phrase that suggests either passivity in the face of his fate . . . or possibly a leap from the bluff into the arms of death.

What Du Bois appears to be writing here is a narrative of a double *unconsciousness*. The white community has its beloved John, as does the Black community, but "neither world thought the other's thought, save with a vague unrest" (189). At crucial moments, both of the Johns are blind to each other's existence. In the opera house, for example, Black John does not see white John at all, while white John, quick to speak of his warm feelings for his childhood playmate, is whipped to equally quick rage by what he imagines to be the sight of an uppity Negro. Each can recognize the other only after the return south—and each recognition scene is both tragic and too late. White John, for example, realizes his brother was the "darky" who tried to "force" himself into a seat beside his date at the opera, and the recollection crystallizes the judge's determination to fire dark John from his teaching post. Black John, meanwhile, does not recall white John as his childhood playmate at all until after he has bludgeoned the youth to death. Du Bois's argument is clear: the failure to think one another's thought always has, and can only have, tragic consequences.

Viewed from the perspective of its pastoral moments, however, "Of the Coming of John" reveals itself to be squarely within the received tradition of southern pastoral. For one, Black John has adopted values that are as aristocratic and chivalric as any southern cavalier's. His sensitivity to Wagner, his intellectual superiority to everyone in Altamaha, from the judge to the kindly yet ignorant and bigoted church members, marks his aristocracy as being that of the spirit and of education, but it is an aristocracy nonetheless. Nor should we forget that it is his chivalric care for his womenfolk that drew him back to the South. Du Bois's treatment of those womenfolk is worthy of remark as well. Depicted as both lacking in intelligence and physically helpless, they are described always in terms of the environment—not, significantly, the land, to which Du Bois appears to be unable to imagine a positive relationship, but to an entity that one can regard only as the very image of inconquerability: the Atlantic Ocean, symbol of both the Great Mother and the Middle Passage, and as such repository of humankind's deepest drives and desires. If we read her as Great Mother, the sea motif here appears to function as an emblem of what Jung would have called the dark side of the Great Mother, she who beckons then destroys.[27] It is, after all, John's vision of his mother and sister—a vision linked explicitly to the sea—that draws him back to Altamaha and his death. Their vulnerability as territory to be conquered demands his protection; their sanctity as the Ideal Order to be upheld demands his allegiance. It is John's adherence to these values that both ennobles and destroys him.

A passage from "The Damnation of Women" is instructive.

> I shall forgive the white South much in its final judgment day: I shall forgive its slavery, for slavery is a world-old habit; I shall forgive its fighting for a well-lost cause, and for remembering that struggle with tender tears; I shall forgive its so-called "pride of race," the passion of its hot blood, and even its dear, old, laughable strutting and posing; but one thing I shall never forgive, neither in this world nor the world to come: its wanton and continued and persistent insulting of the black womanhood which it sought and seeks to prostitute to its lust. I cannot forget that it is such Southern gentlemen into whose hands smug Northern hypocrites of today are seeking to place our women's eternal destiny,—men who insist upon withholding from my mother and wife and daughter those signs and appellations of courtesy and respect which elsewhere he withholds only from bawds and courtesans.[28]

This enumeration of things Du Bois can forgive is quite Victorian in its concern with "manly things between men." As demonstrated by his sympathetic characterization of the judge, Du Bois can indeed forgive slavery, war, manly tears, and manly pride—even that of the strutting, fretting variety. But as demonstrated by the bludgeoning of the judge's son, no Sedgwickian resolution can be possible using the coin of the Black female body. The rape threat is, thus, central to Du Bois's revision of southern pastoral in "Of the Coming of John," though that revision goes no deeper than reversing the poles of the binaries, allying whites with savagery and "uplifted" Blacks with the heights of civilization.

It is, thus, entirely predictable that Black John's inability to prevent the defilement of his sister precipitates physical violence. What does surprise the reader is that what John mourns in his dreamlike trance by the seductive and, ultimately, destructive sea appears to be less Jennie's defilement—she vanishes from the text as completely as if she'd never existed after the rape—than the insult to his own manhood. John's fall into paralytic nostalgia while a mob is ravening for his life makes more sense when examined through the lens of the pastoral. Lost in the romantic dream of power inspired by his memory of the opera house and Lohengrin's bower, Black John chooses death and the irrational near the sea that has become the emblem of both death and the irrational over a life in which his dream can never be fulfilled. Wagner's music acts as both framing device and ironic commentary: the snatch of Wagner John hums signals his preparedness for death. "Freudig gefuhrt, ziehet dahin" translates as "Led happily, move on" (205). The world's "whistle" in John's ears—is it meant to signify that the encounter with the mob has turned the harmony John seeks to harsh cacophony? Or is it the sound of the wind in his ears as he flings himself into the sea? Regardless of the answer, the question arises: Does the embrace of the pastoral represent an artistic dead end for African American artist? For a possible answer, we shall turn to Jean Toomer.

Modernist Primitives in the Southern Garden

The origins of Jean Toomer's *Cane* long ago passed into legend. "On the train from Georgia to Washington, D.C., in November 1921," begins Nellie McKay's account, "Jean Toomer began to write the sketches that became the first section of *Cane*." "Unprepared" for what he "saw and heard in the South—incapable of holding back his creative responses"—Toomer wrote furiously, McKay continues, and the first and third sections were done by Christmas. "I gave with abandon the flow of myself" is how Toomer describes the experience in the passages quoted by McKay. "And as I gave I was given to myself. My soul was resurrected and we were joined. . . . I discovered what I had sought elsewhere, without finding."²⁹

McKay is not the only critic to be driven to raptures by Toomer's unabashedly sensual artistry. Du Bois himself reviewed *Cane* in *The Crisis* in February 1924—and gave it a thundering good review. "Jean Toomer is the first of our writers to *hurl his pen across the very face* of our sex conventionality," wrote Du Bois in what amounted to a rave (emphasis added). Hailing Toomer as the "emancipator," he praised the "splendid careless truth" of the women of *Cane*—"Karintha, an innocent prostitute; Becky, a fallen white woman; Carma, a tender Amazon of unbridled desire, . . . Doris the cheap chorus girl"—and rebuked the small minds that would "shrink and criticize" Toomer's openness about sexuality. The good Victorian in Du Bois was to be baffled by the modernist touches—the "undue striving for effect," the bits that are "difficult or even impossible to understand"—but he ended by giving the young man an approving nod. We will be "watching for the fullness of his strength and for that calm certainty of his art which will undoubtedly come with years."³⁰

No one knew at the time, of course, that this "calm certainty" was never to come, though the dream apparently died hard. "Apostle of beauty," *Opportunity* magazine called Toomer in 1932, as it sorrowed that this "modern Negro" artist had been "poetically quiet for the past eight years."³¹ In 1939, nearly twenty years after Toomer had written "as a means to life as I desire to live it, as an end-in-itself, I have given up art," he was ensconced, firmly if haphazardly, in a budding canon of African American writing. "A lesson in emotional release," Saunders Redding wrote of *Cane* in 1939, describing the book as "hot, colorful, primitive, but more akin to the naïve hysteria of the spirituals than to the sophisticated savagery of jazz and the blues." Toomer "loved the race and the soil that sustained it," added Redding.³² If such descriptive passages seem overdone, then we must remind ourselves of their context—always mentioned though rarely explored: Georgia, whose links to "naïve," hysterical spirituality and "savage" blues and jazz were apparently so plainly manifest as to be completely unworthy of remark. Redding insists that Toomer "loved the race"—but I would argue that there's far more evidence that it's "the race," and those who lust in their hearts for *Cane*'s potent romances of race, that loved Toomer, with an ardor that was almost entirely one-sided.

Of the early commentators, though, it's Du Bois who put his finger most directly on Toomer's appeal. The trip to *Cane*'s aestheticized Georgia takes us directly to the Black borders of color, sex, and primitivism—which, though unstable historically and socially constituted, are also brooding with passion, sullen with the threat of sudden violence, and lavish with beauty. Toomer figures Georgia as Eden after the fall, and his beautiful, (self-)destructive Eves—Karintha, Becky, Louisa, and the rest—bewitch and captivate audiences still. We are riveted by their tragedy—that they are incarcerated within the one category without apparent fluidity or social cachet, a punishment and an incarceration, all rolled into one—even as we revel in Toomer's ironic triumph, that in creating them he created the first collection of fictional Black women with whom there was ever even the remotest possibility of falling in love.

Toomer announces in the book's title that *Cane* will be an extended excursion into the pastoral. Against the shadowy substratum of Hellenic-Hebraic double typologies suggested by its homonym, the word evokes a tragic landscape: layering images of the sugar lands of South Carolina or Georgia or Louisiana—where the plants undulate tall and green over vast acres in the height of summer or lay chopped, supine, and burning after harvest, columns of smoke mounting to a blood-soaked sky in late fall—with Sugar in its sociohistorical sense as the commodity that historians now agree was most responsible for the spread of chattel slavery. The word links the dazzling whiteness of the finished product and the Black hands that for centuries were forced to tend it with the sense of a historic cursing—the notorious cruelty of the sugar islands of the Caribbean, where life expectancy for an adult African could be as little as seven years—for planters found it cheaper to work their hands to death and import fresh ones than to wait for natural increase or to care for aged slaves. This is a tragic landscape indeed.

And just as in previous examples, we see Toomer deploying the pastoral to mediate the encounter with imperialist violence, to slow or speed the slippage toward existential horror. The beautiful, mournful refrain,

> Her skin is like dusk on the eastern horizon,
> O can't you see it, O can't you see it,
> Her skin is like dusk on the eastern horizon
> ... When the sun goes down. (1, 5)

for example, is used to break and unite the action in a story of rape, abortion, and prostitution. Toomer, in contrast to Du Bois, enters fully into the

American pastoral tradition by figuring the landscape as feminine, but he veers wildly from the received tradition. Toomer dares to imbue skin black enough to seem purplish with the divine connotations of sky and the east, he dares to imagine in cadences that recall the slow music of the "Song of Songs" a woman "perfect as dusk ... carrying beauty"—as the women of Georgia at the time of Toomer's visit effortlessly bore heavy burdens on their heads. And yet Toomer is far bolder, carrying the war over representation deep into the enemy territory by narrating a truth so unspeakable that "the pines [had to] whisper [it] to Jesus": Becky, "the white woman who had two Negro sons."

Toomer can be bolder, in part, because he is a far greater artist. His effects are achieved both by intricate mappings of metaphor or metonymy as well as through his virtuosic mastery of the tools of poetic art and his willingness to play "jazz" with them to achieve modernistic idiom. In "Karintha," for example, Toomer's use of alliteration as he depicts a young girl hemmed in on all sides by the lustful gazes of men begins as amusement, as a lark, and ends in menace as the euphonious repetition of soothing nasals—"men," "young men," "old men," "male," "mate"—in the opening paragraph grates with a sinister irony against the literal meaning of the passage and particularly its closing sentence: "This interest of the male, who wishes to *ripen a growing thing too soon*, could mean no good to her" (emphasis added).

In contrast to Du Bois, the benign patriarch and lifelong defender of the right of True (Black) Womanhood to stand on the pedestal, Toomer's women are desiring subjects brought low as much by any of their own actions as by the patriarchy's harsh methods for policing feminine desire. The southern sections of *Cane*, in particular, appear to link patriarchal domination of women, metonymically, with the modern industrial machine's assault on the land. A sawmill, with a looming "pyramidal sawdust pile," acts a reminder of the destructive intrusion of machine into the garden and of man's phallus into the "ripened too soon" Karintha, who aborts her child and embarks in good earnest at the age of twenty, "carrying beauty, perfect as dusk when the sun goes down," upon a life of prostitution.[33] "Black horses drive a mower through weeds" in "Reapers," written in jazzily iambic, fluently accentual heroic couplets, and "a field rat, startled, squealing bleeds" while the blade keeps relentlessly spinning: "Blood-stained, ... cutting weeds and shade" (lines 5–8). Barlo's motorcar precipitates disaster in "Esther." A factory figures as the scene of a lynching in "Blood Burning Moon." One could go on. But I'd like to focus my discussion of *Cane* upon the sketch that ends the first southern section of the book, "Blood-Burning Moon," for it is here that Toomer cuts loose with full force the elements of his art—his mastery of poetic technique, experimentation with form, commitment to history. And it's also here that these engage most strikingly and successfully with the received tradition of southern pastoral. Like "Of the Coming of John," the story pits Black and white "twins" in bitter rivalry for a woman who is neither white nor aristocratic but Black and comely. But unlike Du Bois's innocent, asexual Jennie, Louisa is a desiring subject who, given the choice of a worshipful lover and protector in the form of "Big Boy" Tom Burwell, willfully elects to transgress the color line with Bob Stone, "the younger son of the people she worked for" (28). Remarkably, Toomer does not judge Louisa—splendidly and carelessly, he tells the story as Truth—and uses all the tools in his toolkit to elevate it to a truth tragic and terrific as grand opera.

Let us begin by examining those tools. He starts with devices of parallelism—particularly anaphora and epistrophe, repetitions, respectively, of opening and closing sequences of words—to create an effect that is almost biblical in its portentousness: "*Up from* the stone skeleton wall, *up from* the rotting floor boards and the solid hand-hewn beams of oak of the pre-war cotton factory, *dusk came. Up from* the dusk, the *full moon came.*" It's a fascinating passage given the uses made of dusk in "Karintha." From an ambiguously positive female value, dusk has become a decadent one, emerging from the "skeleton stone walls" and "rotting floor boards" of a factory formerly operated by slave labor. Remember, too, that in "Georgia Dusk," a poem about "night's barbecue" (line 4), that is, lynching, the moon follows hard upon dusk's heels. This feminine symbol in "Blood Burning Moon" is painted a red so brilliant that it seems a portent: "Negro women improvised songs against its spell."

Enter Louisa from stage left. With skin "the color of oak leaves" and breasts "firm and up-pointed like ripe acorns," she seems so much a feature of the natural landscape that she could be a tree. But Louisa is both one of the singing women and the force whose evil influence the women seek to ward off, for two men love Louisa: the Black Tom Burwell, who has many other women, and who yet feels himself obscurely undeserving of the one he desires most; and the white Bob Stone, who has to constantly remind himself to think of her as "nigger" but who, even so, won't share her with Burwell. Louisa has relied on luck and lies to keep each man ignorant of the other, but on the night of the "red nigger moon . . . blood-burning moon," a strangeness trembles in the air. The strangeness infects Louisa's song, making it "agitant and restless":

> Rusty black and tan spotted hounds, lying in the dark corners of porches or prowling around back yards, put their noses in the air and caught its tremor. They began plaintively to yelp and howl. Chickens woke up and cackled. Intermittently, all over the countryside dogs barked and roosters crowed as if heralding a weird dawn or some ungodly awakening.

The passage is worth quoting just for the beautiful cacophony of consonants that mimes the restlessness infecting factory town. But structurally it has an even larger significance—similar to the tuning up of an orchestra before the symphony begins. As Louisa sits on her porch to watch the moon "rising toward a thick cloud-bank that would soon hide it," Toomer intones for the first time the mysterious and evocative refrain: "Red nigger moon. Sinner! / Blood-burning moon. Sinner! / Come out that fact'ry door" (28, 29). Section 2 of "Blood-Burning Moon" returns to the mood of magisterial invocation that opened section 1, but this time what rises "up from" the dusk is the "mellow glow" of the fire at the sugar refinery and the heavily sweet smell of boiling cane. In contrast to the solitude of the women, singing "supper-getting-ready" songs each in the separateness of their individual homes, there is a warm, companionable circle of men chewing cane and telling lies around the thickening cane syrup. It is here, amid gossip about "the white folks, about moonshining and cotton picking, and about sweet nigger gals," that Tom Burwell first hears Bob Stone's name linked with Louisa's. Violence is the immediate result: He knocks one man over, chases others into the woods with his knife, then storms straight to Louisa's porch. After vowing to cut Bob Stone "jes like I cut a nigger" if he discovers the gossip to be true, Tom asks Louisa to sing to him. Here the orchestra tuning up turns choir with full chorus:

> The full moon sank upward into the deep purple of the cloud bank. An old woman brought a lighted lamp and hung it on the common well whose bulky shadow squatted in the middle of the road, opposite Tom and Louisa. . . . As she did so, she sang. Figures shifted, restlesslike, between lamp and window in the front rooms of the shanties. Shadows of the figures fought each other on the gray dust of the road. Figures raised the windows and joined the old woman in song. Louisa and Tom, the whole street singing:
> Red nigger moon. Sinner!
> Blood burning moon! Sinner!
> Come out that fac'try door. (30)

Toomer enters the mind of Bob Stone in section 3 of "Blood-Burning Moon." Sneaking out into the gloom to meet Louisa, we find that Stone is obsessed with the notion of having "lost ground"—a ground explicitly figured as Louisa, whom he imagines tending the fire in the kitchen of his family plantation. His feelings toward Louisa are an uneasy mixture of shame, desire, and ownership in which he must remind himself again and again that, while she is lovely and desirable, it is only in a "nigger way." That fact seems to hold little comfort for him, however, when he overhears the same group of gossips talking and learns he has a rival for Louisa's affections.

In a rage that parallels Big Boy Burwell's, Stone crashes into the canebrake. "Cane leaves cut his face and lips. He tasted blood. He threw himself down and dug his fingers in the ground. The earth was cool. Cane roots took the fever from his hands" (32). This exceedingly odd moment of communion with the soil both calms Stone and reminds him that it is time to claim his own personal bit of soil, Louisa's brown body. Finding her absent from their meeting place, Stone, like Burwell, runs in a blind rage to her house, tasting his own blood on his lips and imagining that it is his enemy's. Amid the yelping of dogs, the cackling of chickens, and the crowing of roosters, Stone arrives at Louisa's house and issues a challenge. Fighting first with fists and then with knives—Stone the aggressor at every escalation of the violence—Burwell soon deals his enemy a mortal blow. Covered in blood from his slashed throat, Stone staggers to Broad Street, in the white part of town—and a lynch mob boils up immediately "like ants upon a forage." Arming itself swiftly, with an almost industrial efficiency—with "shotguns, revolvers, rope, kerosene, torches. Two high-powered cars"—it moves to bring Burwell to "justice."

Up to this point, Toomer's lynching narrative has starkly differed from Du Bois's. It is as if Toomer had rewritten Du Bois's lynching narrative—but tossed all the elements of *bildungsroman* in order to make the connections to Sam Hose case more vivid, more direct. Rather than an argument over pay, or the convenient fiction of a wife raped next to her husband's dead body, the argument is directly over the "ground" of the Black woman's body—her ability to choose, the fatal consequences, in paradise after the fall, of her choice. Toomer's success has thus far in *Cane* derived in large part by deploying what Umberto Eco famously called that exquisite equipoise between "the guarantee of the good" and "the shudder of the bad."[34] But the carnivalesque defiance of the action he vividly imagines collapses when the Burwell who has proven himself so valiant in single combat faces the lynch mob. He sinks into the passivity of Du Bois's John. Too paralyzed to run from the mob and too dazed to fight, he submits tamely to having his wrists bound. Silently, he allows the mob to drag him into the abandoned cotton factory, where a stake is driven into the ground and the rotting planks are ripped up to make a bonfire. Tom burns without making a sound—as folk tradition said Sam Hose had burned—and the natural sounds of factory town, the clamor of chickens and dogs, the songs of women, fall silent and are replaced, first, by the "taut hum" of the mob's efficiency and, then, its savage howls: "Its yell echoed against the skeleton stone walls and sounded like a hundred yells. Like a hundred mobs yelling. Its yell thudded against the thick front wall [of the factory] and fell back. Ghost of a yell slipped through the flames and out the great door of the factory. It fluttered like a dying thing down the single street of factory town" (34–35).

Toomer ends "Blood Burning Moon" by invoking the pastoral once again to suture up the ragged edges of the wound left by the savagery of the lynching. Louisa, collapsed on her porch after seeing death claim both her lovers in the span of an hour, hears the "yell" of the mob and, as with the cacophony of chickens in section 1 and the woman at the well in section 2, receives it as an invitation to song. Gazing at the full moon and understanding for the first time its "evil" message, she pours out her guilty, incoherent aria: "Red nigger moon. Sinner! / Blood-burning moon. Sinner! / Come out that fact'ry door" (35).

"Toomer does not impress me as one who knows his Georgia," Du Bois had written in 1924; but he willingly seemed to accept the lie, noting "he [Toomer] paints things that are true, not with Dutch exactness, but rather with an impressionist's sweep of color. He is an artist with words."[35] And it's true that, in artistry, Toomer represents a giant step beyond Du Bois. As for *Cane*'s incursion upon the terrain of southern pastoral, that, too, was on the whole successful.[36] The prose poems and verse in Toomer's so-called novel sketch a vital and diverse folk community as well as a fully imagined and mostly positive relationship between that community and the land. But the periodic intrusion of a distanced gaze—in "Fern" and "Kabnis," to name two examples—comes as a disquieting reminder of Toomer's actual subjectivity vis-à-vis his subject: as ethnographer and artist. His experiments with the pastoral as a tool of modernist incursion into the archive do serve to underline the cruel hierarchies of life in Georgia by demonstrating, tragically and repeatedly, that the existence of the charming premodern peasantry he describes is predicated upon the existence of a tyrannical and violent aristocracy. But Toomer is not one of this folk, only one who seeks to weave his own song about them. His gaze was that of an ethnographer-artist; his letters evince far more concern, for example, with his own fragmented modernist subjectivity than with the lives of his objects of study.[37]

At the last, *Cane*'s project of pastoral revision from within Black double consciousness runs aground precisely where Toomer had begun in the opening lines of "Karintha": the land is still figured as an explicitly feminine entity and, placed in an object position to male subjectivity, remains matter to be acted upon or an Ideal Order to be upheld. Toomer's great feeling for his female characters allows the reader to empathize intensely with them. But that empathy is achieved by manipulating familiar tropes: he inscribes the "tragic" Black female figure into the pastoral space traditionally occupied by the southern white woman. And as in certain versions of white male pastoral—I'm thinking here of Faulkner's tragic heroines Caddie Compson and Temple Drake—he depicts a positive female potential hinted at then spoiled by man's meddling hand ("Karintha," for example) or turning violently destructive ("Blood Burning Moon"). The seductress Louisa, though handled sympathetically to the end, has after all destroyed Stone and Burwell and, indeed, endangered the entire community with her selfish sensation seeking.

After "Blood-Burning Moon's" almost operatic lyric intensity, Toomer oscillates in section 2 of *Cane* from the aggressive, almost angry jump boogie rhythms of "Seventh Street" and "Theater" to the softer cadences of "Box Seat" to the nearly atonal dissonances of "Rhobert" and "Calling Jesus." The lyric intensity of "Harvest Song" reasserts by contrast with the city sections Toomer's romantic antimodernist commitments, but the positive female potential hinted at in section 1 remains a dream unfulfilled. Toomer's "novel" ends with the theater piece "Kabnis"—and the image of a virginal "child woman" praying "Jesus, come" before a mad old man in the soft circle of light formed by the rising sun.

Having asked "O can't you see it" in "Karintha," having proclaimed "the sun is setting on / A song-lit race of slaves" (lines 11–12) in "Song of the Son," Toomer's sunrise brings the "novel" full circle in a manner that underscores its enmeshment in the received tradition of southern pastoral. For where his text has elsewhere committed itself explicitly to a liberatory vision of human sexuality and the regenerative principle in nature, Toomer here seems to suggest that that principle can be fulfilled only *before* a woman discovers her sexuality: only the virginal "gold-glowing child" can be allowed to sing the "birth song" of the land (116).

And so it may appear at first sight that this seeking after the "pure" essence of the Black authentic is similar in impulse to that which motivated the Charleston Renaissance, but the aims are altogether different. The achievement of artists like Du Bois and Toomer is that they seek for origins in order to give birth to innovation; they dip into the well of authenticity as an act of participation in a communal "changing same," learning the beats of an ancient drum so as to make something new. Du Bois combines concertized spirituals with Wagner in order to make something new. Toomer combines the soul-stirring refrains of the blues and the syncopated, uptown, jump-boogie rhythms of ragtime and its child a-borning jazz with downtown imagist and modernist aesthetics to make something new.

The supreme irony from the point of view of this study is, of course, the fact that *The Souls of Black Folk* and *Cane*, texts so deeply implicated in questions of identity and conflicts over inheritance, have yet been so thoroughly disconnected and disembodied from the actual human and cultural landscape by which both texts were inspired. This a landscape where, I must remind you, that these very conflicts—of scientific/mythopoeic notions of humanity, of political notions of citizenship, or of geographical notions of land—played out, passionately and violently, over a period not of years but of centuries. And yet a dominant critical tradition within African American studies privileging migration over rootedness, emancipation over incarceration has, in effect, disinherited the Black artist in general and the southern Black artist in particular, trapping the "primitive" in discourses of "the blues" or the "Afrocentric" that, while beautifully articulated, attractive, and smart, often never quite succeed in connecting some really important critical dots.

It might be stretching a metaphor to say that, so far as the critics are concerned, *The Souls of Black Folk* and *Cane* may as well have been set on Mars as in Georgia—but I don't think it stretches the metaphor by much. The centripetal force of discipline has been at work, of course—the tendency by specialists of whatever derivation to read what their colleagues and rivals are reading. But another factor is the reality that critics follow where artists lead. So successful were Du Bois and Toomer in painting themselves as "moderns"—as "New Negroes," though that was a box Toomer was thrust into much against his will—that the "primitives" against whom they marked their difference end up "disappeared" as an actuality from the texts (hence from the criticism) even as they bade fair to achieve immortality as myth and memory structure. Du Bois's and Toomer's "primitives" were fun—hot, colorful, naïve, and savage, as Redding said—but that they were essentially inauthentic (and we should enjoy the juxtaposition of those terms) goes without saying. The primitive is, after all, founded upon and deeply implicated in double consciousness, which carries elements of recognition and *mis*recognition, which is about identification but also about *mis*identification. "Maroons" at the border of the modern, the primitive remains bound in certain ineluctable ways. It cannot be educated ("It doesn't want to speak English") without altering ("it'll spoil him,—ruin him") its essential nature. Free these figures may be sexually—but that sexual license carries a terrific cost.

The distinctions that are most critical to contemporary notions of the Gullah Geechee Coast are, of course, distinctions of landscape, lineage, and language—none of them areas in which the body of knowledge was sufficiently advanced or sufficiently free from white supremacy during the period of our study to make a difference even for a thinker of Du Bois's caliber or an artist of Toomer's. Neither man fully understood the Africanisms present in lowcountry culture, though the former's grasp of the sociohistorical facts would have certainly been firmer; neither man succeeds in or even fully imagines the challenges of creating a literary form of the spoken dialect, though Toomer, with his modernist's eye for the main chance of found materials, without question, exceeds Du Bois here. Thus, with the eyes of African American writers and their critics turned firmly toward the modern, the "new," it's left to white southerners, and particularly white southern visual artists, to tell the story of the Negroes they know best—the Negroes who stayed home and whom they sought to incarcerate in a genteel painterly Jim Crow prison as securely as they had incarcerated them in chattel slavery.

CHAPTER 5

What Miss Ann Saw
The Imperial Eyes of Charleston Renaissance Painting

> The past is the safest place there is.
> —BRUCE JACKSON, Foreword to Lydia Parrish et al., *Slave Songs of the Georgia Sea Islands*

Leon Trotsky is said to have once opined that art was not so much a mirror of society as a hammer with which to shape it. Substitute "paintbrush" for "hammer" and you have the art of the Charleston Renaissance. Indeed, one is never so aware of the fact that Charleston Renaissance culture-makers are engaged in an active exercise in memory—and mythmaking—as when looking at the visual art. In this chapter, we shall examine the work of a group of mostly female artists whose work creates the social reality that it claims to reflect. On their canvases, class interests and the civil religion of Lost Cause ancestor worship converge in ways that go far beyond simply casting a glance of complacent approval in the general direction of Charleston's past. Renaissance art, we shall see, evinces an engagement with the Black body in ways uneasily reminiscent of the structures of domination associated with slavery—at the same time, the artists restage, reenact, and transform the primal scenes of slavery in ways that purge Charleston's beauty of all guilt. Indeed, Renaissance art was even more obviously than most other forms of cultural endeavor during this period an exercise in domination, a coordinated exercise of the empire of the eye to diminish the stature of the formerly enslaved and reassert the importance of the former slaveholders.

We noted in chapter 3 that Charleston Renaissance was a term of relatively recent vintage. Indeed, it emerged public discourse in 1985 when the Gibbes Museum of Art organized its "Charleston in the Age of *Porgy and Bess*" exhibition to commemorate the fiftieth anniversary of Heyward's folk opera,[1] and art and literary critics seized upon the coinage with enthusiasm. Boyd Saunders and Ann McAden were inspired to produce *Alfred Hutty and the Charleston Renaissance* (1990). Charles R. Anderson's brief memoir, *Charles-*

ton: A Golden Memory* (1992), included a chapter on "A Little Renaissance in the 1930s." But the most influential popularizers of the term have to have been the art critic Martha Severens, both through her articles in the *Magazine Antiques* and through her lavishly illustrated *The Charleston Renaissance* (1998), and the collector and gallery owner Robert M. Hicklin Jr., an early and influential champion of southern art as a category worthy of serious interest and scholarship.

Twenty years on, adoption of the term has done the work it was intended to do, helping to rescue from obscurity a group of artists, both male and female, northern and southern, who between 1915 and 1940 produced a tremendous body of work set in and telling a cohesive story about Charleston and the Carolina lowcountry. And though acceptance of this so-called renaissance met with resistance,[2] the renaissance-making impulse proved irresistible. Charleston's Gibbes Museum of Art renamed one of its galleries and one of its collections after the Renaissance. New book titles have fountained forth—James M. Hutchisson's *DuBose Heyward: A Charleston Gentleman and the World of Porgy and Bess* (2000); Harlan Greene's *Mr. Skylark: John Bennett and the Charleston Renaissance* (2001), focusing on a relatively unsung figure who was the linchpin of the Poetry Society of South Carolina; Hutchisson and Greene's edited collection, *Renaissance in Charleston: Art and Life in the Carolina Low Country, 1900–1940* (2003); Hutchisson's *A DuBose Heyward Reader* (2003); Hicklin's *Two-Lane South: The Charleston Renaissance Gallery* (2007), to name just a few—and continue to expand the official canon. But before even more scholars and popularizers rush to leap on the bandwagon, it might be well to follow the example of Joan Kelly-Gadol, who, nearly five decades ago, in one of the landmark essays of women's history, asked not "was there a Renaissance?"—speaking, of course, of the Italian Renaissance—but rather "a Renaissance for whom?" It is this question that I propose we allow to linger in the background as we embark on our exploration.

Charleston's "little renaissance" ran counter to all the most important trends in twentieth-century American art. The artists, no less than the art patrons, explicitly rejected modernism: "Simply an expression of radicalism," sniffed Alfred Hutty, when Solomon Guggenheim held the first American exhibit of his "non-objective" art collection at Charleston's Gibbes in 1936.[3] "Renaissance" art itself tended to be nostalgic rather than progressive, figurative rather than abstract, sentimental rather than expressionistic—firmly rooted in the soil and the "soul" of a city the artists loved. Hutty, an artist associated with New York's Woodstock colony who "discovered" Charleston in 1919 at the height of World War I during a trip south to scout out attractive towns in which to winter, summed up the feeling of the Charleston group in a famed wire to his wife: "Come quickly, have found heaven."[4] To a great degree complacent and inward-looking,⁵ the artists associated with the group eschewed the searching and self-criticism of regional art movements that were roughly contemporaneous with theirs, the Harlem and southern literary renaissances, instead proclaiming a particular and unsurpassed Beauty—often and loudly—as their region's great heritage while pounding the drum of that Beauty under the auspices of the cultural groups that created and maintained Charleston's renaissance: the Poetry Society of South Carolina and the Society for the Preservation of Old Dwellings, both founded in 1920; the Society for the Preservation of Spirituals and the Charleston Etcher's Club, both founded in 1923.

This class of creative spirits and art patrons was to assert again and again that their interests and aims were primarily aesthetic, but they were also part of a broader national conversation—being conducted by painters such as Thomas Hart Benton and Grant Wood, by writers in various regional movements, and by visionary developers such as Henry Ford at Greenfield Village and John D. Rockefeller Jr. at Colonial Williamsburg—over the meaning of regional identity and its potential to relieve the anomie and exhaustions of American modernity. By fits and starts and over many years, the Charleston group carved out a "renaissance vision" of their city's past. It was an aristocratic one, with paintings that stressed a heritage of magnificent (if often crumbling) homes and writings that threw a haze over a long-ago "golden age." Even where "renaissance" artists contemplated the present, it was with an agenda, as the predominance of elite homes and neighborhoods, the concern with monumental architecture, appear a clear attempt to use elite cultural forms to communicate and transmit elite values.⁶

Provocatively and significantly, alongside this vision of mastery and power, Renaissance visual artists return again and again to the figure of the Gullah Negro. Indeed, here, renaissance artists showed they had far more in common with the moderns than they realized: for while modernist artists were appropriating African and other "primitive" motifs and forms to reinvigorate what they considered a "dead" tradition of European representation, Charleston Renaissance artists were doing something not terribly different, appropriating the Black body itself in a preoccupation verging on obsession with the role of African Americans in general and Gullahs in particular in the story of the ideal society they were constructing. Black bodies appear everywhere in the artists' canvases—as tiny figures in the shadow of iconic Charleston mansions, as central figures in rural and urban scenes. Stephanie Yuhl calls them "actors on [the] constructed stage" of the "genteel" and "refined" spaces that frame them. And, indeed, one is forcibly reminded of Homi Bhabha's invocation of the term "overlooked" to describe these figures that are simultaneously under surveillance, psychically disavowed, and yet "overdetermined . . . projected, made stereotypical and symptomatic" of complex social realities.⁷

The complex social reality in Charleston—and, indeed, across the South—

during this period was that of the intersection of Jim Crow segregation with the emerging culture of consumption. The city had witnessed the collapse of rice production, the boll weevil–assisted demise of long-staple cotton, and the boom and bust of phosphate mining. Stymied in the search for a commodity that would restore the city to wealth and prominence, elite cultural leaders gradually concluded that their most lucrative asset was . . . the city itself, preserved as if in a museum, by its poverty and irrelevance.[8] A more conscious preservation and shrewd marketing of this commodity—to wealthy northerners such as Henry and Clare Booth Luce who bought the old Henry Laurens estate of Mepkin, Benjamin Kittredge who wrought the transformation of Dean Hall into Cypress Gardens, Solomon Guggenheim who bought an island across the Cooper River from the city, Nelson Doubleday who owned an estate in nearby Yemassee, and the countless others who came as seasonal visitors or remained to enrich the city's social life—permitted the transformation of Charleston from a decayed and dying backwater to a mecca for those seeking a "quaint," "romantic," "old-worldly" atmosphere.[9]

Elizabeth O'Neill Verner, one of the few artists of the movement to write her own text for her coffee table books, was a master at evoking this atmosphere. "'For Lord's sake, where is you come from, 'Becca darlin'?'" Verner writes in *Mellowed by Time: A Charleston Notebook* (1941), making a creditable attempt at rendering the rhythms of Gullah. The passage continues,

> ". . . I ain't know that you is in town; somebody is tell me you is gone Nort' to lib wid you daughter," a surprised voice said one morning on the narrow street just beyond my window. I glanced out and saw Rebecca push her cart, piled high with wilted produce, closer to the curb.
>
> "I done bin gone and I come back," she said. "I don' like it up dere."
>
> "Dat's so? Well, I ain't gone away myself," said her friend, "so I don' know."
>
> "You best stay right here where you is belong, sister," Rebecca advised. "Chas'n ain't no place for lebe. Seem like Chas'n keep all the odder place I see from seem natchel. I suits dis place cause it don't change none."

The artist muses, in conclusion, "It was easy to see that *dear old simple Rebecca* would not fit comfortably into a Harlem atmosphere, but wasn't it nice to think she could come home and find it had not changed" (emphasis added).[10]

Verner's work—widely hailed as celebratory of its African American subjects—stands revealed as a provocative example of Bhabha's interlocking schemes of surveillance and projection. Gullah speakers in Verner's—and, indeed, in the vast majority of renaissance texts—express only those emotions and espouse only those values that are culturally approved. The purportedly "celebratory" aesthetic is, in fact, an active agent of a system of subjection, which coerces, corrects, and confines her subjects.[11] At the same time, using "quaint" anecdotes such as these to frame her etchings allows her to establish her own class credentials in the minds of her readers and consumers: by parading bonds of sympathy with and benevolent paternalism toward African Americans, she dons the hoop skirt of the plantation chatelaine, effectively disguising her role here as a working professional laboring mightily to attract patronage and to support her family. Thus, two figures occupy Verner's stage: the one genteel, refined, aristocratic; the other its polar opposite, primitive, poor, yet content.

Let us consider a further example: "One day I sat for hours in the company of a flower woman in a tattered coat covering layers of dresses, holding in her hand a pitiful bunch of jonquils wrapped in moss. Such tiny, wilted jonquils, hardly recognizable as such, but all that she had to bring into town that day.... I heard tales of poverty that I could scarcely credit, but I knew that they were true, for I had visited her cabin. I had seen the patch of hard ground just outside the shanty with its clay chimney, sufficiently askew to suit a cubist's canvas." The passage is painfully illustrative of Verner's distanced, aestheticizing gaze. She is concerned with ratcheting up the emotional stakes of her tale—stressing the details of the single, wilted bunch of flowers and the woman's tatterdemalion clothing—even as she reveals herself, through her visit to the "shanty," to be participating in the rituals of *noblesse oblige* that are the domain of the remnant of the planter elite. Of course, what she sees when she arrives is the "cubist" detail of the woman's clay chimney, not the contrast between the woman's poverty and her own quite comfortable existence in the artists' enclave on Atlantic Street in downtown Charleston. And the conclusion of the anecdote is a vigorous affirmation of the status quo. "Had I not known her so well I would have been wrung with pity over her poverty. It was useless to pity her, however. The face which I was trying to paint was carved deep around eyes and mouth with the lines of contentment.... She seemed perfectly happy."[12]

While many contributed to Charleston's cultural movement, Severens notes that there were only four visual artists who were cultural leaders with national reputations.[13] Verner (1883–1979) was the youngest of these—and, it should be noted, the only one of the South Carolinians without an aristocratic pedigree. The others included Hutty (1877–1954), who, though born in Michigan, alternated his residence between Charleston and Woodstock, New York, until his death; Anna Heyward Taylor (1879–1956), a Columbia, South Carolina, native, widely traveled and highly educated for the standards of her time, who moved to Charleston permanently in 1929; and the great lady and (arguably) most significant artist of the movement, Alice Ravenel Huger Smith (1876–1958), a "blueblood" of impeccable English and Huguenot lineage. The four lived and had studios within three blocks of each other—collaborating with, teaching, mentoring, and sometimes even competing with each other.[14]

"In general, [white Charleston] artists tended to portray African-

Americans sympathetically, in harmony with their settings and the rest of the population," writes Severens of the racial dynamic of renaissance work. "They did not choose to dwell on the deprivation and discrimination suffered by their Black neighbors. These conditions were merely accepted." The same can, unfortunately, be argued of much of the art criticism of Charleston's renaissance. Though this is a failing that is being corrected,[15] critics have been content merely to note the presence of flower women, street peddlers, and agricultural workers in the canvases without bothering theorize about what they were doing there. But systems of racial coercion and containment aren't always visible unless one is looking for them.

That is to say, such systems are clear when we shift our attention from a technically superb watercolor such as Smith's *Ready for the Harvest* (Figure 1) to the advertising images typical in style and content of the 1877 to 1923 period, which historian Rayford Logan described as the "nadir" of African American life.[16] One such example, an advertisement for the United Fur Co., bears the caption "An Unwelcome Surprise."[17] The focal point of the ad, at the far-left position, is a figure of fun—a Black man being threatened by a skunk. His comic terror is echoed by that of a second Black man located on a sharp diagonal at far right, while the spectator's amusement is reflected by that of two figures stationed at the center of the frame: two hunters, well-dressed, well-groomed, and white—presumably the figures with which a consumer of furs, also figured as white, would be most likely to identify. The contemporary reaction to the ad is immediate, perhaps even visceral. One is offended by the ragged clothing and stylized features of the two virtually indistinguishable "darky" figures, recognizing them immediately as heirs to minstrelsy's Jim Crow. One understands instinctively that images such as these—part of the inescapable visual context of the art of the Charleston group—have but one function: to reduce the complex social reality and indeed the very humanity of African Americans to what Ralph Ellison presciently described as a "sign," one that evokes an atmosphere in which comic Blackness may be enjoyed while suppressing the white audience's moral identification both with the racist aggression inherent in this form of pleasure taking and with the human ambiguities submerged beneath the blackface mask.[18]

Historian Grace Hale is among those who have argued that images such as this were part of the making of southern white identity from the "nadir" to World War II. In marketing terms, she argues, contemptible caricatures such as these are designed to appeal to consumers figured as white by generating an ever-exfoliating variety of objects of consumption—from cartoons and trading cards, children's games and dolls, tea cosies, and salt and pepper shakers to ads for everything from laundry detergent to pancake mix— that mark the "other" as comically "Black."[19] But a close reading of Ellison might persuade one to push the explanation further—from the comic into the chthonic. That is to say, if we can imagine both art and artifacts as existing in a matrix of social enactments, ranging from the "innocently" amusing to the emotionlessly legalistic to the horrifyingly punitive, it becomes clear that a painting such as Smith's—which seems to be gesturing toward the dignity and even the nobility of its humble subject—is not, in fact, the polar opposite of a mammy cookie jar. Instead, both may be imagined as existing on a continuum that iterates and reiterates in psychic terms the segregation of the American imaginary—a segregation whose social and legal dimensions were being expressed in the proliferation of "Jim Crow" legislation and whose punitive extremes were marked during the same period by the rise in spectacle lynching. And since it is visual context that is our primary concern, let us not forget that the imagery of that savage spectacle had become an indelible component of the context in which Charleston Renaissance artists operated as well—through the circulation of penny postcards of lynchings throughout the South and even into the North.[20]

Given the isolation and the relative lack of schooling among key figures in the movement—Smith, educated at a lady's academy and never much of a traveler, leaps to mind—there is no evidence that any of the artists saw any of the magnificent examples of African American genre painting created in the middle and late nineteenth century by artists such as William Sidney Mount or Winslow Homer. Indeed, John Michael Vlach in *The Planter's Prospect* (2002) is struck by the degree to which there is "almost no recognition [among southern painters] of useful antecedents or historical models." But while evidence of a dialogue with tradition is lacking in the *production* of the paintings, this certainly is not the case with their *reception*. Through traveling exhibitions, in costly coffee table art volumes, and through commemorative postcards, the work of the Charleston artists circulated far beyond the city's environs. Their "landscapes of longing" found eager adherents among an educated, widely traveled elite steeped in art world antecedents and contexts.[21]

In the art of the Charleston Renaissance, social/spectatorial control is presented less as longed-for ideal or as an arena of contestation than as accomplished fact, and the effect is achieved by placing African American figures within the context of the city's architectural legacy. Let us consider two iconic views of the steeple of St. Michael's Church: *Looking Up Meeting Street*, by Charleston native Verner, and *St. Michael's* (Figures 2 and 3), by seasonal visitor and noted Tonalist painter Birge Harrison (1854–1929). Leaving aside the differences in size and media, style and point of view, the similarities at the level of narration—the stories they tell and those they attempt to conceal—are compelling. Most obviously, the images are realistic. That is to say, through fidelity to "objective" details of color and line, they assure the spectator that she or he is viewing a stable representation of an unchanged and unchanging world. It's a civilized world, as attested by the magnificent edifice looming in each background. And once again, it's a world of ideal beauty. So much for what the paintings seek to convey. What of their strategic absences, disjunctures, and erasures? Those are revealed in photographs of the same city intersection taken in 1910, five years before the earliest of our iconic views and fully eighteen years before the last. In plain view, one sees a streetcar and streetcar rails, telephone poles and cable car wires, African American figures in spanking white service attire, dapper white men in business attire. Turning once again to the paintings, one is struck by the dearth of cars or streetcars, of telephone poles and wires, of men, of whites, of anyone of any race in business attire. They're clearly meant as symbolic erasures, intended to lift both the images and the spectators viewing them out of time and contingency and to transport them to a romanticized, idealized past.

Art critics of the Charleston Renaissance have noted that the paintings comment on modernity, but they have been silent—with the exceptions of Yuhl and Vlach—on the point that, in South during this period, narratives about modernity are also narratives about race. Severens, for example, chose 1915 as the starting point for the "renaissance" because this was the year that World War I closed Europe to the peripatetic droves of artists and monied elites who had traveled there for decades for reasons of both artistic and social aspiration. But 1915 was also the year that *Birth of a Nation* sparked protests and revived the KKK from coast to coast in the United States. Just as significantly, it was the year that fifty years of "Tom" shows and mawkish Lost Cause mythologizing in story and song intersected with the nationwide commemorations of the semicentennial of the Civil War—and the decision to *exclude* African American veterans from those commemorations.

Against this backdrop, Charleston Renaissance canvases—as media for expressing and exchanging value as well as for expressing meaning—played a complex role in speaking to the wishes and desires of (white) producers and audiences. Circulating as commodities—paintings that could be sold, etchings that could be reproduced in book or postcard form—they attained symbolic force as "speaking texts" that communicated a distinctive narrative about the South even as they functioned as "social hieroglyphs," artifacts that are emblematic of the social relations they are meant to conceal.[22] Renaissance canvases speak to the desire for beauty, for a living connection to the past, for a less avidly acquisitive and hurried lifestyle. They conceal their interest in class and racial distancing and class and racial containment by highlighting harmonious social arrangements in which African Americans appear to be securely and contentedly "in their place." This was a narrative tailor-made for a South relentlessly using law and custom to purge both public and private spaces of the African American's contaminating presence—and for a northern buying public exhausted, as many have argued, by massive dislocations at home: immigration, urbanization, industrialization with its attendant labor strife, and, not least, African American migration.[23]

Great numbers of renaissance-era paintings from this period are available for viewing—at the Gibbes Museum of Art's Charleston Renaissance Gallery and the Greenville (South Carolina) County Museum of Art's Southern Art Collection, in the critical volumes by Severens and Saunders and McAden, and in the many extant copies of Smith's and Verner's coffee table art volumes, to name just some of the sources. And while there are problems with theorizing about art solely from the viewing of reproductions, one can still make striking observations about thematic content. I've noted four overall strategies of racial containment/distancing to which renaissance artists appear to resort again and again.

The first strategy is *emphasizing the differences of scale between towering edifices and tiny African American figures.* This, of course, may be read simply as a function of the genre of architectural monumentalism, a great favorite among both painters and etchers of the period. But such an argument would be persuasive only if race did not appear to be such a factor in the selection of human figures. African American females, females with children, and old men appear in these works in striking numbers—while emblems of modernity, such as vigorous young men of any race, modern transportation, and so on, are nearly absent. All these choices underscore the social hierarchies upon which this ideal world rests.

The second strategy is *limiting the depiction of African Americans to certain acceptable types.* Remember that Charleston was a city whose population was more than 50 percent African American until World War II and that residential segregation was virtually nonexistent. Renaissance artists would have had an infinite array of African American "types" to choose from: professionals, artisans, a mulatto elite second only to that of New Orleans in size and wealth. But the artists invariably opted to depict women of the servant class, most often in the full-length skirts and head wraps that suggested domestic work, along with street hucksters, agricultural workers, and "pickaninnies."

The third strategy is *a caricatured sameness of expression.* An excellent example of this is to be found in *The Jenkins' Orphanage Band* (Figure 4), a drypoint etching by Hutty. Here, the spectator's gaze moves in quite close to the tableau of street musicians, but only so that the artist may engage in a form of caricature that's different only in degree, not in kind, from those found in advertising. As if the painting were the embodiment of the sheet music for the ragtime tune "All Coons Look Alike to Me," all the children do indeed look alike: all of the profiles are slightly different views of the same profile, while the boys facing out from the canvas are doing so with slightly different versions of the same face. The band (Figure 5) was known for its natty professional attire as well as its high-energy performances of marches and jazz tunes.²⁴ It should also be noted that the Reverend Daniel Jenkins (Figure 6)—a figure of some prominence and business acumen, running as many as four touring bands that performed nationally and internationally out of offices in Charleston and New York—was even profiled in *Time* magazine in 1931. In Hutty's rendering, however, no hint of this Jenkins or this Jenkins Band appears. The uniforms appear baggy and ill-matched, and the lack of joy or even cohesion in the performance is remarkable.²⁵ To be sure, different aesthetics govern African American and white band performances to this day—one has only to compare the Southern University or Grambling University band performances exhibited annually at the Bayou Classic with any predominantly white band from any other bowl-game performance to note the striking layering of African American social dance aesthetics upon the metronomic militarism of traditional band movement. Hutty's depiction "reads" this alternative aesthetic, however, as a lack of aesthetic. The tiny drum major in the foreground may conduct, but no one's eyes look his way. The bass drum player is a strong focal point for the picture, but the position of his head—sharply turned to the left—dissipates the focus, disrupts any possibility of reading unity. The figures framing the drum player echo the effect—each appears to exist in his own world. One face directly engages the spectator's gaze only with a challenging, even sullen, glare. As for the spectators within the canvas—the bow-legged, animalistic girl-children at the bottom left and the boy in the wide-brimmed hat in the left background—these offer no purchase for spectator identification either.

All in all, *The Jenkins' Orphanage Band* is a highly ambivalent piece—perhaps reflecting Hutty's awareness of the band's controversial position in the city. Though Jenkins and his orphanage had their elite defenders—Verner was one of his most passionate advocates²⁶—the orphanage and its band were the target of a determined campaign to end its performances on the city's streets and, indeed, remove the institution from quarters it had inhabited in the historic Marine Hospital since 1892.²⁷ Despite howls of protest from African American residents of the area, the "sanitization" went forward in 1938 and 1939, and Rev. Jenkins and his orphanage were removed to a site along the Ashley River, ten miles out of town.

And the final strategy is *the erasure of the facial expression altogether.* This, the reduction of the African American figure to a sign with a vengeance, we see in Anna Heyward Taylor's (1879–1956) 1933 watercolor, *The Strike* (Figure 7). Taylor, it should be noted, was one of the Charleston Renaissance artists most in touch with trends in the larger art world. She was trained at the Provincetown, Massachusetts, artist colony, and her work veered more toward abstraction than that of her peers.²⁸ But abstraction need not convey lack of interest in fidelity to detail—and yet the details of Taylor's mill setting are full of errors.²⁹ Most egregiously, the artist seems blissfully unaware of the fact that

Blacks were barred from employment in textile mills during this period. More tellingly, there are no pickets, placards, or demands for fair treatment from these strikers; instead, we are presented with what a 1934 reviewer called "a semi-savage dance." The painting does indeed "vibrate with color and action," but its moral intelligibility has evaporated with the passage of the years.[30]

As the foregoing discussion should have made clear, paintings—like other forms of media—present us with far more than just a set of distinctive views: they have a narrative and even a performative function. In an active, world-making fashion, they articulate a set of norms that work to compel certain forms of spectator identification and to articulate and reinforce spectatorial identity. The visual synecdoche by which this is achieved is quite seamless, working at the level of the unconscious.[31] As John Berger has written, "Seeing comes before words. The child looks and recognizes before it can speak." And indeed, the spectator looks and sees not a painting but "reality." Though a constructed artifact, the painting denies its status as a made thing, calling into being instead "an identity of the Real and the Imaginary" that can be quite difficult to resist.[32]

Images have tremendous power: they have the ability to condition, confine, and even coerce the members of a social matrix because, in effect, they are the visual language of the tacit social and psychological contract that describes and enforces the social norm.[33] As artists of renown as well as members, in many cases, of elite local families, the Charleston group wielded tremendous cultural capital within their sphere. By asserting their control of the image of the past, they asserted their continued legitimacy—as individuals and as a class—to direct the city's future. We shall proceed from here to an in-depth exploration of how that power was wielded by a central figure of the Charleston Renaissance—and how it was challenged by an artist unfairly forced to its periphery.

If any single figure can be said to embody the Charleston group's social standing and values, it would have to be Alice Ravenel Huger Smith: "Miss Alice"—who exhibited widely and enjoyed remarkable success as an illustrator, printmaker, and watercolorist despite the fact that she almost never left home and was almost entirely self-taught.[34] Her patrons included Mrs. Marshall Field and Mrs. Solomon Guggenheim, and at the peak of her earning power—1930, *after* the stock market crash, mind you—she sold $9,030 in work, or a remarkable $155,500 in 2020 dollars.[35] Her renown reached its zenith in 1937, when she was awarded an honorary doctorate of letters from Mount Holyoke College during its centennial anniversary festivities. Perhaps most remarkable of all, she achieved all these things without ever surrendering her status or tarnishing her image as a lowcountry "gentlewoman."[36]

Indeed, her identity as "a lily and a woman of steel" appears to have been at the heart of her appeal.[37] Smith's art told a story with vast popular appeal

FIG. 1. Alice Ravenel Huger Smith (1876–1958), *Ready for the Harvest*, from the series, *A Carolina Rice Plantation of the Fifties*, 1935, watercolor on paper. Courtesy of the Gibbes Museum of Art/Carolina Art Association. In paintings such as these, the African American appears as one with the landscape.

FIG. 2. Elizabeth O'Neill Verner (1883–1979), *Looking Up Meeting Street*, ca. 1928, black ink on etching on paper. Used with permission of David Hamilton of the Tradd Street Press d/b/a Verner Gallery LLC. A favorite trope of the Charleston School is portraying an African American domestic worker (often with a child) framed by a massive monumentalist structure suggestive of the chasm between the *ancien regime* and its servile class.

FIG. 3. Lovell Birge Harrison (1854–1929), *St. Michael's*, 1919, oil painting. Collection of the Butler Institute of American Art, Youngstown, Ohio. Harrison's tonalist style painting provides another example of the trope of the servant figure in the monumentalist cityscape.

FIG. 4. Alfred Hutty (1877–1954), *The Jenkins' Orphanage Band*, 1933, Gibbes Museum of Art/Carolina Art Association. Take careful note of the facial representations; not only are the faces similar, there is more than a hint of the simian in the representation of Charleston's top tourist attraction.

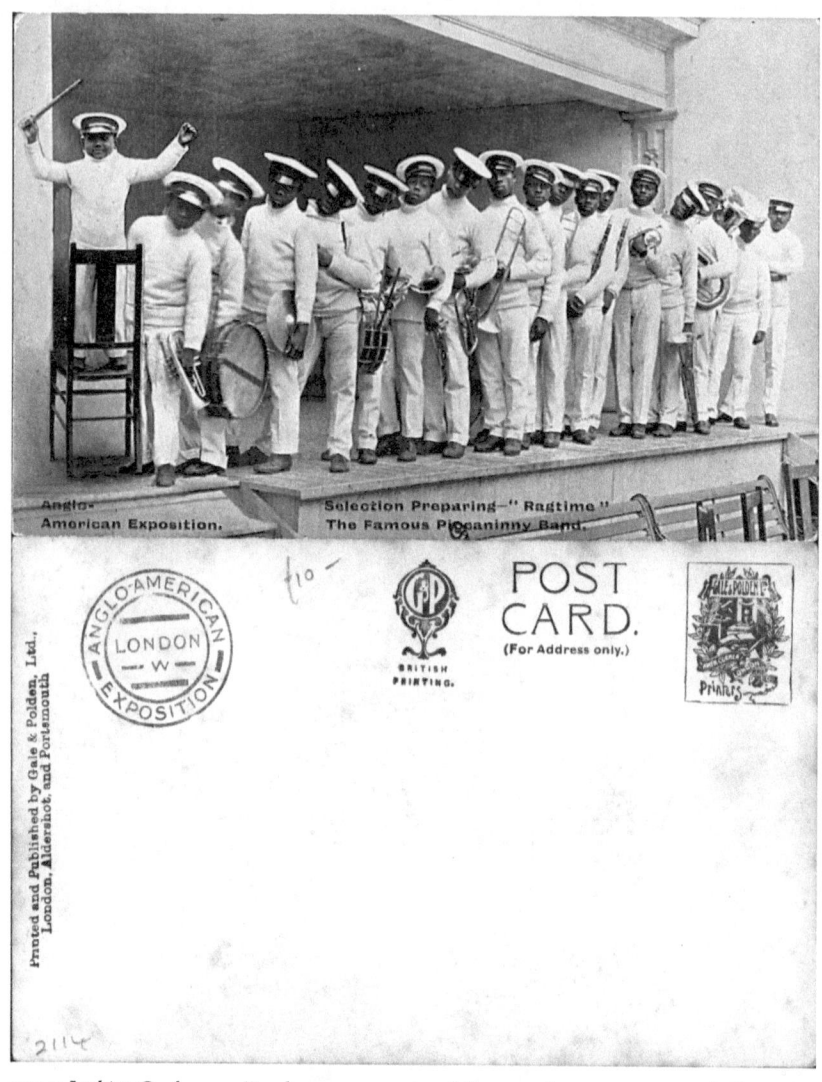

FIG. 5. Jenkins Orphanage Band, ca. 1914, postcard. By way of contrast, postcards from actual band performances reveal the professional appearance one would expect from a group that played in the inaugural parades of Presidents Theodore Roosevelt and William Howard Taft and that appeared at the 1904 St. Louis Worlds Fair. This photo is from the 1914 Anglo-American Exposition in London, where the band performed for members of the British Royal Family.

FIG. 6. Elizabeth O'Neill Verner, (1833–1979), *Rev. Daniel Jenkins*, 1933, pastel. Avery Institute for African American Research, on loan from the City of Charleston. Verner's portrait of the reverend provides another counterpoint to the Hutty piece, revealing a sympathetic gaze that humanizes and celebrates this controversial figure in a visual language much more reminiscent of Edwin Augustus Harleston's than even her own local color images of Charleston.

FIG. 7. Anna Heyward Taylor (1879–1956), *The Strike*, 1933, watercolor on board. Collection of the Greenville County Museum of Art, museum purchase with funds from the 1996 Museum Antiques Show. Taylor's image is roughly contemporaneous with the Uprising of '34, the nationwide textile mill strikes that reset the national calculus between capital and labor. Taylor's ahistorical take reveals the imaginative hold of African American figures on artists of the Charleston School.

FIG. 8. Alice Ravenel Huger Smith (1876–1958), *Sunday Afternoon at the Great House*, from the series, *A Carolina Rice Plantation of the Fifties*, 1935, watercolor on paper. Image courtesy of the Gibbes Museum of Art/Carolina Art Association. A beautifully rendered work of rememory in celebration of an idealized plantation order.

FIG. 9. Edwin Augustus Harleston (1882–1931), *Portrait of Aaron Douglas, Artist*, 1930, oil on canvas. Image courtesy of the Gibbes Museum of Art/Carolina Art Association. Harleston and Douglas collaborated on a series of historic murals at Fisk University; this was Harleston's homage to the leading artist of the Harlem Renaissance.

FIG. 10. Aaron Douglas (1899–1979), *The Emperor Jones*, 1925, from the series, *Defiance*. Used with the permission of the Amistad Research Center, Tulane University. Harleston's skill and technique were essential to the execution of the Fisk murals, but Douglas's was the undisputed star of the Harlem Renaissance. Note the ways modernism creates a bridge back across the colonial encounter permitting the creole artist to reconnect with Africanist expressive roots.

FIG. 11. Edwin Augustus Harleston (1882–1931), *Mary*, 1921, oil on canvas. Used with permission of the Ted Ashton Phillips estate. The racial ambiguity of Charleston's "brown" society, on display in this painting, was deeply disturbing to the sensibilities of the Charleston School.

FIG. 12. Anna Heyward Taylor (1879–1956), *Promise' Lan' Church*, 1930, woodblock print on paper. Collection of the Greenville County Museum of Art, gift of Mariana Taylor Manning. In Taylor's work, on the other hand, modernist technique serves an anti-modernist agenda. The relatively abstract visual language communicates a story of (imperialist) nostalgia—of longing for an ideal yet vanished past.

during the 1915 to 1940 period, a story in which the South figured as a tragically vanquished and vanishing civilization. The fact that she herself was part and parcel of the story she sought to tell only added to her work's authenticity—and thereby its sales appeal. Briefly, Smith's story is this: Through Charleston's "vast cousinship" network, she was related to the most luminous names in the city's Anglo-Huguenot social register. She was raised on tales of Charleston's glorious past by her grandmother, Eliza Middleton Huger Smith, and father, the Confederate veteran and antiquarian historian Daniel Elliott Huger Smith. Had it not been for the dislocations of war and Reconstruction and the early twentieth-century collapse of the rice industry, it is likely that Smith would have inherited some portion of her family's vast rice holdings along the legendary Combahee River and made the advantageous marriage that was the lot of girls of her class.[38] Instead, the plantations were lost and Smith was forced to live modestly on the "ruins" of Charleston's slave imperium, absorbing from her numerous family a passionate loyalty to their highly selective vision of antebellum culture and an equally passionate will to communicate that vision to the wider world.

The various book projects with which the artist began to associate herself in her late thirties tell the tale quite plainly. In her illustrations for *A Woman Rice Planter* (1914) and *Twenty Drawings of the Pringle House on King Street, South Carolina* (1914), Smith expressed her concern with helping to preserve the endangered heritage of her Pringle cousins. *The Dwelling Houses of Charleston*, published in 1917 with text by her father, became the bible of the city's nascent preservation movement in the 1920s.[39] Still other projects—a book on the nineteenth-century Charleston miniaturist Charles Fraser, illustrations for the Society for the Preservation of Spirituals' *The Carolina Low-Country* (1931), and the reprint of Sass's *Adventures in Green Places* (1935)— documented related concerns: with lowcountry antiquarian history, with the preservation of "vanishing" Gullah spirituals, and with a lowcountry variation on agrarian values we associate in the South with the Nashville Fugitives.

But her masterwork—the exhibit and book into which she clearly poured both heart and soul—was *A Carolina Rice Plantation of the Fifties* (1936), a monumental project that included thirty watercolor paintings by the artist, with an introduction by Sass and excerpts from her father's unpublished memoir. This, clearly, was intended to be the artist's magnum opus, a tribute to her recently deceased father, with paintings composing a series of "memory sketches" of the Carolina rice plantation, a world that had entirely passed away by the time of the initial exhibition of the works.[40] Smith certainly drew upon actual visual memory of the lowcountry landscape just as she drew upon personal and family memory to create the eighty-six sketches that illustrated Elizabeth Allston Pringle's *A Woman Rice Planter* (1914). But we must be clear that the final remnants of rice cultivation in South Carolina ended, for all intents and purposes, in 1911, when the last in a series of catastrophic hurricanes destroyed the dikes and closed the book on cultivation of the fabled "Carolina gold" rice;[41] therefore, Smith's direct knowledge of plantation cultivation was, shall we say, limited.

Of the images produced for the Pringle work, it's interesting to note that eleven were reproduced or reimagined, either in whole or in part, for her rice series.[42] The vast majority of what the artist pictured, however, was a fabrication, unencumbered by any firsthand knowledge of conditions on her family's antebellum rice plantations. Beginning with the first painting, *Sunday Morning at the Great House* (Figure 8), and continuing through the last, *A Lagoon by the Sea*, the volume represents an extraordinary exercise in aristocratic self-fashioning. The imperial spectatorial eye follows the artist's eye as it takes a retrospective and intensely nostalgic look back to an ideally beautiful, pastoral Golden Age. The paintings convey an emphatically antipositivist vision—the past as prelapsarian paradise. And absolutely central to the whole exercise is Smith's conception of the role of the enslaved Gullah Negro within the plantation economy.

Sunday Morning at the Great House, the first painting in the book, provides the key for interpreting all the successive paintings in Smith's series. Set during sacred time—Sunday—in a setting hallowed by the cult of the Lost Cause, the painting imagines the plantation as an idealizing and harmonizing social norm. We are in the realm of what Mircea Eliade describes as "sacred history." The painting is revealed truth—as it were, a "true history of what took place at the beginning of time" and, thus, both a model and a justification for all subsequent human actions.[43] The action of the painting, meanwhile, is contained within one great ellipse: civilization, in the form of the Big House, dominates the right half of the frame; the primitive, in the form of the great avenue of oaks into which the enslaved, in their Sunday finery, merge almost as if part of the landscape itself, dominates the left half of the frame. At the center of the ellipse is a patriarchal figure—the planter in Panama hat, gloves, and cane, greeting an African American male who appears to be wagging his finger in admonition or instruction. But this vaguely threatening gesture is undercut by the bland imperturbability of the planter's mien and manner as well as by the suggestions of mutuality elsewhere. A Black woman observes the tableau of man and master with an affable smile. At right, another Black woman, posture hunched by age or subservience, clasps the hand of the smiling plantation mistress. At left, meanwhile, two white boys exchange grins with a shoeless Black playmate.

The painting is a triumphal celebration of the social and racial norms in which the artist passionately believed. In Smith's view, the structures of consent that underlay slavery were its most important aspects; thus, we see her concern with depicting mutual dependency, daily contacts/kindnesses, mutual bonds of affection. The structures of violence that were inextricably linked with these structures of feeling are entirely absent from Smith's frame, and yet there is little doubt as to the identities of masters and mastered. The white patriarch is the center of both the painting and this world, a potent and persuasive symbol of racial hierarchy naturalized by more familiar family hierarchies. Furthermore, the physical intimacy implied by the presence of master and mistress amid the grouping of field hands is belied by several symbols of social distance: the archetypal "young miss" and "old mistress" figures on the gallery and the liminal "dah" with child stationed on the stairs between the two main groupings.[44] The careful placement of characters within the scene dispels the incipient threat posed by the finger-wagging Black male. Indeed, Smith's message cannot be mistaken. We see, in the artist's own words, "the dominance of the man of civilization, of morals, and education, over the absolute savage," at the same time that we see "such close interests between the *employer and employed* that the result was the happy family life so characteristic of Southern establishments" (emphasis added).[45] Interestingly, after this point, the white family virtually disappears from Smith's narrative. With only three exceptions, the remainder of the paintings in the series are landscapes (ten) or representations of the enslaved in the rice fields (sixteen). Apparently, the principle of white spectatorial presence has been so firmly established in the opening canvases that it does not need reiteration.

Smith's vision of slavery, by contrast, is offered up again and again and again. Distanced and faceless, it is the *instrumentality* of the enslaved rather than their individuality that interests the artist. Indeed, Smith's gaze is an imperial one, her narrative one of ownership and mastery. The enslaved appear to have so passionately autochthonous a relationship to the land that, in some canvases, they seem servants as much of the rice as of their masters. Moreover, Smith is careful to portray rice cultivation as an endeavor that does not require much in the way of effort. Her typical strategy is to focus on a single worker at a moment of contemplation or rest in the foreground, while others labor in the background at such a distance that faces, forms, and work implements are almost entirely obscured (see *Ready for the Harvest*). Where whites reenter the narrative, it is generally to make a point, by way of contrast, about the separation of the races (the segregated views of *The Parish Church* and *The Plantation Church*), the natural subservience of the enslaved laborer (*The Stack Yard*), or that laborer's natural unfitness to labor without white supervision (*Mending a Break in a Rice-Field Bank*). Smith is, of course, doing no more than any artist: articulating her subject position by producing and reproducing with her artist's "eye" a convincing "I." But this process of identity making has much in common with that of sign making—the results can be unstable. Even Smith's triumphal vision contains hairline cracks, odd disjunctures, outright fractures. In an interesting irony, while Smith created her series as a tribute to a recently deceased and dearly loved father, her paintings, in key respects, obscure the vision of plantation life that appears in the memoir by the elder Smith published along with the series.

The author's father was hardly a percipient observer of the enslaved community: of Pinckney, his family's cowherd, he wrote only half in jest, "[I]n my most secret soul, I used to wonder sometimes whether he invented the Gullah tongue or remembered it." But compared with his daughter, the elder Smith was a stickler for accuracy. He described the parish church as integrated—a detail his daughter, a product of Charleston's Jim Crow era, was careful to erase by offering for the audience's delectation paintings of two segregated churches, *The Parish Church*, for the gentry, and *The Plantation Church*, for the enslaved. Far more significantly, the elder Smith never attempted to deny the scope of the labors involved in carving out a rice plantation from wilderness swamp. Of the workers, he wrote, "I do not believe that any New Englander could plow a furrow as straight as some of our boys. I have never seen a ditcher who could sink a quarter-drain like any 'full-hand,' straight up and down, as broad at the bottom as at the top, the sides and bottom as smooth and even as a billiard-table.[46] Such carpenters do not exist now; from cutting down the pine-trees to hanging the window blinds, they built the great house and the barns and the mill and all the other houses. . . . In fine they did anything and everything well except reading and writing. *The few who had such knowledge used it badly*" (emphasis added).[47]

An uneasy mixture may be seen here: pride in the achievements of Black workers and fear of their agency struggling against ego demands for personal deference and absolute economic subjugation. Most strongly, the narrative mourns the near-total obliteration of the structure of privilege that surrounded the elder Smith and his loved ones. Again and again, he laments types—of people, of relationships, of places—"that [have] ceased to exist."[48] His daughter's act of filial devotion is quite moving in its way. Her desire appears to have been not just to restore her father's vanished world but to improve upon it, by suturing up the ragged seams; cleaning up the messy habits of social miscegenation that marred the seemliness of the façade; and, most importantly, creating the perfect slave: noble, loyal, but irredeemably inferior, indeed, little more than a beast of burden, at one with the landscape, contented, and regarding his masters with a reverence verging on awe.

The paintings convey an obvious emotional charge that, along with the fortuitous coincidence of the publication of *Gone with the Wind*, resulted in a series of enraptured press notices as they wound their way about the country in a two-year traveling exhibition, accompanied by a magnificent color edition from William Morrow. The social relations that the paintings conceal, however, are far more provocative than the sentiment they are meant to evoke. That is to say, it is, of course, a commonplace that, as a species, we find pleasure in looking, but the spectatorial pleasures provided by these paintings have much less to do with the innocent pleasures one derives from the "picturesque" than they do with guilty, imperial pleasures of implied possession and dominion.[49] The spectator looks with covetousness, with avidity; what she or he sees, she or he—at least potentially, psychically—owns.

Most importantly, the production and consumption of these paintings conceal an economic imperative that forcibly recalls the domestic economy of slavery. That is to say, the rice series allowed the younger Smith, in fabular terms, to remake not only her father's world but also his role. By participating in the reproduction, the sale, and the consumption of Black bodies, she reenacted in ritual fashion her class's historical relationship with African Americans on these shores. Seventy years after the crash of the oxymoronic "slave civilization," Smith and her educated, elite audience of art patrons and book buyers were selling and buying the fantasy of plantation and slave ownership. And the text accompanying the images offered soothing assurances of the harmlessness of the activity. "'Slavery' is not a good name for the institution as it existed on the plantations of the Carolina lowcountry," wrote Smith's cousin, Sass, in his accompanying essay on "The Rice Coast: Its Story and Meaning": "The planter did not speak of his Negroes as slaves; he called them his 'people' and as he spoke of them so he thought of them—they were his people, not his chattels, and many of them were his loved and devoted friends."[50]

And the text and art did their work. The *New York Times Book Review* was convinced that life "in the Low Country of this period was really a delightful one" and congratulated Smith on the "special historical service" she had rendered to posterity. The *Washington Star* found the paintings to be "without [sentimental] exaggeration," while the *Saturday Review*'s nationally renowned cultural critic, Henry Seidel Canby, stressed their "real historical value." His peroration could have been contributed by Sass: "Here was a culture which to a high degree developed an extraordinary sense of responsibility, and which encouraged the art of living, which has since been so generally lost. And it left its mark upon a countryside which these pictures commemorate."[51]

Today's intellectual sensibilities—trained in the rigorous pursuit of (an often chimerical) scientific objectivity—may be outraged at such a purposeful mingling of fact and fancy. But Smith's sun-drenched imagery, her almost palpable yearning for a vanished pastoral Golden Age, the shimmering surfaces of her impressionist watercolors, struck a powerful chord among her contemporaries. It was Smith's genius—at a time of Depression and defeat for the nation at large—to be able to tap into and, in some sense, direct the course of a set of sentimental, yet powerful, cultural yearnings for a simpler, better world. Sentimentality has come on hard times in the twentieth century. One of its most acutely observant critics is the novelist and essayist James Baldwin, who has argued that this "ostentatious parading of excessive and spurious emotion, is the mark of dishonesty, the inability to feel."[52] But I'd like to suggest that Smith's sentimentality was not just a symbol or sign of that inability but actually an instrument or agent, actively preventing the type of moral identification that would have necessitated the reevaluation of the position of the African American—and thus of her own class. Smith intended her rice series as a monument to an ideal world. The function it actually performed was far more complex: it was, in point of fact, both a monument to and a desperate attempt to shore up a set of not entirely vanished but severely threatened power relations.

The paintings so insistently reiterated the position of the Gullah slaves on the plantations because it was their apparent *consent* that was crucial to maintaining the image of benevolent paternalism that Smith celebrated. Without that consent, the whip behind the smiling mask was revealed and the planter class's legitimacy endangered. Smith's paintings, thus, represent a raid on her class's frequently articulated feelings/fears of betrayal: its consciousness that, despite the mutual dependencies, the individual kindnesses, and the love on which they staked their hopes, Gullah Geechee enslaved persons and free, given the slightest opportunity to do so, would refuse their roles as stage props in a Lost Cause–inflected social drama. The paintings express an understandable—but ultimately vain—impulse to keep an illusion intact, an illusion that African Americans shattered daily with their ungovernable and unaccountable insistence on pursuing their own lives.

The contrasts between the paintings we have been viewing and *Portrait of Aaron Douglas, Artist* (Figure 9) are stark. Douglas (1898–1979) was a close associate of Alain Locke's and one of the darlings of that other renaissance up north: the New Negro, or Harlem, Renaissance. As for the man who painted the canvas, he, too, reveals himself in interesting and compelling ways. Once again we're confronting a realistic, idealizing artistic sensibility, but instead of the African American figuring as part of the background, he takes center stage as subject. And what is it that's in the background of this painting? It's a detail from "The Poet"—part of a massive murals project that Douglas had just completed for the Fisk University Library. Significantly, however, that background takes the form of an Italian Renaissance diptych, at once quoting a sacral moment in the history of European fine art and inscribing Douglas—and the African-inflected style of American modernism that he was pioneering (Figure 10)—into that history. The maker of this sophisticated and deeply subversive painting was Douglas's assistant in creating the Fisk murals: his name was Edwin Augustus Harleston (1882–1931), and he, too, lived in Charleston, South Carolina.

Harleston is a figure who should have figured prominently in Charleston's renaissance. He had all the right credentials—a college degree and six years of rigorous beaux arts training at the School of the Museum of Fine Arts in Boston under Edmund Charles Tarbell (1862–1938) and Frank Weston Benson (1862–1951), conservative portraitists who were much admired in Charleston and who, in fact, were featured in an exhibition at the Gibbes in 1905.[53] So yes, Harleston *should* have been welcomed into the Charleston Renaissance. But he was an African American—and not just any African American: he was part of a mulatto elite that Charlestonians preferred to pretend did not exist. As Daniel Elliott Huger Smith wrote in his memoir, "A great deal of nonsense has been written about the cross-breeding of the races in the period of slavery. In fact, on the plantations the percentage of mulattoes was very small. Of course there were more in the cities, but yet today (1913) *the negro race in the State remains black.* The reverse of this is equally true of the whites at the South. The percentage of black blood that has crept into them is infinitely small even among the lower classes. It is probable that there was a greater intermingling of the races at the North, where it was permitted, if not encouraged, than at the South where it was frowned on and prohibited."[54]

We had occasion in chapter 1 to take note of and debunk some of the discourses of the "purity" of South Carolina's white and Black "races." It's worth pointing out that there was real hysteria in Charleston during the period of the renaissance on such questions. John Bennett, one of the founders of the Poetry Society, had to endure nearly a decade of public disgrace and social ostracization merely for reading at a Federation of Charleston Women's Clubs event a ghost story about an antebellum octoroon who sold her soul to the devil so that her children could pass for white.[55] If mere fiction could excite such an extreme reaction, then one can hardly even imagine the level of distress Harleston's existence must have occasioned—for not only was he part of Charleston "brown" elite, he was no less part of Charleston's "vast cousinage" than Smith herself. Harleston's grandfather was William Harleston, a white planter who divided his property equally between his white brother and his Black wife (yes, wife) and children. His great-great-great grandfather, meanwhile, was John Harleston, who immigrated to Charleston in 1699 and whose descendants were pillars of the community, lending their names and their time, treasure, and talent to numerous civic and charitable works.[56] In a city that loudly and insistently proclaimed an unshakeable faith in its own racial purity, Harleston's connections could never be openly acknowledged or discussed.

No less distasteful to Charleston's elite were the artist's political convictions. The brown Harlestons rose to prosperity under Republican federal administrations, anathema to the Democratic sympathies of the white elite. The young painter was also a devotee of Du Bois and a cofounder of the Charleston chapter of the National Association for the Advancement of Colored People. By 1919, the chapter had grown to eight hundred members, and it was strong enough to spearhead a successful campaign to end the exclusion of Black teachers from Charleston's public schools. All these factors—Harleston's claim to gentry status, his political assertiveness, his family's wealth and prominence, and relative independence of white control—made the man far too direct a challenge to the values of the Charleston Renaissance.[57] Rather than welcoming him, its leading lights excluded him and mocked him.

The indignities Harleston suffered came in all shapes and sizes. In order to practice his *plein air* technique, he had to disguise himself as a custodian and sneak into the city's world-famous Magnolia Gardens (which, ironically, were cocreated by and maintained over many generations by a single family of African American gardeners).[58] After he won a national competition and was offered a one-man show by Charleston's mayor, Thomas Stoney, in 1926, the invitation was suddenly—if not mysteriously—revoked. "My dear Mr. Harleston," wrote Laura Bragg, director of the Charleston Museum, which was to have sponsored the show, "Unforeseen circumstances made it necessary for me to have a conference with the Mayor in regard to your exhibit and we decided that, in consequence of this, the exhibit would hurt and not help you at the present time. I, therefore, have to tell you that it will be necessary to postpone an exhibit of your portraits until a time when it can be given with benefit to you."[59] The painter would have been well aware that the "time when it can be given with benefit to you" was, in fact, to be "never."

The memory of Harleston's presumption appears to have lingered—unpleasantly. DuBose Heyward offered an uncharacteristically vicious caricature of the artist—and of Charleston's "brown" elite—in his 1929 bestseller *Mamba's Daughters* (to be discussed at greater length in Chapter 7). But within two years of the publication of that book, Harleston was dead—felled by pneumonia at the age of forty-nine. Fortunately, Harleston's paintings survive, allowing us to decide for ourselves whether, as Heyward charged, a "subtle racial element is missing" from them.

We begin with Harleston's portrait of *Mary* (Figure 11), dated 1921,[60] a painting of one of those Negroes "who give the effect of not being negroes at all" who so disturbed Heyward.[61] At first glance, one notes the dark palette and dramatic lighting effects that reveal an affinity for seventeenth-century Dutch portraiture, but Harleston's interpretation of these effects is without doubt of his own time. He uses strong, painterly—nearly impressionistic—brushstrokes that dissolve the lines of the forms replacing them with restless groupings of strongly contending colors, light, and shadows. One encounters *flesh* in this painting—soft, rounded flesh that invites the touch. Indeed, Mary's skin is rendered with an enormous "truth" to tone. There is a hint of distancing evident. Mary's eyes are set slightly above eye level, forcing the spectator, in effect, to "look up" to her, as if to a parent or other social superior. But the warmth and vulnerability of those eyes cancel out the distance, drawing the spectator into a moment of penetrating intimacy. The work is, in fact, highly subversive: Mary's lightness of skin foregrounds the highly creolized nature of Charleston's Black—and by implication, its white—population.

Looking at other examples of Harleston's oeuvre, one is hard put to find the missing racial element. The painter doesn't neglect the genre figures that are so ubiquitous in the work of "renaissance" artists. He has a *Charleston Shrimp Man*, and his *Honey Man* wears the snow-white apron and bowler hat with which Ralph Bennett, the real-life figure from the streets of Charleston, appears outfitted in contemporary photographs,[62] but always Harleston's representational choices work to subvert the minstrel formula. The central figure in *The Bible Student*, for example, could readily be mistaken for one of the neutered "old uncle" figures that were so ubiquitous in popular entertainments during the period—but for the fact that, instead of regaling a white child with folk tales, he's shown reading the Bible, a potent symbol of moral and racial uplift. Harleston's Harmon Award–winning *The Old Servant* provides another example, showing us a woman in the costume of an aged "auntie," but portraying her surrounded by the rich, draped backdrops of elite portraiture. The painting takes a further poke in the eye of the white elite: according to Charleston lore, the woman in the painting cooked breakfast for Robert Smalls, the Black pilot, Civil War hero, and Reconstruction-era congressman, the morning he made his historic break for freedom by stealing the steamboat he piloted and delivering it safely into the arms of the Union blockade of Charleston Harbor.

Harleston is, to my mind, a compelling figure, caught in an ironic, painful double bind: excluded by Charleston's renaissance, to which he should have belonged by taste and background, by virtue of its racism; peripheral to the Harlem Renaissance because Alain Locke's call for the Black artist to embrace Africa and modernism came after Harleston was already formed as an artist. And yet his paintings of African Americans are among the most important created in this period. In the renaissances in both Charleston and Harlem, African Americans figure as ritual objects: effectually, they are a stage upon which negative fears of or positive fantasies about Blackness—whether the chthonic Blackness of the white unconscious or the social Blackness of the everyday—may be ritually invoked and dismissed or celebrated. Harleston's portraits, however, of the "Talented Tenth," the noble poor, Black professionals and servicemen, and white philanthropists seem symbolic of nothing so much as each subject's humanity: at this period—perhaps at any period—the most radically transgressive act of all.

Today, his reputation is on the rise—due largely to the efforts of two people: his niece, Edwina Whitlock, who finally got her uncle his one-man show, a traveling exhibition that included a stop at the Gibbes, in 1985; and his distant cousin, Edward Ball, who won the American Book Award for *Slaves in the Family* in 1998 and whose follow-up work, *The Sweet Hell Inside*, was a social history of Charleston pegged to the Harleston family. The painter was relegated to a scant few pages of text and a single color plate at the end of Severens's *The Charleston Renaissance*, but the Gibbes Museum of Art has begun collecting his work—work that, as of 2007, was finally being exhibited *inside* the Charleston Renaissance Gallery, rather than outside in the hallway in what was long an ironic and, one hopes, unwitting replication of the segregation to which the artist was subjected during his lifetime. One may be cheered that Edwin Augustus Harleston has finally gotten his due, but he remains an exceedingly apt symbol for Charleston and its renaissance, from its inception a renaissance by the few, for the few, and for the white.

CHAPTER 6

All God's Chillen Got Traveling Shoes
Modern Subjects, Florida Roots, Diasporic Routes

> You're a lost crowd, you educated Negroes and you will only find yourself in the roots of your own people.... Turn your back on all these tiresome clever European novels and read about Russian peasants, the story and struggle of their lowly, patient, hard-riven life.... Be interested in native Africa dialects and though you don't understand be humble before their simple beauty instead of despising them.
>
> —CLAUDE MCKAY, *Banjo*

> I got shoes, you got shoes, all God's children got shoes
> When I get to heaven gonna put on my shoes
> And gonna walk all over God's Heaven
> Heaven, Heaven
> Everybody talking bout Heaven ain't goin there
> Walk all over God's Heaven...
>
> —African American spiritual

Over the course of the past three chapters we have been presented with what we might think of as opposing perspectives on a familiar travel scenario: that of the worldly tourist departing from a cosmopolitan center to study, and be refreshed by, the folkways and folksay of local natives in their rural habitats far from the madding crowds of modernity.[1] Of course, the Charleston- and Harlem-based culture-makers were completely at odds over the question of the Negro's political role in American democracy, but we have noted the moments of hidden attunement between these camps on the ways in which "mastery" of Gullah Geechee materials, expressed through pilgrimages into the past and production of nostalgic texts aimed at reassembling that past in a "usable" form, served as enabling structures in establishing claims to cultural purity, authenticity, and, hence, authority.

In the case of the Charleston Renaissance song preservationists and painters we have discussed, the nostalgia was of the imperialist sort, and the relationship these culture workers were so eager to establish with an authentic Blackness that was also "pure" argued, by way of metonymy, a case for the "purity" of the white race as well and its "natural" position of dominance in the social and political hierarchy. For non–Gullah Geechee artists of the New Negro Renaissance, on the other hand, the cultural role of so-called Old Negroes was more complex. Recall that during the period even such matters as the singing of Negro spirituals could be controversial among the upwardly mobile and self-conscious members of the Talented Tenth—Howard University students went so far as to stage a brief rebellion against the traditional practice.[2] Cultural and artistic leaders, some of them at least, proved more enlightened: Du Bois made folklore central to his project of democratic nation building, arguing that the creations and consciousness of the enslaved were, in fact, foundational to the development of American notions of liberty and that the originality of their contributions to national life proved that, in the realm of culture, all were equals regardless of race.[3] Toomer, meanwhile, found his poet's imagination fired by Georgia's "everlasting song . . . caroling softly souls of slavery"—even if his performance was, for him, a swan song.[4]

So it's clear the New Negroes' aims were the opposite of the Old Charlestonians'—the one group seeking to bring African Americans from the margins to the center and elevate them to the status of culture heroes, the other determined to thrust the Negro as far from the center of social and political discourse as possible. But their means were not as different as they might at first blush appear. Both groups valorized the Gullah Geechee way of life as source and fountainhead of cultural authority, but that authority never percolated down to the folk themselves. The folk remained "in their place," figuratively and literally. Here it might be helpful to remember that both the Harlemites and Charlestonians had aspirations to aristocracy, and to remember as well that one can't establish a peerage, not even a "fur-coat peerage" in Zora Neale Hurston's biting phrase, without peasants.[5] Ultimately, neither group could imagine the Gullah Geechee, either as individuals or as a culture, outside the framework of a "vanishing," "dying" primitive; for Harlemites and Charlestonians alike, Gullah Geechee, the ultimate "roots" culture, remained fixed—indeed, incarcerated—in a place and in a time that were regrettably, inevitably passing away.

At the same time, however, a starkly divergent view was being offered by one who understood Gullah Geechee culture as *traveling* culture.

> First off, he was a whisper, a will to hope, a wish to find something worthy of laughter and song. Then the whisper put on flesh. His footsteps sounded across the world in slow but musical rhythm as if the world he walked on was

a singing drum. . . . The sign of this man was a laugh, and his singing-symbol was a drum-beat. . . .

He had come from Africa. He came walking on the waves of sound. Then he took on flesh after he got here. The sea captains of ships knew that they brought slaves in their ships. They knew about those black bodies huddled down there in the middle passage, being hauled across the waters to helplessness. John de Conquer was walking the very winds that filled the sails of the ships. He followed over them like the albatross.

It is no accident that High John de Conquer has evaded the ears of white people. They were not supposed to know. You can't know what folks won't tell you. If they, the white people, heard some scraps, they could not understand because they had nothing to hear things like that with. They were not looking for any hope in those days and it was not much of a strain for them to find something to laugh over. Old John would have been out of place for them.

Old Massa met our hope-bringer all right, but when Old Massa met him, he was not going by his right name. He was traveling, and touristing around the plantations as the laugh-provoking Brer Rabbit. So Old Massa and Old Miss and their young ones laughed with and at Brer Rabbit and wished him well. And all the time, there was High John de Conquer playing his tricks of making a way out of no-way. Hitting a straight lick with a crooked stick. Winning the jack pot with no other stake but a laugh. Fighting a mighty battle without outside-showing force, and winning his war from within. Really winning in a permanent way, for he was winning with the soul of the black man whole and free.[6]

The passage is from "High John de Conquer," an essay published in *American Mercury*, while its author, the peripatetic Zora Neale Hurston, was, suggestively enough, living on a houseboat. The year this essay was published, 1943, marked a year of remarkable highs and lows in Hurston's relations with her reading public. The zenith came when she learned in February that her 1942 autobiography, *Dust Tracks on a Road*, had won the Anisfield-Wolf Book Award in the category of best treatment of race relations. The honor carried a cash purse in the then-jaw-dropping amount of one thousand dollars ($17,600 in 2020 dollars) plus a cover feature in the *Saturday Review of Literature*, the sponsor of the award. The low came hard on the heels of the high, as the cover story that should have been a source of pride and joy for Hurston included quotes that set off a firestorm of criticism in the Black press that permanently tarnished her image. In a passage Hurston swore was a misquote and distortion of her actual statements, the feature claimed Hurston had said Negroes were better off in the South than the North. Those would have been fighting words in and of themselves, but the writer, Douglas Gilbert, went further: "In short, the Jim Crow system works," he quoted her as saying. Within a week, an incendiary rebuke followed from no less a personage than Roy Wilkins, the NAACP's assistant executive secretary at the time; his editorial in New York's *Amsterdam News* accused the author of peddling "arrant and even vicious nonsense" in order to sell books.[7]

In the weeks that followed, Hurston attempted to push back. "Nothing has ever upset me so much as this printed thing with Douglas Gilbert. It is so untrue, so twisted," Hurston wailed to one of her dwindling number of African American allies, Claude Barnett, founder and director of the Associated Negro Press service. What she had said was far more complex, she said: she had simply pointed out the existence of racism in the North, too, and noted that at least southern Blacks knew where they stood. This apparently was far too nuanced for Gilbert and the editors of the *Saturday Review*, which appears to have had its own agenda in supporting Hurston's memoir. Hurston was to conclude her letter with a solemn pledge: "The iron has entered my soul. Since the god of tolerance has forsaken me, I am ready for anything to overthrow Anglo-Saxon supremacy, however desperate."[8] Unfortunately, the damage was done. One by one, the gatekeepers of African American high culture would turn their backs on her over the next decade and a half, as her inexplicable personal loyalties, quirkily antiassimilationist stances, and shrill anticommunist views placed her increasingly out of step with mainstream African American political thought.[9] Her end, in an anonymous grave in a Florida cemetery in 1960, has become part and parcel of her legend.

Hurston, taught by a beloved mother to "jump at the sun,"[10] had dared an audacious dream in the 1920s: to be a writer and a scholar, to travel the world and make a big noise in it. She was born in 1891 of working-class roots in Notasulga, Alabama, but raised from infancy by upwardly mobile parents in Eatonville, Florida, at the southernmost extremity of the Gullah Geechee Coast; Hurston's early atmosphere was an all-Black town free, in large part, from the withering white gaze and from the worst of the suffocating class distinctions that marred intraracial relations in large urban centers of the South such as Jacksonville, Savannah, and Charleston. Indeed, Hurston's upbringing was paralleled only by Claude McKay among her Harlem Renaissance–era peers:[11] immersed in an Afro-creole folk world and folk consciousness, she was a native of the imaginative landscape that had for generations so fascinated sympathetic tourists on both sides of the color line.

Hurston was to travel out of that space as a naïf, seeking education and city polish, and eventually to return to it, a fully modern subject, all the while remaining remarkably unselfconscious about and unashamed of her roots. We cannot stress enough her singularity in this regard. In a world of fakes, Hurston was the real McCoy—a walking, talking source of Afro-creole authority who combined a clear-eyed vision of working-class Black folk with a rare virtuosity as a writer and a hard-earned status as one of the only academically trained African American anthropologists of her day. Over the course of decades of intense labor, Hurston substantially achieved "my dreams! my vaulting ambition!":[12] she became a force for "introducing African American culture into the project that Margaret Mead called the 'Giant Rescue operation' of recording and salvaging dying cultures" while also "injecting anthropological methods into Harlem Renaissance artistry."[13] No one was to thank her for it—at least not until long after her death. Indeed, her inability to fully claim the cultural *authority* that her cultural *authenticity* should have brought her will be the subject of this chapter.

Before proceeding to Hurston's life and works, however, this notion of Gullah Geechee culture as "traveling culture" requires a bit more unpacking. In part I we discussed both the waves of forced migration that brought West Africans of many conditions and nations to coastal South Carolina and some of the key processes that forged this polyglot nation within a nation into a recognizable unity on the basis of language, lineage, and landscape. In addition, in chapter 3 we explored the elite genealogies celebrating the Anglo-Barbadian roots of Charleston's ruling caste. We are less familiar, however, with the circum-Caribbean forms of exchange that connected the Antilles archipelago and Gullah Geechee Coast through shared African cultural and linguistic roots and migratory routes. In the next section, we return to our triangular topos, particularly the third leg of the triangle, *landscape*, to elaborate this crucial bit of backstory for understanding Hurston.

As we've noted in discussions of the pastoral, "landscape" can be suggestive—too suggestive, in fact—of single landscapes. The Carolina lowcountry. The Sea Islands. The city of Charleston. The architects of the National Park Service's "Special Resource Study" performed yeoman's service in exploding that mythos forever when they demonstrated so conclusively that the Gullah Geechee "homeland," as we might call it, covered a four-state region of the U.S. South. Not even that analysis, however, goes far enough in disturbing our notions of the "rootedness" of this community and acknowledging Gullah Geechee peoples' complex agency in a continuously unfolding colonial moment[14]—for when we cast our nets farther afield, we see the Afro-creole networks in which they are embedded are much more expansive, that, indeed, Zora Neale Hurston's central Florida roots shine a bright light on the routes of the Afro-creoles communities that were to become her special study. In delving more deeply into the Gullah Geechee nation's history, we find that we may speak most fruitfully about language, lineage, and *landscapes*—particularly but not exclusively of the Black Atlantic, as Florida, the Anglophone Caribbean, and even pockets of the American West and the Texican borderlands emerge as topoi in which Gullah Geechee language communities have survived: evidence that Gullah peoples, both enslaved and seeking freedom, put on their traveling shoes in order to exercise a complex, and heretofore unacknowledged, agency over their own fates.

Florida Roots and Routes

In the contemporary popular imagination, Florida exists less as a no-man's-land than as an *everyman's* land: a heterotopia peopled by characters from Mickey Mouse to Shamu, settled by snowbirds and migrants from almost anywhere else, blessed—or cursed, depending on your point of view—by the visitations of upward of a hundred million annual tourists drawn by the ebb and flow of the events calendar: Biker Week, the Daytona 500, Spring Break, not to mention the year-round delights of beaches, sunshine, and shopping. Native Floridians, though thin on the ground by comparison, know to look deeper. They know the state's heritage has been a complex, multicultural brew from the moment of First Contact.

Few Floridians have shown as keen an awareness of these facts as Zora Neale Hurston, who, on the opening pages of her memoir, described the Sunshine State as a "dark and bloody country" where "Spanish French, English, Indian and American blood had been bountifully shed" for nigh for two centuries.[15] And if the omission of "African blood" from the initial catalog strikes the modern sensibility as curious, we should be clear that the omission was a brief one. In the history I shall be outlining in this brief section, we have the advantage of Hurston in terms of access to sixty years of historiography based on research into colonial archives unavailable to her as an independent writer and scholar working with neither institutional support nor meaningful guidance. The soundness of her instincts and the prescience of her insights are thus the more remarkable given the constraints under which she labored.

Today, we know things Hurston intuited and may make claims that would have been vigorously contested in the mid-1940s—we know, for example, that every single sixteenth-century Spanish expedition to "La Florida" included Africans, both enslaved and free. That Africans traveled with Juan Ponce de León on his travels in search of the "fountain of youth" as well as with Hernán "Cortés the Killer" during his 1519 conquest of Mexico.[16] Indeed, a 1702 account from the capital of Spanish Florida, St. Augustine, noted that "[b]y 1589, the [indigenous], white, and black populations of the Spanish settlement totaled almost fifteen thousand, and outside St. Augustine there already existed the makings of a distinct Negro community which would grow with time."[17] This "distinct community," recognized as early as the 1580s, was fortified and officially christened Gracia Real de Santa Teresa de Mose in 1738.[18] Appearing both as "Fort Mose" (Mo-zay) and "Fort Moosa" in the historical record,[19] it constituted the first legally established free African settlement in North America.[20]

Now we must be clear: multicultural St. Augustine—comprising Europeans of many nations, free and enslaved Africans, and their indigenous allies—was *not* a Gullah Geechee community; for one, Spanish not English was the language of economic and political power. But this site, as an entrepôt of relatively free cultural exchange among persons of the *tres de sangre*, creoles of multiple lineages, whose occulted knowledge to this day roils imperialist discourses of *de pura sangre*, most assuredly *was* a magnet for the escaping Afro-Carolinians and (later) -Georgians who were to *become* Gullah Geechee. Little did the Anglo-Americans dwelling a few hundred miles to the Spanish capital's north know how tightly woven their fates were to become. All that was known to the denizens of the Charles Town settlement, established in 1670 as a colony of Barbados with free, indentured, and enslaved emigrants mostly from the Caribbean, was that there was a threat on the horizon.

St. Augustine thus quickly became "a constant subject of public discussion" as a "likely refuge" for escaped servants of both races during the Carolina colony's early years, according to historian Peter Wood.[21] Indeed, the colony was just a teenager when the earliest documented Carolina runaways appeared in the records of the Spanish and English: a group of eleven, including two women and a nursing child, arrived by boat from Saint George, Carolina, in 1687, setting off what was to become an explosive power struggle between the two great powers.[22] These maroons (from the French *marron*, meaning "feral" or "fugitive") were to become so numerous that King Charles II of Spain was prompted in 1693 to establish an official policy concerning their fate. His royal *cédula*, issued November 7, gave "liberty to all [runaways] . . . the men as well as the women . . . so that by their example and by my liberality others will do the same."[23] Indeed, his majesty virtually issued an engraved invitation to enslaved Afro-creoles living in his enemy's domains to put on their traveling shoes and beat feet to Florida.

The new rules of the game represented both a provocation to the English as well as an escalation in Spain's efforts to undermine the toehold the enemy had established in lands the Spanish had long claimed as their own, and exacerbating the danger for the Carolinians was the fact that, by the time of the king's proclamation, enslaved persons were well on their way to becoming the majority population in South Carolina. Wood is still an authoritative source on the processes of demographic change. The numbers of Africans and English were roughly equal just shy of forty years after the colony's founding in 1708, running at about four thousand each.[24] These Africans constituted an original generation of "pioneers," as the English had called them—a "founder generation," "the region's first real 'Afro-Americans'"[25]—and it was their resourcefulness in what would later be called "making a way with no way" and "hitting a straight lick with a crooked stick" that would be a critical, perhaps even a definitive, factor in sustaining the colony before the American Revolution.²⁶ It was, after all, the enslaved not the English who had familiarity with the fauna of the New World, especially deadly predators such as sharks, alligators, big cats, and venomous snakes.²⁷ It was the enslaved not the English who were able to "walk in the *feenda*,"²⁸ that is to say, who possessed the practical skills as woodsmen and watermen, as well as the spiritual attunement to cope with dense semitropical forests and the maze of creeks and waterways that constituted the great lowcountry swamps. Most importantly, it was the enslaved not the English who possessed the cultural competence to communicate with the Amerindians and to effect a knowledge transfer as to medicinal lore, agricultural practices, and edible plants based on their "comparable personal and ancestral experiences in the subtropical coastlands of the southern Atlantic."²⁹

Despite cultural differences between these communities of color and the English colonists' creative attempts to exacerbate them, cultural exchange between captives and the indigenous inhabitants was an established fact of colonial existence and critically important to the colony's survival. Indigenous allies could sometimes be depended on to return or hunt down runaways— but often not. War, disease, and a cruel trade with the Caribbean in Amerindian slaves was to deplete the numbers of the original inhabitants of Carolina over time, but their knowledge base lived on mostly with the Afro-creole pioneer generation and became part of that occulted knowledge that the enslaved held close, along with their secret lexicon to describe it, as ammunition in their war of wits with the enslavers. Simultaneously, the increasingly successful adoption of rice in the early 1700s began to necessitate importations directly from the Senegambian rice-growing regions as well as from the Kongo-Angola, resulting in a concomitant re-Africanization of the lowcountry's pioneer generation. And the colony's racial balance began tipping sharply and dangerously in favor of the Afro-creoles.

A critical year came about in 1720. Only a dozen years after reporting rough equality among free and enslaved colonists, a detailed census submitted to London recorded a free population of 6,525 and enslaved persons numbering 18,393: from parity to a three-to-one ratio in little more than a decade. Indeed, the total number of humans trafficked between 1706 and 1723 was a relatively modest 4,504; between 1724 and 1739, however, Charles Town was inundated with some 32,233 captive Africans—more than seven times the numbers of the previous two decades.³⁰ The speed and scale of the trafficking were transformative: uniquely among North American colonies, Carolina swiftly became "more like a Negro country than a country of white men."³¹

So it was that the Carolinas and Georgia became a matrix in which the symbolic and all too real deaths of African subjects rebirthed a new Afro-Atlantic subjectivity: the Afro-creole subjects who, in the fullness of time, were to be known as the Gullah Geechee. This development of a distinctly oppositional consciousness was to be a key soul survival mechanism for the enslaved, permitting the preservation and transmission of oral lore including stories, song, and an intact lexicon that represents "the distilled remnants of a larger corpus known and used throughout the Lowcountry" across centuries of time.[32] It also left the colony uniquely vulnerable, for enslavement was not a settled status: not for Black pioneers who had been granted remarkable liberties and allowed to participate even in the colony's defense, and certainly not for newcomers who had quite recently been free and who were far from resigned to their fate. Florida remained a thorn in the side of the English— as Spanish "coast guards" targeted English ships and plundered them of their goods, including their human cargo; as Spanish governors turned a blind eye to cross-border raids by African maroons and their Seminole allies seeking to reunite families or punish former masters; and as Africans simply continued vanishing into the swamps to reappear in Florida, sometimes singly or in family groups, sometimes in bands of up to fifty at a time. How to maintain control of this restive population? It was a matter of the gravest concern.

The great fear of the English colonists—debated at sessions of the legislature, in pleadings to the Spanish at St. Augustine, and in formal complaints to the British Crown—was that the instability would provoke a general insurrection.[33] That fear was realized in September 1739 with the Stono Rebellion. A contemporary account is worth quoting at some length.

> On the 9th day of September last, being Sunday, which is the day the Planters allow them to work for themselves, Some Angola Negroes assembled to the number of Twenty; and one who was called Jemmy was their Captain. They surprised a Warehouse belonging to Mr. Hutchenson at a place called Stonehow [Stono]; they there killed Mr. Robert Bathurst and Mr. Gibbs, plundered the House and took a pretty many small Arms and Powder, which were there for Sale. Next they plundered and burnt Mr. Godfrey's house and killed him, his Daughter and Son. They then turned back and marched Southward along Pons, *which is the Road through Georgia to Augustine* [emphasis added].
>
> They passed Mr. Wallace's Tavern towards daybreak, and said they would not hurt him, for he was a good Man and kind to his Slaves, but they broke open and plundered Mr. Lemy's House and killed him, his wife and Child. They marched on towards Mr. Rose's resolving to kill him; but he was saved by a Negroe who, having hid him, went out and pacified the others. Several Negroes joined them, they calling out Liberty, marched on with Colours displayed and two Drums beating, pursuing all the white people they met with, and killing Man Woman and Child when they could come up to them.[34]

This was the planters' worst fear realized. Later, much later, the colony's leaders were to focus on the high number of Kongo-Angola nationals among the most recently trafficked groups of slaves and to debate curtailing traffic, especially from that region. Still other colonial leaders were to single out the use of drums for communication and outlaw their use, among many other punitive "Negroe Acts" passed in the wake of the violence. (This was to prove a stroke of genius, according to Africanist scholar Janheinz Jahn, as "without the drums it was impossible to call the Orishas, the ancestors were silent, and the [Christian] proselytizers seemed to have a free hand.")[35] But as a heavily armed militia dispersed the rebels—whose number had swelled "above Sixty, some say a hundred," according to the colonial source—then methodically set about tracking, capturing, and executing the remaining fugitives amid the months of instability that followed,[36] attention turned quickly to the "outside agitator" to the south.

Here, Georgia, under its governor, Gen. James Oglethorpe, took the lead. Seizing on the pretext of war between the English and the Spanish in New Grenada[37]—the improbably named War of Jenkins' Ear (1739–48)—Oglethorpe launched an assault on St. Augustine the following June aimed at eliminating the threat of Fort Mose. After initial success in a short siege, however, the colonists were to suffer an ignominious defeat, with Oglethorpe losing over 60 percent of his fighting force in a single counterattack by the Spanish. The Mose militia, composed of maroons and their Seminole allies and led by one Capt. Francisco Menendez—himself an Afro-creole escapee from slavery in South Carolina[38]—was key to swinging the battle. The demoralized English were forced to fall back across the border, vowing to fight another day.

I hope it is clear that this lengthy excursion into the colonial history is more than just a digression. Not only do we seek to more firmly establish the roots of the language and knowledge community who were to become the Gullah Geechee, but we are also concerned with the routes they traveled in and through our settled conceptions of the landscapes of early America. I have tried here to be mindful of the advice of Katherine McKittrick, whose work grounds itself in recognition that the landscapes of the everyday have a way of obfuscating all evidence of struggle and that such concealment tends, for non-dominant groups, to bolster discourses of where they do and do not "naturally" belong.[39] We have, therefore, spent so much time on the forgotten centuries and unremembered conflicts of the Columbian encounter in order to challenge geographies of domination established only in the late nineteenth century or even later—and even then only after massive and bloody contestation.

Casting our glance back, at the landscapes of the middle seventeenth and eighteenth centuries, we see clearly that the geographies of the Gullah Geechee Coast were, to quote McKittrick, "an alterable not a static domain,"[40] and that the human tides moving across this domain flowed in many directions. As the interests of the Anglo-American colonists and the home country diverged, some of those tides flowed . . . toward the British? For example, the expulsions of royalists from the Carolinas and Georgia following the Revolutionary War led to mass migrations from the lowcountry in 1783 and 1784. For the Gullah Geechee, this was in the main a forced repatriation of already enslaved peoples. Those populations, however, were emancipated thirty years before persons on the mainland, and the resettlements were transformative for the Bahamas, according to Cartwright, "more than doubling the population of the capital, Nassau, and providing initial settlement for most of the Out Islands. . . . Gullah Geechee migration to the Bahamas was, in fact, so formative . . . that John Holm has described contemporary Gullah and Bahamian as 'sister dialects' of an eighteenth-century Sea Island plantation creole."[41]

Further complicating notions of a static population, the Caribbean flows of Gullah Geechee peoples deepened during the War of 1812, this time at the agency of the enslaved. Promised freedom by the British Royal Navy in exchange for aid against the United States, Sea Island Gullah Geechees opted for a chance at freedom over the certainty of continued servitude. The British lost their gamble and their war but did not renege on their bets with their Gullah Geechee allies, eventually resettling them as free farmers in Trinidad from 1815–16. Here, Gullah Geechee "praise societies" proved foundational for what Cartwright has called "one of the most cross-culturally open faiths of the Anglo-Caribbean world: the Spiritual Baptists, also known as the Shouters," whose practices "juxtapose and accumulate ritualistic traditions from Orisha, Hindu, Muslim, Catholic, and Pentecostal traditions."[42]

But the deepest flows in the human tides of the Gullah Geechee Coast were also in some ways the most deeply hidden. Here I speak of the subterranean tides that flowed in the direction of the Seminole nation, alongside whom the maroons adopted into the tribe and known as the Black Seminoles were to fight three wars with the U.S. government. It has not been well understood that the Seminole Wars—ostensibly beginning in between 1821, though the conflicts, as we have demonstrated, had simmered for centuries longer—were wars over slavery. The Seminoles, having adopted Africans into their tribe, would not bend on the point of returning them to former masters, and so the freedom struggle—fought over battlegrounds ranging from north Florida to Pensacola to Lake Okeechobee—ground on until the conflicts' official end in 1858.

The aftermath of those wars left survivors in widely scattered enclaves who lost contact with and memory of each other, though retaining vivid tales of the battle for their Florida homeland as well as the imprint of Gullah on their speech. The first of these enclaves may be found in the Bahamas, among the so-called Black Indians of Andros Island who made their way to freedom there at the conclusion of the First Seminole War in 1818. Three larger groupings flowed westward as a result of the negotiated settlement that followed the end of the Second Seminole War in 1842. The first are known as the Seminole Freedmen, and they're still to be found living in what was then Indian Territory and what is now Seminole County, Oklahoma, as per the terms of the original treaty. The second group, the Mascogos, live near Nacimiento in Coahuila state, Mexico; they are descendants of a band led by Coacoochee (or Wild Cat), who rose to the chiefdom of the tribe after the betrayal of Osceola and rejected life within the orbit of the slaveholding Creeks in Oklahoma. The third band, the Scouts, are descendants of a band of Black Seminoles led by John Horse, an ally of Wild Cat, who moved his fighting force back across the border to Bracketville, Texas, at the conclusion of the Civil War. Here, they served with distinction at the invitation of the U.S. Cavalry; their unit, the so-called Seminole Negro Indian Scouts,[43] were Indian interpreters and guides, a bulwark against the Comanches in the struggle for control of South Texas. Back in Florida, meanwhile, where the Seminole Wars dragged on until the 1858 surrender of Billy Bowlegs, a small band refused to leave the state, choosing marronage in the Big Cypress Swamp (next door to the Everglades) over exile in Oklahoma.[44] There are about fifty Black Seminoles remaining among the roughly thirty-five hundred casino-rich Seminoles living near the Fort Pierce Reservation. While their language status is unknown, linguists researching the Brackettville and Oklahoma communities found Gullah still being spoken in those enclaves as late as 1980, though the communities were unknown to each other and the connection with the Carolinas and Georgia had been completely forgotten.[45] Truly, the remarkable travels of the Gullah Geechee tongue bear out the notion that lowcountry Carolina, Georgia, and Florida swamps were the "sacred groves" for the African "Guardian of Souls," whom Toomer imagined as "Feasting on strange cassava, / Yielding to new words and a weak palabra"[46]—yielding, yet still resisting, still holding onto secret ways that disturb settled notions of modernity, settled notions of geography, long after they were believed to have vanished from the landscape.[47]

We have noted before that while the Black creative force was the heart and soul of the Harlem Renaissance, the number of New Negro writers who concerned themselves with the creative energies spiraling up from the "Negro farthest down" was relatively few.[48] Fewer than a dozen names leap to mind. If we further narrow the focus to artists who gave book-length treatment to the lives of the rural poor, we are left with only four names: Claude McKay and Eric Walrond from the Caribbean and Sterling Brown and Zora Neale Hurston from the United States. Of the two U.S.-born artists, I shall be arguing that it was Hurston whose achievement in weaving with her life and works a meaningful answer to Countee Cullen's poignant question, "What is Africa to me?" was unique.

Hurston alone among the artists drawn to the creative flame of Harlem had the acute perception to discern the fine threads connecting the Carolinas, Georgia, Florida, and the islands of the Antilles to altars guarded by the African Guardian of Souls along with the painterly gift with words and the scholarly training to properly interpret and communicate what she perceived. It has been argued that Hurston's folk inhabited an essentialist utopia removed from modernity in ways that made meaningful struggle to better the conditions of their lives impossible, but this I believe is to reduce her to the colorful darky act that she interposed between her inner self and the gatekeepers to the worlds she sought to enter. Rather, I find myself more persuaded by claims that Hurston's work is organized around the exploration of "heterotopias"—heterogeneous, egalitarian spaces where the marginalized give voice to their subjectivity in relative freedom and produce independent assessments of their lives that challenge the borders and subvert the hegemonic maps drawn by colonial patriarchs and anxious assimilationists.[49] Who better to expose and explore the heterotopos of the Gullah Geechee Coast than one birthed from Senegambian/Kongo roots, however occulted, than one molded in the crucible of New World experiences of enslavement and survival of the same? Who better than one such as Hurston?

For an artist such as Toomer, the Guardian of Souls was a metaphor, a primitivist artistic device to be cherished while useful then discarded after its novelty was exhausted. For many other artists of the Harlem Renaissance primitivism was a fashion, a fad. For Hurston the Guardian was no metaphor but a rather a soul force whose call evoked a response that would lead her down strange roads and over tremendous obstacles. Having been gifted with the "spy-glass of Anthropology" by her intellectual father, Franz Boas, Hurston accepted the glad and sacred mission to go forth and "collect Negro folk-lore."[50] Receiving the call as a challenge to reveal the African presence in the Americas, including both its deeply buried traumas and the still-available sources of rebirth and renewal this heritage made available, Hurston embarked upon an epic circum-Caribbean quest that was to carry her wherever in the New World Black folk were to be found and she could scrounge up the research funds to collect their lore. So it is that we at last turn our attention to Hurston's travels, from the Sea Islands to Lake Okeechobee, from New Orleans to Jamaica, from the Bahamas to Honduras, in search of the sources of Black authenticity in the Americas. It was an authenticity she was to try, and only many years after her death succeed in, locating within the abjected motherland and mother tongues of Africa.

Walkin' All over God's Heaven

The story of how nine-month-old Hurston became a "traveling woman" occurs near the opening of *Dust Tracks on a Road*, and it's a typically knee-slapping performance with more than a whiff of the tall tale about it. Beginning with a pan of cornbread and a curious sow, Hurston describes the sow pushing her way into the family's front door to investigate the cornbread and the screams of terror that brought her mother running from the spring where she'd gone to wash greens. "Her heart must have stood still when she saw the sow in there because hogs have been known to eat human flesh," Hurston writes, but in her deft handling, suspense turns quickly to laughter.

> But I was not taking this thing sitting down. I had been placed by a chair, and when my mother got inside the door, I had pulled myself up by that chair and was getting around it right smart....
>
> With no more suggestions from the sow or anybody else, it seems that I just took to walking and kept the thing a'going. The strangest thing about it was that once I found the use of my feet, they took to wandering. I always wanted to go. I would wander off in the woods all alone, following some inside urge to go places. This alarmed my mother a great deal. She used to say that she believed a woman who was an enemy of hers had sprinkled "travel dust" around the doorstep the day I was born. That was the only explanation she could find.[51]

Hurston was an artist of mature sensibility when she was dragooned by her publisher into writing her memoir. She did so unwillingly, and so it's perhaps not surprising that an artist who has been called "famously Janus-faced and ... noted for dissembling and secrecy" would adopt a bit of the method she had described her Florida informants using on nosey whites in *Mules and Men* to shield the secrets of their souls.[52] Fabulizing—a narrative method with which Hurston experimented in *Jonah's Gourd Vine* and which matured in *Their Eyes Were Watching God*—becomes seamless in *Dust Tracks on a Road*, proffering the buffer of a "featherbed resistance" of "laughter and pleasantries" between the parts of her story she wished her audience to remember and the parts she sincerely hoped they would forget to question.[53]

The anecdote sounds a sour note to contemporary ears because it serves to remind us that Hurston wrote for an audience ill-accustomed to thinking of Black women as anything but domestic help. But the charming folk trappings have a purpose beyond mere entertainment: they also allow the anecdote to work as a recuperative reframing of Hurston's unusual and perhaps unnerving record of professional achievement. Recall that Hurston is near the zenith of her career when she's writing *Dust Tracks on a Road*: she had published three of her four novels, along with two collections of folklore and dozens of short stories and articles in the premiere magazines of the day. She had made her mark in the theater with successful shows introducing "authentic" Afro-American music and dance to white audiences and worked on collections of Black music for the Library of Congress and Black folklore for the Works Progress Administration's Florida Writers' Project. She had reached heights of professional recognition no Black woman before her had ever reached with inductions into the American Folklore Society, the American Anthropological Association, and the American Association for the Advancement of Science, among others.

This woman—fearsomely accomplished (intimidatingly unrelatable?)—Hurston manages to efface in *Dust Tracks on a Road* by framing her otherwise perplexingly peripatetic life within a safe space, for her audience, of "Negro laughter," in which they are invited imaginatively to inhabit the subjectivity of towheaded youngsters dandled in the lap of a loving dark "uncle" or "auntie" spinning animal tales. For Hurston's Black readers these fabular passages might have rung jarringly against sensibilities honed to detect the slightest taint of minstrelsy, its safe orbit, as Hurston's formidable foe Richard Wright put the matter in a crushing review of *Their Eyes Were Watching God* "between laughter and tears."[54] But as critic Carla Kaplan has explained, feather-bed resistance is no mere play, nor is it "Tomming": "It is deception necessitated by social inequality." As an African American, as a woman, Hurston faced resistance, envy, and relentless negative appraisals of her person and her work. In response she had developed coping mechanisms for navigating the white world that themselves opened her to criticism and scorn. Of all her contemporaries, Arna Bontemps seemed to have understood her particular strategy best: "She knew how to handle white folks," he told Hurston biographer Robert Hemenway.[55] Balanced on a knife edge in *Dust Tracks on a Road* between what she needed to say, what her publisher would allow her to say, and what the buying public would accept, we see Hurston "handling white folks" at a high level.

Culturally, it's a performance of signifying:[56] changing the joke to slip the yoke of her audience's expectations. The humor is double-edged, with Hurston acting as a "two-headed doctor" slyly highlighting her audience's ignorance while situating her tale within an alternative Afro-creole geography of conjure, a heterotopia whose subversive possibilities resonated throughout Hurston's oeuvre. Renato Rosaldo has written of conjure as *metaphor* in Hurston—a mode of ironic self-portraiture that depicts her situation while also commenting on "the two-sidedness of her status."[57] Conjure also works as *methodology* in Hurston,[58] a mode of testimony that hints at the existence of arcane feminine powers while also, in the context of this specific passage, thematically setting up the experiences of orphaning that she says "began my wanderings."[59] Notes of laughter and tears, indeed, but played by a master musician, as in a series of extraordinarily complex narrative acts, she reveals and conceals the selves she wishes her audience to see.

Of course, we now know that this is partly a performance of powerlessness: that the book that alternately disappointed and infuriated Black audiences while also winning a thousand-dollar prize from white audiences for "advancing" race relations had been heavily censored. Excised material included an extended critique of imperialism in which missionary work and organized religion, "screaming for blood in Jesus' name," were not spared, nor were Europe's great powers or the "international hypocrite" of the United States. These chapters might have seasoned the views of Hurston critics who deplored her as an apolitical clown, but then, of course, that Hurston would never have been elevated to the status of race spokeswoman by the *Saturday Review*, which lauded the memoir for its "humor, color, and good sense" and for the absence of the *"race consciousness that spoils* so much Negro literature" (emphasis added).[60] The incident is in many ways exemplary of the contradictions of Hurston's life and work, particularly of matters she simply could not explain to the satisfaction of her warring audiences.

We know, of course, a great deal about the things she *would* not explain about her life: for example, the only recently settled mystery of her age. Scholars in the 1990s have agreed upon a consensus birth year of 1891 based on the discovery of the Hurston family Bible and cross-referencing with census records.[61] But it remains something of a feat that none of the birthdates Hurston supplied for various purposes over the course of her life was accurate. To be sure, fudging one's age was a common practice, particularly for southern women of a certain generation, but Hurston's creative use of the calendar was in another category altogether. She reported her birth year variously as 1898, 1899, 1900, 1901, 1902, 1905, even 1910;[62] added up, these represent not just a minor vanity but missing *years* in her biography—at a minimum seven of them, at a maximum nineteen.

Similarly, Hurston proved cagey about her relationship to the "the Negro farthest down," often fostering the impression, especially with white patrons, that she herself was of working-class or even peasant origins. This is an impression her memoir never *quite* manages to dispel, but in point of fact John Hurston's position as pastor of Zion Hope Baptist Church provided handsomely for his extensive family during Hurston's childhood, and his prominence in the councils of church and town only grew over time.[63] On the land he bought in Eatonville, he built a two-story, eight-room house and barn where a five-acre garden, a citrus grove, and both chickens and hogs amply provisioned the family. The woman who felt orphaned and who certainly cultivated an image of early poverty was, in fact, "raised with the trappings of a substantial middle-class life and the prestige of being the minister's daughter," the critic Pamela Bordelon notes.[64] Physical hunger was something she likely did not experience until she was well beyond the reach of two loving (if not necessarily understanding) brothers, living on her own in her mid-twenties in Baltimore, Washington, and Harlem.

Had Hurston been able to conform, it's likely that her lot would have been more comfortable. But she had hungers of the spirit that were difficult to sate—hunger, for something far beyond the life of a wife or domestic—a "slave ship in shoes," as she called that life—that was society's expectation for her. Hers were transgressive, quite extraordinary hungers, and while Hurston seems to have decided any price was worth paying—even the price of a life of dissembling and performance—in order to travel to the horizon and back again, she was to have to do battle with society's external structures her whole life long to define herself, to find her literary voice,[65] and to determine a path forward.

Hurston seems to have considered two models for the life she wished to create early on. At Howard,

> The teacher who most influenced me was Dr. Lorenzo Dow Turner [yes, that Turner, the author of *Africanisms in the Gullah Dialect*], head of the English department. He was tall, lean, with a head of wavy black hair above his thin, aesthetic, tan-colored face. He was a Harvard man and knew his subject. His delivery was soft and restrained. . . . Listening to him I decided that I must be an English teacher and lean over my desk and discourse on the eighteenth century poets, and explain the roots of the modern novel. Children just getting born were going to hear about Addison, Poe, De Quincey, Steele, Coleridge, Keats and Shelley from me, leaning nonchalantly over my desk.[66]

But that vision dissipated like morning fog when she talked her way into Barnard College and fell under the spell of Dr. Franz Boas, "the King of Kings." In Boas, Hurston found a kindred spirit:

> [F]ull of youth and fun, [a man who] abhors dull, stodgy arguments. Get to the point is his idea. Don't raise a point which you cannot defend. He wants facts, not guesses, and he can pin you down so expertly that you soon lose the habit of talking all over your face. Either that, or you leave off anthropology.

Abruptly, she writes, she "gave up my dream of leaning over a desk and explaining Addison and Steele to the sprouting generations."[67]

In truth, Hurston did not give up on literature. It was, after all, her inimitable way of arranging a bright spatter of words upon a page, her beautifully concrete gift for description, that had won her entrée to the literary circles of New York City and all its bright promise. It was the force of her personality that allowed her to carve out a space in that competitive atmosphere and win friends, allies, and patrons there. In stepping off this fast track to apprentice herself to both anthropology *and* literature, however, Hurston was to find herself torn between two worlds, two approaches. Her literary gift was a coat of many colors; the standard for communication in anthropology was, by contrast, a shroud of dull scientific objectivity. Publishers wanted the colorful Hurston promised by her associations with proven sellers like Fannie Hurst, Carl Van Vechten, and Langston Hughes. Gatekeepers such as Alain Locke, Du Bois, Charles S. Johnson, and Carter G. Woodson needed a "credit to the race."

On the other hand, her demanding "Papa Franz" offered a language and a methodology for examining the world she had known from the "earliest rocking of [her] cradle": the world of Brer Rabbit and Squinch Owl and High John de Conquer. Boas encouraged the immersive approach to participant observation that Hurston helped to pioneer; in Hurston's ability to "bring a more subjective and novelistic style to ethnographic work and a more ethnographic tone to literature," he saw potential to advance the culturally relativistic direction he sought for his field.[68] From the perspective of later developments, it's clear that Boas was prescient, as Hurston's example has directly and indirectly influenced such luminaries as Clifford Geertz, James Clifford, and George Marcus.[69] But what is now standard practice—a strategy of decolonization in a field founded in hegemonic practices—was in 1926, the year Hurston began doing field work under Boas's direction, in its infancy. Hurston's literary approach to folklore was firmly rejected by establishment anthropologists;[70] her anthropological approach to literature, meanwhile, was to mystify and alienate key gatekeepers among the "Negrotarians" and "Niggerati" whom she, perhaps too often, mocked.

There were a few broad areas of agreement between Hurston and establishment Black voices. Hurston's view of the African American sermon tradition largely accorded with that of fellow Floridian James Weldon Johnson, who had made them the focus of his 1922 book of verse, *God's Trombones*. Hurston was a fairly frequent collaborator with Johnson's musician brother, J. Rosamond, and while she often chaffed the elder brother for his grand manner—calling him "Lord Jim" and other teasing nicknames—she seems to have regarded him with real affection. It was to Johnson that she poured out her heart when the *New York Times'* review of her first novel, *Jonah's Gourd Vine*, scoffed at her rendering of the protagonist's sermons. "I never saw such a lack of information about us," she lamented. "It just seems that he is unwilling to believe that a Negro preacher could have so much poetry in him. When you and I (who seem to be the only ones *even among Negroes* who recognize the barbaric poetry in their sermons) know that there are hundreds of preachers who are equaling that sermon weekly" (emphasis added).[71] Johnson had, indeed, described old-time sermons in the preface to *God's Trombones* as a form of "conscious and unconscious art" that combined poetry with movement "in what was actually a very rhythmic dance." Furthermore, Johnson had argued that the folk art form of old-time Negro preachers had, in fact, constituted a separate form of English: "[T]hough they actually used dialect in their ordinary intercourse, [these preachers] stepped out from its narrow confines when they preached. They were all saturated with the sublime phraseology of the Hebrew prophets and steeped in the idioms of King James English, so when they preached and warmed to their work they spoke another language, a language far removed from traditional Negro dialect. It was really a fusion of Negro idioms with Bible English; and in this there may have been, after all, some kinship with the innate grandiloquence of their old African tongues." Johnson, though raised in an elite family with roots in the Bahamas and Florida, was able to call on childhood memories of dances and drumming in Nassau's African Village and ring shouts at Gullah Geechee sanctified churches in Jacksonville.[72] He concluded with a sniff, "To place in the mouths of the talented old-time Negro preachers a language that is a literary imitation of Mississippi cotton-field dialect is sheer burlesque."[73]

Similarly, Hurston and Johnson shared an approach to the authentic rendering of folk speech without descending into minstrel caricature. Noting in the preface to *The Book of American Negro Poetry* that the dialect of the minstrel stage is "an instrument with but two full stops, humor and pathos," Johnson went on to argue, "What the colored poet in the United States needs to do is something like what Synge did for the Irish; he needs to find a form that will express the racial spirit by symbols from within rather than by symbols from without, such as the mere mutilation of English spelling and pronunciation. He needs a form that is freer and larger than dialect, but which will still hold the racial flavor; a form expressing the imagery, the idioms, the peculiar turns of thought, and the distinctive humor and pathos, too, of the Negro, but which will also be capable of voicing the deepest and highest emotions and aspirations, and allow of the widest ranges of subjects."[74] Poet and critic Sterling Brown was to echo Johnson in his essay "On Dialect Usage." Arguing that "readers are repelled by pages sprinkled with misspellings, commas and apostrophe," Brown stressed that "[t]ruth to idiom is more important than truth to pronunciation." Though he and Hurston were more often than not at odds on matters political, Brown was to single Hurston out for praise in this essay precisely on the heading of capturing "truth to the manner of speaking" in her "stories of Florida negroes."[75] Indeed, one can hardly imagine an instrument more finely attuned to a place and its people than the Hurston of *Their Eyes Were Watching God*—as passages such as the revelation of the pear tree, the "sermon on the mule," the personification of Lake Okeechobee as a "monstropolous" monster roaring out of his banks, and so many others demonstrate.

But aside from these examples, few of Hurston's opinions on matters related to art and to the folk found favor with Harlem Renaissance gatekeepers. She never seems to have passed on an opportunity, for example, to take a poke at the august presence of W. E. B. Du Bois—dubbed "Dr. Dubious" in one of her funnier wisecracks.[76] Hurston's participation in the short-lived *Fire!! A Quarterly Devoted to Younger Negro Artists* had of course aligned her as early as 1926 with the insurgent youth wing of the Harlem arts movement—young men and women like Richard Bruce Nugent, Wallace Thurman, Gwendolyn Bennett, and Langston Hughes. But in Hurston's case, the antipathy cut deeper than just a desire to tweak the goatee of an old fogey tastemaker. Indeed, Hurston seems to have violently disagreed with the whole premise of *The Souls of Black Folk*: "The idea that the whole body of spirituals are 'sorrow songs' is ridiculous. They cover a wide range of subjects from a peeve at gossipers to Death and Judgment." This broadside swipe at Du Bois is one of the central propositions of "Spirituals and Neo-Spirituals," published in Nancy Cunard's 1934 anthology *Negro*. Hurston's desire is to argue for the protection of "real spirituals"—the spiritual songs and religious practices she had encountered and documented in her journeyings throughout Florida and the Bahamas. Du Bois, she implies, in elevating the Fisk and Hampton singers, had missed the point.

"There never has been a presentation of genuine Negro spirituals to any audience anywhere," Hurston argues. "What is being sung by the concert artists and glee clubs are the works of Negro composers or adaptors *based* on the spirituals." Listing the chief African American interpreters of the songs—Harry T. Burleigh, Rosamond Johnson, Lawrence Brown, Nathaniel Dett, Hall Johnson, and John Work—she says, "All good work and beautiful, but *not* spirituals." For all their success and fame, she says, Fisk University's renowned Jubilee Singers are no more than an outgrowth of glee club singing. "They have spread their interpretation over America and Europe. Hampton and Tuskegee have not been unheard. But with all the glee clubs and soloists, *there has not been one genuine spiritual presented*" (emphasis added).[77] This is strong stuff, to be sure—and at first blush it seems little different from the stance taken by the Charleston Renaissance Society for the Preservation of Spirituals. Moreover, in stating the case so emphatically—naming names and taking numbers, as it were—Hurston was potentially antagonizing allies such as collaborators Rosamond Johnson and Hall Johnson (no relation) and, in some cases, stirring lifelong enmities.

But as a folklorist who had been documenting the Afro-creole roots of southern culture and working to achieve her vision of the "real black theatre" for the better part of a decade, Hurston was sure of her ground and marshaled her evidence carefully. And here we see how easily her analysis outstrips the trite generalities of the Charleston preservationists. Real spirituals, as opposed to neo-spirituals, she says, are never sung solo or in quartets—but always in groups. The harmonies are jagged not regular and the dissonances are "important and not to be ironed out by the trained musician." Most importantly, each singing of a song is "a new creation. . . . No two times singing is alike, so that we must consider the rendition of a song not as a final thing, but as a mood. It won't be the same thing next Sunday."

This set of assertions shows an interesting evolution in Hurston's thinking since her first folklore foray in 1926. She had begun her work under Boas's tutelage with a concern to preserve a "dying culture"—and often expressed her mission in those terms in grant requests and correspondence with patrons and fellow folklorists. But in "Spirituals and Neo-spirituals," she makes the remarkable statement that "[c]ontrary to popular belief their creation is not confined to the slavery period. Like the folk-tales the spirituals are being made and forgotten every day." Spirituals are not a dying culture—they are a *living* culture. Here, Hurston anticipates the work of later anthropologists, folklorists, and ethnomusicologists who are far better positioned to make direct comparisons between Africanist and Afro-creole materials.

In "Characteristics of Negro Expression," also published in *Negro*, Hurston wrote,

> Negro folklore is not a thing of the past. It is still in the making. Its great variety shows the adaptability of the black man: nothing is too old or too new, domestic or foreign, high or low, for his use. God and the Devil are paired, and are treated no more reverently than Rockefeller and Ford. Both of these men are prominent in folklore, Ford being particularly strong, and they talk and act like good-natured stevedores or mill-hands. Old Massa is sometimes a smart man and often a fool. The automobile is ranged alongside of the ox-cart. The angels and the apostles walk and talk like section hands. And all through it walks Jack, the greatest culture hero of the South; Jack beats them all—even the Devil, who is often smarter than God.[78]

Hurston's lively prose appears to have detracted, for her contemporary readers, from the fact that all her assertions were based in direct observations. In exploring Afro-creole practices including "shouting," "seeking religion," and spirit possession, in looking for the logic behind everything from the "capers" that Brer Rabbit cut to the songs sung in turpentine camps to the funerary and grave decoration rituals practiced even in proper Eatonville homes, Hurston was uncovering and providing the earliest interpretive documentation of the Senegambian-Kongo roots of what a later generation of artists and scholars was to describe variously as a blues sensibility, as a blues aesthetic, as Gullah Geechee culture. These practices of actively "producing God" during worship, calling the spirits down during work, play, and all the routines of everyday life, were routes to resilience and survival for a formerly enslaved people in a hostile and ever-unfolding colonial moment, and Hurston was determined that they be properly understood.[79]

By 1938, she is sure enough of her ground to state confidently in "Go Gator and Muddy the Water"—written for the Florida Writers' Project's proposed volume on *The Florida Negro*—"Folklore is the boiled-down juice of human living. It does not belong to any special time place, nor people." Refusing to incarcerate folk culture in the past, she continues, "Folklore in Florida is still in the making. Folk tunes, tales, and characters are still emerging from the lush glades of primitive imagination before they can be finally drained by formal education and mechanical inventions."[80] These are audacious arguments, to be sure, and not, in the main, greeted as glad tidings by African American tastemakers. They flew directly in the face of pronouncements by "Lord Jim" Johnson, with whom Hurston had found common ground in so many areas. Writing in *Harper's* magazine a decade earlier, Johnson had mused that blues expression was effectively over: "It is more than probable that with the ending of the creative period of the Blues, which seems to be at hand, the whole folk creative effort of the Negro in the United States will come to a close. All the psychological and environmental forces are working to that end."[81] Johnson's predictions may have been premature, but they found fervent adherents among the African American scholarly establishment. By the mid-1930s, sociologist E. Franklin Frazier was championing the notion of the Great Migration as a "second emancipation of the plantation Negro," noting that even the so-called pathologies of urbanization represented "a step toward reorganization of life on a more intelligent basis."[82] Charles S. Johnson, writing in the *American Sociological Review*, had forcefully stated, "Actually, the Negro in America has very little if any African cultural heritage." The survival of "old folk-beliefs and customs," including medical practices, etiquette, speech idioms, and so forth, Johnson attributed to "cultural lag" and labeled these "backward," "stagnant," and "offer[ing] no advantage."[83] Indeed, during this period it was a mainstream view to consider folk consciousness as a deviant form of social organization, a "backward state of mind which had to be given up, actively be destroyed," according to critic Günter Lenz, for the Negro to reach his so-called potential as a Democratic citizen.[84]

Against such a backdrop, one can clearly see the ways in which Hurston's continued attempts to explore and explain African American expression would have troubled the waters for a Talented Tenth readership actively experiencing stereotype threat in regard to its folk roots. As contemporary readers, we are struck by the prescience of the extraordinary set of observations and arguments set forth in "The Sanctified Church"; these were carefully researched and informed by the insights gleaned from writing *Jonah's Gourd Vine* and Hurston's further travels through the Carolinas and Georgia, Jamaica, and Haiti. Hurston, for example, contends in that piece that the emergent "sanctified" congregations—the Church of God in Christ and the Saints of God in Christ, in particular—were not new religions as was generally believed but a very old form of worship asserting itself in protest against "the high-brow tendency of Negro Protestant congregations" as they gained more education and wealth. She goes even further: "In fact," she says, "the Negro has not been Christianized as extensively as is generally believed"—a statement that likely landed like a thunderclap among Hurston's collaborators on *The Florida Negro*, whose first draft was produced under supervision of Hurston's frenemy Sterling Brown, director of the Works Progress Administration's Office on Negro Affairs in Washington, D.C.[85] Here, Hurston was treading in dangerous territory indeed: suggestions as to the "Africanness" of African American religion practices were edging far too close to cultural sensitivities about the ways in which Black spirituality had been stereotyped under white supremacy.

The body of knowledge was certainly advanced by Hurston's striking insights—for example, connecting the "real" Negro spirituals to an African heritage of drum-like "dance-possible" rhythms, vividly describing the "priest before the altar chanting his barbaric thunder-poem" and the service itself as a ritual "drama with music."[86] But the same could not be said for the cause of Talented Tenth–style racial uplift, especially in the context of a national media-induced moral panic that amounted to a "voodoo craze" during the decades of the 1920s and 1930s. Against the backdrop of images of "bloodthirsty voodooists" "appeasing and conjuring African spirits with spells, blood sacrifices, and wild drum rhythms" disseminated by a sensationalistic press and "zombie" books and films, Hurston's accounts of the complexity of Black spiritual practice were over her peers' and much of the potential audience's heads.[87] Complicating matters was the fact that Hurston's and Brown's views of Negro music and the folk more generally had diverged as her relationship with Alain Locke, his mentor (and once hers), had soured. During work on Florida guides, Hurston had quipped to her boss, Florida Writer's Project director Carita Doggett Corse, about the rivalry, calling Brown the federal FWP director Henry Alsberg's "pet darkey." "I laugh at the little phenagling [Alsberg] does to give Sterling the edge over me. BUT, he cannot make him no new head with inside trimmings and that's where he falls down. You ought to see Sterling exhibiting his jealousy as I top him time after time," she wrote in late 1938.[88]

Sneers notwithstanding, Hurston was to find herself outmaneuvered. Despite providing "fabulous material" for the project, Hurston's contributions were "all but eviscerated" from the state guide, in part because she, an African American employee, committed the unforgivable sin of outshining her white peers: counterintuitively, the material was considered "too good" for inclusion. Stetson Kennedy, Hurston's white colleague during the production of the guides, recalls, "There we were doing our best to see that everything that went into the Guide was couched ... in staid Federalese ... and there was Zora turning in these veritable prose poems of African eloquence and imagery.... Inevitably, the inferior triumphed over the superior," and only the folktales themselves made their way into the Florida guide. Similarly, Black coworkers intent on projecting an image of acculturation and assimilation appear to have whittled down her contributions to *The Florida Negro* to the point of negligibility. The final version of *The Florida Negro* was not released until 1993, and all Hurston's writings had been deleted from the manuscript. Hurston's friend and ally Corse later admitted, "I feel that the principle oversight in my direction of the project was my failure to realise that Zora should have written the Negro book ... but she was forty years ahead of her time."[89] Indeed, if not for the recovery of the Florida materials by Pamela Bordelon, our understanding of the evolution of Hurston's thought, not to mention this allegedly apolitical artist's courageous work to document the deadly conditions in Florida's turpentine camps, would be considerably impoverished.

As we see in the passages we have examined, the Hurston of the prose essays is confident in the strength of her writing and research; she is thus bold in her pronouncements and even combative in defending her points. Increasingly, however, her boldness seems to have antagonized the community of scholars, nettled that the writing was "too good"—in an ironic echo of Hurston's Florida coworkers. The prevailing sentiment seems to have been that without a traditional institutional affiliation (though those doors were closed to her for reasons of racial prejudice) and without traditional scholarly publications (doors Hurston chose to close due to her need for money and her New York publishers' demands for an audience-pleasing persona), this journeywoman scholar should have the decency to sit quietly and keep her trap shut. Similarly, Hurston's Black peers looked askance. The denizens of the jooks, turpentine camps, sanctified churches, and hoodoo assemblies from whom she gathered materials did not have access to books; meanwhile, the Talented Tenth gatekeepers upon whom she depended for positive word of mouth were, by turns, scandalized or offended by her efforts. The unwritten expectation of those days was that when folklore collectors delved into the slave past, it was with the understanding that the stories they told were to "uplift" the race and advance the cause of integration. By testifying to an alternative consciousness that looked askance at mainstream white culture, at the efforts of the integrationists at the NAACP, *and* at the oppositional style of the Communist Party, Hurston found herself increasingly occupying the position of bone of contention.

Her racy personal style did not help. Sterling Brown, at the end of his life, cackled to two interviewers over a story that no doubt at the time had given unutterable offense: "Zora Neale Hurston sitting over there [pointing], keeping us entranced. She was a better liar than I am, a wonderful liar! Just had us in stitches. She gets up to leave. Being of the folk, she had a cigarette holder from here to yonder with a cigarette in it [gestures] and a long ash and stands at the door and tells us goodbye and flicks them damn ashes right down on [my wife] Daisy's rug. Daisy took care of the house. Daisy looked at her flick those ashes, and Zora took her damn big foot and rubbed them into the damn rug and said 'good for the roaches.' She knew damn well we didn't have no roaches. Daisy could have killed her," Brown said.[90] Hurston once described the "primitive" mind as "quick to sunshine and quick to anger. Some little word, look or gesture can move them either to love or to sticking a knife between your ribs";⁹¹ she might well have been speaking of her own modus operandi. It's difficult to say what provoked Hurston to this display, but outrageous behavior combined with acid observations—about everyone—won her no friends and turned many a onetime ally to foe.

She satirized Marcus Garvey in 1928 and, a decade later, lambasted her onetime sponsor Alain Locke so mercilessly that the magazine *Opportunity* refused to print the piece. In between, a matter of personal jealousy appears to have sparked the *Mule Bone* affair, ending her affectionate relations and all potential future collaboration with Langston Hughes, a popular figure who had been a key ally in Hurston's war on bourgeois cant and hypocrisy.⁹² Characteristically, Hurston never commented in print on her feelings about the affair. But eighteen months later, she wrote wistfully to her "godmother," Charlotte Osgood Mason, "New York is painful to me now. I feel so out of place." In other letters from this period, Hurston seems well aware of the realities of her situation: "You must hang with the gang or be shot in the back. . . . Don't disturb the existing order of things. Get on the band wagon, that is the backs of the poor Negro and ride his misery to glory. . . . He must not walk in daylight and disturb the cogitations of the intellectuals."⁹³ But knowing all this, Hurston is also incapable of refraining from poking the beast. One of the concluding sections of *Dust Tracks on a Road* describes a group of elite interlocutors curious about her research. "[S]etting their mouths in 'the Boston Crimp,'" Hurston says they start asking her "about the great differences between the ordinary Negro and the 'better-thinking Negro.' I [showed] . . . my irritation by saying I did not know who the better-thinking Negro was. I knew who the think-they-are-better Negroes were, but the better-thinkers were another matter."⁹⁴

We must not attempt, however, to lay all Hurston's difficulties at the door of personal prickliness. There's a strong argument to be made that the building blocks of the wall against which she was hurling herself were made of abjection—that shame about African origins that we explored at length in chapter 1 and that has lingered in the backdrop of our discussions of Talented Tenth reactions to the spirituals. Abjection has been one of the most powerful tools of the oppressor in the war of control over the subaltern consciousness since the dawning moments of the colonial encounter. Hurston's work rubbed very much against the grain of the New Negroes'—and the wider culture's—sense of the abject status of her subject matter.

One can just imagine Talented Tenth audiences recoiling in genteel horror at Hurston's attempts to illuminate the "truth" of Hoodoo, Voodoo, and Conjure. In sections of *Mules and Men*, in selected essays, and especially in *Tell My Horse*, Hurston was to argue for a culturally relativistic understanding of African-derived religious practices, disputing the conventional understanding of these rites as "black magic" and "satanism." Instead, she argued, Voodoo was a "religion of creation and life," of feminine power, and women's agency.[95] In the process, Wendy Dutton has argued, "[Hurston] established a tradition of black women writers at the same time that she illuminated the tradition of black women in conjure. She eulogized priestesses like Marie Leveau [sic] as if they were role models and she also produced a portrait of herself, a woman on her own, moving amid magic with ease."[96] This was an ease, we must emphasize, that was *not* shared by her audience.

Hurston was calling for a radical revision in Americans' and African Americans' conception of spirituality—finding parallels between conceptions of the invisible realm of ghosts, ancestors, and gods in the United States, the Caribbean, and Africa; arguing for the importance of dreams, meditation, fasting, and visions; connecting spirit possession in Africa with practices in U.S. sanctified churches. Her instincts were at times unerring: her speculations about the science of Voodoo—that the secret of the zombie was to be sought for in the houngan's African-derived knowledge of the properties of various ethnobotanical drugs and poisons—were especially provocative and eventually proven correct, although it took until 1981.[97] But her refusal to shy away from the sexual dimensions of these practices—the descriptions in *Tell My Horse* of the "love baths" that prepared the virgin for the marriage bed, the kiss of worship Voodoo practitioners bestowed upon the priestess's "organ of creation," and other details—would have been profoundly shocking and possibly the last straw for a class that Du Bois himself had described as beset by "sex squeamishness."[98]

It is, however, *Barracoon*—Hurston's book-length manuscript about Cudjo Lewis, born Oluale Kossula, the last living survivor of the Atlantic slave trade—that is most instructive in illuminating issues of abjection and her audience. Consider this passage from early in Lewis's/Kossula's account:

> When we at de plantation on Sunday we so glad we ain' gotee no work to do ... we dance lak in de Afficky soil. De American colored folks, you understand me, dey say we savage and den dey laugh at us and doan come say nothin' to us. ... But Free George, he come to us and tell us not to dance on Sunday. Den he tell us what Sunday is. We doan know what it is before. Nobody in Afficky soil doan tell us 'bout no Sunday. Den we doan dance no mo' on de Sunday.[99]

Kossula's rejection by Africans born in America is a small incident but still, to contemporary sensibilities, shocking. The Alabama-born slaves laugh African dances to scorn while shuddering at the sacrilege of dancing to pagan gods on Sunday. It's left to a freedman to explain to Kossula and his community the nature of their transgression: "Nobody in Afficky soil doan tell us 'bout no Sunday" is his succinct response. Kossula explains that the Africans are willing to accommodate themselves to the hostile environment by avoiding dancing on Sunday. But the withdrawal to "Africatown" after emancipation suggests Kossula and his kin needed stronger ways to protect their occulted African ways from the curiosity and hostility of outsiders on both sides of the color line.

Though Hurston compiled the first book-length version of the Cudjo Lewis manuscript as early as 1927, she was never to find a publisher for it in her lifetime and had to content herself with weaving short snippets of the Cudjo Lewis/Kossula story into her memoir, followed by a short piece in *American Mercury* in 1944. It wasn't until 2018 that *Barracoon* finally saw print, quickly becoming an "instant classic" as the publishing industry catchphrase goes, a *New York Times* bestseller that was showered with prestige prizes: *Time* magazine's Best Nonfiction Book of 2018, the New York Public Library's Best Book of 2018, the *Economist*'s Book of the Year, and so on.

In 1927, however, this story of trauma and violence complicated simplistic slavery-to-emancipation narratives in ways that neither white nor Black audiences were ready to hear. Kossula was not stolen away from his home by greedy whites, as Black audiences would have expected to hear; his village was attacked by the militaristic Dahomey, its inhabitants slaughtered, and the survivors tossed into the maw of the slave trade for one reason and one reason only: gold. This instance of slave trading, on the other hand, was not located far in the distant past, as a white audience might have expected to hear—but occurred only five years before the final emancipation of the enslaved. Nor did that emancipation provide a triumphant resolution to Kossula's story. He had to endure the tragic loss of all six of his children and his beloved wife. Disabled in a steam engine accident and left unable to work, he decided to begin the creation of Africatown, an act of withdrawal to a place of "refuge and memory."[100] But Hurston's visits revealed there was no refuge for Kossula from the horrifying flashbacks he endured; there was no hiding place from his despondency. In *Dust Tracks on a Road*, the Kossula section concluded on a heartrending note: "'I feel lonely for my folks [in Africa]. They don't know [what became of me]. Maybe they ask everybody go there where Kossola [sic]. I know they hunt for me.' There was a tragic catch in his voice like the whimper of a lost dog. After seventy-five years, he still had that tragic sense of loss. That yearning for blood and cultural ties. That sense of mutilation. It gave me something to feel about."

As it turned out, Hurston had few fellow travelers in her desire to remember and "feel about" those memories. Her contemporaries, like the descendants of Africa who derided Kossula and his kin, wished to forget, not to remember, the past. In 1931, the year she returned to *Barracoon* and began attempting to place it with various publishers, the deepening depression and the fate of the Scottsboro Boys seemed of far more moment to Hurston's peers than her explorations of the complex connections between the African past and the American present. And something deeper is at work, too. Genevieve Sexton's work on *Barracoon* is provocative in exploring the dynamics of the adoption of what she calls a "compromised self" for the sake of survival. The rejection of African cultural practices is a key part of the process; in the exigency of the moment, the abjected self must become more or less entirely complicit in denying the past in order to craft a new version of self and community that will substitute for the old.[101] But Hurston carried within her the memory and the experience of other possibilities for self and community—Hurston's life and work explored heterotopias of subversion and survival against which the New Negroes, lifting as they climbed the ladder of respectability and uplift, had firmly closed their psychic doors.

Hurston was to continue recovering hidden histories with work on Fort Moosa and the Black Seminoles; to continue discovering links between folktale traditions in the Carolinas, Georgia, Florida, and the Caribbean; to continue working on novels that continued to be rejected by publishers for whom she was "old news"; and especially to continue shocking the sensibilities of the Black bourgeoisie with her conservative takes on the issues of the day. Today, we see Hurston as a clear-eyed observer of Black people and the Afro-creole roots and routes of their sojourn in the New World. Unfortunately, it appears she saw some things too clearly and attracted the sun god's curse on seers who get too sassy. She could not be contained but could be punished by the elites who envied and feared her, and punish her they did. New York became a decidedly unfriendly place for Hurston after her falling out with Hughes. Job offers and offers of support for her graduate studies were to land like manna from heaven in her lap—an academic position at Fisk University, two full years in pursuit of a Ph.D. from the Rosenwald Foundation—only to be qualified or abruptly withdrawn. After wowing Alan Lomax with her field-collecting skills, her feud with Brown left her stripped of authority and even authorship in the Florida WPA project. She was consistently misread, discounted, and dismissed for both her creative work and her scholarship. And in a final blow, the Black press destroyed her personal reputation by misreporting scurrilous accusations of sexual abuse of a minor at the very time she was launching her comeback project: *Seraph on the Suwanee*, a novel in which her Black gaze was for the first time to be turned on white lives. It is touching that at this extremity—a period when she seriously contemplated suicide—Langston Hughes was one of those who was prepared to come to court to testify in her defense.[102]

She was destined, unfortunately, to die a prophet without honor among those whose favor would have allowed her to make a living from her work: misread, misinterpreted, and censored by publishers; patronized and condescended to for reasons of race and gender by the community of scholars; misunderstood and rejected for reasons of gender and class by the "Negrotarians" and "Niggerati" whom she, perhaps too often and too acerbically, taunted. Despite her contradictions, however, it's Hurston whose reputation has survived the vicissitudes of time. We honor the way Hurston's travels—her crossings and interactions across multiple points of the African diaspora—trouble the waters of privileged pastoral discourses of holism, history, and hierarchy. We are enthralled by her way of drawing so-called primitive cultures into complex cosmopolitan connections and conversations. Hers was a restless movement that patriarchal Black heterosexism and racialist white supremacism sought to still—and succeeded for a while in doing so. Yet it can be argued that it was this native of an allegedly carceral Gullah Geechee Coast culture who, more than any other figure of the Harlem Renaissance, set African American artistry, particularly women's artistry, flowing.

CHAPTER 7

Plenty o' Nothin
Spectacular Blackness and Global Miscegenation in Porgy and Bess

> The dream of a simple life, "of a disencumbered, stripped down life has the potential to become a socially disruptive force, but also, given its historic sponsorship by hegemonic groups (like the Puritan fathers and the Founders) to become an ultrarespectable plank in American civil religion and thus as much of a placebo as *e pluribus unum*."
>
> —LAWRENCE BUELL, "American Pastoral Ideology Reappraised"

In 1999, *Mamba's Daughters*—a rip-roaring melodrama of race, rape, and revenge written by Charleston's favorite son, DuBose Heyward—came to the stage for the very first time in the city that framed its setting. The venue was the Spoleto Festival U.S.A., which for twenty-two years had claimed Charleston as its second home; the vehicle was a critically acclaimed revival of the show by New York's Target Margin theater company. But though the production trailed in its wake Obies for star Heather Gillespie, and a special citation for the creative team, though rave reviews had greeted the show in the *New York Times*—"Talk about a revival! With amazing grace, the director David Herskovitz summons the animating spirit of the old melodrama and allows us to experience it as something fresh"[1]—the audience in Charleston was not unanimous in sharing the thrill.

The source of the dissent might initially have seemed a mere matter of highbrow versus middlebrow taste. Herskovitz and his creative team had chosen to mount a "deconstructed" drama. That is to say, characters were cast without regard to race, though the race assigned them in the original text was indicated by black, white, or yellow patches on their costumes. Gillespie's performance was, indeed, award worthy—an Anglo-Caribbean family background gave her an advantage in rendering Gullah Geechee speech that the African American cast mates did not appear to share. But the acting in general was stilted and flat—intentionally so, according to a Q&A after the show with the director, dramaturge, and star. The idea, as the dramaturge explained it, was to make a radical comment on the blood-and-thunder melodrama at the spine of Heyward's sprawling novel, in effect, allowing a countercultural perspective to emerge. At the session I attended, the audience listened politely to the high-flown theoretical answers to its questions for quite some time. Then a cultured voice with a tremolo associated with advanced age lofted down from the balcony; it belonged to a gentleman who described himself as an African American and a retired college professor from Tennessee. He gave a vivid description of his frustrated longing as a boy growing up in the segregated South to travel to New York to see Ethel Waters in the 1938 stage version of the play—and expressed his disappointment, sixty years later, to find so little substance behind what had been a lifelong dream. The question he asked was one to which no one on the stage—not the director or the dramaturge or the star—seemed to have an answer:

"But without the melodrama, what do you have?"

We can't be certain whether the elderly gentleman was complaining that, without melodrama and its intense emotional engagement, he found the play lacking; whether he was making a subtler complaint about the "deconstructed," and hence missing, racial element; or whether he meant something quite different from either of these. But his question is a highly pertinent one—one that has, in one fashion or another, dogged Heyward's heels for decades. This is, after all, a writer who managed to create one of the most indelible portraits of a city and a cultural milieu in southern literature—not to mention in the performance history of the American stage. And yet Heyward's work has had a difficult time situating itself within the canon of twentieth-century American literature. Despite a generous body of work—several books of poems, five novels, plays, essays, and more—Heyward is traditionally neglected by critics of southern writing, who rarely even mention him in comparison with contemporaries like Faulkner and the Nashville Agrarians; he is ignored, too, by African Americanist critics who quite reasonably privilege the work of his contemporaries and sometime rivals among the "New Negroes."

Of course, in the project of literary recovery that we tout as the Charleston Renaissance, Heyward is a culture hero. This is a development that can hardly surprise but that carries dangers even as it gathers momentum. All of the works—whether good (the novels *Porgy* and *Mamba's Daughters*), bad (the limp Civil War novel *Peter Ashley*, the potboiler miscegenation melodrama *Brass Ankle*), or indifferent (the poems)—are in the process of being kidnapped by discourses of "beautiful, historic" Charleston and "renaissance." Indeed, the critic hoping to shed new light on Heyward's place in American fictions of race faces a situation in which *A DuBose Heyward Reader* (2003) has become airport reading for tourists entering and leaving the city before any of the most important questions raised by his work can be asked much less answered.

So, in this chapter we shall look deeply at the novel that was Heyward's signal achievement, *Porgy*, examining its roots in literary, social, and personal histories of the Gullah Geechee Coast and paying close attention to the process by which the subsequent stage versions, through a gradual process of cultural amnesia that eroded memory of their specific antecedents as well as all "authentically" vernacular elements, mutated into a work whose appeal has become so "universal" that *New York Times* opera critic Anthony Tommasini argued that racial casting was no longer relevant and white singers ought to be allowed to perform the roles.[2]

We shall be concerned, of course, with the discourses analyzed in previous chapters—discourses of authenticity, the pastoral, and the primitive that gave the novel, and the play and opera inspired by the novel, such resonance and such an important role in the national and global racial imaginary. Bringing this constellation of issues into focus is the slight and somewhat unlikely figure of DuBose Heyward, a man whose complex acts of literary minstrelsy—what critic Joseph Roach calls "reversed ventriloquism . . . black music pouring from a white face"[3]—have confounded generations of critics and whose history-making collaboration with George Gershwin set the stage for similar twentieth-century acts of simulation and impersonation from Elvis Presley to Eminem.[4] In analyzing the processes that led to the production and consumption of *Porgy and Bess* as a global megahit, we shall be arguing for an underlying poetics of desire and envy, of love and theft, as Eric Lott might say, rooted in the geography of the Gullah Geechee Coast—both landscape and the unique cultural forms that arose there—as well as in the history of structural inequities upon which relationships across race and class were based and from which they have yet to be liberated.

"Knowing the Negro": A Southern Artist's Racial Mountain

Although Heyward's novels take place, for the most part, in Charleston, to understand them fully, we must turn first to New York City, where a group of writers and intellectuals were flinging themselves like moths against the candle flame of something felt as the "modern"—and seeking, even more assiduously, to give their experiments a name. We begin with two quotes, illustrating two points of view, two literary strategies for producing fictions of race. The first comes courtesy of Carl Van Vechten, the man at the center of one of those boiling cauldrons of experimentation "up North." A prolific essayist, art and music critic, novelist, and all-around bon vivant who took an early—and lonely—stand on behalf of integration in both the arts and social life, Van Vechten has been hailed as a chief architect—and reviled as a cheap huckster—of the Harlem Renaissance. It seems clear that Van Vechten's intentions were noble—and equally clear that he is doomed to remain an ambivalent figure in the annals of the era. And his own words offer a reason why.

There's no escaping the savage, if unintended, irony of his oft-quoted essay, written in response to a questionnaire circulated among writers and published in 1926 for the NAACP's *Crisis* magazine. Intended as a call to arms to the African American artist, the words shriek down through the decades like fingernails across a blackboard: "The squalor of Negro life, the vice of Negro life, offer a wealth of novel, exotic, picturesque material to the artist. On the other hand, there is very little difference if any between the life of a wealthy or cultured Negro and that of a white man of the same class. The question is: are Negro writers going to write about this exotic material while it is still fresh or will they continue to make a free gift of it to white authors who will exploit it until not a drop of vitality remains?"[5]

An apparently contrasting notion of literary method—not to mention of literary decorum—is offered by Heyward:

> In the well-bred southern drawing room of a decade ago, the "Negro Problem" was never mentioned. And so the authors who undertook to interpret Negro life divided themselves into two general classes: those who deal altogether delightfully with the Negro of the past, and those who took the Negro's sense of humor as a keynote, caricatured it beyond recognition, and produced a comedian so detached from life that he could be laughed at heartily without the least disloyalty to the taboo.
>
> Now the task that confronts the South today is simply this: to readjust its standards of good taste in manners if you will. But for art, its own code of good taste, [must be] based upon a fearless and veracious moulding of the raw human material that lies beneath its hand.[6]

These are brief excerpts from much longer pieces. Even so, obvious differences of audience and aim leap to the eye. Van Vechten's essay is offered to an educated, cultivated audience of Negroes and progressive whites; the author strikes the pose of a "man of experience" offering advice to apprentices in a trade in which he is master. Most importantly, Van Vechten foregrounds an issue that was central during this period of dueling renaissances: the issue of contestation for literary and artistic "ownership" of African American materials. Van Vechten gives notice here that African American artists, through a lingering Victorian sex squeamishness or a misguided notion of racial uplift, are in danger of making a "free gift" of potentially "fresh," "exotic" materials to exploitation-minded whites. But while the unconscious paternalism and racism of his phrasing jars upon our contemporary sensibilities—and indeed evoked a thundering response from the *Crisis* editor, W. E. B. Du Bois—none of Van Vechten's most important literary friendships suffered any lasting harm. He continued to *épater le bourgeois* of his time by working across lines of color and class to discover new talent and promote it through his essays; to steer new writers to his publisher, Knopf; to document the great talent of his era through his photography; and, most importantly, to establish important literary and art collections documenting the Harlem Renaissance at Fisk and Yale universities. Van Vechten and Hughes exchanged long gossipy letters on the creative world that they inhabited to the end of their lives; similarly, Van Vechten's friendship with James Weldon Johnson remained so strong that each man named the other the literary executor of his estate.

Heyward's essay, meanwhile, represents us with quite a different case. Titled "The New Note in Southern Literature," it was published in 1925 in the *Bookman*, a literary journal that offered a listing of bestsellers—the first in the country, according to the Library of Congress—and that also just happened to be owned by *Porgy*'s publisher, the George H. Doran Co. of New York. The readership for the *Bookman* would have been conservative and largely northern, people for whom ideas of southern literature were more likely shaped by H. L. Mencken's savage 1920 satire, "The Sahara of the Bozarts," than by southern letters themselves. Indeed, the southern literature that Heyward defines and defends so assertively here is, at this time, much more wish than reality. Of the Nashville Agrarians, only Donald Davidson, Allen Tate, and John Crowe Ransom had even begun to publish poems, and their signature work *I'll Take My Stand* was half a decade away. Of the writers later associated with the Southern Literary Renaissance, only Ellen Glasgow had a significant record of publication. William Faulkner was an unknown: his first novel would not be published until 1926. New Critics Robert Penn Warren and Caroline Gordon wouldn't appear in print until 1929 and 1931, respectively. Even Heyward's reputation before *Porgy* was based on one and a half books of poetry; the lucky happenstance of being selected, based on his friendship with Yale Younger Poets prize winner Hervey Allen, to edit a "Southern number" of *Poetry*; and a few seasons at the MacDowell Colony.

Genteel and gentle where Van Vechten is brash and bracing, Heyward nonetheless stakes out some bold claims in this essay: the authority to speak for southern literature and the authority to speak for and about the Negro. We have seen that his authority on the matter of southern literature rests upon somewhat slender justification. On the second matter, however, that of speaking of and for the Negro, Heyward is on much firmer ground because his authority has been established by centuries worth of precedent: the southerner's special claim that he "knows the Negro." But what precisely did "knowing the Negro" mean in the case of DuBose Heyward? Did he have a right to claim such a special status?

It appears that, in certain critical respects, he did. For Heyward, "knowing the Negro" certainly meant knowing the Negro's language at a much deeper, more intimate level than virtually any other "blackface" writer of the period—for the Charleston Negro's language, Gullah Geechee, was also Heyward's own. Like his contemporary Julia Peterkin, author of the Pulitzer Prize–winning "Gullah Geechee novel" *Scarlet Sister Mary* (1927), Heyward was raised by an African American "dah" and lived on terms of physical proximity, and even intimacy, with lower-class African Americans that would be difficult to imagine in the thoroughly gentrified, and now residentially segregated, contemporary city. While Peterkin's fictional world revolved around her plantation, Lang Syne in Calhoun County, near the state capital city, Columbia, Heyward's vision shifted among a broader spectrum of "types": domestic servants in the homes of the elite, the African American families to whom he sold burial insurance in his first paid job, the field hands whom he supervised on an aunt's plantation during his summers, and the stevedores whose violent, hypermasculine subculture he observed working as a cotton checker on the Charleston docks.[7]

Heyward was bilingual in Gullah Geechee; his own speech bore the stamp of what was most likely his first language: a northern visitor to the "ravishing old city" in 1923 described the newly married author as "an adorable boy who talks about 'cyars' and 'gyardens.'"[8] But even if we did not have such direct testimony, other associations would speak to his facility. He was a founding member of the Society for the Preservation of Spirituals, whose public concerts of Gullah Geechee spirituals complete with the polyrhythmic hand and body jive known as "shouting" we encountered in chapter 3. Even more to the point, his mother was a successful "dialect recitalist" whose performances earned as much as fifty dollars for a ninety-minute program at a time when a loaf of bread cost five cents.[9] Most persuasively, there's the evidence of the novels themselves, which elevate Gullah Geechee speech, one of the most antique of American vernaculars, to the level of literature. Let us look briefly at a passage from *Porgy*, in which two respectable, churchgoing characters from Catfish Row speculate on the scandal of Porgy's relationship with Bess:

> "I tell yuh dat nigger happy," [Peter] said to Serena one evening while they were smoking their pipes together on her washing bench.
>
> "Go 'long wid yuh!" she retorted. "Dat 'oman ain't de kin' tuh mek man happy. It tek a killer like Crown tuh hol' she down."
>
> "Dat may be so," agreed the old man sagely. "But Porgy don' know dat yit. An' 'side. Ef a man is de kin' wut needs er 'oman, he goin' be happy regahdless. Him dress she up in he own eye till she look lak de Queen of Sheba tuh um. Porgy t'ink right now dat he gots a she-gawd in he room." . . . And he emitted an indiscreet chuckle, which was too much for his friend.
>
> "Yuh po', ole, wall-eyed, sof'-headed gran'daddy! Ain't yuh 'shame' tuh set dey befo' me, an' talk sweet-mout' 'bout dat muderin' Crown Bess? Ef I wuz yo' age, an' er man, I'd sabe my sof' wo'd fer de Gawd-fearin' ladies. (63–64)[10]

This snippet of speech hints at what was, in fact, a thoroughgoing commitment. For Heyward, giving a faithful rendering of Gullah Geechee language was not just a matter of grammar but a matter of art. He captures here an intimate, unguarded moment that transcends the "delightful . . . Negro of the past" and the "comedian . . . detached from life" criticized in his essay. Simultaneously wise, wry, and laugh-out-loud funny, the characters here are emphatically *not* Ellisonian "ritual objects" but performers in their own drama, sharing the homely, slightly salacious, wisdom of elders, then lapsing into a barrage of invective that is squarely within the African American tradition of verbal art. This, apparently, was what Heyward meant when he spoke of a "fearless and veracious moulding of . . . raw human material" as the "new note" in southern literature. It was to be achieved in Heyward's oeuvre, in part, by the creation of a *literary* Gullah.

This was a signal achievement of the renaissance period in South Carolina, one that Heyward shared with only two others and for which the discipline of southern studies has never fully given him credit.[11] Linguistics teaches us that the literary form of a spoken dialect cannot arise until the dialect has achieved a critical mass of native speakers with the educational attainment, the artistic ambition, and the cultural confidence to attempt such a creation. Writers of the Harlem Renaissance filled these conditions over and over again during the early twentieth century: Claude McKay, for example, working with Gullah Geechee's Jamaican cousin both in verse and in his luminous prose; Langston Hughes creating the blues form in poetry; Zora Neale Hurston transforming folk orature into artistically rendered prose.[12] The surprise comes in having to recognize that some of the earliest native American speakers to make this leap with Gullah Geechee were, in fact, of European descent: the lady-of-the-manor-cum-novelist Julia Peterkin, who bragged in her memoir, "I spoke Gullah before I spoke English," and the genteel charmer, Heyward.[13]

With this recognition comes another intriguing set of propositions. For if we accept Gwen Bergner's extension of Lacanian theory—her assertion that racial differentiation, no less than gender differentiation, occurs at the level of the unconscious with language acquisition and that both processes, that is, becoming a racial subject and speaking a language, require an unconscious accommodation to a society's symbolic order, in effect an act of learning to speak the "Name-of-the-White-Father" (xxvi) and submitting to his authority—then one can't help but wonder what it means for that emerging subject when the first language in question, in fact, *belongs* to an Other, particularly an Other such as the Gullah Geechee: differentiated so radically in social terms from one's own identity. Stuart Hall has written, speaking of Frantz Fanon's prescience in seeking to apply poststructuralist and psychoanalytic theory to the "primordial—and primordially resistant structures of racism," that "an account of racism which has no purchase on the inner landscape and the unconscious mechanisms of its effects is, at best, half the story." We shall try to avoid telling half the story in our analyses of *Porgy* and *Porgy and Bess*.

We have demonstrated so far in this chapter that Heyward's engagement with African American culture was passionate. In addition, we have a chorus of Charleston Renaissance critics—from Martha Severens to James Hutchisson to Harlan Greene—to assure us that his respect for African American culture was also progressive, at least in contrast to the attitude of a Negrophobe like Sass or the unseen hand that shut the door on Edwin Harleston's exhibition at the Charleston Museum. We have it on good authority as well that at least some of Heyward's relationships across the color line—particularly after he began collaborating with his wife and working with African American performers to realize his works on the stage—were personal, too, in the fashion, though perhaps not to the same degree, that Van Vechten's relationships with African Americans were personal.

Even so, there are questions well beyond those around Heyward's social milieu that have yet to be probed, questions such as the following: In what ways are genre or even mode—for example, melodrama, the gothic, or the pastoral—relevant to a discussion of Heyward's blackface novels? As the text moves from page to stage, what are the implications of the *performative* in Heyward's relationship to the African American folk? Are his "blackface" fictions and acts of oratory/kinesthetic imitation a particularly sophisticated form of what Ralph Ellison called "the darky act"? A partly unconscious reenactment of a "circum-Atlantic" memory/culture to which he was native and thus a rightful heir?[14] Or some combination of these elements? And what about his relationships with the urban sophisticates cast to play the denizens of Catfish Row? The answers to these questions will lead us, by circuitous paths, over large rocks, and through some very tall weeds, deep into the heart of this southern artist's "racial mountain."

It was Hughes, of course, who introduced the discourse of a "racial mountain" into American letters, referring in a 1926 essay in the *Nation* to the dilemma of an aspiring writer who expressed his frustrated longing "to be a poet—[but] not a Negro poet." Hughes diagnosed the writer's ailment as a secret, unacknowledged shame about his race and culture. It turns out that, in psychoanalytic terms, the comparison may be apt on both sides of the color line as Heyward, in his life and relationships, struggled with issues of personal identity and artistic identification, professional ambition and racial desire, that were no less tangled than those faced by Hughes's unnamed interlocutor. In his art, Heyward furthermore faced the challenge of accurately rendering a "folk" community and embedding it in the modern world—an endeavor filled with dangers that we have probed in previous chapters.

To recapitulate quickly, "folk" and "primitive" are categories deployed in order to police the racial, sexual, and social borders of modernity. Confusions about these categories exist on both sides of the color line, and our discussions of Harlem and Charleston Renaissance figures have revealed sometimes-dueling strategies for mediating these confusions. On the one hand, we have the artists of the Charleston Renaissance—whose "retrospective," "nostalgic" works offer up visions of "simplicity" among a sometimes "rural," sometimes urban, but always "primitive" "Folk." The awareness of modernity is always pushed just out of the frame, and while the essentialist vision of the Folk may be positive, and fully embraced, there is also a parallel movement toward imperialist nostalgia: a pose of mourning the world of innocence and simplicity that one is, in fact, complicit in bringing to an end.

On the other hand, with the artists of the Harlem Renaissance—artists who were "modern," "urban," "experimental," and "progressive"—the Folk offered the attraction of an "authentic" racial community. Unfortunately, "that allure itself is often represented as uncanny—a dangerous nostalgia for an experience inaccessible to modern subjects and inextricably linked to racist exploitation."[15] Indeed, Alain Locke's essays on culture return again and again to the notion of an authentically African essence, or "folk spirit," that nonetheless is figured as one of the "deep resources of the past."[16] Art that crossed the stringently policed temporal border, art in which the Folk appear not merely as historical, aesthetic figures but also as contemporary, social figures—as in the work of, say, Zora Neale Hurston—tended to elicit at times harsh denunciation.[17]

Our analysis of Heyward will examine these categories as well as their psychoanalytic dimensions as we focus on three general areas. First, we shall consider *contexts*, Heyward's inspiration by and encounters with African Americans as subjects and as (sometimes rival) artists, considering particularly the ways in which events reveal attitudes that are, by turns, loving yet dismissive, drenched in nostalgia yet objective and detached, emulative yet occasionally viciously proprietorial. Second, we will look at selected *texts*—particularly the first and third novels, featuring Gullah Geechee protagonists attempting to navigate the stormy waters of the modern. And finally we shall probe the process by which *Porgy*, a moderately successful "serious" novel, was translated into the smash international hit *Porgy and Bess*, theorizing particularly on the ways in which bodies in motion make Story accessible to what Joseph Roach has called the "kinesthetic imaginary" of national and global cultures. It is my hope that thoroughgoing attention to these areas will allow us to tie up the threads of our previous discussions and begin to draw a few conclusions about the geographies and genealogies of desire for Black bodies and Black culture expressed in the literature and art inspired by the Gullah Geechee Coast.

Genealogy of a Performance: From a Southern City's Streets to the Page

Somewhere in the world today, on an opera or even a musical theater stage, Porgy weeps and storms his love, Bess struggles with her inner demons, and Crown lies in wait to kill, to die, to claim his final victory. But while place names like Catfish Row retain their resonance with tourist visitors to Charleston, while "Summertime" remains one of the most frequently covered songs in the American songbook, very few people know that Porgy was a real person—indeed, it was only in undertaking this research that I discovered the fact and realized, as well, that his story had an unexpected personal dimension. Who was Porgy? For this section of our narrative we will rely on the oral recollections of three women, all of them deceased, two of them born and raised in Charleston who, though in their eighties when I interviewed them in 1995, retained vivid memories of Charleston in the 1920s and the man the world came to know as Porgy.

That man was, in fact, named Samuel Smalls, a disabled panhandler with a fine, loud singing voice who drove a goat cart through the streets of Charleston. My grandmother, Anna Hall Hamilton, knew him as a girl growing up on Charleston's Neck, the area north of downtown that joins the peninsula to the mainland. Historical home to free Blacks, to slaves "living out" and hiring their time for wages, as well as to runaways evading their owners by hiding in plain sight amid the crowds,[18] the Neck has always been a sort of creolized third space "between the strictness of Charleston's genteel social codes and the more generous, forgiving amorality of Nature."[19] The Neck's association with Black Charleston persisted into Heyward's time and well beyond. For much of the twentieth century, Afro-Charlestonians like the Hamiltons and our kin among the Desaussures, Halls, and Bradleys worked small farms, fished and crabbed the polluted waters of the Ashley and Cooper rivers, and held down menial jobs at the fertilizer plants and paper mills whose choking fumes wreathed the city when the wind was from the north. After hours, they went about their lives in suburban and North Charleston neighborhoods like Silver Hill, where my father was born, as well as Rosemont, Accabee, Union Heights, and Liberty Hill—all in relative isolation from the city's whites.

Such isolation was most emphatically not in operation in downtown Charleston, where residential segregation along the typical southern pattern was a relatively late development associated with white flight of the Civil Rights Era. Here, African Americans lived cheek to jowl with whites throughout the historic district, at now long-gentrified addresses on Tradd, Water, Legare (pronounced luh-GREE), Rutledge, and East Bay streets. Granted, many of these Blacks were quite poor,[20] part of the country-to-city migration that followed the collapse of rice culture in the early twentieth century. But, whether poor or well-to-do, their music, styles of dress and dance, expressive postures—"styling," if you will[21]—had for generations been part and parcel of the carnival of Charleston's streets, creating a miscegenated space that some found bracing, others disturbing, that Jim Crow laws were increasingly intended to police, but that even so managed to burst from all restraints to travel to New York City and spawn the worldwide dance phenomenon, the Charleston.

Sarah Dowling, the second of my informants on Samuel Smalls, was part of that miscegenated space, having grown up South of Broad on Tradd Street among Black and white neighbors. Her marriage to the Reverend John E. Dowling, head of the Jenkins Orphanage for many years after the death of the institution's founder, the Reverend Daniel Jenkins, placed her at a swinging hinge of the elite social world of the Charleston Renaissance—the Heywards and Elizabeth Verner were passionate advocates for Jenkins and his charges—and the desperate conditions of urban blight from which she and her husband worked to rescue an average of 350 homeless children every year. It should be noted that these connections placed Mrs. Dowling squarely in the Jazz Age as well. As early as 1896, Jenkins' Pickaninny Band had an established repertoire of traditional marches, spirituals, and popular cakewalks and rags. By 1914, the Jenkins Orphanage Band had played the St. Louis World's Fair and the Hippodrome in London and had marched in the inaugural parades of both Theodore Roosevelt and William Taft. Despite its worldwide fame (not to mention a shrewd business model that earned, according to a 1935 *Time* magazine article, $75,000 to $100,000 a year to support the orphanage),[22] controversies over historic preservation and gentrification eroded the support the institution enjoyed among residents of the rapidly gentrifying neighborhood South of Broad. So it was that in the thirties, Rev. Jenkins and his assistants, Dowling and William Blake, began making plans for the removal of the orphanage from its location next to the grim hulk of the City Jail on Franklin Street to farmland far from the city center along the Ashley River, where Jenkins dreamed the children would play in the open air, eat food they'd grown with their own hands, and gain an elementary school education. Jenkins died in 1937 and the move from downtown came in 1939, but Dowling kept alive the band's tradition of fund-raising tours, especially to New York, where band members received a bit of city polish before returning home or simply went AWOL to join big bands led by Duke Ellington, Bennie Moten, and Count Basie.[23] That Mrs. Dowling knew both Samuel Smalls and Dorothy Heyward shines an interesting sidelight on DuBose Heyward's creation—for the Sam Smalls she and my grandmother describe bears little resemblance to DuBose Heyward's saintly Porgy.[24]

"Us chillen been scared of him, that Sam," Anna Hamilton said in an interview conducted in November 1994, just months before her death. "They said he was a 'bad man,' and you know any time they call someone that, you kinda look at 'em out your eye sideway."[25]

My grandmother claimed, and subsequent research confirmed, that Sam lived not on Cabbage Row, but on the "Neck" of the peninsula, at the Green Tenement on Mount Pleasant Street. And while he ranged all over the peninsula in his goat cart, the place he spent most of his time was Long Alley, another road on the Neck with a post office and a much racier attraction. "What did they call it? The Bull Pen! That's right. The Bull Pen!" she recalled in the musical Gullah she spoke until her dying day. Then she dropped her voice and curled her lip in disapproval. "That was the gambling place."

"Oh, Lawd, you'd see him just going along, just a-singing, a body in a cart with two wheels. . . . I don't know if he had no feet. He mighta had a knee. But he would spring out that wagon and spring in that door, and the goat would stay there all day. You could always tell when he been there—when that goat been out there in the Long Alley."

Smalls was, in fact, a thoroughly unsavory character: a gambler and, it was whispered, a pimp. "Oh, he was a mean man, a drunk and whatnot. And that Bess business!" Mrs. Dowling added with a scornful snort. "It wasn't no Bess. They just wrote it up as a story and put all this Sporting Life and stuff in it." "No, they wasn't no Bess," Grandmother agreed, "but he had plenty of girlfriend. He used to beat 'em, beat 'em with his little goat whip."

This portrait of Smalls is echoed by a surprising source: Ethel Waters, the jazz and blues song stylist and film star. Waters, who grew up in a tough Baltimore neighborhood not unlike the Neck, claimed in her autobiography, *His Eye Is on the Sparrow*, that she "knew the original Porgy in real life." Describing him as "a short, stocky man with no legs and enormous strength in his hands and arms," she added, Frank Wilson, who played the role in the first stage version, "just [didn't have] Porgy's build or physical strength. So I couldn't believe in him when he kills a man with his bare hands."[26] Apparently, neither Waters nor anyone else who knew him had trouble believing that of Sam Smalls. And no one was surprised that, by the end of the decade, he had come to a bad end, one shrouded in mystery.

"Sam was buried north to south," notes Alphonso Brown, a local historian and owner-operator of Charleston's popular Gullah Tours. "Now everybody knows that the spirit of a man buried north to south will not find peace—but this was not, as some folks have written, a sign that the [Black] community rejected Sam, wanted to prevent him from going to God." Instead, Brown argues, this burial practice was grounded in African religious practices and indicated that Sam's people believed he'd been killed by a "root" worker. "Sam's spirit would not rest until he revenged himself on whoever had put the root on him," Brown explained.[27]

White Charlestonians certainly noticed Smalls—his goat cart and reportedly magnificent singing voice made him hard to miss. It is a fact, though, that he would never have become central to the myth of the city had not Heyward, seeking some way of catapulting the divide between himself—a self-educated though talented provincial—and the witty, cultivated sophisticates at the MacDowell Colony for writers, begun to look closer to home for the stuff of fiction. On March 24, 1924, a sensational item about Smalls in the local paper's crime report, virtually the only section where happenings in the African American community were assured of appearing, caught Heyward's attention: "Cripple Accused of Firing at Woman" read the headline. The item went on to recount that Smalls, "commonly seen on King Street with his goat and wagon," apparently had fired "several shot[s] at Maggie Barnes, at 4 Romney Street," then fled the scene in his goat wagon. "Just think of that old wreck having enough manhood left to do a thing like that" was Heyward's wondering reaction before setting pen to paper to explore why.[28]

At one level the short unhappy life of Sam Smalls—gambler, pimp, and community bogeyman used to frighten children into good behavior—is absolutely banal. One finds desperate men in dangerous circumstances like him in small towns and big cities from Charleston to Calcutta. But the apotheosis of Sam from banal reality to myth is achieved in aesthetic terms by splitting the man into three characters: Porgy, a gentlemanly beggar whose poet's temperament and physical infirmities recall his creator's;[29] Sporting Life, the handsome, seductive pimp and drug pusher; and Crown, who mingles elements of the "bad man" of folk tradition with the "beast rapist" of the white American racial imaginary. Real life might well have found Sam Smalls to be—as W. H. Auden opined of Don Giovanni and Tristan—a "dead bore,"[30] but by fracturing him into Porgy, Sporting Life, and Crown—each man fighting for the love of a passionate, beautiful, but fatally weak woman—Heyward was to transcend his tawdry local materials and achieve that passionate focus on a single-minded desire that Auden claimed was the true mark of grand opera. Indeed, we shall see that as Porgy's story moved from page to its first reiteration for the stage—the author's somewhat accidental collaboration with his wife on the Broadway smash *Porgy*—to its final form—the Heyward-Gershwin collaboration *Porgy and Bess*—its creators achieved so exquisite an attunement to popular tastes and the spirit of the times that their creation was able to conquer not just Broadway but the world.

The plot of *Porgy* differs in key respects from that of *Porgy and Bess*; therefore, it bears a quick recap. *Porgy* tells the tale of a disabled beggar who witnesses a murder during a dice game and, in a gesture of chivalry, decides to give shelter to the murderer's woman, the beautiful, dissolute Bess. Neighbors in the tenement where Porgy lives, Catfish Row, are united in their opposition to Porgy's association with "dat muderin' Crown Bess," but realize over time that Porgy and Bess make each other happy and that their happiness only increases when they take in a child orphaned by a hurricane. The idyll is brief, however. The murderer, Crown, returns for Bess, and Porgy, defending his family, strangles Crown to death. The police detain him for contempt of court—basically, fleeing when summoned to the morgue to identify the body—but, never dreaming that he could have been the killer, allow Porgy to return triumphantly to the Row. The triumph takes a tragic turn, however, when our hero learns that while he was away, a group of men down on the wharves has "ganged" the grief-stricken Bess, gotten her drunk, and taken her away on a "ribber boat" to Savannah to resume, it is implied, her old life as a prostitute. The novel ends with an uncompromisingly grim focus on Porgy, stunned with his loss, sinking into a tragically early old age "alone in an irony of sunlight" (196).

The book is beautifully written, stylistically and thematically ambitious, and quite moving—indeed, with the exception of Peterkin, who is just beginning to publish right around the same time, *Porgy*'s only peers in representation of African American subject matter are by African Americans. Reviewers seemed to agree that Heyward had achieved something special. Harry Hervey, writing for the *New York Evening Post*, for example, called the novel "a series of throbbing moments, a ghost of Africa stalking on American soil." Ellen Glasgow said *Porgy* was "born a classic. Nothing finer has occurred in American literature since *Uncle Remus*." The *Nation* found it "a fresh and finished picture of the simple Southern Negro. And because he writes with poetry and penetration his story is a moving one; because he writes with detachment and tenderness . . . a fusion of comedy and tragedy is delicately achieved." Indeed, no less a fan than Langston Hughes called Heyward one who saw, "with his white eyes, wonderful, poetic qualities in the inhabitants of Catfish Row that makes them come alive."[31] In assessments up to the late 1980s, words like "simple," "passionate," and "alive" were occurring with monotonous regularity. Those critics who did not dismiss Heyward out of hand—Du Bois, for example, was deeply annoyed that Heyward wrote about the Black underworld rather than turning that same penetrating insight on white culture[32]—were more or less uniformly enthralled by his "precise" and "penetrating" insights into the "essential" realities of African American life.

But what precisely was it, we must inquire, that was so compelling about Heyward's representations of Catfish Row?

Part of the appeal certainly lay in Heyward's skill at evoking the "dream of a simple life," that pastoral nostalgia whose power as an organizing trope for American thought and culture we have explored at some length. Of course, in asserting that pastoralism is essential to understanding the text, we must also account for the undeniable fact that the action of the novel almost never strays from the urban environment of the city of Charleston. But there's ample evidence to argue that pastoral is embodied not in *Porgy*'s landscape but in the *persons* of the novel's Gullah Geechee protagonists.

We noted in the previous chapter the passionately autochthonous relationship to the land of the Gullah Geechee figures in, for example, Alice Ravenel Huger Smith's paintings. With Catfish Row, Heyward simply moves those figures two generations forward in time, dramatizing the final stages of the postbellum country-to-city migration that emptied the plantation districts of their labor force, a blow from which rice cultivation never recovered. Though living in the city, Porgy and his neighbors remain premodern—the literary embodiment of "the old types," the plantation Negroes, whom Charleston Renaissance artists painted and Society for the Preservation of Spirituals singers imitated. The relationships between Catfish Row and the city's Old Guard are both implied and explicitly stated. Serena Robbins, the social arbiter of the Row, "is a born white-folks nigger," her husband brags just before the murder that sets the plot in motion. "She fambly belong tuh Gob'ner Rutledge. Ain't yer see Miss Rutledge sheself come tuh visit she when she sick. And dem chillen ob mine, dem is raise wid *ways*."[33] The emphasis in this passage, we must note, was original. The most sympathetic white character in the book, meanwhile, is the lawyer Archdale, whose portfolio of duties for the Rutledge family includes "look[ing] after their colored folks," that is, their former slaves (60).

The "colored folks" of the Row may, thus, be bereft of their historic relationship to the land, but not of the "radical innocence of spirit" that that relationship implies.[34] Their relationships with their "white folk" also linger, along with enough of "the old ways" to qualify them, in the novel's frame, as an authentically autochthonous and even ideal folk community: supportive in times of joy as well as in danger, with its own music and rituals, folkways, and even holidays.[35] A poetics of "wistful envy" (116) for the primitive's vaunted capacity for joy commingles with pastoral nostalgia to structure an ultimately conservative and hegemonic portrait of lives that are untrammeled, uncomplicated, happy, even "free." This is one reason for the novel's appeal. But there is another, perhaps even more powerful, and that is the exquisite equipoise Heyward achieves in what Umberto Eco has called the desire of the American consumer to have it both ways: to rely on the "guarantee of the Good" while thrilling to the "shudder of the Bad."[36]

Yes, there are saints on Catfish Row. There's the wounded quest figure Porgy. He's racially pure—Heyward describes his skin as "black with the almost purple blackness of unadulterated Congo blood"—not to mention a philosopher, a poet: the influence of Africa gives something "Eastern and mystic [to] the intense introspection of his look" and makes him whisper delicate little prayers—"Oh, little stars, roll me some light! . . . Roll me a sun and a moon!" (13)—rather than grunt or shout to his dice. Also arrayed on the side of the angels are Maria, the "vast and moist" (50) cook shop proprietress who combines maternal care with a terrifying physical strength and indomitable will; and Serena Robbins, highly religious, aligned with the Old Guard, and an arbiter of social destinies on the Row. But though these "good" characters are, indeed, very, very good, it's the bad ones who are better.

There's Sporting Life, of course, a mulatto trickster figure whose clothes speak of city polish and whose pockets are full of city dope. Vain, deceitful, dangerous to the social order—the widow Serena Robbins, for example, begs him to leave before his loose talk about white women ends in a lynching—he is an obvious product of miscegenation whose rejection of the folk community's values and embrace of all that the white South feared make him a potent symbol of the destructive force of the modern.[37] Even more threatening is Crown, whom Heyward perhaps intended to make a Faustian villain with a terrifying bargain with the devil—though what he succeeds in creating is more along the lines of a racial caricature every bit as extreme as anything out of Thomas Dixon.

This is how Heyward describes Crown's wanton murder of Serena Robbins's husband. Note that emphases are added.

> With a low *snarl*, straight from his *crouching* position, Crown hurled his tremendous weight forward, shattering the lamp, and bowling Robbins against the wall.... The oil from the broken lamp ... blazed up ruddily. Crown was *crouched* for a second *spring*, with *lips drawn from gleaming teeth*. The light fell strong upon *thrusting jaw*, and threw the *sloping brow* into shadow. One hand touched the ground lightly, balancing the *massive torso*. The other arm held the cotton-hook forward, ready, like a *prehensile claw*.... A *heady, bestial stench* absorbed all other odors. A fringe of shadowy watchers crept from cavernous doorways, *sensed it* [the scent?], and commenced to *wail eerily*. (19–20)

The italics tell the story. Crown is described entirely in terms of overwhelming physical power and animalistic threat. His postures, gestures, physiognomy—not to mention his smell—owe more to the gorilla than to the human. A figure of raw, naked aggression, his killing rage and his ease in escaping the authorities threaten the stability of the whole community—not just the African American portion of it.[38]

There's only one character who doesn't fear the murderer's violent streak. She is the third in our trio of "bad" characters, Crown's woman, Bess. When we first meet her, she is stumbling drunk, possibly high on drugs, but in any case so far gone that "the acid of utter degradation" has etched "hard lines" about her mouth and Maria can spy a human soul "flickering [only] feebly" in her eyes as she gives her a meal. Though warned to "eat and trabble, sistah," Bess refuses and latches onto Porgy for "the good money" he "gits fum the w'ite folks" (53). His gentleness tames Bess's ferocity, eventually earning her the grudging acceptance of Maria and Serena. Still, she cannot resist the lure of Sporting Life's happy dus'—a small folded paper of which transforms her into "a maddened woman whirl[ing] like a dervish . . . call[ing] horribly upon her God, striking and clawing wildly" (85). Still less can she refuse Crown's "hot hands." The description of the meeting of the long-separated lovers on Kittiwah Island leaves no doubt as to the nature of Bess's relationship with the killer and foreshadows her eventual fate:

> At the low door of the hut she paused and turned toward him. He laughed suddenly and hotly at what he saw in her face.
> "I know yuh ain't change," he said. "With yuh an' me it always goin' tuh be de same. See?"
> He snatched her body toward him with such force that her breath was forced from her in a sharp gasp. Then she inhaled deeply, threw back her head, and sent a wild laugh out of the clearing.
> Crown swung her about and threw her face forward into the hut. (121)

Porgy's wise, sorrowing tone of nostalgia for a Golden Age, Heyward's general high-mindedness, and his lapidary prose almost prevent us from seeing the obvious—that this is a story that revolves around hot sex, drugs, murder, and mayhem ratcheted to a gothic pitch of horror by the fact that Heyward creates in Catfish Row a more or less perfect panopticon. That is to say, Gullah Geechee identity is figured as a site of freedom from bourgeois social codes—Heyward describes, for example, his "wistful envy" of the movement of Gullah Geechee bodies "exotic as the Congo, and still able to abandon themselves to the wild joy of fantastic play" moving through the streets in colors like a "tropic garden," their dance, dress, and song "intoxicat[ing], . . . madden[ing]" to the senses, "seeming to pull every ray of color from the dun buildings, leaving the sunlight sane, flat, dead" with their passing (114–15). But simultaneously, Heyward's Gullah Geechee are incarcerated in an identity that is synonymous with lack—lack of means, lack of education, and indeed a basic lack of freedom of movement.

Physically, we should note, Catfish Row is not a row at all but a massive three-story brick structure organized around a court, a court that has but one entrance and one exit—in other words, a trap. It's a trap that's haunted by the specter of the glories of the faded plantation regime—Heyward devotes loving attention to describing flagstones that "even beneath the accumulated grime of a century, glimmered with faint and varying pastel shades in direct sunlight"; "high-ceilinged rooms, with . . . battered colonial mantels and broken decorations of Adam designs in plasters" where "governors had come and gone, and ambassadors of kings had schemed and danced."[39] But in its current debased form, as in its previous glorious one, the structure acts a theater of surveillance, discipline, and punishment where African Americans endure and observe their peers enduring various forms of interrogation and ill-treatment by police, coroners, lawyers, landlords, pawnbrokers, and other agents of the disciplinary authority of the symbolic order.

There is no safety in the Row. A steady stream of key characters—Peter, Bess, and finally Porgy—are extracted from it by these authorities and imprisoned for varying periods in the City Jail, a grim hulk built in a Gothic Revival style that Maurie McInnis has identified as "central to the architectural language of slave control" that emerged as an important design element in the city in the wake of the twin terrors of Denmark Vesey and the Nullification Crisis.[40] The jail was part of a "landscape of correction" at what had once been the western edge of the city: a complex of buildings that served as sites of regulation, discipline, and punishment for the city, and especially for its African American population. These buildings included the city's poorhouse; the workhouse where fastidious masters sent their disobedient slaves to be punished; and the medical college that, into Heyward's time, lingered as a specter of terror for poor African Americans. In *Porgy*'s opening chapter, for example, collecting funds to bury Serena Robbins's husband is given added urgency by a mourner's observation that "he gots tuh get buried termorrer ... or de boahd ob healt' will take um, an' give um tuh de students" at the medical school.[41]

From birth to death there is no escape from the panopticon of race. But the worst fate appears to be that living death suffered by the unfortunates incarcerated in the city jail, which Heyward takes pains to describe in some detail:

> The jail in which Bess was incarcerated [after the incident with the "happy dus'"] was no better, and no worse, than many others of its period, and the score of negro women with whom she found herself could not be said to suffer acutely under their imprisonment. When life reaches a certain level of misery, it envelopes itself in a protective anesthesia which deadens the senses to extremes....
>
> By day [the prisoners] were at liberty to exercise in the jail yard, a square of about half an acre surrounded by a high brick wall containing not so much as a single blade of grass. Like a great basin, the yard caught and held the heat which poured from the August sun until it seemed to overflow the rim, and quiver, as though the immense vessel had been jarred from without. But the soaring walls gave always a narrow strip of shade to which the prisoners clung, moving round the sides as the day advanced, with the accuracy of the hand of a sundial.
>
> Before nightfall the prisoners were herded into the steaming interior of the building, and Bess and the other women were locked in a steel cage, which resembled a large dog-pound and stood in the center or a high, square room,

with a passageway round it. A peculiarly offensive moisture clung to the ceiling, and streamed in little rivulets down the walls. An almost unbreatheable stench clogged the atmosphere....

The jailers ... locked them up, gave them a sufficiency of hominy and white pork to sustain life, allowed them to see their visitors, talk and sing to their heart's content. If they were suffering from tuberculosis, or one of a hundred nameless and communicable diseases, when they entered, it was none of the County's affair. And if they left showing that ash-pallor so unmistakable in a negro [as a harbinger of death], it was as lamentable as it was unavoidable. But when all was said and done, what must one expect if one added to the handicap of a dark skin the indiscretion of swallowing cocaine and indulging in a crap game? (92–93)

Thus, we see that Catfish Row, center of Heyward's celebrated folk community, is, in fact, little more than a jail in which inhabitants are incarcerated as surely as they are incarcerated in their dark skins and their Gullah Geechee superstitions. When they leave, it's only to go to literal jails where their poverty and illiteracy leave them completely at the mercy of an indifferent or hostile authority. Heyward adopts a tone of bitter irony toward that jail, but it is, in fact, the city itself that is the perfect jail: a panopticon where African Americans are always under surveillance, unable to escape. Freedom is to be found where there are no humans, places like Kittiwah—where we find Crown sickening for the sound of a human voice but living quite comfortably in a homey little shack of driftwood and palmetto fronds—or in the forests "far to the north" of the Neck and even of neighborhoods like Accabee and Silver Hill, to which Porgy tries to flee when sought for questioning in Crown's death.

To be sure, in depicting Bess as the persecuted maiden trapped in the nightmare landscape of gothic horror, Heyward shatters several important social taboos and seems to establish his bona fides as a southern progressive. It is suggestive, too, that Heyward—his upper body permanently disabled by adolescent bouts with polio and typhoid fever—chose Samuel Smalls, similarly confined in the prison of his body, as the model for his protagonist. But the relentlessness of the characters' entrapment and Heyward's ambivalent representation of racism considerably soften the impact of any apparent critique or identification. We are told at the beginning of the novel that Porgy lived in the Golden Age of beggary—a period when "a man begged, presumably, because he was hungry, much as a man of more energetic temperament became a stevedore from the same cause" (11). This characterization has the effect of naturalizing the African American's place in the southern symbolic order, offering no hint that race or class might play a role in the equation.

Indeed, racism in *Porgy* tends to be individualized, rather than a basic structure of society, and identified with whites, but *not* those of Heyward's class or ethnicity. For example, Heyward swiftly sketches in a "fat German" shopkeeper who laughs at a Negro funeral, a "vile-mouthed, bearded Teuton" who repossesses Negro furniture with blows and terrifying curses (29, 37), and brutal, sneering, Irish policemen who again and again terrorize the residents of the Row. We are meant to deplore and despise all these characters. Upper-class whites, on the other hand, might appear to be indifferent, as in the case of the judge who rules on Porgy's case or the warden too enervated by the August heat to improve conditions at the jail—but more often, as with the lawyer Archdale or the nameless lady in the window who admires Porgy's song, they are sympathetic. Indeed, the social contract operating in Heyward's fictional Charleston appears to be grounded upon a reinscription of the authority of the planter class.[42] The sympathetic characters in the novel belong either to the planter class or to the Gullah Geechee, the peasant folk whom Heyward portrays as serving them and who, though emancipated, do not question their lot in life. The unsympathetic characters tend to be characters who represent a modern threat to the struggling remnants of that ancien régime.

Those include African American characters observed attempting to better their class positions. Only three Black characters in the novel are depicted as having escaped the grinding poverty of the Row, and all have used less than savory methods to do so: the "yellow-skinned" undertaker with the extortionate rates, the lawyer who sells phony divorces to a Negro clientele, and the dope-dealing Sporting Life who excuses his crimes with the justification that he is only seeking "adwantages" (56) in life. The undertaker receives a fleeting mention, and the lawyer's discomfiture at Archdale's hands is treated as a scene of high comedy. But the threats to the social order posed by the trickster / bad man figures, Sporting Life and Crown, are more serious—indeed, they are central to the plot—and so must be treated at length.

Sporting Life—"a slender young octoroon" whose first words are, "Yuh sho got good-lookin' white gals in dis town" (55)—embodies the most stringently enforced of Charleston's many racial prohibitions, the miscegenation taboo, in body and in speech. Crown, meanwhile, completely outside and indifferent to the social order, poses the challenge of utter and unrepentant lawlessness. These threats are allowed to loom large in the narrative, then they are neutralized by figures guaranteed to appeal to the sensibilities of an audience figured as white and bourgeois: the "mammies," Serena and Maria, who join forces against Sporting Life; and Porgy, the artist and man of feeling whose seeming weakness is revealed as strength when he slays Crown, the dragon of the piece. Even the disappearance of Bess, while tragic for Porgy, is necessary to the ritual drama. The threat of her disturbing, animal sexuality must be eliminated to preserve the social order.

It's interesting to note here that the accounts told by my grandmother and

Mrs. Dowling share many elements in common with *Porgy*: the gambling, the threat of violence, the lurid intimations of sexual depravity, drinking, possibly even drugs—though, of course, in the interviews, these details are provided in a veiled language with prim averted glances and eyerolls of disgust that do not translate to print. What Heyward adds to the mix is his vision of Gullah Geechee culture—a culture that has elements of community, simplicity, and dignity that he admires; but also a culture of violence, Hoodoo, and "hysterical" religion to which he ultimately condescends. Heyward stirs his distorted view of Gullah Geechee culture into a potent brew of grotesque bodies, murder, hot sex—neatly capturing the tension between "the guarantee of the Good" and "the shudder of the Bad" and evoking, in the process, fears and fantasies about race within an ultimately antimodernist, paternalistic frame that also allows these fears to be laid to rest. Balancing deftly the tastes of a white South still reeling from the blows of civil war and postwar economic collapse and a white North alarmed by the swelling ranks of immigrants and disaffected southern Blacks within its midst, Heyward achieves a novel widely admired for its literary qualities. But he does not yet have a bona fide hit on his hands. To achieve that milestone, he'll require bodies in motion—African American bodies singing and dancing—and his story, too, will have to be stripped down, disencumbered of all extraneous elements, refined and poured into the vessel of the body so that it can make the leap from the page to the stage. To create the proper formula, he'll require, first and foremost, the right collaborator.

Preparing to Launch: From the Page to the Stage

The textual *Porgy*'s action takes place in a geography that appears to be ludic—to borrow Roland Barthes's term for performative signification marked by freedom, subversion, and spontaneity—but that careful analysis shows is, in fact, carefully controlled by "master" metaphors of incarceration and confinement. Similarly, the story of the novel's transformation into a play and then an opera has been told as a straightforward tale of the triumph of pluck, luck, and talent,[43] but in fact the cultural forces that accompanied this process were fraught with conflict and contestation.

Evidence of precisely how fraught is suggested in this letter written to Heyward by his amanuensis, John Bennett, the fiction writer and folklore collector who was a cofounder of the Poetry Society of South Carolina and one of the mainstays of Charleston's literary and artistic coterie. The letter was written in 1932—*after* Dorothy Heyward's stage adaptation of the novel became a runaway Broadway smash in 1927–28, *after* Al Jolson's radio adaptation and his repeated attempts to secure the rights for film and musical versions, but *before* Heyward signed the crucial contracts with George Gershwin in 1933.

Please note that, except where indicated otherwise, the emphases in the passage are added.

> Dear Old Top:—
>
> I am enclosing you a letter from my boyhood... and life-long friend, [the theatrical producer] George C. Tyler, of New York....
>
> I believe there is here the *opportunity for a great killing*. Review "Journey's End," and "What Price Glory"; put the Negro there *just as he was*, with all his fears, his grotesque hours of courage and well-nigh delirious service... remembering the TWO NEGROES who, in one trench, threw aside their useless muskets and fought it out to an astounding finish, bare-hand, trench-knife, brickbat, stick, hand-to-hand, head-to-belly, for life's sweet sake, *crazy as two wild savages, as battling creatures of all sorts are*... and, by golly, whipped, slew, and captured that invading troop of twenty Germans....
>
> not HEROES, but just MEN, *Negroes, as you know them*, with every *characteristic of the race*... crazy valor, turned to humiliating fear... their emotions, their lusts, their weaknesses, and their pitiful disappointments and small rewards....
>
> Scenes on the road to the front, in the dug-out and the covered trench... I suggest just the one, last great battle in the trench where the cornered negroes... TWO of 'em... fought... *like things demented*... against the *startled sanity* of a troop of German soldiery... confronted by two *mad, demented black devils*....
>
> I shall at once write G.T.C. that I have *communicated his suggestion to you* [emphasis original].... I believe a good story of this kind would cap-sheaf the Negro, and *put the Harlem out of it for good*.[44]

Again, the emphases tell the tale. Perhaps we should not be too critical of Bennett's overriding concern with "the opportunity for a great killing"—the time period was, after all, the Great Depression. But Bennett's paternalistic condescension to the objects of his gaze, his primitivist fascination with "savage" Black masculinity—these are glaringly overt. The letter reveals an aggressive appropriative process in which African American stories and cultural material—"Negroes" as the white South "knew" them, as primitive clay of a consistency just right for shaping into saleable forms—are being seized for the interlocking processes of consumption and production of "hot" theatrical properties.

This should not surprise us. *Porgy* may have been "born in the Golden Age," but the Heywards were clearly children of a global age: full participants in the codes of transatlantic modernism whose sensational celebration (and commodification) of racial essences marked the aesthetic production of everything from Picasso's *l'art nègre* to the global phenomenon of "the Charleston," from Paul Whiteman's "jazz" to the literary sensation of *Cane* and the popular powerhouse *Nigger Heaven*.⁴⁵ Both the Heywards had ambitions to establish themselves as artists of national standing—ambitions that, despite the failure of Heyward's second novel *Angel* (1926) and the drubbing Dorothy Heyward's light farces *Jonica* (1930) and *Cinderelative* (1931) had received from the critics, the couple was beginning to realize. But a shadow of doubt loomed over the proceedings: a consciousness that African Americans were aware of and, at times, quite resistant to the process of being ground out as intellectual property; the simultaneous recognition that African Americans artists, though disadvantaged by the color bar, could come to pose stiff competition in the arms race for artistic authenticity and so one, therefore, needed to strive to "put the Harlem out of it for good."

This argument may, at first, seem a contradiction of what we know of Heyward's professional relationships with African American performers—with people, for example, like Ethel Waters, who starred in *Mamba's Daughters* and wrote warmly of the couple in her autobiography, or James Weldon Johnson, who defended *Porgy and Bess* in *Black Manhattan* and who was happy to allow "Lift Every Voice and Sing," the "Negro National Anthem," to be used in the print version of *Mamba's Daughters*. It may seem equally at odds with the Heywards' commitment to authenticity in ventriloquizing Gullah Geechee voices and representing Gullah Geechee culture. But while Heyward transgressed many of Charleston's rigid social taboos in his career—indeed, the way he met Ethel Waters, at Georgette Harvey's glittering mixed-race bash for Rouben Mamoulian, the director of *Porgy and Bess*, would have been considered a grave social sin in the proper Charleston society that was his social milieu—his relationships across the color line had a certain internal consistency that does not, in fact, appear to have challenged the inherent logic of Jim Crow.⁴⁶

That is to say, what is often poorly understood about the slave and Jim Crow eras is that physical contact, even intimacy, between the races—being unavoidable given the population ratios—could be permitted and even encouraged under certain conditions: the chief one being that such interactions did not challenge the status quo, the racial hierarchy. For example, in the interactions of a mistress and her maid—or a sporting man and his guide—friendliness, sociability, even insolence in the latter could be tolerated without violence to the Jim Crow code because the former's social position in the hierarchy was unassailable. The question is, does the playwright who socializes with his all-Black cast—let us be clear, in Manhattan, at the apex of the Jazz Age, not at home among his less open-minded peers—establish his bona fides as a genuine southern progressive by so doing? Is this more a case of, in a paraphrase of the popular ad campaign, "What happens in Manhattan stays in Manhattan"? Or is something else going on?

Perhaps that question can be best approached by considering the author's relationships across the color line with men who are like himself: not performers of exceptional talent hoping to rise above the herd—the workers of the creative world—but the capitalists, the writers or artists whose ambition it might be to employ those "workers" as they struggled to perfect their craft and jostled for a share of the public's attention. Looking at two of these relationships—with Jean Toomer and Edwin Harleston—may help us to answer more definitively the question about the limits of Heyward's progressive tendencies.

It may come as something of a surprise to learn that Heyward and Toomer were acquainted—if somewhat tangentially—and that their brief encounter was not a happy one. Their acquaintance begins with a letter to the secretary of the Poetry Society of South Carolina, Rex Fuller, on February 19, 1923. Noting that his interest "was focused and stimulated by the Southern number of *Poetry*," guest edited by Heyward and featuring a fair sampling of Charleston writers, Toomer requested—and received—a nonresident membership to the PSSC.[47] The question of race does not appear to have entered Toomer's mind—though for John Bennett, relaxing with the *New York Times Book Review* after a hard day's work editing the PSSC *Year Book*'s roster of members and list of member activities, it precipitated a crisis. Spotting an advertisement for *Cane* that called it "a book about negroes by a negro,"[48] Bennett recalled seeing Toomer's name among the nonresident members and quickly pounded out a near-hysterical letter to Heyward. The emphases, it should be noted, are his own.

> Whether this individual joined the Society with the deliberate intention of starting trouble for us if ejected, or of causing a row by discovery that the Poetry Society of South Carolina had a negro member, I do not know. I fear all this may come out with the publication of this book in the Fall, by BONI & LIVERIGHT. There must be reviews of the author and book procured by B. & L. in papers seen by our members resident and non-resident. There may possibly be inserted somewhere, in some paper unaware of the row, or delighted with it, the fact that TOOMER, the author of "Cane," "a book about negroes by a negro," is a MEMBER OF THE POETRY SOCIETY OF SOUTH CAROLINA.
>
> Now, what is to be done? Strike out the book-notice and expunge the name from the list of members? Refuse further membership by stating that TOOMER obtained such on false pretenses . . . ?
>
> How to prevent more TOOMERS, and more BOOBS from becoming members of various sorts . . . is another searching query. . . .
>
> It is to laugh! Eh? Or not to laugh?[49]

Bennett's fears were realized. Somehow the news of a "colored" member did leak out, prompting letters of protest from some society members.[50] Even the eventual compromise—removing the list of "activities" in total from the 1923 *Year Book*—occasioned "gossip" in Charleston.[51] Meanwhile, the revocation of Toomer's membership occasioned the same in Harlem circles, as attested by Toomer's November 7, 1923, letter to Walter White in which he denies knowledge of the controversy. Toomer, somewhat defensively citing his desire to stay "in touch with Southern literary matters," explains in detail his interactions with the society: "[As for my] inclusion in the Society's Year Book[,] I have not seen this book as yet, and so, whether or not I'm there, I do not know. But nothing that has happened thus far, that I am aware of, would lead me to expect an exclusion. . . . Where Mr. Spingarn received his information, I do not know."[52]

Heyward's side of the correspondence—if it exists—has not been found, so it cannot shed light on his reactions to the controversy. But we do have some evidence of Heyward's reactions to another mixed-race artist with pretensions: Edwin Augustus Harleston, whose proposed exhibition of paintings at the Charleston Museum had been scheduled and abruptly canceled in 1926, within the time horizon in which Heyward was beginning to sketch out ideas for the 1929 novel that he clearly intended as his masterwork, *Mamba's Daughters*. Harleston, in fact, makes an appearance in *Mamba's Daughters*, a none too flattering one, as the character Frank North, member of an effete and pretentious mulatto elite that Heyward gleefully parodies.

The choice of the name North is suggestive—gesturing toward the direction of the character's aspirations, unlike a name like Harleston, one of the most storied names in the Charleston social register, which points directly and quite awkwardly to social practices of blood mixture that the "code" demanded that Heyward ignore. This awkwardness about the origins of skin color also infects Heyward's characterization of his heroine, Lissa, "light bronze" in color even though both her grandmother and mother are very dark. We are assured that she is not a product of miscegenation, but apparently a genetic sport—beautiful, refined, artistically gifted—one of nature's aristocrats. North is inevitably drawn to Lissa—and in this scene tries to impress her with a viewing of his paintings.

> The studio was a large, airy second-story room, and a number of portraits were already hung, while many more were stacked against the walls. The group scattered, examining the paintings and exclaiming over them. Lissa was left standing alone before two portraits, a man and a woman in middle life. Then she recognized them as the Broadens. She wondered why she had been so slow in knowing them. The likenesses were good, she could see that the features were those of her host and hostess of a few nights ago. What was the difference? . . . Then in a swift revealing moment she had the answer. In spite of the fact that the drawing was well done and the features characteris-

tically negro, they gave an effect of not being negroes at all, but white people painted in darker shades—some subtle racial element was lacking....

North came and stood beside her, looking eagerly at her face for her verdict. She tried to find words for her inchoate impressions.

"I can see you know a heap about painting. Those pictures are just like Mr. and Mrs. Broaden, only they don't look like coloured people and the Broadens do." North was slightly dashed in spirit. "That's a matter of artistic technique," he explained. "You learn to paint in the academy by a certain method, a method that has been used by great artists, then you apply that technique to your own subjects. After all, if the pictures look like them, that's about all that we can do, isn't it?" (243–44)[53]

It's fascinating to note Heyward appears most disturbed by the achievement for which we have praised Harleston in the previous chapter: North's paintings "are just like" their subjects, and yet "they don't look like colored people." Instead of conveying a "subtle racial element"—or perhaps we could translate that as "projecting a stereotypical notion of racial phenotype"—North's paintings present a world of "white people painted in darker shades," where the question "What was the difference?" seems queasily unanswerable. Whether Heyward posits his paint-by-numbers notion of North's/Harleston's technique because he is convinced of its truth, or whether his concern is simply to draw a stronger contrast with Lissa's "native from the dirt up" (333) musical talent, is simply impossible to say from the available evidence. What we can argue, however, is that Lissa's gift for song is not threatening, can indeed be celebrated, because it is not just stereotypically Negro, it's archetypally so, while North's talent threatens because, nurtured by years of study in an elite northern institution, it challenges the very notion of innate racial inferiority. Lissa's singularity—we are assured again and again of her uniqueness—and her peculiarly American genius for song—Africa's racial gift, to return to terms that W. E. B. Du Bois would have understood, shaped, though untainted, by European training—in no wise constitutes a threat to the status quo equivalent to that posed by a Negro like North—financially secure, academically trained, perhaps with the means and opportunity to protest against unfair treatment (as Harleston did by founding Charleston's chapter of the NAACP) and to compete against similarly endowed whites.

In the final pages of *Mamba's Daughters*, this submerged conflict becomes even more overt. Saint Wentworth, Lissa's white patron and the moral center of the novel, has traveled to New York to see Lissa's debut on the opera stage. Flanked by his mother and sister, he sits in the audience musing about Lissa's artistry—"Primitive?—Sophisticated?—Neither—both"; dreaming that his son—"the *boy*"—may succeed where the father has failed and paint or write or even sing; wondering if Lissa's achievement signifies that he should, upon his return home, start offering the Negro banker, Broaden, the courtesy of calling him "Mister." "'Black menace,'" Saint muses, as he wonders what his friends would think. "Absurd, looking from this distance" (335). But the novel leaves the question unresolved.

On the one hand, *Mamba's Daughters* seems to offer the hope that art will eventually trump prejudice—a hope that many of the artists and philosophical architects of that other renaissance up north shared. And indeed, Heyward's faith in Black performed art is strong. The novel—written during the period in which Dorothy and DuBose Heyward were hard at work on the stage adaptation of *Porgy* for Broadway—is suffused with his love of Black music and Black performance: traveling from dignified churches where "authentic" spirituals are never sung to the revival meetings of the "holy rollers"; giving voice to the musical cries of street vendors and rhythmic work songs down on the wharves; even traveling to country dancehalls far to the north of the city to describe the roots of that worldwide dance sensation, the Charleston. But his own role in bringing that great getting-up morning to pass was to be an ambivalent one.

All these elements, we should note, also make their way into the Heyward-and-Heyward stage version of *Porgy* (not to mention *Porgy and Bess*)—though the Gullah Geechee speech had to be almost immediately jettisoned. In spite of the fact that *Porgy*'s original stage directions called for Gullah Geechee to be spoken, then gradually "tempered to the audience's ear,"[54] northern audiences simply rebelled at even a few moments of unintelligibility, according to a rueful account by Dorothy Heyward. "The whole of the play became a translation," she was to write later, "the language of 'Porgy' ... so thoroughly tempered to the Northern ear that, should it ever fall on the astonished ear of Porgy's prototype, he would never know what it was all about."[55]

Ironically, with this exchange of racial authenticity for a concomitant gain in "universality," *Porgy* was to become a veritable moneymaking machine on Broadway. It ran a total of 367 performances at two theaters in 1927 and 1928 and returned for 34 more performances in 1929 after a successful regional tour.[56] James Weldon Johnson was to include an enthralled account in *Black Manhattan*, raving that "*Porgy* loomed high above every Negro drama that had ever been produced."[57] If the play's success points up the limits of the Jazz Age audience's interest in and acceptance of racial authenticity, it also created conditions that pointed out the limits of Heyward's tentative vision of racial equality through art. For all Heyward's respect for African American musical ability, there was simply no question that when it came time to create a musical version of *Porgy*, white collaborators would be doing the making. George Gershwin—the "prince of Broadway," Dorothy Heyward called him in her unpublished autobiography—was always DuBose Heyward's first choice. But even that choice was to be complicated and contested one.

The story of how Gershwin discovered Porgy is an oft-told tale. As early as 1920 Gershwin had expressed his ambition to write "operettas that represent the life and spirit of this country.... After that may come opera."[58] In 1925, he spoke several times with critics on this theme, telling a correspondent for *Musical America*, "I think [jazz opera] should be a Negro opera, almost a Negro 'Scheherazade.' Negro, because it is not incongruous for a Negro to live jazz. It would not be absurd on the stage. The mood could change from ecstasy to lyricism plausibly because the Negro has so much of both in his nature. The book, I think, should be an imaginative, whimsical thing like a Carl Van Vechten story; and I would like to see him write the libretto."

Later that year, Gershwin told an interviewer for *Musical Canada* that Van Vechten was, in fact, working on helping him find a suitable book for his "jazz opera": "I shall certainly write an opera.... I shall write it for niggers. Blacks sing beautifully. They are always singing; they have it in their blood. They have jazz in their blood, too, and I have no doubt that they will be able to do full justice to a jazz opera.... I do not think there will be undue difficulty about finding principals for the solo parts. There will probably be a nigger orchestra."[59] We should note that strong prejudices barred African Americans from the opera stage—the color bar at New York's Metropolitan Opera was not broken until 1947 and, despite Marian Anderson's heralded debut in 1955, the Met did not have a Black singer on full-time contract until 1962.[60] Thus, Gershwin's determination to make use of African American singers and musical idioms was, in its way and for its time, remarkable—regardless of his beliefs on the blood quantum of Black musicality or the language he used to express it. But his friend Van Vechten was not, in fact, to be a partner in this venture. Instead, in 1926, longtime friends Lou and Emily Paley gave Gershwin a copy of *Porgy*, which, legend has it, the composer devoured in a single night.[61]

We are told that Gershwin fell in love with the novel, determined immediately that he wanted to collaborate with Heyward on an opera version and wrote him to that effect—but he, too, had a rival for the honor: the "jazz singer" and blackface entertainer Al Jolson, whose interest in the role verged, according to Alpert, on obsession. While Gershwin delayed going to work on the project that was to become *Porgy and Bess* for nearly nine years—diverted by other projects and also by a dispassionate artistic self-assessment that he wanted time to study orchestration and build a body of work that would prepare him for the serious undertaking he had in mind—Jolson pursued the role with fervor. On the heels of the Heyward-and-Heyward Broadway production in 1927–28, he asked for and received permission for a radio adaptation and followed that with an offer of $30,000 for the rights to a "talking picture" version. "It sounded like big money to us," Dorothy Heyward wrote in her unpublished autobiography. "There was no one to tell us he price would one day rise to a million."

The stock market crash of 1929 killed that project. But the contest for Porgy's soul was renewed in 1932 when Jolson approached the Heywards' Broadway producers with a new proposition: a stage musical version of *Porgy* featuring the hit-making team from *Show Boat*, Jerome Kern and Oscar Hammerstein II. Jolson, of course, would star—in blackface. Dorothy Heyward describes what happened next in her unpublished autobiography. "DuBose objected that Gershwin was to write the musical. 'When?' was the answer from the Theatre Guild. To a couple, habitually hard up, the Jolson musical was a sore temptation." But it was a temptation the Heywards were able to resist. The impasse broke when "[DuBose] phoned George in New York and left out all the fancy persuasion. He said, 'I think Al Jolson is great, but I want a Negro. I have the greatest admiration for Jerome Kern, but I want you. I have the greatest admiration for Oscar Hammerstein, but I want myself. I've been thinking about and planning this opera for seven years. I'll go on waiting. But please make it within the next seven.' George answered, 'I'll drop everything and start work tomorrow.'"[62] And Gershwin was as good as his word, finally writing Heyward amid a busy production schedule and the planning of a trip abroad to inform him that he was at last ready to begin serious exploration of the collaboration based on his novel.[63]

Let's consider the unfolding of events for just a moment before moving on. The Jolson project was certainly attractive financially—with one of the most bankable stars of the era, it would have been an almost surefire hit in tough financial times, in contrast to the risky labor of love that was all Gershwin would promise. Ultimately, both Gershwin and Heyward seem to have come together on the basis of shared passions and shared prejudices. Both men loved African American music and shared a conviction that its fusion with European forms represented entirely new possibilities for art.[64] At the same time, both men had a passion for "authenticity" that neither was willing to compromise. Jolson's offer was solid gold—gold that Heyward was able to resist with the mantra "I want a negro," while Gershwin, too, had turned down a commission, including a $5,000 bonus, to mount a new American opera for the Met when he realized he could adapt *Porgy* at the venue only if he used Met (i.e., white) singers for the roles.[65]

If blackface minstrelsy was indeed "people's culture" in the nineteenth century, a form elevating Black types to national mythology, then this decision signals a sea change, a shift in taste: the white performer with his burnt cork and sad clown's lips is no longer held by the national kinesthetic imaginary to be an adequate representation of the original. If mimicry is indeed "at once resemblance and threat," as Bhabha has written,[66] then we see played out in Jolson's exclusion the recapitulation of an ancient and bitter backstage drama: a performance in which the leading roles are in the process of being recast. Roach's perceptive observation—that "[e]ven as parody, performances... raise the possibility of replacement of the authors of the representation by those whom they imagined into existence as their definitive opposites"—is quite apropos here.[67] Jolson's contested and ultimately denied desire to play the role of Porgy brings into sharp focus a cultural shift in which he became emblematic not of the folk, but of the fake.

But mimicry's threat cuts in more than one direction. The Heyward-Gershwin collaboration represents an attempt to speak not just for *but also in the voice of* the American Negro. On the one hand, the endeavor could be justified by Heyward's Gullah Geechee roots, by Gershwin's genius at transforming the sounds and rhythms he heard uptown in Harlem—among many others, we must be clear—into a product that, though commercial, was never merely slick.[68] On the other hand, if we consider the actual effect of all this mirroring and doubling—the fact that the mirror effect of Heyward and Gershwin's original masking would be redoubled yet again by overturning performance convention to place African American singers in the roles—we would have to conclude that this might impose special burdens of authenticity upon the collaboration: questions less of whether singers capable of tackling the roles could be found, the types of questions that occupied producers, but of whether such singers, when found, could embrace the music they were asked to sing. This was a burden that could not be satisfied as simply as it was during the heyday of minstrelsy—I'm recalling here the nineteenth-century convention of the quasi-mystical encounter, as described by Eric Lott, in which Black performance was transmitted to white mimic in a process as miraculous as it was brief. Here, it appears that, with the composition of *Porgy and Bess*, Heyward's passion for the music demanded, and Gershwin's own perfectionism would accept no less than, a ritualistic immersion in the cultural landscape of the Gullah Geechee Coast and the music that had emerged from it.

Gershwin made only two visits to Charleston during the twenty months—as the critic Joseph Swain notes "a prodigious length of concentrated effort for any Broadway composer"[69]—it took to compose and orchestrate *Porgy and Bess*, but they seem to have been transformative. The first was a brief holiday visit between December 1933 and January 1934 in which Gershwin experienced the songs of Gullah Geechee street vendors and was impressed by a spiritual, "Oh, Dr. Jesus," sung at Macedonia AME Church. Both of these elements—transmuted into the street songs of the "Honey Man,"[70] "Strawberry Woman," and "Crab Man" and into the hymn "Oh, Doctor Jesus" that saves a fevered Bess's life—appear in the final score.[71]

But Heyward's adamant insistence that Gershwin had barely scratched the surface of the region's musical riches brought the composer back for a second visit that stretched over five weeks in June and July 1934—and it's this visit that has entered Charleston Renaissance legend. Arriving with his cousin, painter Henry Botkin, and his valet, Paul Mueller—as well as his golf clubs and paints—the dapper Gershwin found himself in a four-room cottage on the ocean side of Folly Beach, directly opposite the Heywards' beach cottage, Follywood. The three men were completely inadequate to the domestic arrangements—the house had no closets, hot water, or telephone, though Gershwin, to his vast surprise, found a Jewish delicatessen. Dorothy Heyward solved the problem by engaging a maid.[72]

Gershwin marinated in music while in South Carolina—he heard performances by the Society for the Preservation of Spirituals at a private home and repaid the favor by playing portions of the opera for his hosts. He traveled down the coast to Rockville, on Wadmalaw Island, and listened to Black singers from the cast of *Plantation Echoes* performing at the home of Edings Whaley Wilson.[73] "James Island with its large population of primitive Gullah Negroes lay adjacent, and furnished us with a laboratory in which to rest our theories, as well as an inexhaustible source of folk material," wrote Heyward.[74] And while Gershwin's cousin Botkin tried his hand at painting scenes and characters from *Porgy and Bess*, for Gershwin there were also the inevitable visits to churches.

Heyward, for example, describes a visit to a sanctified church in Folly Beach where spirituals were sung in the old way: "The Gullah Negro prides himself on what he calls 'shouting.' This is a complicated rhythmic pattern beaten out by feet and hands as an accompaniment to the spirituals, and is indubitably an African survival. I shall never forget the night when, at a Negro meeting on a remote sea island, George started 'shouting' with them. And eventually to their huge delight stole the show from their champion 'shouter.' I think that he is probably the only white man in America who could have done it."[75] Gershwin seems to have agreed. He told Anne Brown, the twenty-year-old Juilliard student whom he cast very much against type as his original Bess, that one of the church elders told him afterward, in a passage that recalls the minstrelsy initiation ritual described by Lott, "By God, you sure can beat out them rhythms, boy. I'm over seventy years old and I ain't never seen no po' little white man take off and fly like you. *You could be my own son*" (emphasis added).[76]

Of course there was another incident in a church, recounted in Dorothy Heyward's unpublished autobiography, that is somewhat less flattering to the composer.

> Once we took George to a Holy Rollers church [near the couple's summer home, Dawn Hill, in Hendersonville, N.C.]. . . . As we sat inconspicuously in the back row, our hosts managed to forget all about us and really went to town. . . . They began to leap up and down the aisles and to talk in unknown tongues. I had never heard this before—nor since. And I did not hear nearly enough of it then. I was beginning to feel on the very verge of doing some leaping myself and taking a crack at an unknown tongue when George's iron

grip on my arm lifted me right out of my seat and out the door. DuBose, who had been fascinated and entranced, followed us in bewilderment.

He said, "You didn't like it?"

George said, "I've never been so scared in my life. Why those people were carried out of themselves. They could have torn us to pieces without knowing what they were doing."

The thought that the gentle people we knew the congregation to be by day, suddenly turning into fiends by night, amused DuBose and me as a strange Northern idea. But it was not a wasted evening. In November, 1934, George wrote DuBose, "I start and finish the storm scene with six different prayers sung simultaneously . . . the effect we heard as we stood outside the Holy Rollers Church."[77]

The anecdote reveals much more about this trio of moderns than its teller may have realized: the fascinated, fetishizing gaze of two tourist consumers being disrupted, at least for a moment, by the third's dread at confronting too directly the uncanniness of the Other; the fact that even this experience may then be transformed by the alchemy of artistic creation into a *beautiful uncanny* that heightens the terror of one of the most powerful scenes in the opera's second act.

So, yes, Gershwin encountered music in South Carolina that was to influence his composition in ways large and small. "Authentic" touches include spirituals ("Oh, Doctor Jesus," "Oh, Dere's Somebody Knockin' at the Door") lifted in whole and in part from their original sources, street cries, work songs sung by Black longshoremen at the Charleston docks ("It Takes a Long Pull to Get There"). The literature on the admixture of additional elements in the score—jazz, blues, Hebrew sacred music, Russian folk elements, Yiddish and "American" musical theater, and classical orchestration—is vast, fascinating, and well worth taking the time and trouble to explore.

But for our purposes what may be most provocative is the notion that musical ideas may have been the *least* of what Gershwin sought and found in South Carolina. That is, the summer idyll with the Heywards appears to have allowed Gershwin to immerse himself in both a romantically alien landscape and a powerful experience of radical rural innocence for which he—one of F. Scott Fitzgerald's "Beautiful People," living amid the sophistication, the corruption, and the gay dissipations of Manhattan—may have deeply hungered without necessarily even realizing it. The anecdotes about Gershwin "going native"—swimming, golfing, going shirtless and unshaven, tanning brown as a "nut," in contrast to his immaculate dress and bearing in New York City—abound.

And music critics have drawn attention to the impact these experiences had on the musical language of the piece: that sense Gershwin is able to convey of a story unfolding in a timeless wilderness at the edge of an eternal sea, as Wilfrid Mellers argues in his remarkable study, *Singing in the Wilderness*. The opera's theme, Mellers persuasively argues, is "the search for an equilibrium between the 'black' jungle and the 'white' town that exist, whatever the color of our skin, within us all."[78] This was the human universal that Gershwin perceived nearly a decade before writing the opera, in his earliest reading of *Porgy*: Catfish Row as a Black Eden, alienated and oppressed by the modern, equally embattled by the corruption of authorities without and human vice within. Stripped of all vernacular elements that might hinder comprehension, wrapped in a gorgeous, unforgettable score, and "authentically" embodied within the persons of a Black cast whose vocal talent and star quality were rivaled only by their good looks, these universals were to drive *Porgy and Bess* to the center of national—and global—kinesthetic imaginaries and to keep it there for nearly two decades.

The iconic status that *Porgy and Bess* was eventually to assume in global culture was a fate that seemed by no means certain when the show finally opened on Broadway on October 10, 1935, after nearly a decade of delays, a month of arduous rehearsals, a concert performance at Carnegie Hall, and tryouts in Boston. Despite a rapturous reception on opening night, with an audience of luminaries—Hollywood's Katharine Hepburn and Joan Crawford, bestselling novelist Edna Ferber, famed violinist Fritz Kreisler, and Algonquin Round Table writer Robert E. Sherwood—erupting into applause throughout, even bringing the show to a full halt on "I Got Plenty o' Nuttin,'"[79] the critics immediately began sharpening their knives, and the drone of controversy—"Is it an opera?" "Is it musical theater?" "Is it authentically Negro?" "Is it warmed-over Tin Pan Alley?"—seemed to overwhelm the positive word of mouth.

A few quotes reveal the tone of the debate.

Duke Ellington was annoyed, saying Gershwin had "borrowed from everyone from Liszt to Dickie Wells kazoo." Virgil Thomson, apparently forgetting that he himself had tried his hand at a "Negro opera" in 1934—*Four Saints in Three Acts*, with a libretto by Gertrude Stein—damned it in *Modern Music* as a "libretto that never should have been accepted on a subject that never should have been chosen [by] a man who should never have attempted it.... Folk-lore subjects recounted by an outsider are only valid as long as the folk in question is unable to speak for itself, which is certainly not true of the Negro in 1935."[80] Nettled, William Youngren, writing in the *New Republic*, shot back, "Nor was it true of Spaniards and Spanish Gypsies 60 years earlier, but one is grateful that such fine scruples did not keep Bizet from composing *Carmen*."[81]

It's difficult to say what role the controversy played in depressing ticket sales, but the show closed after only 124 New York performances—an unprecedented hit for an opera, a ruinous financial failure by Broadway's standards. And that might have been the end... but for the fact that Gershwin died less than eighteen months later of a brain tumor—the event's suddenness, its tragedy, bringing renewed attention to all his work but especially to this most ambitious of his works. Immediately, there were memorial concerts featuring Todd Duncan (Porgy), Anne Brown (Bess), and Ruby Elzy (Serena). Less than a year later a series of revivals began, each one more popular, critically acclaimed, and financially successful than the one before. The first was a Merle Armitage production in Los Angeles and San Francisco in 1936, aborted by the Great Southern California Flood. This was followed, first, by DuBose Heyward's death in 1940 and, next, by Cheryl Crawford's drastically cut version in 1941—which, among other omissions, sought to cut Heyward's name from the credits. Crawford's version vastly outperformed the original, with 286 performances on Broadway, a forty-eight-city tour, and a return engagement in New York that didn't close until 1944. Hard on the heels of that success, the U.S. government gave the show its imprimatur, permitting a ninety-minute USO version in 1944 that was said to have "exactly suited" the nation's wartime mood. And after Europe had clearly signaled its interest, staging versions with white singers in Copenhagen, Moscow, Zurich, Stockholm, and other music capitals during and after the war, Robert Breen and Blevins Davis made *Porgy and Bess* a global phenomenon, a so-called cultural ambassador for American values, enlisting U.S. State Department support to take the show to major performance venues on four continents from 1952 to 1956.

Throughout this chapter we have worked diligently to unravel putatively seamless myths about the origins of *Porgy* and *Porgy and Bess*. But it's here—at the moment when the deaths of its creators allow the story to achieve, as it were, escape velocity from their intentions—that the work of art begins to take its place in the global imaginary. While the hybrid elements of its composition carried certain potentials, it's during the wartime and immediate postwar years that the show begins to fulfill its circum-Atlantic promise, gradually becoming something more than a show: becoming, rather, a ludic space, a performative vortex alternating Foucauldian oppression with carnivalesque release.[82]

Porgy and Bess displays its Foucauldian face most unambiguously within the U.S. cultural context—as revealed by the persistence of, and the persistent denial of, controversies of race in its performance and reception history. Broadway historian Joseph Swain, for example, may have thought that he was putting to rest a controversy then sixty years old when he wrote in 1990, "The social and political implications of *Porgy and Bess* for the black community are very real and quite complex, and require discussion, but ultimately they are irrelevant to any dramatic appraisal of the work. This may be difficult to swallow for some.... But such defects lie apart from the musical-dramatic issues with which the composer is wrestling, and modern opera goers forget politics as part of their suspension of disbelief that allows them to enter into the medium in the first place." While acknowledging the complexities of the social and racial issues involved, acknowledging indeed that *someone* must at *some point* discuss them, Swain simply avoids the issues, arguing for the separation of art from context. This is a strategy of evasion and denial that's different only in degree from Alpert's strategy of dismissing audience discomfort with stereotyping out of hand or Tommasini's of insisting that, while such concerns might have been relevant in the past, they have been transcended and no longer need concern either critics or audiences. Each strategy absolves the work—and the artists—by extracting them from their social history and excusing them from any complicity in social practices of exclusion and oppression. Such evasions, ironically, ensure that the controversies will continue to fester by leaving the disciplinary superstructure of disadvantage both underexamined and unchallenged.

The fact is, if we consider Swain's "reasonable," middle position, he is mistaken on all points. On the one hand, there's considerable evidence that the opera's "social defects" do, in fact, inhibit its ability to evoke that willing "suspension of belief" that is necessary to enjoying a work of theater. Arguing otherwise requires ignoring the inconvenient fact that the opera enjoyed its heyday of financial success and popularity during decades when racial apartheid in the United States was at its strongest. The first attempt at a production in the post–*Brown v. Board* era, as this retrograde worldview was collapsing, was the disastrous 1959 Samuel Goldwyn film version, starring Sidney Poitier, Dorothy Dandridge, Pearl Bailey, and Sammy Davis Jr.—so embarrassing a failure due to withering reviews and a highly effective NAACP boycott of segregated southern theaters that Goldwyn yanked the film from theaters in disgust and left instructions in his will that it was to be removed from distribution.[83] Despite highly praised productions that have belatedly ushered *Porgy and Bess* into the opera repertory—at the Houston Grand Opera in 1976, the Metropolitan Opera (at last!) in 1985 (with revivals in 1989 and 1990), Trevor Nunn's Glyndebourne production in 1986 (expanded and videotaped for television in 1993), Covent Garden (1992), and limited performances at the New York City Opera in 2000 and 2002[84]—*Porgy and Bess* has for long periods been absent from the repertory.[85]

More importantly, Swain's argument that sociracial issues can—or should—be separated from musical-dramatic ones simply founders on the rocks of the facts, for Gershwin iterated and reiterated again and again in interviews that his aims were not only musical and dramatic but social and racial too. He states, with an insistence that verges on monotony, his desire both to create a new idiom in music and to do it with African American styles and singers. And if his stated words offer any reason for doubt, his social interactions with his cast throw his apparent sincerity into sharp relief. A few anecdotes may serve to illustrate the point. Todd Duncan and Anne Brown—stars of the original Broadway production whose reminiscences were not recorded until the 1990s and not published until 2004—recall in vivid detail Gershwin's attempt to overcome their initial skepticism. Both classically trained—Duncan, son of a pianist from Danville, Kentucky, was on the voice faculty at Howard University; Brown, a doctor's daughter from Baltimore, was a student at Juilliard—they came to audition for Gershwin with chips firmly planted on shoulders. Duncan, for example, notes, "My training had been strictly classical and I *simply had no interest in any show business stuff*. But when I received a phone call from George Gershwin, well, it was pretty difficult to say no. So up to New York I went on the train one day. I sang an old Italian aria that day, 'Lungi dal caro bene.' Well, number one, he didn't understand because he thought I was going to sing 'Shortnin' Bread' or 'Ol' Man River' or some Negro spiritual—something 'niggery,' you know. That's what he thought. But I sang what I loved and what I wanted to sing" (emphasis added).

Gershwin stopped Duncan from singing after twelve measures, gave him some stage business to perform, then asked him to start again. After only twelve measures, Gershwin stopped Duncan again—greatly annoying him—and offered him the title role. "Now guess what I had the nerve to say? I didn't say, 'Yes, I'll be glad to be your Porgy.' . . . I said, 'Mr. Gershwin, I have to hear your music first.' Oh, he loved it! He just loved it! He then said, 'Well, we can arrange that. Could you come back next week?'"[86]

Brown tells quite a similar story about her audition:

> I sang a French aria by Massenet, several German lieder, Russian songs in English, even a Gershwin melody. And George Gershwin was full of praise. And then he asked me to sing a Negro spiritual. Well, unless one is nearly as old as I am and has lived in the United States before the Second World War and understood the insidious damage racial prejudice can afflict on both the victim and the racist, it may be difficult to understand my reaction at that moment. I said, "Well, weren't you satisfied with what I sang?" And he said, "Yes, of course, it was lovely—beautiful." "But why do people always ask Negro singers to sing spirituals as if that is the only thing that they should be singing and not German lieder or French arias." I was very much on the defensive. George Gershwin simply looked long at me and he said, "Ah huh, I understand." And I realized that he *did* understand and then I wanted more than anything else to sing a spiritual for him. How dumb I had been! Wasn't this to be an opera about Negroes? "I didn't bring any accompaniment for a spiritual," I said, "but I could sing one without accompaniment if you would like." "Oh, yes, please do," he said. So I sang a spiritual, "A City Called Heaven." And when I finished I knew that I had never sung it better nor would I ever sing it better.[87]

Though Brown was as physically unlike Bess as could be imagined—all schoolgirlish innocence and café au lait skin—Gershwin soon decided that he had to have her as Bess and was even prepared to fight his producers to get her.[88]

The performance history of the original cast production is full of moments like these: moments in which both members of the cast and Broadway's crown prince reveal themselves as being fully aware of—and actively negotiating—the complex social, racial, and musical dynamics at play in their interactions. As anecdote piles on anecdote—Duncan threatening to settle things "man to man" with Gershwin for paying too-pointed attention to his wife, with Gershwin's honest apology cementing their friendship; Gershwin patiently teaching John Bubbles, who taught Fred Astaire to tap but could not read music, to learn the timing of Sporting Life's songs by dancing them; Gershwin chaffing his cast of middle-class northerners and midwesterners for their vast ignorance of southern and street culture; Gershwin hosting intimate lunches, showing up at Black parties, even offering to bunk with Duncan in a "colored" home on the road rather than staying in segregated hotels—what quickly becomes clear is that, even though the power dynamics between composer and cast were in no way equal, the performers also felt themselves to be partners in the enterprise of achieving his vision. They were clear that what they were participating in was not Black, nor white, but Gershwin's singular contribution to what we might call "the changing same"; and they expressed no apparent alienation from their labor with him.

Duncan tells a particularly moving anecdote in which Ruby Elzy—whose Serena performs the show-stopping aria "My Man's Gone Now"—gave a rendition of the spiritual "Oh, Doctor Jedus" at rehearsal that was so powerful that the entire cast and crew were held rapt long moments after she finished. Gershwin, moving slowly as if spellbound from the back of the theater to the front, seemed moved nearly to tears. "He knew then"—indeed, they all knew, Duncan says—"that he had put on paper accurately and truthfully something from the depth of the soul of a South Carolina Negro woman who feels the need of help and carries her troubles to God."[89]

Of course there were all too many reminders that the rough equality of the collaboration went no further than the theater footlights. One of those reminders came during rehearsals with what initially seemed a compliment: Duncan was flattered one day to notice that Lawrence Tibbett of the Metropolitan Opera—then considered the greatest baritone in the world—seemed to have begun haunting the rehearsal hall, attending almost daily for several weeks. The cast's pleasure in the great man's attention quickly turned to shocked hurt and disappointment when they realized that RCA, Gershwin's record company, had hired Met stars Tibbett and Helen Jepson for the official cast recording. Brown notes, "We were all so young in the business that we knew that there was simply nothing to be done about it." Gershwin, she says, apologized for the slight with the words, "I would prefer that you and Todd would sing these parts but I don't have much to say about it. This is business."[90]

A potential crisis was narrowly averted near the end of the run by Gershwin. Upon learning that the final performance was to occur at Washington's segregated National Theatre, Duncan and Brown dug their heels in and threatened a boycott. Brown recalled, "And I can remember as if it were yesterday that the other members who stood around me, particularly Matthews who sang Jake ... said, 'You can't refuse. Who do you think you are? This is your first experience on the stage and you think you can say where you will sing and where you will not? Well, you'll be blacklisted for the rest of your career.' And I said, 'I don't give a damn.... I'm not going to sing in Washington.'" This time Gershwin took a hand. He strong-armed his producers at the Theatre Guild, who reached a compromise with the National Theatre management to suspend the policy for the week of the run. The following week, Brown noted satirically in her interview, the National rolled out the red carpet for Ethel Waters—playing once again to a whites-only audience.[91]

These struggles highlight a phenomenon that is central to understanding the Foucauldian underpinnings of *Porgy and Bess*'s U.S. performance history: that while giving means of employment, self-determination, self-expression, and of course stardom to so many Blacks in the entertainment industry, it has also served as a tool of white supremacist cultural imperialism. These effects have been passive—by seeming to insist through a kind of performative synecdoche that a single circa-1925 community of desperately impoverished Gullah Geechees could stand for all African Americans—and also active—through the patchwork quilt of segregation policies at theaters beyond the borders of New York City that prevented the mass of African Americans from ever seeing or encountering the show outside of a handful of song hits for the first three decades of the show's performance history. There is a sense in which *Porgy and Bess* exists *only* as stereotype—not just in African American cultural memory but in most of American cultural memory too. A song hit like the perennially popular "I Got Plenty o' Nuttin'," for example, removed from the context of Duncan's performance, ends up sounding like nothing more than the most retrograde of banjo songs—rather than the bitter protest piece that Gershwin intended it to be and that Duncan performed it as.

By contrast, audiences abroad were precisely attuned to nuances that escaped—or were repressed by—their U.S. counterparts. We have seen that in the United States questions of the opera's authenticity—one might go so far as to say its racial purity—were paramount. Those who saw beyond this simple binary tended to be disturbed by the view. "The trouble with the whole thing," grumbled Stark Young—the Agrarian writer of the bestselling Civil

War romance *So Red the Rose* and *New Republic* critic—was that it was "neither black nor white."[92] European audiences and critics, on the other hand, seemed thrilled by the "newness" and "originality" of this spectacle of compositional and performative miscegenation. European critics, moreover, appeared to feel less need to evaluate and dismiss what they were viewing on purely racial grounds. For example, when William Warfield and Leontyne Price headlined the first Breen-Davis tour in September 1952, there were fourteen curtain calls at the Vienna Volksoper and twenty-one at Berlin's Titania Palast. And the critics—rather than bogging down into questions of "Is it opera?" and "Is it authentic?"—instead argued the finer distinctions among *jazzoper* and *volksoper*, eventually concluding that Gershwin had surpassed the efforts of composers like Smetana, Weill, and Menotti. By incorporating elements of folk, jazz, and modern life into his work, he had instead created a new kind of opera, an opera of "hyperrealism" that emerged *directly* from the folk, jazz, and modern life.[93]

Well aware of the U.S. government's propaganda aims, they nonetheless professed themselves to be charmed—no less by the cast than by Gershwin's remarkable score. Indeed, the cast—a large group by the standards of touring opera as Breen decided to double-cast the roles to ensure that his singers would always be fresh—created waves of good will wherever they traveled. Warfield, for example, became a sensation in Vienna at a benefit concert of German *lieder*, which, of course, he sung with a flawless accent. Black mannequins appeared in fashionable shop windows throughout the capitals of Europe, as the comings and goings of the cast—operatically trained, multilingual, stylishly dressed, their sophistication rivaled only by their talent and good looks—generated the type of massive press coverage one associates with megastars such as Michael Jackson and Madonna. The United States may have figured as a land of lynchings in much of the communist and socialist press, but these African Americans—ironically, mingling freely with European elites and walking fearlessly into doors that in the United States would have been closed to them—were far from seeming visibly deprived or oppressed.[94] So the elites of three continents celebrated their presence; indeed, members of the company experienced slurs and segregation almost exclusively in the United States.[95]

And this was the area that offered the sharpest contrast between European and U.S. reception histories. In the twenty years since *Porgy and Bess* had opened on Broadway, a show intended to shatter stereotypes had gradually become an instrument of American apartheid, employing an elite of African American talent, while exposing them—along with potential African American fans—to insult and exclusion. In Europe, on the other hand, *Porgy and Bess* had always been symbolic of the freedom of the human spirit in the face of oppressive structures of society. The earliest European production was a Danish translation of the work mounted—with white singers in dark makeup—by the Danish Royal Opera in March 1943. Producing a *Negeroper*—by a Jewish composer, no less—was a clear act of provocation in Nazi-occupied Denmark, and it drew an official protest from the SS officer acting as the Reich's plenipotentiary. The company managed a full run of eighteen performances in 1943 anyway, plus four more in 1944 until a bomb threat cut short the run—reflecting, perhaps even heightening, a national mood in which, during the same period, the Danish Underground was working to rescue the country's persecuted Jewish minority.[96] In the postwar period, as victorious Allies and defeated Axis powers realigned themselves along the fault lines of the Cold War, a bottled-up demand for musical forms deemed "degenerate" by fascist and totalitarian regimes was given free rein.

And, for a brief period of years, *Porgy and Bess* conquered the world.

And so we circle back to the question that we started with: What are we to make of *Porgy* and *Porgy and Bess*? Are they acts of love and a mimicry born of love? Or are they just another "darky act" that traps the love object like a butterfly in amber, freezing moving, breathing, expressing, culture-making beings into performances that can be repeated again and again? I think the answer is yes—to all the questions. Heyward's and Gershwin's *are* acts of love, but the unequal power dynamics between these artists and the culture they're representing and the performers with whom they interact cannot be denied. And the long shelf life, successful commoditization, and continued popularity of the works they created mean that the business interests that control the commodity may, even after the artists' deaths, continue to demand a particular type of representation/performance whether or not the subjugated culture and/or artists from that culture want to provide such performances. The commodity interests, furthermore, are in a position to reward certain kinds of performances, thus eliciting more of them, and to threaten the existence of others simply by ignoring, or refusing to reward, them. Indeed, a type of mimicry that becomes popular enough can intervene in, change, even threaten the very viability of the culture it claims to love. This is a love that doesn't just steal—it strangles.

Let us consider, briefly, the counterexample of James P. Johnson, the stride piano master and Gershwin contemporary whose gigantic stature among jazz pianists is indicated by his lineage: Fats Waller, Willie "the Lion" Smith, Count Basie, Duke Ellington, Art Tatum, and Thelonious Monk.[97] Johnson was a New York legend: a member of James Reese Europe's Hellfighter bands in 1920 and 1921 and the man who wrote the worldwide dance hit "Charleston" for *Runnin' Wild*, the 1924 Black-cast musical that was Flournoy Miller's follow-up to *Shuffle Along* (1921). Johnson never achieved anything like Gershwin's success, even though he almost certainly influenced Gershwin's technique and though both men evinced omnivorous desires to master genres from jazz to Broadway to symphonic music and opera. The serious works Johnson wrote in his lifetime, such as the Gullah Geechee–inspired symphonic piece *Yamacraw*, were ignored in his lifetime and are forgotten today; the ownership of his songs, rather than enriching his heirs, is divided among large publishers like EMI and Warner Brothers. While library shelves groan with volumes devoted to Gershwin, Johnson is a mere footnote in Gunther Schuller's magisterial two-volume history of jazz.

The city of Charleston has suffered a similar fate, at least in relation to *Porgy and Bess*—increasingly, as the city has become irrelevant to the forces grinding it out as intellectual property, the opera has been found wanting by critics such as the late Virginia Mixson Geraty, a tireless advocate of Gullah Geechee language and culture, who introduced her Gullah Geechee translation of *Porgy* in 1990 as a counterweight to the ever more refined versions of the original that made it virtually unrecognizable in the city that inspired it.[98] Elizabeth Verner Hamilton, daughter of the Charleston Renaissance artist Elizabeth O'Neill Verner and a friend of the Heywards, used almost Geraty's exact words in expressing her thoughts: "I don't like *Porgy and Bess*. I don't like it because it's too refined. It's not the black people I knew back then and it's certainly not about the black people DuBose Heyward was writing about. These people were terribly poor, terribly educated Negroes who were almost abandoned after 'The War' when they didn't have any money and no master to look after them. Families lived one family to a room, six, seven children to a family; no public education for them."[99]

As for the reactions of African Americans closer to Sam Smalls's home? They, too, are negative—and tinged with anger. Anger that white Charlestonians remained so opposed to integrated seating that *Porgy and Bess* circled the globe four times before the unofficial boycott on a "home" production fell in 1970. Anger over the treatment of Sam Smalls's mother. Over the decades, the local paper dispatched reporters on three separate occasions to chronicle the travails of "Porgy's" mother, Elvira Gibbs. The headlines of the ensuing stories—"Porgy's Mother Still Lives in Charleston" in 1951, "Porgy's Mother Still Alive—Unaware of Fame Which World Gave 'Goat Sammy'" in 1959, and finally "Little Fame, Much Pain—Mother of 'Porgy,' Elvira Gibbs Dies" in 1961[100]—reveal an unseemly fascination with the ignorance, poverty, and violence of the city's "underworld," even as it seems to have occurred to no one that a few thousand dollars skimmed off the millions in profits generated by *Porgy and Bess* would have bought Mrs. Gibbs a house and kept her in comfort throughout the last decade of her life.[101]

Mrs. Dowling had fond memories of performing in *Porgy and Bess* when it finally came to Charleston during the city's tricentennial celebration in 1970, but she also expressed a seething anger at the way folklore collectors interested in early Charleston and the Jenkins Orphanage Band had exploited her over the years. She vividly recounted telling a woman with a grant from South Carolina Educational Television that she was "fed up" with collectors trooping in, taking her stories, and giving her little or no compensation. Red-faced, the woman "stuck ten dollars in my hand" as she left. Grandmother, on the other hand—a woman abandoned by her husband during the Depression, with four mouths to feed and a much more daunting set of circumstances than had faced Janie Screven Heyward two generations before her—had more pressing concerns than the fate of Sam Smalls and was only vaguely aware of the long and turbulent fictional career he'd enjoyed after his death.

"Didn't they make a movie about him?" she asked at one point in our talk.

Still, in considering the tension between Goat Cart Sam and Porgy, she may have summed up the ironies of the situation best when I told her, yes, they had:

"Oh, Goat Cart Sam, Goat Cart Sam, dead and gone and they still making money off him," she sighed.

AFTERWORD

South of Tomorrow

Sullivan's Island is a tiny finger of barrier island curving into Charleston Harbor from the east. Part of the network of fortifications that protected the city from attack by the sea, it's the site of Fort Moultrie: a military installation surrounded for much of its history by a dense and mysterious lowcountry swamp. Pvt. Edgar Allan Poe was stationed here in the 1840s for a time he'd commemorate by inventing the detective story.[1] Just to the east and south of the fort, there's a submerged jetty that provides both excellent fishing for locals and a frequently deadly hazard for unwary sailors. Just across the water, within clear sight of the lighthouse on the "point," are the ruined colonial fort Castle Pinckney, Fort Sumter of Civil War fame, and the steeple-studded skyline of historic Charleston.

People come to Sullivan's, a charming village of around nineteen hundred with one of the highest per capita income ranges in the county, to get away from the tourist hordes in the historic district. They drive over the Ben Sawyer Bridge from Mount Pleasant, crossing mud flats, marsh, and the cane-straight edge of the Intracoastal Waterway in search of seafood—the island has a couple of legendary restaurants—or the road to the white-sand beaches on Isle of Palms, a barrier island one creek to the north. Those who meander the little town's streets are charmed by the slumberous ease, the rambling houses painted aqua and pink and white, many of them still, in the fashion of the island's early architectural legacy, set on stilts, their lines softened, nearly obscured, by oleander, palmetto, and moss-draped live oak. These remnants of the wetland that once completely covered the island add an air of age and history to the place, an air enhanced by buildings like Stella Maris, one of the oldest Catholic parishes in the area, with its statue of Our Lady Star of the Sea set in the dome. Not even the new lighthouse, a structure with all the charm of an air traffic control tower, can dispel the atmosphere.

But we are here not for atmosphere but to linger, just for a moment, at the end of our long journey into the history and meaning of Gullah Geechee culture, at Fort Moultrie, which has guarded the approaches to the harbor from the Atlantic Ocean since colonial times. On this bright June day, suspended sweating between cloudless skies and a sea still and flat as a shining blue plate, it's hard to imagine the fort as a place of secrets kept, stories untold. But a plaque erected outside the massive complex by the U.S. Department of Archives and History reminds us that this nearly all-white enclave once had a darker hue. From the eighteenth century to the first decade of the nineteenth, it was the place to which enslaved Africans were transshipped and quarantined before sale in Charleston and points deeper in the continent's interior. Only one other region of the South, the Port of New Orleans, even came close in terms of numbers.

The plaque is silver on black, about the height of a tall man. It's been there only since 1999,[2] but set among the Revolutionary War guns and Civil War breastworks of the fort, it looks to be much older. It's placed not on the ocean side, the side toward which the romantic in me likes to imagine that my ancestors yearned for all their days, but near the crypt of Osceola, chief of the Seminole nation, on the side facing the river and Stella Maris Church. South Carolina's Indians seem longer ago and even further away than its slaves, but it's well to remind ourselves that Osceola died a lifelong hostage to the Seminole Wars in 1838, around the time Stella Maris parish was gearing up to serve Irish immigrant labor on the island.[3] So it's fitting, after all, that the tribute to the enslaved should be placed near the tribute to Osceola—his people did, after all, fight three wars to protect the Gullah-speaking Carolina and Georgia runaways among them who'd been accepted as brothers and sisters into the tribe.[4]

Given so much rich context, it seems a shame that the words on the plaque are written in that stiff governmentese that aims for historical accuracy, yet clings to the hope of not offending. "THIS IS SULLIVAN'S ISLAND," the plaque proclaims. "A place where . . . Africans were brought to this country in extreme conditions of human bondage . . . and contributed to the greatness of our country." Striving for the sonorous anaphoras most familiar to us from Walt Whitman, Abraham Lincoln, and the Bible, the text repeats "a place where" again and again before details of oppression or triumph. It ends, "This memorial rekindles the memory of a dismal time in American history, but it also serves as a reminder of a people who, despite injustice and intolerance—past and present, have retained the unique values, strengths and potential that flow from our West African culture which came to this nation through the middle passage."

Language written by committee to serve national rather than local purposes rarely gets the opportunity to soar. But the location remains significant as perhaps the only one in the city, amid a cultural landscape dense with memorials to white supremacy, where all the human populations whose members shed and mingled their blood in the making of the nation—Native, African, and European—receive official recognition through the designation of historic markers and sites. The Middle Passage plaque thus speaks of an alternative story in which the balance has begun ever so slightly to shift, and the physical marker itself has become an anchor for alternative rituals of public memory. One such ritual, held in 2000, was significant enough that it deserves a closer look.

As documented in a series of news stories around July 4, 2000, date of the ritual performance announcing the establishment and aims of the Gullah/Geechee People Foundation as well as in the memories of the three-hundred-odd participants, the performance began with a procession from the Atlantic Ocean—"symbolic as the site of our ancestors' debarkation," said Elder Halim Gullahbemi, one of founders of the organization and a guiding spirit behind the ceremony.[5] Their destination was a large open field on the grounds of Fort Moultrie, the putative site of the "pest house" where captive slaves were quarantined. Costumed women ritually "swept the way" at the head of the procession, followed by drummers whose role was to "call down the spirits." Between these groups and several hundred friends and observers stood Marquetta Goodwine, an "art-ivist" and cultural leader from St. Helena Island, South Carolina, who had recently given an address in Gullah before the United Nations Human Rights Council in Sweden. Goodwine appeared as a strikingly tall, slim figure in news photographs, her dark skin glowing against rich purple robes and heavy jewelry, her long, slim hands bound in chains signifying the ancestors' condition upon arrival. After libations to the ancestors, tributes to Osceola, and a brief ceremony "enstooling" Goodwine as "Queen Quet" of "the Gullah Geechee Nation," the bonds were released.[6]

Gullahbemi described the event as "a beautiful ceremony" on "a beautiful day," but his organization was interested in far more than just the staging of twenty-first-century tableaux vivants, as was evidenced by the presence of Dr. Yussuf Kly from the International Human Rights Association for American Minorities, a British Columbia–based NGO that holds consultative status with the United Nations. Kly's remarks recognized Gullah Geechee African Americans residing in the southeastern United States as a distinctive community with recognizable foodways, customs, and language—"all of which qualifies us as a nation under international law," explained Gullahbemi. As a nation, he added, "we have human and cultural rights, including the right not to be assimilated by the majority culture."[7] In a broad-ranging conversation, Elder Gullahbemi described his organization's philosophical and cultural aims, and the language he used amounted to a search for a third cultural way—a locus from which Gullah Geechee people could participate in as well as critique contemporary culture, while revitalizing traditional and historical harmonies between humans, nature, and society. In his "all-inclusive" vision, as Gullahbemi said of Gullah Geechee people, "We stand in the middle ground."

Middle ground. The hunger for an alternative space in a post-creole moment that is not yet postcolonial seems powerful indeed.

So it's fitting that our excursion in *Romancing the Gullah* through the mythic imaginary of the Gullah Geechee Coast brings us to the Middle Passage plaque at Fort Moultrie to hear the words of the nascent Gullah Geechee People Nation, so that we may, as a final gesture, confront the temptation to dismiss the activity. It would be a simple enough matter, for example, to construct a critique of this new wave of tradition building based on what Appiah called in his challenge to Du Bois its intrinsic racism—or "essentialism." And such a critique might be well-founded . . . or it might well be that the kind of "ideological decolonization" that is Appiah's dream may be an impossible dream, too. That's one of the questions that remains to be answered.

What *is* certain is that the Gullah Geechee Coast's history, literary and otherwise, is still unfolding from the inflection point represented by the 2000 ceremony. The National Trust for Historic Preservation declaration in 2004, followed by the National Park Service's "Special Resource Study" in 2005 and the establishment of the Gullah Geechee Cultural Heritage Corridor along with the commission to oversee it in 2006, allowed a robust local infrastructure to be established where before (ill-informed) conjecture and (biased) speculation had filled all gaps in knowledge. Questions of ownership and interpretation of folk knowledge and ways now are inclusive of Gullah Geechee views and voices in ways never seen before.

For example, retiring Spoleto Festival U.S.A. director Nigel Redden's parting gift to the city for the fortieth anniversary of the festival was a spanking-new production of *Porgy and Bess*, featuring an innovative production design by "Gullah artist" Jonathan Green that, for the first time, emphasized the color and vibrancy of Gullah Geechee street style rather than the drab Depression-era poverty characteristic of so many previous productions. That same year, 2016, Coastal Carolina University announced the establishment of the Charles Joyner Institute for Gullah and African Diaspora Studies; among other programs, the institute hosts the annual International Gullah Geechee African Diaspora Conference, bringing together scholars, practitioners, artists, and community members in a rarely seen, collaborative, and inclusive initiative of collection, interpretation, and preservation. The most eagerly anticipated event of 2023, meanwhile, was the opening of the International African American Museum at Gadsden's Wharf, a point of final debarkation for the enslaved in downtown Charleston. Founded with a mission to "honor the untold stories of the African American journey at one of our country's most sacred sites," the museum represents a previously unimaginable sea change in the recognition of Gullah Geechee African American peoples in the landscape of their culture's violent birth.

So concludes this examination of the literatures associated with the creole languages, landscapes, and lineages of the Gullah Geechee Coast. There is of course so much more to be said about this topic: about the Caribbean contemporaries of the writers examined, about the eruption of Gullah Geechee settings and symbols during the Black Arts Movement and beyond. Having a context for these books gives us fresh eyes with which to see both serious literature and sensationalist potboilers of the 1970s, 1980s, and 1990s, even as new contemporary writers of the diaspora continue to mine the vein in the twenty-first century. And so I say it is now—now that we have with this study established, across disciplines and across lines of color and region, a genealogy, a history, and a narrative that can bring the region's "shadow canon" into the light—it's now that the work can really begin. I look forward to the conversation.

NOTES

Foreword

1. The others are Tidewater Virginia-Chesapeake region and the mouth of the Mississippi, encompassing the Delta region and the city of New Orleans. Note the salience of waterways and historic ports to all three regions.
2. Smith, Hawes, and Darlington.
3. Berman; Dukakis.
4. Diamond and Bash.
5. D. L. Brown and Phillip.
6. Ghansah. *Lieux des memoires* is from Pierre Nora's designations for sites of collective memory, *lieux de memoire*, marked sites of civic memory receiving sanction and support from official sources, versus *milieux de memoire*, unmarked sites of social memory kept alive by community transmission.
7. Gajanan.
8. Roldán and Monk.
9. For example, Frank Dawson and James C. Hemphill, editors of the Charleston *News and Courier* from 1873 to 1910 (in Kytle and Roberts 116–21), and Mary B. Poppenheim, Charleston-born president-general of the United Daughters of the Confederacy and publisher of the *Keystone*, a monthly women's journal that fiercely advocated for indoctrination of southern children, among other "lost" causes (121–35). Meanwhile, Mary C. Simms Oliphant's various Lost Cause histories of South Carolina were still being taught in lowcountry high schools as late as 1976; lawmakers educated under that regime were responsible for five bills debated in the South Carolina House Education Committee during the 2021–22 session censoring the teaching of slavery in the state's public schools. https://www.statehousereport.com/2022/03/04/big-story-grassroots-groups-organize-against-bills-limiting-of-history-teaching/.
10. See Ghansah.
11. Chang 498–99.
12. Chang 499.
13. Foucault, "Of Other Spaces."
14. Toledo's monologue from August Wilson 57–58.

Chapter 1. Mother Tongues and the King's English

1. Salikoko Mufwene makes this important point—that Lowcountry residents are often "shocked by the application of the terms *Gullah* and *creole* to how they speak, [they] say they are speaking English!" See "What Is African American English?" 29.
2. Dunbar, "The Poet."
3. Behar 177.
4. Spivak, *Post-colonial Critic* 156.
5. See James Clifford's *Routes*.

6. Rosaldo 69–70.
7. Baraka 186.
8. Carter 120.
9. K. Hamilton, "Dialect" 35
10. Asante 24.
11. L. D. Turner 11–12.
12. Herskovits 276.
13. Savannah Unit, Georgia Writers' Project, Works Progress Administration 162.
14. L. Young.
15. On February 8, 1968, students angry at continued segregation at All Star Bowling Lane gathered around a bonfire on the campus. Police fired into the crowd of protestors, killing three students—Samuel Hammond, Delano Middleton, and Henry Smith—and wounding twenty-seven others. The Orangeburg Massacre was virtually ignored by the national press, especially when compared to the saturation coverage granted the Kent State killings later that year. See Bass and Nelson.
16. Yes, *the* Moon River from the song of the same name written by Johnny Mercer and Henry Mancini and sung by Audrey Hepburn in *Breakfast at Tiffany's* (1961). It won the Academy Award for Best Original Song in 1961.
17. Merida and Fletcher 61–62 and 73.
18. Gonzales 10.
19. Qtd. in Herskovits 276.
20. Starting with Peter Wood's *Black Majority* (1974) and continuing through Daniel Littlefield's *Rice and Slaves* (1981), Charles Joyner's *Down by the Riverside* (1984), Patricia Jones-Jackson's *When Roots Die* (1987), and Margaret Washington Creel's *"A Peculiar People"* (1988).
21. Merida and Fletcher speculate that the lingering tension between grandfather and grandson could be attributed to Thomas's choices as he began that climb: his "drift away from the church," his divorce, and perhaps even his shift to a rigid right-wing orthodoxy that far exceeded Anderson's own philosophy of self-sufficiency and self-help (81–83).
22. Nettle and Romaine 136.
23. Fanon 25.
24. G. Bailey 38; Cukor-Avila 94.
25. K. Hamilton, "Dialect" 36.
26. Krupat 73.
27. Crystal 83.
28. Cosby 3–4.
29. Rampersad, "Cosby Criticism."
30. Singh and Schmidt 13.
31. Walker calls the women in Jean Toomer's *Cane* "exquisite butterflies trapped in an evil honey" (231).
32. In the essay "Natural Poetics, Forced Poetics" (1976), Glissant outlines a conception of "nation language" as a poetics into which the enslaved individual is "forced" to disguise his attempts to retain his culture while adapting to his new conditions. Brathwaite calls this a "prison language" (16), and his own definition of nation language is much bolder and much freer. For Brathwaite, the nation language *itself* comes to embody the potential for liberation from the psychological shackles Fanon describes in *Black Skin, White Masks*.
33. Brathwaite 13.
34. With the noteworthy exception of African American women writers during the Black Arts Movement and in its immediate aftermath.

Chapter 2. Toward a Triangular Topos

1. K. Morgan 907.
2. Cartwright, *Sacral Grooves* 37.
3. Most recently, culinary historian David Shields, in his eagerness to establish a provenance for the legendary "Carolina Gold" rice, all but erases African agency in the establishment of the crop in South Carolina. His argument shows far too much deference to early twentieth-century sources well known for Lost Cause bias while minimizing Judith Carney's important anthropological study *Black Rice* (2001) and ignoring the towering contributions of Daniel C. Littlefield's *Rice and Slaves* (1981) and especially Peter Wood's *Black Majority* (1974) to this debate. See Shields 236.
4. Burroughs.
5. Please note that this section is indebted to Scott Herring's essay on "Rural" and Burgett and Hendler's essay on "Space," in Romaine and Greeson, *Keywords*.
6. Burroughs.
7. B. Smith; SC Picture Project, "Colleton County: Donnelly WMA," https://bit.ly/3jfqwEd.
8. Cartwright, *Sacral Grooves* 37.
9. Vileisis 5–6.
10. To cite headlines just from this year alone, see the following: E. Williams, "Contested S.C. Eco-resort Plan, Flagged as 'Greenwashing,' Up for Key Decision Soon"; Swenson, "Goldfinch Urging State to Oppose Baruch Claim to Marsh."
11. The original 1663 charter to the Carolina colony from Charles II of England named eight "absolute lords and proprietors"—later simply called lords proprietors. The colony's Fundamental Constitutions also established orders of nobility—from baron to cassique to landgrave—based on land ownership. But this attempt at establishing a hereditary nobility proved unworkable and was swiftly abandoned, according to Walter Edgar's *South Carolina: A History* 36, 43.
12. Hartigan 41–42.
13. See Anthony Wilson's *Shadow and Shelter*, especially the introduction and first chapter, for a comprehensive discussion.
14. Patricia Jones-Jackson and Judith Carney have noted resemblances between the topography of the Gullah Geechee Coast and that of the rice-growing regions of the western Sudan. Jones-Jackson 7; Carney 84–89.
15. Cf. Robert O'Meally's introduction to E. C. L. Adams, *Tales of the Congaree*, especially the description of the spiritual meaning of the forest, or *feenda*, as described by one of Adams's informants; R. M. Brown 311.
16. Compare Wilson's "animal self" with my discussion of Fanon's "jungle" in chapter 1.
17. Anthony Wilson 15.
18. A comprehensive account of this vast literature is to be found in Mazzotti and Bauer.
19. Mazzotti and Bauer 6–7.
20. Charles Stewart 1.
21. Qtd. in Mazzotti and Bauer 1.
22. Greeson 25, 29.
23. Crèvecoeur 158–59.
24. Drawn from Jean Bodin's theories, ca. 1566. See Bodin.
25. Charles Stewart 9.
26. Anthony Wilson performs a provocative reading of their correspondence (7–8).
27. In Query 14, "Laws," Jefferson goes so far as to assert his suspicion that whites, In-

dians, and Blacks represent separate human species. See David Waldstreicher's edition of *Notes on the State of Virginia*.

28. Irving 199.
29. Bongie 158.
30. Charles Stewart 2.
31. Crèvecoeur 41, 43, 39.
32. A. Anjana Mebane-Cruz, personal communication, 2010.
33. Indeed, historians have argued persuasively that it was Bacon's Rebellion that helped to create modern categories of race, as the Black codes passed in its wake—and adopted as models across the South—conferred numerous benefits on poor whites while systematically stripping slaves, freedmen, mulattoes, and Indians of all rights under the law. The ultimate effect was to create what has been called elsewhere "the possessive investment in whiteness" that has limited working-class coalition building across the color line ever since. See E. S. Morgan's *American Slavery, American Freedom*. Also see Theodore Allen's flawed, but still useful, *Invention of the White Race*.
34. Klein 668–73.
35. Gilroy, *Black Atlantic* 42.
36. Manning 258.
37. U.S. Census Bureau, "National Population Projections."
38. U.S. Census Bureau, "Population in Colonial and Continental Periods."
39. Qtd. in Peter Wood 132.
40. Qtd. in Kytle and Roberts.
41. Higgins 118.
42. Mebane-Cruz, personal communication, 2010.
43. Edgar 22.
44. Mebane-Cruz, personal communication, 2010.
45. Angelina Grimke's *Appeal to the Christian Women of the South* (1836) is the only such appeal by a southern woman addressed to southern women. It was burned by southern postmasters, and she was threatened with arrest should she ever return. Grimke went on, with her sister Sarah, to assist her husband, Theodore Weld, with the writing and editing of *American Slavery as It Is: Testimony of a Thousand Witnesses* (1839).
46. Tindall 299.
47. Edgar 485–86.
48. Barry 34.
49. For further reading on the civic religion that sprung up around Civil War remembrances, two sources are indispensable. A national perspective is offered by David Blight in *Race and Reunion*. A greater focus on region comes with Gaines Foster's *Ghosts of the Confederacy*.
50. National Park Service, "Low Country" 4.
51. The New York Public Library's Schomburg Center for Research in Black Culture has brought together tremendous documentary resources in this area to create "In Motion: The African American Migration Experience," available at https://www.inmotionaame.org.
52. Described in Zora Neale Hurston's *Barracoon*.
53. Berlin 66–67.
54. Goodwine and Clarity Press Gullah Project 54.
55. Said xxv.
56. A good general introduction to current theories in genetics and human prehistory is offered by the Oxford University–based medical doctor and geneticist Stephen Oppenheimer in *The Real Eve*.

57. The notes on the slave trade come from Pollitzer, *Gullah People* 25–26. The geographical equivalences are provided with the assistance of Google Earth.

58. See particularly Gomez 27–37 and chaps. 3–4 of Pollitzer, *Gullah People*.

59. Manning 258.

60. For purposes of comparison, in 1850, 22 percent of slaves were associated with hemp production, 14 percent with tobacco, and 6 percent with sugar, according to Steckel n. 112.

61. Vinovskis 106; Steckel 86. This seems the definitive answer to claims of slave "immunity" to malaria. Those among the enslaved *who survived to adulthood* did indeed have a virtual immunity. But it was purchased at the cost of a terrible mortality rate during childhood.

62. Vinovskis 465. Citing these statistics is in no way meant to minimize the horrific toll suffered by Amerindians, who lacked immunities to Eurasian disease, or of whites in the colonial and antebellum periods, whose encounters with malaria and yellow fever along the coasts were every bit as deadly.

63. Qtd. in Pollitzer, *Gullah People* 69–70.

64. Along with Gomez and Pollitzer there are two other important sources on slave ethnicity in the Gullah Geechee context: Creel, *"A Peculiar People"* and Peter Wood, *Black Majority*.

65. Baugh 29.

66. See Herskovits, *Myth of the Negro Past*, particularly chap. 1, for a summary of the racist theories in history, sociology, and anthropology that were predominant from the Civil War to the Second World War.

67. Jackson, "Foreword."

68. Mufwene, "Ecology of Gullah's Survival" 69.

69. Harvin D3.

70. Later in the twentieth century it would allow a rereading and recontextualizing of classic Black feminist work by Paule Marshall, Gloria Naylor, Toni Morrison, and Julie Dash, among others.

Chapter 3. Pastoral Scenes of the Gallant South

1. During this period South Carolina was claimed by the Spanish and considered a part of Florida. Qtd. in Cothran, *Gardens of Historic Charleston*.

2. Cartwright, *Reading Africa* 205.

3. Yuhl, *Golden Haze* 12.

4. As documented by journalist Clothilde R. Martin, the state's plantation districts, from Berkeley County to Beaufort County, teemed with a who's-who of northern wealthy, escaping the chill of their New York estates for a season of hunting and entertaining in South Carolina's mild climate. See Cuthbert and Hoffius.

5. The concept of "usable past" is of venerable age in American studies, originating with Van Wyck Brooks's *America's Coming of Age* (1915). Yuhl, *Golden Haze* 8, 10.

6. Martens and Robertson.

7. Moten.

8. Waring's career as a segregationist and particularly his persecution of his uncle, U.S. district judge J. Waties Waring, over the judge's courageous and lonely desegregation stand, is recounted at length in Roberts and Klibanoff.

9. Donna Haraway's definition of the "plantationoscene," qtd. in Martens and Robertson.

10. The terms are original to C. L. R. James's *Black Jacobins* (1938), but this discussion is much indebted to Fred Moten's exploration of their implications in *Black and Blur* (2017).

11. As imagined by Du Bois et al.

12. The "singing tree" is a powerful metaphor in Jean Toomer's *Cane* ("Song of the Son"), in Langston Hughes's "Jazzonia," and in Keith Cartwright's *Reading Africa into American Literature*.

13. DuBose Heyward, *Porgy* 11.

14. Blair 550.

15. We should note that these traditional categories have been at least in part reclaimed by the recent proliferation of "keywords for cultural studies" series among publishers such as New York University Press and the University of Georgia Press, among others.

16. This discussion is influenced by three key texts: Leo Marx's *Machine in the Garden*; Lewis P. Simpson's *Dispossessed Garden*; and Elizabeth Jane Harrison's *Female Pastoral*. In addition, three other texts will be important in making the pivot from pastoral to gothic: Anthony Wilson's *Shadow and Shelter*, discussed in chapter 2, along with David Miller's *Dark Eden* and Cartwright's *Reading Africa into American Literature*.

17. I'm using "mode" to indicate a set of codes, or literary conventions, within genre that constrain both the powers of action available to characters as well as the methods used by writers to achieve their designs. For example, the "high mimetic" is a mode that accounts for the hyperreality of characters within the historical epic and contemporary high fantasy genres. The sentimental and the ironic are modes, while autobiography is a genre that might make use of them. Similarly, the gothic and the pastoral are modes, and melodrama and drama are genres that frequently deploy them.

18. Santesso 15; Rosaldo 71.

19. Marx makes a distinction between "complex" and "simple" pastoral in *The Machine in the Garden*, in which, in the complex pastoral, a pattern of disruption signals that the pastoral space is idealized and unachievable. It can be argued that a sufficiently disruptive irruption of the real into the ideal space pivots the work from the pastoral into the gothic space.

20. Slotkin, *Fatal Environment* 11.

21. From Henry Wadsworth Longfellow's "Retribution," in *Poetic Aphorisms* (1846). Wadsworth, we should note, was an avowed abolitionist, having published his *Poems on Slavery* only four years before the aphorisms. It is quite likely that when thinking of the "mills of God," he was musing on the fate of the plantation South.

22. This, in a series of highly influential works: *Regeneration through Violence: The Mythology of the American Frontier, 1600–1860* (1973), *The Fatal Environment: The Myth of the Frontier in the Age of Industrialization, 1800–1890* (1985), and *Gunfighter Nation: The Myth of the Frontier in Twentieth-Century America* (1992).

23. From the wanderings of conquistadors and incursions of the French in the sixteenth and seventeenth centuries through the Yamassee, the Cherokee "removal," and the Seminole Wars of the eighteenth and nineteenth centuries. Where appropriate in this and later chapters we shall explore these histories.

24. Berry 10, 14.

25. Rosaldo 69–70.

26. Cottom.

27. The digital images were printed with a sepia tone and were inspired by Civil War photography and the letters of Walt Whitman.

28. Pujol, personal communication, 21 Oct. 2005.

29. McKittrick x.

30. Yuhl, *Golden Haze* 132.

31. Wilgus 344–64.

32. A useful summary may be found in Mahar 19–23. Also see Epstein 141–44.

33. Yuhl, *Golden Haze* 114.

34. Bennett was a children's book author from Ohio who, after marrying into the Charleston elite, also mined the Southern gothic vein with books such as *The Treasure of Peyre Gaillard* (1906), *Madame Margot: A Grotesque Legend of Old Charleston* (1921), and *The Doctor to the Dead: Grotesque Legends and Folk Tales of Old Charleston* (1946). Meanwhile, the Columbia-area doctor Adams was actually befriended by Langston Hughes and was the only collector among this group to win serious attention from African American literary critics with his *Congaree Sketches* (1927), *Nigger to Nigger* (1928), and *Potee's Gal: A Drama of Negro Life Near the Big Congaree Swamps* (1929), all collected in the 1987 volume *Tales of the Congaree* from University of North Carolina Press.

35. Yuhl speaks of the general competitiveness between Renaissance members (*Golden Haze* 114–15), but with the exception of the Stoney anecdote, the authors and anecdotes are drawn from my own reading of the publication record.

36. Du Bois, *Souls of Black Folk* 536–37.

37. K. Morgan 907.

38. Sass's work spanned the long-running local newspaper column "Woods and Waters," publication in national magazines like the *Saturday Evening Post*, and three collections of essays.

39. Sass 5.

40. R. Williams.

41. Cothran, *Gardens of Historic Charleston* 26.

42. Sass 14.

43. Maurie McInnis in *In Pursuit of Refinement: Charlestonians Abroad, 1740 to 1860* (1999) and *The Politics of Taste in Antebellum Charleston* (2005); and Stephanie Yuhl in her dissertation "High Culture in the Low Country" and the book based on it, *Golden Haze of Memory*. We shall speak of these matters further in chapter 5.

44. Žižek and Daly, *Conversations* 29.

45. Ciucevich.

46. As reflected in the 354 songs on 366 cylinders recorded in Darien, Ga., and surrounding areas from Feb. 1926–1927, AFC 1928/002: Robert Winslow Gordon Cylinder Collection, American Folklife Center, Library of Congress.

47. Charles C. Jones Sr. 266. Also qtd. in Cartwright, *Sacral Grooves* 38.

48. Ellison, "Change the Joke" 56–64.

Chapter 4. "I Can Peep through Muddy Waters"

1. Guzzio.

2. This is particularly interesting in Du Bois's case. While Toomer fled the state from which his father hailed after less than a year, Du Bois spent a total of twenty-three years (1897 to 1910, and then 1934 to 1944), the bulk of his academic career, at Atlanta University. For a recent volume describing how foundational these years were in terms of the development of the discipline of sociology, see Aldon D. Morris's recent title *The Scholar Denied* .

3. For example, Keith Cartwright's work. Also John Wharton Lowe's *The Calypso Magnolia*.

4. For example, Charles C. Jones's *Negro Myths from the Georgia Coast* (1888) and Ambrose Gonzales's *The Black Border* (1922), among others.

5. The official setting for the novel is, curiously, Alabama—though possibly, given Du Bois's animus toward Booker T. Washington, this, too, is a provocation.

6. See the "Jean Toomer (1894–1967)" entry in *The New Georgia Encyclopedia*, www.georgiaencyclopedia.org.
7. Gilroy, *Black Atlantic* 112.
8. Kelley 1402.
9. Du Bois, *Dusk of Dawn* 22–23.
10. Toomer, "Crock of Problems" 55.
11. Toomer, "Crock of Problems" 58.
12. Qtd. in Webb 206–7.
13. Wall, "Resounding Souls" 222.
14. In *Cane* and in many other texts as well. Cheryl Wall is among the many who note the resonance of *Souls* down through the decades for James Weldon Johnson, Toomer, Ralph Ellison, and Toni Morrison, among others. See "Resounding Souls."
15. Du Bois, *Souls of Black Folk* 204.
16. Du Bois, *Conservation of Races*.
17. Du Bois, *Conservation of Races* 205.
18. Stepto 66.
19. A one-sentence summary cannot hope to do justice to Appiah's complex, subtle explication of Crummell's and Du Bois's thought and writings. See chapter 2, "Illusions of Race," in *In My Father's House*.
20. I should note that Appiah's views on Du Bois have attracted controversy. For a good example of the tone and range of the criticism, see Bell, Groshoz, and Stewart, with particular attention to the essays by Lucius Outlaw, Robert Gooding-Williams, and Bernard R. Boxill.
21. As detailed in Le Vin and Wells-Barnett.
22. By way of context, there were 115 total lynchings in Georgia in the same decade, according to Capeci and Knight.
23. Žižek and Daly, *Conversations* 69–70, emphasis original.
24. Du Bois, "My Evolving Program" 63.
25. Žižek and Daly, *Conversations* 10–11.
26. Ellison, "Change the Joke" 49. An extension of the argument Ellison makes in "Change the Joke and Slip the Yoke."
27. Jung 222.
28. Du Bois, "Damnation" 958.
29. All quotations from the actual text of *Cane* are from the 1975 Norton critical edition.
30. Durham, *Merrill Studies in Cane* 41–42.
31. Qtd. in Durham, *Merrill Studies in Cane* 45.
32. Redding.
33. Similar to the function of the horse-drawn mower in "Reapers," the trains in "Becky," Barlo's motorcar in "Esther," and the cane refinery in "Blood Burning Moon."
34. Eco.
35. Qtd. in Toomer, *Cane* 41.
36. If not always in the eyes of contemporary white reviewers. One anonymous review in the *Springfield Republican* called it not just a "vaudeville" but more damningly one that was hard to follow. See Durham, *Merrill Studies in Cane* 34.
37. Consider Toomer's 19 July 1922 letter to Waldo Frank during a stay at Harper's Ferry, West Virginia: "Life here has not the vividity and distinction of that of middle Georgia. Racial attitudes, on both sides, are ever so much more tolerant, even friendly. Oppression and ugly emotions seem nowhere in evidence. And there are no folk-songs. A more stringent grip, I guess, is necessary to force them through." In Toomer, *Letters* 10.

Chapter 5. What Miss Ann Saw

1. Severens, *Charleston Renaissance* 16.
2. Stephanie Yuhl's dissertation did not make use of the term, insisting that "artists of the Charleston Group" was more historically accurate. By the time of her book publication, however, she had accepted the inevitable. See "High Culture in the Low Country"; also see *Golden Haze of Memory*.
3. Qtd. in Greene, *Master Skylark* 343n.
4. Qtd. in Saunders and McAden 13.
5. Yuhl, "High Culture" 18; Greene, *Master Skylark* 156–57.
6. Marcus 16–17; McKittrick xiii–xiv.
7. Yuhl, "High Culture" 8; Bhabha 236.
8. Don Doyle's description in *New Men, New Cities, New South* is particularly apt: "Old Charleston, besieged and subverted, retreated to the safe territory South of Broad, with its old mansions and its old ways. As the new century progressed, the old city became a museum, a sanctuary of artifacts and values that no longer ruled the South" (188).
9. Greene, *Master Skylark* 236; Yuhl, "High Culture" 8.
10. Verner, *Mellowed by Time* 2.
11. Foucault, *Discipline and Punish* 172.
12. Verner, *Mellowed by Time* 27–28.
13. Severens, *Charleston Renaissance* 13.
14. An "intense professional rivalry" for subjects and patrons between Hutty and Verner (46) is described in Saunders and McAden 46. And Taylor is also said to have disliked Verner, thinking she gave herself inappropriate airs for one of her lowly origins, according to Farrow.
15. Estill Curtis Pennington was one of the earliest to attempt an analysis of the racial content of southern art, but his *Look Away: Reality and Sentiment in Southern Art* (1989) completely ignores Charleston artists, an indication of how recently their stock has risen, and is further hampered by his lack of access to Eric Lott's *Love and Theft* (1993) and the many fine studies of minstrelsy that followed. Stephanie Yuhl's "High Culture in the Low Country" (1998) and the follow-up *Golden Haze of Memory* (2005) remain the best, most comprehensive recent works on the Charleston Renaissance period. Also see John Michael Vlach's *The Planter's Prospect: Privilege and Slavery in Plantation Paintings* (2002) for a work that successfully places Charleston Renaissance art in a regional historic context.
16. Actually, in *The Negro in American Life and Thought: The Nadir, 1877–1901* (1954), Logan argued that race relations improved after 1901. John Hope Franklin and Henry Arthur Callis vigorously disagreed, citing the Red Summer of 1919 and arguing for the later date. Logan eventually came to agree with them in *The Betrayal of the Negro, from Rutherford B. Hayes to Woodrow Wilson* (1965).
17. Reproduction sign for the United Fur Co., captioned "An Unwelcome Surprise," from the collection of the U.C. Berkeley Folklore Archive: plate 23 in Patricia A. Turner's *Celluloid Mammies and Ceramic Uncles*.
18. Ellison, "Change the Joke" 49.
19. Turner coined the phrase "contemptible collectibles" in *Celluloid Mammies and Ceramic Uncles*.
20. One such postcard, dated 1902 and depicting a lynching in a coastal Georgia swamp, was circulated by Wright's Kodak in Savannah, Georgia, and bore the handwritten inscription, "Warning The answer of the Anglo-Saxon race to black brutes who would attack the Womanhood of the South—." The image was of the burned remains of an armless,

legless, headless torso hanging from a scaffold with groups of whites casually chatting below. Plate 53 in James Allen, *Without Sanctuary: Lynching Photography in America* (2000).

21. Smith's patrons included, for example, Mrs. Marshall Field and Mrs. Solomon Guggenheim. She was reviewed in respected New York publications and even, in 1937, received an honorary doctorate from Mount Holyoke College (Yuhl "High Culture" 100; Vlach, *Planter's Prospect* 151). "Landscapes of longing" is a term applied by Estill C. Pennington to southern landscape art, particularly of the nineteenth century, in which the evocation of nostalgia and a fantasy landscape into which the viewer might project herself or himself are paramount (147).

22. Mitchell 15.

23. David Blight is one of many who gives a persuasive account of rapidity and comprehensiveness of the change confronted by American society after 1865. See "Quarrel Forgotten or a Revolution Remembered?" 160, 155. Also consider the arguments on the roots of antimodernist nostalgia in the 1875–1925 period offered by Michael Kammen 294–296; Lears xvi–xix.

24. Indeed, throughout the teens and twenties, a steady stream of Jenkins Orphanage Band members "ran away" from the band's annual tours to become valued members of the orchestras of Louis Armstrong, Chick Webb, Lionel Hampton, and many others. The band's story and the evolution of its style are documented in two books: Jeffrey P. Green's *Edmund Thornton Jenkins* and John Chilton's *Jazz Nursery*.

25. Hutty demonstrates in other work that he's capable of accurately rendering African American facial features, but the bodies of African Americans are always caricatured, with ill-fitting clothing over sloping shoulders, apishly long arms, high rear ends, and bowed legs, as apparent in Saunders and McAden.

26. One of two Verner portraits of a middle-class African American subject was a drypoint etching titled *The Reverend Jenkins* (1933), which rejects the mawkish clichés more typical of her flower sellers and servants and uses instead elite codes of representation more typically reserved for high-status sitters.

27. Green 9.

28. Severens, *Charleston Renaissance* 30–32; Vlach, *Planter's Prospect* 44–45.

29. Severens points out that the large tubes in the backdrop are parts of the cotton gin that separate cotton seed from fiber, items used at an early stage of the process, while the bins in the foreground contain spindles, used at a late stage, in the finishing process, and usually segregated into another room (*Charleston Renaissance* 87–88). Segregation in the mills is discussed in G. Wright 44–46.

30. Qtd. in Severens, *Charleston Renaissance* 88.

31. In which the part stands for the whole, e.g., the steeple of a historic church can stand for the "civilization" founded by Charleston's slaveholding aristocracy, while a Black woman with a basket balanced on her head stands for the alien, unassimilable "Other."

32. Culler 114; Berger 7; Mitchell 15.

33. This discussion is heavily indebted to the description of "order" in the meting out of disciplinary punishments in Michel Foucault's *Discipline and Punish* 195–96.

34. But for a few local art classes, her only influences were an extensive portfolio of original Japanese prints collected and shared with Smith by her cousin, Motte Allston Read (Severens, *Smith* 121); the tonalist painter Birge Harrison, who offered informal criticism while using an old dependency behind Smith's family home as a studio between 1906 and 1911 (Severens, *Charleston Renaissance* 50–52); and a quartet of "lady etchers"—Chicago's Helen Hyde and Bertha Jaques, Boston's Ellen Day Hale, and Philadelphia's Gabrielle Clements—who taught Smith the technique in the early 1920s (Yuhl, "High Culture" 125).

35. Calculated using Lawrence H. Officer and Samuel H. Williamson's currency conversion method, described in "Computing 'Real Value' over Time with a Conversion between U.K. Pounds and U.S. Dollars, 1830–2007" (MeasuringWorth, 2008), www.measuringworth.com. The sum is all the more remarkable given the fact that a note in the artist's ledger claimed her actual living expenses were paid by family legacies. Severens, *Charleston Renaissance* 13.

36. Petteys 654; Helen Gardner McCormick, "Biography," in *Alice Ravenel Huger Smith* 4.

37. Qtd. in Yuhl, "High Culture" 98.

38. There are at least eleven "rice rivers" surrounding the port city of Charleston: from north to south, the Waccamaw, the Pee Dee, the Black, the Sampit, the Santee, the Cooper, the Ashley, the Edisto, the Ashepoo, the Combahee, and the Savannah. Elizabeth W. Allston Pringle's *A Woman Rice Planter* (1914) was a Pee Dee memoir, while Alice Ravenel Huger Smith's *A Carolina Rice Plantation of the Fifties* (1936), which included selections from the unpublished memoirs of the artist's father, Daniel Elliott Huger Smith, and Duncan Clinch Heyward's *Seed From Madagascar* (1939), commemorated the Combahee region.

39. Yuhl, "High Culture" 94.

40. "Memory sketches" denotes Birge Harrison's technique of painting from memory, passed on to Smith during their informal sessions together, according to Severens (*Smith* 52). The technique consisted of direct observation of a scene, accompanied perhaps by quick pencil sketches, with meditation on the details of the scene, and finally the actual process of painting back in her studio. She defended the method thus in 1926: "I do not mean guessing. I mean remembering. Just as there is no guessing at a history lesson or at mathematics" (qtd. in Yuhl, "High Culture" 105).

41. There were, in fact, seven hurricanes in twenty years: two in 1893 and one each in 1894, 1898, 1906, 1910, and 1911. These flooded the fields with salty or brackish water and destroyed ditches, dikes, and drainage systems painstakingly constructed over centuries of cultivation (Edgar 479).

42. Vlach, *Planter's Prospect* 170.

43. Eliade 23.

44. While "mammy" is the more common term for an African American nursemaid figure, there were regional variations on this usage. In Charleston, such a woman was called "mauma" or by the Gullah term "dah."

45. Alice Ravenel Huger Smith, "Doorways" 296.

46. "Full-hand" is a reference to the task system of distributing labor. A full hand did a full day's task—on the Daniel Smith plantation, a half acre, though the amounts varied somewhat from plantation to plantation depending on the difficulty of the task and the age, infirmity, or pregnancy status of the worker. A ten-year-old, for example, might be assigned a quarter task or more, depending on ability.

47. Alice Ravenel Huger Smith, *Carolina Rice Plantation* 68–69.

48. Alice Ravenel Huger Smith, *Carolina Rice Plantation* 59.

49. The essays in W. J. T. Mitchell's *Landscape and Power* (1994) make provocative reading in the consideration of such issues.

50. Alice Ravenel Huger Smith, *Carolina Rice Plantation* 39.

51. C. McD. Puckette, "Life on Carolina's Rice Plantations," *New York Times Book Review* 3 Jan. 1937; "Watercolors of a Carolina Rice Plantation to Be Exhibited," *Washington Star* 9 Jan. 1937; Henry Seidel Canby, "The Rice Coast in Art," *Saturday Review* 5 Dec. 1936; News clippings, Alice Ravenel Huger Smith Scrapbook, Gibbes Museum of Art, Charleston, S.C.

52. Baldwin 14.

53. One year after the museum opened. Indeed, this was far more in the way of education than any of the other homegrown "stars" of the Charleston group had. DuBose Heyward was an indifferent student, a high school dropout whose mother could not afford to send him to college. Alice Smith, meanwhile, was educated mostly at home, and Elizabeth O'Neill Verner attended a ladies academy in Columbia, then received a year of art school.

54. Alice Ravenel Huger Smith, *Carolina Rice Plantation* 77–78, emphasis original.

55. Greene, *Master Skylark* 122–27.

56. Edward Ball gives a fascinating glimpse of family viewed across the color line in his encounter with his distant cousin, Edwina Harleston Whitlock (niece of Edwin), in *Slaves in the Family* 272–75.

57. McDaniel 9–13; Ball 279.

58. McDaniel 240.

59. Laura M. Bragg, Charleston, S.C., to Edwin A. Harleston, Charleston, S.C., 22 Apr. 1926, typewritten letter, Whitlock Papers, South Carolina Historic Society, qtd. in McDaniel 220–21.

60. The date is a matter of some dispute; this may be a canvas from later in Harleston's career, ca. 1929 or 1930. Ted Ashton Phillips, personal communication, 15 Jan. 2001.

61. DuBose Heyward, *Mamba's Daughters* 245.

62. See the text and photographs in Lettie Gay and Blanche Rhett's *200 Years of Charleston Cooking* (224–25).

Chapter 6. All God's Chillen Got Traveling Shoes

1. Inspired by the Amitar Ghosh anecdote from James Clifford's *Routes* 2.
2. Hurston, "Hue and Cry" 338.
3. Sundquist 465–66.
4. Turner, *Cane: An Authoritative Text* 14.
5. Hurston, "My People! My People!," chapter of *Dust Tracks on a Road* 731.
6. Hurston, "High John de Conquer" 451.
7. Wall, *Zora Neale Hurston: Novels and Stories* 1026.
8. Hurston, Letter to Claude Barnett, 4? Feb. 1943, in Kaplan 474–75.
9. Hurston's eccentric loyalties often landed her in hot water with African American peers. Her support of George Smathers, signer of the Southern Manifesto, was in line with her own opposition to *Brown v. Board*, but deeply unpopular with Afro-Floridians who voted overwhelmingly for his liberal Democratic opponent. Kaplan 595–97.
10. Hurston, *Dust Tracks on a Road* 572.
11. McKay, the son of peasant farmers in Jamaica, was another writer whose fluent use of dialect and insistence on exploring the lives—including the sex lives—of working-class Afro-creole subjects called down the wrath of race propagandists such as W. E. B. Du Bois. John Wharton Lowe has argued that McKay's work, particularly the novel *Banana Bottom*, was a key influence on Hurston's *Their Eyes Were Watching God*. See Lowe 198–247.
12. Zora Neale Hurston, Letter to Annie Nathan Meyer, Jan. 1926, in Kaplan 77.
13. Kaplan 50–51.
14. Clifford 3.
15. Hurston, *Dust Tracks on a Road* 561.
16. Francis, Mormino, and Sanderson.
17. P. Wood 51fn.
18. National Park Service, "African Americans."

19. Indeed, Hurston published one of the first modern accounts of the settlement and its travails with the English. "Communications."

20. "Legally established" is in contrast with "maroon" settlements, established by self-liberating bands of runaways typically though not always in concert with indigenous inhabitants. Maroons were known to join natives in their wars against the invaders and to return to plantations to reunite families and liberate friends. *Marronage* was common throughout the Caribbean and the Americas, with the earliest accounts of Africans joining forces with the Taino reported by the Spanish governor of Hispaniola in 1503. See Landers, "Central African Presence" 234.

21. P. Wood 51 and 51n.

22. This proclamation was reaffirmed in 1733, with the stipulation that runaways would owe four years of service to the Crown in exchange for their freedom. Landers, "Spanish Sanctuary" 297, 300.

23. Qtd. in Landers, "Spanish Sanctuary" 298.

24. P. Wood 143.

25. R. M. Brown 302; P. Wood 96.

26. "Making a way with no way" and "hitting a straight lick with a crooked stick" are two of Zora Neale Hurston's favorite folk phrases.

27. Janet Schaw's 1775 description of an alligator hunt notes that "the negroes . . . are very dextrous at this work," capturing a large specimen without white direction or much in the way of assistance. See Schaw, "Journal of an English Lady," in Lixl 45.

28. *Feenda* can also be spelled *finda* or *nfinda*—a West-Central African word for forest that implies both the physical entity and a place of contact with the "invisible" realms of ancestors, gods, and spirits. R. M. Brown 294–95.

29. P. Wood 95–96, 116–17.

30. P. Wood 147 and 151.

31. Swiss emigrant Samuel Dyssli (1737), qtd. in P. Wood 132.

32. R. M. Brown 295.

33. P. Wood 304–5.

34. Candler et al. vol. 22, pt. 2, 232–36. Some scholars credit the account to Gen. James Oglethorpe, founder and leader of the Georgia colony. Also printed in M. E. Smith, *Stono*.

35. "Residual African Elements in the Blues" (1961), in Dundes 95–103.

36. Rumors of conspiracies continued to circulate and actual plots to be discovered, culminating in June 1740, when 150 to 200 enslaved persons rebelled near Goose Creek, north of Charleston. This revolt had no real chance of success; the band was unable to obtain arms and, even if they had been, had no direct road, as the Stono rebels did, through Georgia to St. Augustine. P. Wood 318–19.

37. New Grenada was the jurisdiction or viceroyalty that included the modern states of Panama, Ecuador, Colombia, and Venezuela as well as northern Peru, northwestern Brazil, Guyana, southwestern Suriname, and the islands of Trinidad and Tobago.

38. Riordan 30.

39. McKittrick xi–xii.

40. McKittrick xvii.

41. Cartwright, *Sacral Grooves* 44.

42. Cartwright, *Sacral Grooves* 45–46.

43. Opala.

44. Seminole Nation Museum.

45. Opala.

46. Toomer, "Conversion," in *Cane* 28.

47. Cartwright puns on sacred groves/grooves and invokes Toomer's "Conversion" in his exploration of Afro-creole agency in unsettling Western notions of modernity. He writes, "Along with Deleuze and Guattari, we find '[c]ollective assemblages of enunciation' moving in rhizomatic patterns, 'agglomerating very diverse acts, not only linguistic, but also perceptive, mimetic, gestural and cognitive' in a 'throng of dialects, patois, slangs, and specialized languages.' The lowcountry's creole language (Gullah or Geechee) offers vital perspective on complex machineries of globalization and counter cultural feedback." *Sacral Grooves* 37.

48. Hurston uses this phrase describing her performances for Charlotte Osgood Mason in *Dust Tracks on a Road* 689.

49. Hazel Carby's critiques of Hurston appear in multiple publications, but here I'm paraphrasing from "Politics of Fiction, Anthropology, and the Folk." Dale Pattinson makes sensitive use of Foucault's notion of the "heterotopia" in "Sites of Resistance."

50. Hurston, "Mules and Men" 9.

51. Hurston, *Dust Tracks on a Road* 580.

52. Kaplan 13.

53. Hurston, "Mules and Men" 10. This is a play on the opening of *Their Eyes Were Watching God*. See Wall, *Zora Neale Hurston: Novels and Stories* 175.

54. R. Wright.

55. Qtd. in Kaplan 27.

56. Signifying is a form of verbal art and culturally specific irony of which Hurston was a past master. The art offers speakers the ability to demonstrate their mastery of rhythm and rhyme, improvise on the verbal play of others, and express ideas, opinions, and feelings by indirection. "One who signifies says without really saying, criticizes without criticizing, insults without really insulting," writes Theodore Mason Jr. in "Signifying."

57. Rosaldo 180.

58. The method is one that would be embraced by future generations of African American writers and scholars. For an excellent summary account and a genealogy of this exploration of Hurston's method, see Pryse and Spillers.

59. Hurston, *Dust Tracks on a Road* 618.

60. Quotes from Kaplan 437–38.

61. Bordelon 3.

62. Kaplan 37.

63. He did not, for example, decline into irrelevance after her mother's death, as Hurston's memoir insists. His election to the Baptist Convention and terms as mayor occurred after his remarriage and Hurston's expulsion from the family home. Bordelon 7.

64. Bordelon 5.

65. Indeed, the critical literature exploring what Cheryl Wall called "the connection between voice and selfhood, between the power of speech and personal status" is vast and has only grown since she wrote *Women of the Harlem Renaissance* (142).

66. Hurston, *Dust Tracks on a Road* 680.

67. Hurston, *Dust Tracks on a Road* 685–86.

68. Salamone 217.

69. Salamone 218.

70. Even Hurston's own biographer, Robert Hemenway, expressed the prevailing view in 1980 that "writing as an artist rather than as a folklorist or historian" (101) was a flaw rather than an approach with its own logic and validity. Elsewhere, he called it a "vocational schizophrenia" (63). See Sexton 192 and Dutton 138.

71. Hurston had based the sermon in her novel on one she collected from Rev. C. C. Lovelace of Eau Gallie, Florida, and published in Nancy Cunard's *Negro* anthology. Hurston to James Weldon Johnson, 8 May 1934, in Kaplan 302.

72. J. W. Johnson, *Along This Way* 158, 179.
73. J. W. Johnson, "Preface," in *God's Trombones* 838–39.
74. J. W. Johnson, "Preface," in *The Book of American Negro Poetry* 713–14.
75. Qtd. in Sexton 200.
76. Qtd. in Kaplan 17.
77. Hurston, "Spirituals and Neo-spirituals" 870.
78. Hurston, "Characteristics of Negro Expression" 836.
79. Jahn 98–99.
80. Hurston, "Go Gator and Muddy the Water" 69.
81. J. W. Johnson, "Race Prejudice" 775.
82. Frazier, "Certain Aspects" 77; Frazier, "Changing Status" 390.
83. C. S. Johnson, "Education of the Negro Child" 264, 266.
84. Lenz, "Southern Exposures" 10.
85. Catherine Stewart 170.
86. Hurston, "Sanctified Church" 95–96.
87. Cooper 41.
88. Hurston to Corse, 3 Dec. 1938, Kaplan 417–18.
89. Kennedy and Corse, qtd. in Catherine Stewart 172–73.
90. Tidwell and Wright 813–14.
91. Hurston, *Dust Tracks on a Road* 689.
92. Wall, "Chronology," in *Zora Neale Hurston: Folklore, Memoirs, and Other Writings* 966, 972. Hughes certainly suggests feminine competition is at the root of the matter in *The Big Sea*, writing, "She felt that if the play were ever produced I would only take my half of the money and spend it on a girl she didn't like." Hurston biographer Robert Hemenway and Hughes biographer Arnold Rampersad echo this interpretation. See "The Mule Bone Controversy," in Hurston and Hughes, *Mule Bone* 139, 171, 203.
93. Hurston to Charlotte Osgood Mason, 16 Sept. 1932, Kaplan 272; Hurston to Mason, 15 Oct. 1931, Kaplan 234. For a point of comparison, the *Mule Bone* crack-up occurred in February 1931.
94. Hurston, *Dust Tracks on a Road* 731.
95. Hurston, *Tell My Horse* 113.
96. Dutton 147–48.
97. As described in Davis.
98. Hurston, *Tell My Horse* 17–18, 113–14.
99. Qtd. in Sexton 204.
100. Threadcraft.
101. Hurston, *Dust Tracks on a Road* 715; Sexton 205.
102. Kaplan 447.

Chapter 7. Plenty o' Nothin

1. Marks.
2. This would involve breaking George Gershwin's will and testament—both Gershwin and Heyward believed that "blacking up" by white singers would do irreparable damage to the unprecedented sense of verisimilitude to Negro life they believed the opera had established. Cf. Tommasini.
3. Roach 69.

4. Here I do not mean to suggest that there has not been sensitive and thoughtful criticism of Heyward's work. But not until Yuhl did modern race criticism informed by African American studies perspectives in history and literature become a part of the conversation.

5. Van Vechten 219.

6. Heyward, "New Note."

7. Hutchisson 8–9.

8. Letter, 10 April 1923 (43/2151) South Carolina Historical Society.

9. At some point during her son's adolescence, Janie Screven Heyward's love of collecting and writing stories, poetry, and comic or sentimental Gullah tales became a real vocation: she became a "dialect recitalist," eventually winning local acclaim and a small regional reputation. The J. S. Heyward Notebooks at the South Carolina Historical Society simply bulge with the Gullah poems, stories, and anecdotes that Janie Heyward wrote between 1882 and 1914—as well as the news clips, letters, family stories, and diary entries that were the grist for her mill. Her first book of poetry, *Wild Roses*, found a New York publisher and saw print in 1905—just as her "dreamy" son, then around twenty, was starting to stabilize the family's finances with the insurance business he cofounded. As the son's efforts removed more and more of the financial load from his mother's shoulders, the elder Heyward went on the lecture circuit and served as a radio program hostess—eventually charging as much as fifty dollars for a ninety-minute lecture program at a time when a loaf of bread cost five cents.

10. All quotations from DuBose Heyward, *Porgy* (1925).

11. The writers are both South Carolinians: Julia Peterkin, who wrote six novels, story collections, and memoirs between 1924 and 1934, winning the Pulitzer Prize in 1929 for *Scarlet Sister Mary*; and E. C. L. Adams, whose *Congaree Sketches* (1927) and *Nigger to Nigger* (1928) won the approval of no less a critic than Sterling Brown. There is a copious and perceptive literature on Peterkin. For a contemporary evaluation of Adams's work, see Brown's "Folk Literature" 228. A more recent evaluation appears in Robert O'Meally's critical edition of Adams's selected works titled *Tales of the Congaree* (1987). See particularly the introduction.

12. "Orature" is a term borrowed from Kenyan novelist and director Ngugi wa Thiong'o by way of Joseph Roach. By "orature," Thiong'o means that literacy and orality are not opposed forms of communication but modes that have produced one another interactively over time. See Roach 11–12.

13. The phenomenon may seem counterintuitive given the discussion of "language death" in the previous chapters. But linguistics teaches us that while the languages of subject peoples are often overwhelmed by their conquerors, this is not *always* so. Sometimes, as in the case of Fulani overlords in West Africa, the Normans in England, and Cromwell's English overlords in Ireland, it's the *conquerors* whose mother tongues are swept away. The common threads weaving together these widely disparate examples from West Africa, the United Kingdom, and the lowcountry are economic and geographical: all are examples of rural economies operating near to the level of subsistence. Elites in each of these areas could and did become fabulously wealthy, but given their status as absentee landlords living off the fat of the land, they were neither numerous enough nor influential enough in the day-to-day lives of the rural populations to cause language loss among those subject to their will. At the same time, so skewed were the population ratios that the elites themselves lost a portion of their heritage from the economically superior culture. See Nettle and Romaine 128–30. These populations became recognizably hybrid, though perhaps not

to themselves: "A part yet apart, at home and not-home neither 'here' nor 'there,'" in the majority culture (Singh and Schmidt 7). To summarize, in the lowcountry, it seems, surprisingly large numbers of whites weren't just bilingual in Gullah—they were monolingual in it too.

14. Roach uses the concept of a "circum-Atlantic World," in contrast to the transatlantic, to achieve two purposes: first, to complicate linear, "transatlantic" narratives by substituting for them the idea of a vortex, in which commodities and cultural practices continually circulate and recirculate; and second, to foreground the role of violence, the histories of diaspora and genocide that created the culture of modernity.

15. Duck 266.

16. Consider "Black Truth and Black Beauty: A Retrospective Review of the Literature of the Negro for 1932" (1933) or "Sterling Brown: The New Negro Folk Poet" (1934), both collected in Locke, *Critical Temper of Alain Locke*.

17. We have seen how Hurston's critical mauling started with Locke and Du Bois and continued with Richard Wright through to important modern critics such as Paul Gilroy and Hazel Carby.

18. The city annexed the Neck in 1849 because it was a known haunt of runaway slaves. Powers 23.

19. Pujol.

20. Farrow 64–66.

21. This definition of "styling" is derived from architectural critic William Wesley Taylor of the University of Cincinnati (123).

22. *Time*, 26 Aug. 1935.

23. Lonnie Hamilton III, personal communication, 29 Apr. 2008; Chilton.

24. The comments of Anna Hamilton and Sarah Dowling are from interviews with the author—in December 1994 and March 1995 for Hamilton and March 1995 for Dowling.

25. See Bruce Jackson's *Get Your Ass in the Water and Swim Like Me: Narrative Poetry from Black Oral Tradition* (1974) for a provocative introduction to the African American outlaw figure.

26. Waters 238.

27. For information on Bess, see Rosen. The comments of Alphonso Brown are from an interview with the author, 30 Apr. 1999.

28. Qtd. in Crawford 17.

29. Heyward was a polio survivor—the disease permanently weakened his right arm and side and possibly contributed to his early death.

30. "Notes on Music and Opera," in Auden's *Selected Essays*.

31. H. Allen; Killens 43.

32. Du Bois, "Criteria of Negro Art" 1001.

33. John Rutledge (1739–1800) was the first governor of the state of South Carolina and a signer of the U.S. Constitution. His house, on that critical borderline Broad Street, is on the U.S. National Register of Historic Places. DuBose Heyward, *Porgy* 17.

34. Mellers 179.

35. The parade and picnic in part IV satirize early-century July Fourth festivities, a day of celebration for the formerly enslaved, but only for them, as what Heyward calls "the social code" forbade elite white Charleston from so much as acknowledging the day. Also described in Kytle and Roberts.

36. Eco.

37. DuBose Heyward, *Porgy* 13, 18, 57.

38. For a description of the social role and cultural fears of the "bad man," see Jackson, *Get Your Ass in the Water* 30–31.

39. DuBose Heyward, *Porgy* 21–22.

40. McInnis, *Politics of Taste* 225–26.

41. DuBose Heyward, *Porgy* 27.

42. This is central to Grace Hale's argument in the indispensable *Making Whiteness* (87).

43. For decades Hollis Alpert's *The Life and Times of Porgy and Bess* (1990) was the only book-length treatment, though Ellen Noonan's *The Strange Career of Porgy and Bess* (2012) has offered a much-needed update.

44. John Bennett, "To DuBose Heyward," 18 Apr. 1932, DuBose Heyward Papers, South Carolina Historical Society, emphasis original.

45. For cogent analyses of these matters, see Douglas; and Sieglinde Lemke.

46. Waters 237–39. Among many other roles, Harvey played Maria in *Porgy and Bess*.

47. Toomer, *Letters* 132.

48. Qtd. in Durham, "Poetry" 13.

49. Durham, *Merrill Studies in Cane* 11–14.

50. Kerman and Eldridge 95.

51. James 145.

52. Toomer, *Letters* 181–82. Joel Elias Spingarn was the former Columbia University professor of comparative literature who founded Harcourt Brace & Jovanovich publishers. A liberal Jewish Republican and ally of W. E. B. Du Bois, he was a cofounder, the second president, and the chairman of the board of the NAACP from 1913 until his death in 1939. He established the NAACP's Spingarn Medal, for "American Negroes who perform acts of distinguished merit and achievement," in 1913.

53. DuBose Heyward, *Mamba's Daughters*.

54. The original stage directions to the play specify that Gullah is to be spoken as the curtain rises, though "[t]he audience understands none of it.... Like the laughter and movement, the twanging of a guitar from an upper window, the dancing of an urchin with a loose, shuffling step, it is a part of the picture of Catfish Row as it really is—an alien scene, a people as little known to most Americans as the people of the Congo.... Gradually it seems to the audience that they are beginning to understand this foreign language. In reality, the 'Gullah' is being tempered to their ears, spoken more distinctly with the African words omitted" (Dorothy Heyward 1).

55. Of course, Gullah speakers were perfectly capable of understanding English—they simply didn't always choose to speak it. Dorothy Heyward 2.

56. Statistics for all Broadway plays may be found in the International Broadway Database, http://www.ibdb.com/production.asp?ID=10467. There was also a brief Broadway revival of thirty-four performances in 1929, as was customary after a regional tour.

57. J. W. Johnson, *Black Manhattan* 795.

58. Qtd. in Pollack 567.

59. Pollack 568.

60. "Helen L. Phillips." According to a 9 Aug. 2005 obituary in the *Los Angeles Times*, Helen L. Phillips was hired as an extra for five performances in a Metropolitan Opera production of Mascagni's *Cavalleria Rusticana* from Dec. 1947 to Feb. 1948. Quoting a Met archivist, the story also notes that the Marian Anderson debut came in 1955, with the role of Ulrica in Verdi's *A Masked Ball*, and that the first Black contract player for the Met was Elinor Harper.

61. Lou Paley was a lyricist and sometime collaborator with Gershwin, who hosted a salon with his wife, also the sister to Ira Gershwin's wife.

62. Dorothy Heyward, DuBose Heyward Papers.
63. George Gershwin to DuBose Heyward, 29 Mar. 1932.
64. Gershwin offers this view in just about every interview he gave on the subject.
65. Pollack 574.
66. Bhabha 86.
67. Roach 6.
68. Gershwin is said to have told a friend that his fascination with "Negro rags, blues, and spirituals" dated from 1905, when he first heard James Reese Europe's band playing at the Barron Wilkins, at Seventh Avenue and 134th Street, a private club with an exclusive, white clientele. Other influences included W. C. Handy, whom Gershwin presented with a signed copy of the solo version of *Rhapsody in Blue* in 1926, and James P. Johnson, whose gigantic stature among Harlem's stride piano players is indicated by his lineage: Fats Waller, Willie "the Lion" Smith, Count Basie, Duke Ellington, and Art Tatum, on down to Thelonious Monk (Schuller 214). The anecdotes about Europe and Handy are described in Pollack 52–56. Pollack touches on Johnson's career in 74–75, mistakenly attributing his ambition as a pianist—Johnson was a prolific producer of jazz songs, collaborated on several successful Broadway shows (including *Runnin' Wild* from 1921, which gave the world the tune and dance "Charleston"), and composed operas (*'De Organizer*, with a libretto by Langston Hughes) and symphonic music (*Yamekraw: A Negro Rhapsody*)—to a desire to emulate Gershwin. But Gunther Schuller suggests that the influence worked the opposite way—as early as 1920 Johnson was "the undisputed leader of the Harlem piano school (Eubie Blake and Jelly Roll Morton's contributions not withstanding)," he says, pointing to a lineage that was still lively in the 1960s. Johnson played with James Reese Europe's Hellfighters bands in 1920 and 1921, among whom Gershwin is likely first to have encountered him. Schuller also definitively traces Johnson's interest in "serious" music to his broad classical training and the influence of Scott Joplin, particularly Joplin's opera *Treemonisha*.
69. Qtd. in Wyatt and Johnson 193.
70. Ralph Bennet was the real name of the Honey Man. See the text and photographs in Gay and Rhett's *200 Years of Charleston Cooking*, 224–25.
71. Gershwin wrote "Summertime" immediately after this trip as well. The Charleston visit was a brief stopover while the composer was traveling to Palm Beach with friend Emil Mosbacher before a thirty-city tour celebrating the tenth anniversary of *Rhapsody in Blue*. See Swain 205 and Wyatt and Johnson 212.
72. Pollack 578; Dorothy Heyward Papers, South Carolina Historical Society, from her unpublished autobiography.
73. The John A. Lomax Southern States collection contains a recording of this play, written and directed by Rosa Warren Wilson and sung by singers from the New Jerusalem AME Church community on Wadmalaw Island, for performances in and around Charleston in the late 1930s (Hodges).
74. Qtd. in Pollack 578.
75. Armitage 39.
76. Pollack 578.
77. Dorothy Heyward, unpublished autobiography, Dorothy Heyward Manuscript Papers, South Carolina Historical Society.
78. Mellers 181.
79. Pollack 603.
80. Both men later recanted, but it took them twenty years to do so (Schwartz 245).
81. Wyatt and Johnson 201.
82. Roach 30.

83. Alpert 280.

84. The latter of which was the occasion for Tommasini's controversial column.

85. We should note, however, that a mini-revival seems to have been sparked in the last decade beginning with the Gershwin Centennial celebrations in 1996 and 1998. The Nashville Symphony mounted a production in 2006, as did Trevor Nunn at London's Savoy Theatre the same year. The Los Angeles Opera followed in 2007. Three important stagings followed in the 2010s: Audra Macdonald's "stripped-down" version for Broadway in 2012; the revival staged for the fortieth anniversary of the Spoleto Festival U.S.A. in 2017; and the Met's restaging of the classic in 2019. Each of these revivals has borne the imprimatur of African American artists. Suzan-Lori Parks slimmed down the book for Broadway; Gullah artist Jonathan Greene vividly reimagined the visual concepts for Spoleto. The brightness and color of Greene's staging seem to have influenced the visual design for the Met.

86. Qtd. in Wyatt and Johnson 221–22.

87. Wyatt and Johnson 229.

88. Wyatt and Johnson 234.

89. Qtd. in Pollack 597.

90. Qtd. in Wyatt and Johnson 233–34.

91. Wyatt and Johnson 234–35.

92. See, for example, S. Young 338.

93. Pollack 617–18.

94. Woods 28–29.

95. Woods 31.

96. Pollack 613.

97. Schuller 214.

98. Virginia Mixson Geraty, personal communication, April 1998.

99. Farrow 65.

100. All articles appeared in the *Charleston News and Courier*: 11 Mar. 1959, 23 June 1959, and 3 Nov. 1961.

101. Indeed, when Dorothy Heyward learned of Mrs. Elvira Gibbs's existence, her first thought was for her reputation. She eventually offered Mrs. Gibbs five hundred dollars through a friend, Thomas Waring, and was astonished when the family rejected the humiliating conditions attached: that the money would be placed in a bank account and given to M. Virginia Myers, a white neighbor, who would dole payments out to Gibbs at the rate of ten dollars a week. Noonan 250–52.

Afterword

1. I refer, of course, to "The Gold Bug," published 1843. There is also a Gold Bug Island just inland of Sullivan's Island.

2. Park Ranger Michael Allen, personal communication, 27 July 2007.

3. James H. Soltow provides a full discussion of the issues of serving Irish labor in *Stella Maris Church*.

4. William Loren Katz's books *The Black West* and *Black Indians: A Hidden Heritage* did much to popularize the connection between Gullah "maroons" and the Seminole Wars, particularly for young audiences. This story, however, is one that the dominant narrative has not yet been capable of assimilating.

5. July 4 is significant not only as Independence Day but also as the date on which some groups commemorate Denmark Vesey's death. He was executed on 2 July 1822. Halim Gullahbemi, personal communication, 24 July 2007.

6. "Queen Quet" is a diminutive of "Marquetta."

7. Linguist John Baugh offers a provocative discussion of the sociopolitical consequences of the U.S. refusal to grant minority language rights to African Americans—or indeed any minority language speakers in *Beyond Ebonics* 3.

WORKS CITED

Abrahams, Roger. "Black Talk and Black Education." *Florida Reporter* Spring/Summer 1969.
———. *Singing the Master: The Emergence of African American Culture in the Plantation South.* New York: Penguin, 1993.
Adams, Edward C. L. *Tales of the Congaree.* Ed. Robert G. O'Meally. Chapel Hill: University of North Carolina Press, 1987.
Alice Ravenel Huger Smith of Charleston, South Carolina: An Appreciation, on the Occasion of Her Eightieth Birthday. Charleston, S.C.: Privately published, 1956.
Allen, Hervey. *DuBose Heyward: A Critical and Biographical Sketch, Including Contemporary Estimates of His Work.* New York: George H. Doran, 1920.
Allen, James. *Without Sanctuary: Lynching Photography in America.* Santa Fe, N.Mex.: Twin Palms, 2000.
Allen, Michael. Telephone interview, 27 July 2007.
Allen, Theodore. *The Invention of the White Race.* Vol. 2: *The Origin of Racial Oppression in Anglo-America.* New York: Verso, 1997.
Alpert, Hollis. *The Life and Times of Porgy and Bess: The Story of an American Classic.* New York: Knopf, 1990.
Anderson, Charles R. *Charleston: A Golden Memory.* Charleston, S.C.: Wyrick, 1992.
Anziano, Santina. "Lillie: Cupola Usage Study of a Mesolect Gullah Speaker from the Federal Writers Project." M.A. thesis, University of South Carolina, 1998.
Appiah, K. Anthony. *In My Father's House: Africa in the Philosophy of Culture.* New York: Oxford University Press, 1992.
Armitage, Merle, ed. *George Gershwin.* Harlow, U.K.: Longmans, Green, 1938.
Asante, Molefi Kete. "African Elements in African American English." *Africanisms in American Culture.* Ed. Joseph Holloway. Bloomington: Indiana University Press, 1990. 65–92.
Auden, W. H. *Selected Essays.* 1962. London: Faber & Faber, 1964.
Bailey, Guy. "The Relationship between African American Vernacular English and White Vernaculars in the American South: A Sociocultural History and Some Phonological Evidence." *Sociocultural and Historical Contexts of African American English.* Ed. Sonja L. Lanehart. Amsterdam: John Benjamins, 2001. 71–110.
Bailey, Rosalie Vincent. "DuBose Heyward: Poet, Novelist, and Playwright." M.A. thesis, Duke University, 1941.
Baldwin, James. "Everybody's Protest Novel." *Notes of a Native Son.* 4th ed. Boston: Beacon, 1984.
Ball, Edward. *Slaves in the Family.* New York: Farrar, Straus and Giroux, 1998.
Bambara, Toni Cade. "Deep Sight and Rescue Missions." *Lure and Loathing: Essays on Race, Identity, and the Ambivalence of Assimilation.* Ed. Gerald Early. New York: Penguin, 1993. 163–74.
Baraka, Amiri. "The Changing Same (R&B and New Black Music)." 1968. *The LeRoi*

Jones/Amiri Baraka Reader. Ed. William J. Harris. New York: Thunder's Mouth, 1991. 186–209.

Barry, Brewton. "The Mestizos of South Carolina." *American Journal of Sociology* 51.1 (July 1945): 34–41.

Barthes, Roland. *Camera Lucida: Reflections on Photography.* Trans. Richard Howard. New York: Hill & Wang, 1981.

Bascom, William R. "Acculturation among the Gullah Negroes." *American Anthropologist* New Series 43.1 (Jan.–Mar. 1941): 43–50.

Bass, Jack, and Jack Nelson. *The Orangeburg Massacre.* 1970, 1984. Macon, Ga.: Mercer University Press, 1990.

Bateman, Rebecca B. "Africans and Indians: A Comparative Study of the Black Carib and Black Seminole." *Ethnohistory* 37.1 (Winter 1990): 1–24.

Baugh, John. *Beyond Ebonics: Linguistic Pride and Racial Prejudice.* New York: Oxford University Press, 2000.

Behar, Ruth. *The Vulnerable Observer: Anthropology That Breaks Your Heart.* Boston: Beacon, 1996.

Bell, Bernard W., Emily R. Groshoz, and James B. Stewart, eds. *W. E. B. Du Bois on Race and Culture.* New York: Routledge, 1997.

Bennett, John. *The Doctor to the Dead: Grotesque Legends and Folk Tales of Old Charleston.* 1946. Columbia: University of South Carolina Press, 1995.

———. *Madame Margot: A Grotesque Legend of Old Charleston.* 1921. Hardpress, 2013.

Berger, John. *Ways of Seeing.* 1972. London: British Broadcasting Corporation & Penguin, 1977.

Bergner, Gwen. *Taboo Subjects: Race, Sex, and Psychoanalysis.* Minneapolis: University of Minnesota Press, 2005.

Berlin, Ira. "Time, Space, and the Evolution of African-American Society." *Slavery in American Society.* 3rd ed. Ed. Lawrence Goodheart, Richard Brown, and Stephen Rabe. Lexington, Mass.: D.C. Heath, 1993. 34–69.

Berman, Mark. "S.C. Gov. Nikki Haley: Charleston Gunman Should Face the Death Penalty." *Washington Post* 19 June 2015. https://wapo.st/3xhP44A.

Berry, Wendell. *The Hidden Wound.* 1970. Berkeley, Calif.: Counterpoint, 2010.

Bhabha, Homi K. *The Location of Culture.* London: Routledge, 1994.

Blair, Sara. "Cultural Geography and the Place of the Literary." *American Literary History* 10.3 (Autumn 1998): 544–67.

Bland, Sidney. *Preserving Charleston's Past, Shaping Its Future: The Life and Times of Susan Pringle Frost.* Westport, Conn.: Greenwood, 1994.

Blight, David. "Quarrel Forgotten or a Revolution Remembered? Reunion and Race in the Memory of the Civil War, 1875–1913." *Union and Emancipation: Essays on Politics and Race in the Civil War Era.* Ed. David Blight and Brooks D. Simpson. Kent, Ohio: Kent State University Press, 1997. 151–79.

———. *Race and Reunion: The Civil War in American Memory.* Cambridge, Mass.: Harvard University Press, 2001.

Bodin, Jean. *Method for the Easy Comprehension of History.* Ed. Beatrice Reynolds. New York: Octagon, 1966.

Bolton, Ruthie. *Gal: A True Life.* New York: Harcourt Brace, 1994.

Bongie, Chris. "Resisting Memories: The Creole Identities of Lafcadio Hearn and Edouard Glissant." *SubStance* 23.3 (1997): 153–78.

Bordelon, Pamela, ed. *Go Gator and Muddy the Water: Writings by Zora Neale Hurston from the Federal Writers' Project.* New York: Norton, 1999.

Brathwaite, Edward Kamau. *The History of the Voice: The Development of Nation Language in Anglophone Caribbean Poetry*. London: New Beacon, 1984.
Brown, Alphonso. Personal communication, 30 Apr. 1999.
Brown, DeNeen L., and Abby Phillip. "In Charleston, Thousands Join Hands to Show Solidarity, Mourn 'Emanuel Nine.'" *Washington Post* 21 June 2015. https://wapo.st/3fk49fx.
Brown, Ras Michael. "'Walk in the Feenda': West-Central Africans and the Forest in the South Carolina-Georgia Lowcountry." *Central Africans and Cultural Transformations in the American Diaspora*. Ed. Linda M. Heywood. 2002. Cambridge: Cambridge University Press, 2011. 289–318.
Brown, Sterling A. "Folk Literature." *A Son's Return: Selected Essays of Sterling A. Brown*. Ed. Mark Sanders. Boston: Northeastern University Press, 1996. 207–31.
———. "Negro Characters as Seen by White Authors." *Journal of Negro Education* 2.2 (Apr. 1933): 179–203.
———. *A Son's Return: Selected Essays of Sterling A. Brown*. Ed. Mark Sanders. Boston: Northeastern University Press, 1996.
Buell, Lawrence. "American Pastoral Ideology Reappraised." *American Literary History* 1.1 (Spring 1989): 1–29.
Burgett, Bruce, and Glenn Hendler. "Space." *Keywords for Southern Studies*. Ed. Scott Romine and Jennifer Rae Greeson. Athens: University of Georgia Press, 2016. 301–5.
Burroughs, Franklin. "Low Country Legacy." *National Geographic* Nov. 2014. https://www.nationalgeographic.com/magazine/article/ace-basin.
Butler, Judith Butler, Ernesto Laclau, and Slavoj Žižek, eds. *Contingency, Hegemony, Universality: Contemporary Dialogues on the Left*. London: Verso, 2000.
Candler, Allen D., et al., eds. *The Colonial Records of the State of Georgia*. Atlanta: Byrd, 1913.
Capeci, Dominic J., Jr., and Jack C. Knight. "Reckoning with Violence: W. E. B. Du Bois and the 1906 Atlanta Race Riot." *Journal of Southern History* 62.4 (Nov. 1996): 727–66.
Carawan, Guy, recorder. *Been in the Storm So Long: Spirituals and Shouts, Children's Game Songs, and Folktales*. With Benjamin Bligen, Laura Rivers, Esau Jenkins, Bertha Smith, Alice Wine, Mary Pinckney, Janie Hunter, Moving Star Hall Singers. Folkways 3842. Smithsonian Folkways Records, 1967.
Carawan, Guy, and Candie Carawan. *"Aint You Got a Right to the Tree of Life": The People of John's Island, South Carolina—Their Faces, Their Words, and Their Songs*. 1966. Athens: University of Georgia Press, 1994.
Carby, Hazel. "Foreword: Zora Neale Hurston." *Seraph on the Suwanee*. 1948. New York: Harper, 1991.
———. "The Politics of Fiction, Anthropology, and the Folk: Zora Neale Hurston." *New Essays on Their Eyes Were Watching God*. Ed. Michael Awkward. New York: Cambridge University Press, 1990. 71–90.
Carney, Judith. *Black Rice: The African Origins of Rice Cultivation in the Americas*. Cambridge, Mass.: Harvard University Press, 2001.
Carter, Harold. *The Prayer Tradition of Black People*. Valley Forge, Pa.: Judson, 1976.
Cartwright, Keith. *Reading Africa into American Literature: Epics, Fables, and Gothic Tales*. Lexington: University Press of Kentucky, 2002.
———. *Sacral Grooves, Limbo Gateways: Travels in Deep Southern Time. Circum-Caribbean Space, Afro-creole Authority*. Athens: University of Georgia Press, 2013.
Cash, W. J. *The Mind of the South*. 1941. New York: Knopf, 1978.
Cavallero, Dani. *Art for Beginners*. Illus. Carline Vago-Hughes. London: Writers & Readers, 2000.

Chang, Stewart. "Our National Psychosis: Guns, Terror, and Hegemonic Masculinity." *Harvard Civil Liberties Law Review* 53 (Oct. 2018): 495–532.

Chaplin, Joyce E. "Creoles in British America: From Denial to Acceptance." *Creolization: History, Ethnography, Theory*. Ed. Charles Stewart. Walnut Creek, Calif.: Left Coast, 2007. 46–65.

Chilton, John. *A Jazz Nursery: The Story of the Jenkins' Orphanage Bands of Charleston, South Carolina*. London: Bloomsbury, 1980.

Ciucevich, Robert. *Glynn County Historic Resources Survey Report, Glynn County Georgia*. Glynn County Board of Commissioners, July 2009.

Clifford, James. *Routes: Travel and Translation in the Late Twentieth Century*. Cambridge, Mass.: Harvard University Press, 1997.

Clifford, James, and George E. Marcus, eds. *Writing Culture: The Poetics and Politics of Ethnography*. 1986. Berkeley: University of California Press, 2010.

Clinton, Catherine. *The Plantation Mistress*. New York: Pantheon, 1982.

Coclanis, Peter A. "The Sociology of Architecture in Colonial Charleston: Patter and Process in an Eighteenth-Century Southern City." *Journal of Social History* 18.4 (Summer 1985): 605–23.

Cohn, Raymond L. "Deaths of Slaves in the Middle Passage." *Journal of Economic History* 45.3 (Sept. 1985): 685–92.

Conde, Maryse. *The Last of the African Kings*. Trans. Richard Philcox. 1993. Lincoln: University of Nebraska Press, 1997.

Cooper, Melissa L. *Making Gullah: A History of Sapelo Islanders, Race, and the American Imagination*. Chapel Hill: University of North Carolina Press, 2017.

Cosby, Bill. "Dr. Bill Cosby Speaks at the 50th Anniversary Commemoration of the *Brown v. Topeka Board of Education* Supreme Court Decision, May 22, 2004." *Black Scholar* 24.4 (Winter 2004).

Cothran, James R. *Gardens and Historic Plants of the Antebellum South*. Columbia: University of South Carolina Press, 2003.

———. *The Gardens of Historic Charleston*. Columbia: University of South Carolina Press, 1995.

Cottom, Tressie MacMillan. "In the Name of Beauty." *Thick: And Other Essays*. New York: New Press, 2019. 33–72.

Counihan, Clare. "Reading the Figure of Woman in African Literature: Psychoanalysis, Difference, and Desire." *Research in African Literatures* 38.2 (Summer 2007): 161–80.

Courtenay, William A. *The Centennial of Incorporation*. Charleston, S.C., 1883.

Crawford, Richard. "It Ain't Necessarily Soul: Gershwin's 'Porgy and Bess' as a Symbol." *Anuario Interamericano de Investigacion Musical* 8 (1972): 17–38.

Creel, Margaret Washington. *"A Peculiar People": Slave Religion and Community-Culture among the Gullahs*. New York: New York University Press, 1988.

Crèvecoeur, J. Hector St. John de. *Letters from an American Farmer*. 1782, 1912. London: J. M. Dent, 1926.

Crystal, David. *Language Death*. Cambridge: Cambridge University Press, 2000.

Cukor-Avila, Patricia. "Co-existing Grammars: The Relationship between the Evolution of African American and Southern White Vernacular English in the South." *Sociocultural and Historical Contexts of African American English*. Ed. Sonja L. Laneheart. Amsterdam: John Benjamins, 2001. 93–128.

Cullen, Jim. *The Civil War in Popular Culture: A Reusable Past*. Washington, D.C.: Smithsonian Institution, 1995.

Culler, Jonathan. *Literary Theory: A Very Short Introduction*. Oxford: Oxford University Press, 1997.
Cunard, Nancy, ed. *Negro: An Anthology*. 1934. New York: Continuum, 2002.
Cuthbert, Robert B., and Stephen G. Hoffius. *Northern Money and Southern Land: The Lowcountry Sketches of Clothilde R. Martin*. Columbia: University of South Carolina Press, 2009.
Dance, Daryl Cumber. "Zora Neale Hurston." *American Women Writers: Bibliographical Essays*. Ed. Maurice Duke, Jackson R. Bryer, and Thomas M. Inge. Westport, Conn.: Greenwood, 1983. 321–51.
Dash, Julie. *Daughters of the Dust: The Making of an African American Woman's Film*. New York: New Press, 1992.
Davey, Elizabeth. "The Souths of Sterling A. Brown." *Southern Cultures* 5.2 (Summer 1999): 20–45.
Davis, Wade. *The Serpent and the Rainbow: A Harvard Scientist's Astonishing Journey into the Secret Societies of Haitian Voodoo, Zombies, and Magic*. New York: Touchstone, 1985.
Diamond, Jeremy, and Dana Bash. "Nikki Haley Calls for Removal of Confederate Flag from Capitol Grounds." <OSC>cnn</OSC> *Politics* 24 June 2015. https://cnn.it/2Vgs6ov.
Douglas, Ann. *Terrible Honesty: Mongrel Manhattan in the 1920s*. New York: Noonday Press, 1995.
Dowling, Sarah. Personal communication, March 1995.
Doyle, Don H. *New Men, New Cities, New South: Atlanta, Nashville, Charleston, Mobile, 1860–1910*. Chapel Hill: University of North Carolina Press, 1990.
Driskell, David C. *Two Centuries of Black American Art*. New York: Los Angeles County Museum of Art and Knopf, 1976.
Du Bois, W. E. B. *Black Reconstruction: An Essay toward a History of the Part Which Black Folk Played in the Attempt to Reconstruct America, 1860–1880*. New York: Harcourt, Brace, 1935.
———. *The Conservation of Races*. 1897. New York: Arno, 1969.
———. "Criteria of Negro Art." *W. E. B. Du Bois: Writings*. Ed. Nathan Huggins. New York: Library of America, 1986. 993–1002.
———. "The Damnation of Women." *W. E. B. Du Bois: Writings*. Ed. Nathan Huggins. New York: Library of America, 1986. 952–68.
———. *Dusk of Dawn: An Essay toward an Autobiography of a Race Concept*. 9th ed. Ed. Irene Diggs. 1940. New Brunswick, N.J.: Transaction, 2002.
———. "The Freedmen's Bureau." *Atlantic Monthly* 87 (1901): 354–65.
———. "My Evolving Program for Negro Freedom." *What the Negro Wants*. Ed. Rayford W. Logan. Chapel Hill: University of North Carolina Press, 1944. 31–70.
———. "*Porgy* by DuBose Heyward." *W. E. B. Du Bois: Writings*. Ed. Nathan Huggins. New York: Library of America, 1986. 1215.
———. "Reconstruction and Its Benefits." *American Historical Review* 15 (1909–10): 781–99.
———. *The Souls of Black Folk*. New York: A.C. McClurg, 1903.
———. *The Souls of Black Folk*. *W. E. B. Du Bois: Writings*. Ed. Nathan Huggins. New York: Library of America, 1986. 357–547.
DuCille, Ann. "The Occult of True Womanhood: Critical Demeanor and Black Feminist Studies." *Female Subjects in Black and White: Race, Psychoanalysis, Feminism*. Ed. Eliz-

abeth Abel, Barbara Christian, and Helene Moglen. Berkeley: University of California Press, 1997. 21–56.

———. "Postcolonialism and Afrocentricity: Discourse and Dat Course." *The Black Columbiad: Defining Moments in African American Literature and Culture*. Ed. Werner Sollors and Maria Diedrich. Cambridge, Mass.: Harvard University Press, 1994. 28–41.

Duck, Leigh Anne. "'Go There Tuh Know There': Zora Neale Hurston and the Chronotype of the Folk." *American Literary History* 13.2 (Summer 2001): 265–94.

Dukakis, Ali. "Lindsay Graham Says Church Shooting Suspect Roof Was Niece's Classmate." ABC News 18 June 2015. https://abcn.ws/3rQID7b.

Dunbar, Paul Laurence. "The Poet." *The Complete Poems of Paul Laurence Dunbar*. New York: Dodd, Mead, 1913.

Dundes, Alan, ed. *Mother Wit from the Laughing Barrel: Readings in the Interpretation of Afro-American Culture*. New York: Garland, 1981.

Durham, Frank, comp. *The Merrill Studies in Cane*. Columbus, Ohio: Charles E. Merrill, 1971.

———. "The Poetry Society of South Carolina's Turbulent Year: Self-Interest, Atheism, and Jean Toomer." *Southern Humanities Review* 5 (Winter 1971): 76–80. Repr. in Durham, *Studies in Cane*, 11–14.

Dutton, Wendy. "The Problem of Invisibility: Voodoo and Zora Neale Hurston." *Frontiers* 13.2 (1993): 131–52.

Eco, Umberto. "Ecology 1984 and Coca-Cola Made Flesh." *Travels in Hyperreality: Essays*. 1986. San Diego: Harcourt, 1990.

Edgar, Walter. *South Carolina: A History*. Columbia: University of South Carolina Press, 1998.

Eliade, Mircea. *Myths, Dreams, and Mysteries: The Encounter between Contemporary Faiths and Archaic Realities*. Trans. Philip Mairet. 1957. New York: Harper Colophon, 1960.

Ellison, Ralph. "Change the Joke and Slip the Yoke." *Shadow and Act*. 1953. New York: Quality, 1964.

———. "The Shadow and the Act." *Shadow and Act*. 1953. New York: Quality, 1964.

Emery, Amy Fass. "The Zombie in/as the Text: Zora Neale Hurston's *Tell My Horse*." *African American Review* 39.3 (Fall 2005): 327–36.

Epstein, Dena. "Spirituals." *New Encyclopedia of Southern Culture*. Vol. 12: *Music*. Ed. Bill C. Malone. Chapel Hill: University of North Carolina Press, 2008. 141–44.

Fabian, Johannes. *Time and the Other: How Anthropology Makes Its Object*. New York: Columbia University Press, 1983.

Fabre, Genevieve, and Michael Feith, eds. *Jean Toomer and the Harlem Renaissance*. New Brunswick, N.J.: Rutgers University Press, 2001.

Fanon, Frantz. *Black Skin, White Masks*. New York: Grove Press, 1967.

Farrow, David A. "Octogenarian Recalls Charleston of *Porgy and Bess*." *Carolina Style* Summer 1995: 64–66.

Fiedler, Leslie A. *Love and Death in the American Novel*. Rev. Ed. New York: Stein & Day, 1982.

Forbes, Jack D. *Black Africans and Native Americans: Color, Race and Caste in the Evolution of Red-Black Peoples*. New York: Blackwell, 1988.

Foster, Gaines. *Ghosts of the Confederacy: Defeat, the Lost Cause, and the Emergence of the New South, 1865–1913*. New York: Oxford University Press, 1987.

Foucault, Michel. *Discipline and Punish: The Birth of the Prison*. Trans. Alan Sheridan. New York: Pantheon, 1977.

———. *Language, Counter-Memory, Practice: Essays.* Ithaca, N.Y.: Cornell University Press, 1993.
———. "Of Other Spaces: Utopias and Heterotopias." 1967. Trans. Jay Miskowiec. *Architecture, Movement, Continuite* 5 (Oct. 1984): 46–49.
———. *This Is Not a Pipe.* Illus. Rene Magritte. Ed. and trans. James Harkness. Los Angeles: University of California Press, 1983.
Fox-Genovese, Elizabeth. *Within the Plantation Household: Black and White Women of the Old South.* Chapel Hill: University of North Carolina Press, 1988.
Francis, J. Michael, Gary Mormino, and Rachael Sanderson. "Slavery Took Hold in Florida under the Spanish in the 'Forgotten Century' of 1492–1619." *Tampa Bay Times* 29 Aug. 2019. www.tampabay.com/opinion/2019/08/29/before-1619-africans-and-the-early-history-of-spanish-colonial-florida-and-america-column.
Franklin, John Hope. "Mirror for Americans: A Century of Reconstruction History." *American Historical Review* 85.1 (Feb. 1980): 1–14
Fraser, Walter J., Jr. *Charleston! Charleston! The History of a Southern City.* Columbia: University of South Carolina Press, 1989.
Frazier, E. Franklin. "Certain Aspects of Conflict in the Negro Family." *Social Forces* 10.1 (Oct. 1931): 76–84.
———. "The Changing Status of the Negro Family." *Social Forces* 9.3 (Mar. 1931): 386–93.
———. *The Negro Family in the United States.* Chicago: University of Chicago Press, 1939.
French, Christopher C., ed. *Facing History: The Black Image in American Art, 1720–1940.* Washington, D.C.: Bedford Arts and Corcoran Gallery of Art, 1990.
Gajanan, Mahita. "Dylann Roof Had a Handwritten List of Black Churches in Car." *Time* 12 Dec. 2016. https://bit.ly/3rOrdZ2.
Gates, Henry Louis. "Of Negroes Old and New." *Transition* 46 (1974): 44–57.
———. *The Signifying Monkey: A Theory of African American Literary Criticism.* New York: Oxford University Press, 1988.
Gay, Lettie, and Blanche S. Rhett, eds. *200 Years of Charleston Cooking.* Intro. Helen Woodward. New York: Harrison, Smith & Robert Haas, 1930.
Ghansah, Rachel Kaadzi. "A Most American Terrorist: The Making of Dylann Roof." *GQ* 17 Aug. 2017. https://bit.ly/3A3Y132.
Gilroy, Paul. *The Black Atlantic: Modernity and Double Consciousness.* Cambridge, Mass.: Harvard University Press, 1993.
———. *Small Acts: Thoughts on the Politics of Black Cultures.* London: Serpent's Tail, 1994.
Glissant, Edouard. *Faulkner, Mississippi.* 1996. Trans. Barbara B. Lewis and Thomas C. Spear. Chicago: University of Chicago Press, 1999.
———. "Natural Poetics, Forced Poetics." *Caribbean Discourses: Selected Essays.* Trans. J. Michael Dash. 1982. Charlottesville: University of Virginia Press, 1996. 120–33.
———. *Poetics of Relation.* 1990. Trans. Betsy Wing. Ann Arbor: University of Michigan Press, 1990.
Gomez, Michael A. *Exchanging Our Country Marks: The Transformation of African Identities in Colonial and Antebellum America.* Chapel Hill: University of North Carolina Press, 1998.
Gonzales, Ambrose E. *The Black Border: Gullah Stories of the Carolina Coast.* Columbia, S.C.: State, 1922.
Goodwine, Marquetta L., and Clarity Press Gullah Project. *The Legacy of Ibo Landing: Gullah Roots of African American Culture.* Atlanta: Clarity, 1998.
Gordon, Robert Winslow. AFC 1928/002: Robert Winslow Gordon Cylinder Collection, American Folklife Center, Library of Congress, 1922–28.

———. "The Negro Spiritual." *The Carolina Low-Country*. Ed. Augustine T. Smythe et al. New York: Macmillan, 1931. 189–222.

Green, Jeffrey Press. *Edmund Thornton Jenkins: The Life and Times of an American Black Composer, 1894–1926*. Westport, Conn.: Greenwood, 1982.

Greene, Harlan. *Mr. Skylark: John Bennett and the Charleston Renaissance*. Athens: University of Georgia Press, 2001.

———. "'Mister Bennett's Amiable Desire': The Poetry Society of South Carolina and the Charleston Renaissance." *Renaissance in Charleston: Art and Life in the Carolina Low Country, 1900–1940*. Ed. James Hutchisson and Harlan Greene. Athens: University of Georgia Press, 2003. 57–75.

Greeson, Jennifer Rae. *Our South: Geographic Fantasy and the Rise of National Literature*. Cambridge, Mass.: Harvard University Press, 2010.

Griffin, Farrah Jasmine. *"Who Set You Flowin'": The African-American Migration Narrative*. New York: Oxford University Press, 1995.

Gullahbemi, Halim. Telephone interview, 24 July 2007.

Guzzio, Tracie Church. "Jean Toomer." *American Writers: A Collection of Literary Biographies*, suppl. 9 (2002). https://archive.org/details/americanwriterscooo9unse_b6j6.

Hale, Grace. *Making Whiteness: The Culture of Segregation, 1890–1940*. New York: Pantheon, 1998.

Hall, Stuart. "The After-life of Frantz Fanon: Why Fanon? Why Now?" *Why Black Skin, White Masks? The Fact of Blackness: Frantz Fanon and Visual Representation*. Ed. Alan Read. Seattle: Bay Press, 1996. 12–37.

Hamilton, Anna Hall. Personal communication, December 1994 and March 1995.

Hamilton, Kendra. "The Dialect Dilemma." *Black Issues in Higher Education* 21 Apr. 2005.

Hamilton, Kendra, and Ernesto Pujol. "*Water/Table*: Site Specific Art at the Spoleto Festival U.S.A. 2004." Artists' manifesto accompanying exhibition. Charleston, S.C.: Spoleto Festival U.S.A.

Hamilton, Lonnie. Personal communication, 29 Apr. 2008.

Harris, Joel Chandler. *Nights with Uncle Remus: Myths and Legends of the Old Plantation*. 1883. Boston: Houghton Mifflin, 1911.

Harrison, Elizabeth Jane. *Female Pastoral: Women Writers Re-visioning the American South*. Knoxville: University of Tennessee Press, 1991.

Harrison, Ira E., and Faye V. Harrison, eds. *African American Pioneers in Anthropology*. Chicago: University of Illinois Press, 1999.

Hartigan, John, Jr. "Objectifying 'Poor Whites' and 'White Trash' in Detroit." *White Trash: Race and Class in America*. Ed. Matt Wray and Annalee Newitz. New York: Routledge, 1997. 41–56.

Hartman, Sadiya. *Scenes of Subjection: Terror, Slavery, and Self-Making in Nineteenth-Century America*. Oxford: Oxford University Press, 1997.

Harvin, Stephanie. "Marquetta Goodwine: Sea Island 'Art-ivist' Works to Preserve Gullah-Geechee Heritage." *Post and Courier* [Charleston] 1 July 2000: <NSC>d</NSC>1+.

"Helen L. Phillips, 86; Soprano Broke Color Barrier at the Met in 1947." *Los Angeles Times* 9 Aug. 2005. http://articles.latimes.com/2005/aug/09/local/me-phillips9.

Hemenway, Robert. *Zora Neale Hurston: A Literary Biography*. Urbana: University of Illinois Press, 1980.

Herring, Scott. "Rural." *Keywords for Southern Studies*. Ed. Scott Romine and Jennifer Rae Greeson. Athens: University of Georgia Press, 2016. 288–91.

Herskovits, Melville. *The Myth of the Negro Past*. Boston: Beacon, 1958.

Heyward, Dorothy. "Porgy's Native Tongue." Dorothy Heyward Manuscript Papers 180.01.03.04, South Carolina Historical Society.
Heyward, DuBose. *Mamba's Daughters*. New York: Doubleday, 1929.
———. "The Negro in the Low Country." *The Carolina Low-Country*. Ed. Augustine T. Smythe et al. New York: Macmillan, 1931. 169–87.
———. "The New Note in Southern Literature." *Bookman* 61 (April 1925): 153–56.
———. *Porgy*. New York: Doran, 1925.
Heyward, Duncan Clinch. *Seed from Madagascar*. Illus. Carl Julien. Chapel Hill: University of North Carolina Press, 1937.
Hicklin, Robert M., Jr. *Two-Lane South: The Charleston Renaissance Gallery*. Charleston, S.C.: Charleston Renaissance Gallery, 2007.
Higgins, W. Robert. "Charleston: Terminus and Entrepôt of the Colonial Trade." *The African Diaspora: Interpretive Essays*. Ed. Martin L. Kilson and Robert I. Rothberg. Cambridge, Mass.: Harvard University Press, 1970. 114–31.
Hodges, Heather. "'I Heard the Angels Singing': Documenting the Gullah Geechee People of Wadmalaw Island Who Inspired Porgy and Bess." International Gullah Geechee and African Diaspora 2022 Conference, Coastal Carolina University, 26 Feb. 2022.
Hoffman-Jeep, Lynda. "Creating Ethnography: Zora Neale Hurston and Lydia Cabrera." *African American Review* 39.3 (Fall 2005): 337–53.
Holloway, Joseph, ed. *Africanisms in American Culture*. Bloomington: Indiana University Press, 1990.
Holmes, Ethlynne E. "Flower Vendors." *Phylon* 2.2 (1941): 117–18.
Hopkins, Tometro. "Issues in the Study of Afro-Creoles: Afro-Cuban and Gullah." Ph.D. dissertation, Indiana University, 1992.
Houston, Susan H. *Black English in Florida: Sociolinguistic Examination*. Monograph 3. Atlanta: Southeastern Education Laboratory, 1969.
Huggins, Nathan, ed. *W. E. B. Du Bois: Writings*. New York: Library of America, 1986.
Hughes, Langston. *The Big Sea: An Autobiography*. 1940. Intro. Arnold Rampersad. New York: Hill & Wang, 1993.
———. "The Negro Artist and the Racial Mountain." *The Portable Harlem Renaissance Reader*. Ed. David Levering Lewis. New York: Penguin, 1994. 91–94.
Hughes, Robert. *American Visions: The Epic Story of Art in America*. New York: Knopf, 1997.
Hurston, Zora Neale. *Barracoon: The Story of the Last Black Cargo*. Ed. Deborah G. Plant. Intro. Alice Walker. New York: Amistad, 2018.
———. "Characteristics of Negro Expression." *Zora Neale Hurston: Folklore, Memoirs, and Other Writings*. Ed. Cheryl Wall. New York: Library of America, 1995. 830–45.
———. "Communications." *Journal of Negro History* 12.4 (Oct. 1927): 664–69.
———. "Conversions and Visions." *Zora Neale Hurston: Folklore, Memoirs, and Other Writings*. Ed. Cheryl Wall. New York: Library of America, 1995. 846–50.
———. "Cudjo's Own Story of the Last African Slaver." *Journal of Negro History* 12.4 (Oct. 1927): 648–63.
———. *Dust Tracks on a Road*. *Zora Neale Hurston: Folklore, Memoirs, and Other Writings*. Ed. Cheryl Wall. New York: Library of America, 1995. 557–769.
———. "Go Gator and Muddy the Water." *Go Gator and Muddy the Water: Writings by Zora Neale Hurston from the Federal Writers' Project*. Ed. Pamela Bordelon. New York: Norton, 1999. 68–88.
———. "High John de Conquer." *American Mercury* Oct. 1943: 451.

———. "The Hue and Cry about Howard University." *Messenger* 7 Sept. 1925.
———. "John Redding Goes to Sea." *Zora Neale Hurston: Novels and Stories*. Ed. Cheryl Wall. New York: Library of America, 1995. 925–39.
———. *Jonah's Gourd Vine*. *Zora Neale Hurston: Novels and Stories*. Ed. Cheryl Wall. New York: Library of America, 1995. 1–171.
———. *Moses, Man of the Mountain*. *Zora Neale Hurston: Novels and Stories*. Ed. Cheryl Wall. New York: Library of America, 1995. 335–595.
———. *Mules and Men*. *Zora Neale Hurston: Folklore, Memoirs, and Other Writings*. Ed. Cheryl Wall. New York: Library of America, 1995. 1–267.
———. "The Sanctified Church." *Go Gator and Muddy the Water: Writings by Zora Neale Hurston from the Federal Writers' Project*. Ed. Pamela Bordelon. New York: Norton, 1999. 94–98.
———. *Seraph on the Suwanee*. *Zora Neale Hurston: Novels and Stories*. Ed. Cheryl Wall. New York: Library of America, 1995. 597–920.
———. "Shouting." *Zora Neale Hurston: Folklore, Memoirs, and Other Writings*. Ed. Cheryl Wall. New York: Library of America, 1995. 851–53.
———. "Spirituals and Neo-spirituals." *Zora Neale Hurston: Folklore, Memoirs, and Other Writings*. Ed. Cheryl Wall. New York: Library of America, 1995. 869–74.
———. *Tell My Horse: Voodoo and Life in Haiti and Jamaica*. Ed. Henry Louis Gates Jr. New York: Harper, 1990.
———. *Their Eyes Were Watching God*. Ed. Henry Louis Gates Jr. New York: Harper, 1990.
Hurston, Zora Neale, and Langston Hughes. *Mule Bone: A Comedy of Negro Life*. Ed. George Houston Bass and Henry Louis Gates Jr. New York: Harper, 1997.
Hutchisson, James M. *DuBose Heyward: A Charleston Gentleman and the World of Porgy and Bess*. Jackson: University Press of Mississippi, 2000.
———. *A DuBose Heyward Reader*. Athens: University of Georgia Press, 2003.
Hutchisson, James M., and Harlan Greene, eds. *Renaissance in Charleston: Art and Life in the Carolina Low Country, 1900–1940*. Athens: University of Georgia Press, 2003.
Irving, Washington. *Astoria; or, Anecdotes of an Enterprise beyond the Rocky Mountains*. 1836. Augsburg: Jazzybee Verlag, 2017.
Jackson, Bruce. "Foreword." *Slave Songs of the Georgia Sea Islands*. Ed. Lydia Parrish, Creighton Churchill, and Robert MacGimsey. 1942. Hatboro, Pa.: Folklore Associates, 1965.
———. *Get Your Ass in the Water and Swim Like Me: Narrative Poetry from Black Oral Tradition*. Cambridge, Mass.: Harvard University Press, 1974.
Jahn, Janheinz. "Residual African Elements in the Blues." 1961. Repr. *Mother Wit from the Laughing Barrel: Readings in the Interpretation of African Culture*. Ed. Alan Dundes. New York: Garland, 1981. 95–103.
James, C. L. R. *The Black Jacobins: Toussaint L'Ouverture and the San Domingo Revolution*. 1938. 2nd ed., rev. New York: Vintage, 1989.
Jefferson, Thomas. *Notes on the State of Virginia: With Related Documents*. Ed. David Waldstreicher. Boston: Bedford, 2002.
Jenkins, Candice M. *Private Lives, Proper Relations: Regulating Black Intimacy*. Minneapolis: University of Minnesota Press, 2007.
———. "Pure Black: Class, Color, and Intraracial Politics in Toni Morrison's *Paradise*." *Modern Fiction Studies* 52.2 (2006): 270–96.
Jenkins, Wilbert L. *Seizing the New Day: African Americans in Post–Civil War Charleston*. Bloomington: Indiana University Press, 1998.
Johns, Elizabeth. "The Farmer in the Works of William Sidney Mount." *Art and History:*

Images and Their Meaning. Ed. Robert I. Rothberg and Theodore K. Rabb. Cambridge: Cambridge University Press, 1988. 257–75.
Johnson, Charles S. "The Education of the Negro Child." *American Sociological Review* 1.2 (Apr. 1936): 264–72.
———. *Shadow of the Plantation*. Chicago: University of Chicago Press, 1934.
Johnson, James Weldon. *Along This Way*. 1934. *James Weldon Johnson: Writings*. Ed. William L. Andrews. New York: Library of America, 2004. 129–604.
———. *Black Manhattan*. *James Weldon Johnson: Writings*. Ed. William L. Andrews. New York: Library of America, 2004. 767–808.
———, ed. *The Book of American Negro Poetry*. 1922. New York: Harcourt, Brace, 1931.
———. *God's Trombones: Seven Negro Sermons in Verse*. 1922. *James Weldon Johnson: Writings*. Ed. William L. Andrews. New York: Library of America, 2004. 834–67.
———. "Race Prejudice and the Negro Artist." *Harper's* Nov. 1920: 775.
Johnson, James Weldon, and J. Rosamond Johnson, eds. *The Books of American Negro Spirituals, Including the Book of American Negro Spirituals and the Second Book of American Negro Spirituals*. 1925, 1926. New York: Da Capo, 1969.
Jones, Anne Goodwyn. *Tomorrow Is Another Day: The Woman Writer in the South, 1859–1956*. Baton Rouge: Louisiana State University Press, 1981.
Jones, Charles C., Sr. *The Religious Instruction of the Negroes in the United States*. Savannah, Ga.: Thomas Purse, 1842.
Jones, Charles Colcock, Jr. *Negro Myths from the Georgia Coast, Told in the Vernacular*. 1888. Detroit: Singing Tree, 1969.
Jones, Leroi. *Blues People: Negro Music in White America*. 1963. New York: Harper, 2002.
Jones, Lewis Pinckney. *Stormy Petrel: N. G. Gonzales and His State*. Columbia: University of South Carolina Press, 1973.
Jones, Suzanne W. *Race Mixing: Southern Fiction since the Sixties*. Baltimore: Johns Hopkins University Press, 2004.
Jones-Jackson, Patricia. *When Roots Die: Endangered Traditions on the Sea Islands*. Athens: University of Georgia Press, 1987.
Joyner, Charles. *Down by the Riverside: A South Carolina Slave Community*. 1984. Urbana: University of Illinois Press, 2009.
Jung, Carl, ed. Man and His Symbols. New York: Dell, 1968.
Junior League of Charleston. *Charleston Receipts*. Charleston, S.C.: Walker, Evans & Cogswell, 1950.
Kammen, Michael. *Mystic Chords of Memory: The Transformation of Tradition in American Culture*. 1991. New York: Vintage, 1993.
Kaplan, Amy, and Donald E. Pease. *Cultures of United States Imperialism*. Durham, N.C.: Duke University Press, 1993.
Kaplan, Carla. *Zora Neale Hurston: A Life in Letters*. New York: Doubleday, 2002.
Kapsalis, Terri. *Public Privates: Performing Gynecology from Both Ends of the Speculum*. Durham, N.C.: Duke University Press, 1997.
Katz, William Loren. *Black Indians: A Hidden Heritage*. New York: Atheneum, 1986.
———. *The Black West: A Documentary and Pictorial History of the African American Role in the Westward Expansion of the United States*. 1987. Rev. ed. Golden, Colo.: Fulcrum, 2019.
Kelley, Robin D. G. "Notes on Deconstructing the Folk." *American Historical Review* 97.5 (Dec. 1992): 1400–1408.
Kerman, Cynthia, and Richard Eldridge. *The Lives of Jean Toomer: A Hunger for Wholeness*. Baton Rouge: Louisiana State University Press, 1989.

Killens, John O., ed. "Writers: Black and White." *The American Negro Writer and His Roots: Selected Papers from the First Conference of Negro Writers, March, 1959*. New York: American Society of African Culture, 1960.

Klein, Rachel N. "Ordering the Backcountry: The South Carolina Regulation." *William and Mary Quarterly* 38.4 (Oct. 1981): 661–80.

Kristeva, Julia. *Powers of Horror: An Essay on Abjection*. Trans. Leon S. Roudiez. New York: Columbia University Press, 1982.

Krupat, Arnold. "Post-colonialism, Ideology, and Native American Literature." *Postcolonial Theory and the United States: Race, Ethnicity, and Literature*. Ed. Amritjit Singh and Peter Schmidt. Jackson: University Press of Mississippi, 2000.

Kytle, Ethan J., and Blain Roberts. *Denmark Vesey's Garden: Slavery and Memory in the Cradle of the Confederacy*. New York: New Press, 2018.

Landers, Jane. "The Central African Presence in Spanish Maroon Communities." *Central Africans and Cultural Transformations in the American Diaspora*. Ed. Linda M. Heywood. Cambridge: Cambridge University Press, 2002. 227–42.

———. "Spanish Sanctuary: Fugitives in Florida, 1687–1790." *Florida Historical Quarterly* 62.3 (Jan. 1984): 297, 300.

Laneheart, Sonja L., ed. *Sociocultural and Historical Contexts of African American English*. Vol. 27 of *Varieties of English Around the World*. Amsterdam: John Benjamins, 2001.

Langer, Susanne K. *Feeling and Form: A Theory of Art*. New York: Scribner, 1953.

Le Vin, L. Press, and Ida B. Wells-Barnett. *Lynch Law in Georgia: A Six-Weeks' Record in the Center of Southern Civilization, as Faithfully Chronicled by the "Atlanta Journal" and the "Atlanta Constitution": Also the Full Report of Louis Press. Le Vin, the Chicago Detective Sent to Investigate the Burning of Samuel Hose, the Torture and Hanging of Elijah Strickland, the Colored Preacher, and the Lynching of Nine Men for Alleged Arson*. Chicago, 1899.

Lears, T. Jackson. *No Place of Grace: Antimodernism and the Transformation of American Culture, 1880–1920*. 2nd ed. Chicago: University of Chicago Press, 1994.

Léger, Fernand. "Origins of Painting and Representational Value." *Functions of Painting*. Part of *The Documents of 20th Century Art* series. Trans. Alexandra Anderson. Gen. ed. Robert Motherwell. 1965. New York: Viking, 1973.

Leighten, Patricia. "The White Peril and L'art nègre: Picasso, Primitivism, and Anticolonialism." *Art Bulletin* 72.4 (Dec. 1990): 609–30.

Lemke, Sieglinde. *Primitivist Modernism: Black Culture and the Origins of Transatlantic Modernism*. Oxford: Oxford University Press, 1998.

Lennon, John, and Malcolm Foley. *Dark Tourism: The Attraction of Death and Disaster*. London: Thomson, 2006.

Lenz, Gunter H. "Southern Exposures: The Urban Experience and the Re-construction of Black Folk Culture and Community in the Works of Richard Wright and Zora Neale Hurston." *New York Folklore* 7.1 (Summer 1981): 3–39.

Levine, Lawrence W. *Black Culture and Black Consciousness: Afro-American Folk Thought from Slavery to Freedom*. New York: Oxford University Press, 1977. 227–41.

Littlefield, Daniel C. *Rice and Slaves: Ethnicity and the Slave Trade in Colonial South Carolina*. 1981. Chicago: University of Illinois Press, 1997.

Lixl, Andreas, ed. *Memories of Carolinian Immigrants: Autobiographies, Diaries, and Letters from Colonial Times to the Present*. Lanham, Md.: University Press of America, 2009.

Locke, Alain L. R. *The Critical Temper of Alain Locke: A Selection of His Essays on Art and Culture*. Ed. Jeffrey C. Stewart. New York: Garland, 1983.

———. "The Legacy of the Ancestral Arts." *The New Negro*. 1925. New York: Atheneum, 1968. 254–70.

Loewen, James W. *Lies My Teacher Told Me: Everything Your American History Textbook Got Wrong*. New York: Touchstone, 1996.

Lofton, John M., Jr. "Denmark Vesey's Call to Arms." *Journal of Negro History* 33.4 (Oct. 1948): 395–417.

Logan, Rayford Whittington. *The Betrayal of the Negro, from Rutherford B. Hayes to Woodrow Wilson*. 1965. Cambridge: Da Capo, 1997.

———. *The Negro in American Life and Thought: The Nadir, 1877–1901*. New York: Dial Press, 1954.

Lomax, Alan, comp. *Georgia Sea Islands*. Vols. 1–2. *Southern Journey: A Collection of Field Recordings from the South*. Lochrae Music, 1961.

———. *The Land Where the Blues Began*. New York: Pantheon, 1993.

Longfellow, Henry Wadsworth. *Poetic Aphorisms*. 1846.

Lott, Eric. *Love and Theft: Blackface Minstrelsy and the American Working Class*. New York: Oxford University Press, 1993.

"Louise Bennett-Coverley: Poet and Broadcaster Whose Courageous Use of Patois Inspired Jamaicans to Take Pride in Their Language." *Guardian* 2 Aug. 2006. http://www.timesonline.co.uk/tol/comment/obituaries/article696907.ece.

Love, Josephine Harrell, ed. *Edwin A. Harleston: Painter of an Era, 1882–1931*. Detroit: Your Heritage House, 1983.

Lowe, John Wharton. *Calypso Magnolia: The Crosscurrents of Caribbean and Southern Literature*. Chapel Hill: University of North Carolina Press, 2016.

Lutes, Jean. "Lynching Coverage and the American Reporter-Novelist." *American Literary History* 19.2 (2007): 456–81.

Mahar, William J. "Black Music." *The New Encyclopedia of Southern Culture*. Vol. 12: *Music*. Ed. Bill C. Malone. Chapel Hill: University of North Carolina Press, 2008. 19–23.

Manigault-Bryant, James A., and LeRhonda S. Manigault-Bryant. "Conjuring Pasts and Ethnographic Presents in Zora Neale Hurston's Modernity." *Journal of African Religions* 4.2 (2016): 225–35.

Manigault-Bryant, LeRhonda. *Talking to the Dead: Religion, Music, and Lived Memory among Gullah Geechee Women*. Durham, N.C.: Duke University Press, 2014.

Manning, Patrick. "The Slave Trade: The Formal Demography of a Global System." *Social Science History* 14.2 (Summer 1990): 255–79.

Marcus, George. "The Deep Legacies of Dynastic Subjectivity: The Resonances of a Famous Family Identity in Private and Public Spheres." *Elites: Choice, Leadership, and Succession*. Ed. João de Pina-Cabral and Antónia Pedroso de Lima. Oxford: Berg, 2000. 9–29.

Marks, Peter. "Critics Notebook: At Spoleto, the Novelty Is Still Novel." *New York Times* 12 June 1999.

Martens, R. L., and Bill Robertson. "How the Soil Remembers Plantation Slavery." *Edge Effects* 28 Mar. 2019 (updated 28 Apr. 2021). https://edgeeffects.net/soil-memory-plantationocene/.

Marx, Leo. *The Machine in the Garden: Technology and the Pastoral Ideal in America*. Oxford: Oxford University Press, 1964.

Mason, Theodore, Jr. "Signifying." *The Oxford Companion to African American Literature*.

Ed. William L. Andrews, Frances Smith Foster, and Trudier Harris. Oxford: Oxford University Press, 1997. 665–66.

Mazzotti, José Antonio, and Ralph Bauer, eds., *Creole Subjects in the Colonial Americas: Empires, Texts, Identities*. Chapel Hill: University of North Carolina Press, 2009.

McAlester, Virginia Savage. *A Field Guide to American Houses*. New York: Knopf, 1998.

McDaniel, Maurine Akua. "Edwin Augustus Harleston: Portrait Painter, 1882–1931." Ph.D. dissertation, Emory University, 1994.

McInnis, Maurie. *In Pursuit of Refinement: Charlestonians Abroad, 1740 to 1860*. Columbia: University of South Carolina Press, 1999.

———. *The Politics of Taste in Antebellum Charleston*. Chapel Hill: University of North Carolina Press, 2005.

McKay, Claude. *Banjo*. New York: Harcourt, Brace, 1929.

McKay, Ian. *The Quest of the Folk: Antimodernism and Cultural Selection in 20th Century Nova Scotia*. Montreal: McGill-Queen's University Press, 1994.

McKittrick, Katherine. *Demonic Grounds: Black Women and the Cartographies of Struggle*. Minneapolis: University of Minnesota Press, 2006.

Mebane-Cruz, A. Anjana. "The Black Borders of Indianness." Society for the Study Southern Literature Annual Conference, Williamsburg, Va., 2011.

———. Personal communication, 2010.

Mellers, Wilfrid. *Singing in the Wilderness: Music and Ecology in the 20th Century*. Urbana: University of Illinois Press, 2001.

Merida, Kevin, and Michael A. Fletcher. *Supreme Discomfort: The Divided Soul of Clarence Thomas*. New York: Doubleday, 2007.

Merleau-Ponty, Maurice. "Eye and Mind." *The Primacy of Perception and Other Essays on Phenomenological Psychology, the Philosophy of Art, History, and Politics*. Evanston: Northwestern University Press, 1964. 159–90.

Mikell, Gwendolyn. "When Horses Talk: Reflections on Zora Neale Hurston's Haitian Anthropology." *Phylon* 43.3 (1982): 218–30.

Mille, Katherine Wyly. "A Historical Analysis of Tense-Mood-Aspect in Gullah-Creole: A Case of Stable Variation." Ph.D. dissertation, University of South Carolina, 1990.

Miller, Angela. *Empire of the Eye: Landscape Representation and American Cultural Politics, 1825–1875*. Ithaca, N.Y.: Cornell University Press, 1993.

Miller, David. *Dark Eden: The Swamp in Nineteenth-Century American Culture*. Cambridge: Cambridge University Press, 1989.

Mills, Kincaid, Genevieve C. Peterkin, and Aaron McCoullough, eds. *Coming Through: Voices of a South Carolina Gullah Community from Wenn. Oral Histories Collected by Genevieve Chandler*. Columbia: University of South Carolina Press, 2008.

Mitchell, W. J. T. "Introduction" and "Imperial Landscape." Landscape and Power. Ed. W. J. T. Mitchell. Chicago: University of Chicago Press, 1994. 6–34.

Montgomery, Michael. *The Crucible of Carolina: Essays in the Development of Gullah Language and Culture*. Athens: University of Georgia Press, 1994.

Morgan, Edmund S. *American Slavery, American Freedom: The Ordeal of Colonial Virginia*. New York: Norton, 1975.

Morgan, Kenneth. "Slave Sales in Colonial Charleston." *English Historical Review* 113.453 (Sept. 1998): 905–27.

Morgan, Philip D. *Slave Counterpoint: Black Culture in Eighteenth-Century Chesapeake and Lowcountry*. Chapel Hill: University of North Carolina Press, 1998.

Morris, Aldon D. *The Scholar Denied: W. E. B. Du Bois and the Birth of Modern Sociology*. Berkeley: University of California Press, 2015.

Moten, Fred. *Black and Blur: Consent Not to Be a Single Being*. Durham, N.C.: Duke University Press, 2017.
Mufwene, Salikoko S. "The Ecology of Gullah's Survival." *American Speech* 72.1 (Spring 1997): 69–83.
———. "What Is African American English?" *Sociocultural and Historical Contexts of African American English*. Ed. Sonja L. Laneheart. Vol. 27 of *Varieties of English Around the World*. Amsterdam: John Benjamins, 2001.
Nagel, Joane. "Ethnicity, Sexuality and Globalization." *Theory Culture Society* 23 (2006): 545–47.
National Park Service. "African Americans in St. Augustine, 1565–1821." Castillo de San Marcos National Monument, 20 Apr. 2022. https://www.nps.gov/casa/learn/historyculture/african-americans-in-st-augustine-1565-1821.htm.
———. "Low Country Gullah Culture Special Resource Study and Environmental Impact Statement." Atlanta: National Park Service Southeast Region, 2005.
National Trust for Historic Preservation. "11 Most Endangered Historic Places of 2004." www.nationaltrust.org/11Most/2004/gullah-geechee.html.
Naylor, Gloria. *Mama Day*. New York: Tichnor & Fields, 1988.
Nettle, Daniel, and Suzanne Romaine. *Vanishing Voices: The Extinction of the World's Languages*. New York: Oxford University Press, 2000.
Noonan, Ellen. *The Strange Career of Porgy and Bess: Race, Culture, and America's Most Famous Opera*. Chapel Hill: University of North Carolina Press, 2012.
Nora, Pierre. "Between History and Memory." *Representations* 26 (Spring 1989): 7–24.
Ogunleye, Tolagbe. "The Self-Emancipated Africans of Florida: Pan-African Nationalists in the 'New World.'" *Journal of Black Studies* 27.1 (Sept. 1996): 24–38.
Olwell, Robert A. "'Domestick Enemies': Slavery and Political Independence in South Carolina, May 1775–March 1776." *Journal of Southern History* 55.1 (Feb. 1989): 21–48.
———. *Masters, Slaves and Subjects: The Culture of Power in the South Carolina Low Country, 1740–1790*. Ithaca, N.Y.: Cornell University Press, 1998.
O'Meally, Robert G. "Introduction." *Tales of the Congaree*. Ed. In Edward C. L. Adams. Chapel Hill: University of North Carolina Press, 1987. xi–lxix.
Opala, Joseph A. "The Gullah: Rice, Slavery, and the Sierra Leone–American Connection." New Haven, Conn.: Yale University MacMillan Center, 2023.
Oppenheimer, Stephen. *The Real Eve: Modern Man's Journey Out of Africa*. New York: Carroll & Graf, 2004.
Ortega y Gasset, José. "The Dehumanization of Art." *The Dehumanization of Art and other Essays on Art, Culture, and Literature*. 1948. Princeton, N.J.: Princeton University Press, 1968.
Paquet, Sandra Pouchet. "The Ancestor as Foundation in *Their Eyes Were Watching God* and *Tar Baby*." *Callaloo* 13 (1990): 499–515.
Parrish, Lydia. *Slave Songs of the Georgia Sea Islands*. 1942. Trans. Creighton Churchill and Robert MacGimsey. Hatboro, Pa.: Folklore Associates, 1965.
Patterson, Tiffany Ruby. *Zora Neale Hurston and a History of Southern Life*. Philadelphia: Temple University Press, 2005.
Patterson, Tiffany Ruby, and Robin D. G. Kelley. "Unfinished Migrations: Reflections on the African Diaspora and the Making of the Modern World." *African Studies Review* 43.1 (Apr. 2000): 11–45.
Pattinson, Dale. "Sites of Resistance: The Subversive Spaces of *Their Eyes Were Watching God*." *MELUS* 38.4 (Winter 2013): 9–31.

Pennington, Estill C. *Look Away: Reality and Sentiment in Southern Art*. Atlanta: Peachtree, 1989.
Pennington, Patience (Elizabeth W. Allston Pringle). *A Woman Rice Planter*. New York: Macmillan, 1914.
Perry, Gill. *Gender and Art*. New Haven, Conn.: Yale University Press, 1999.
Petteys, Chris. *Dictionary of Women Artists: An International Dictionary of Women Artists Born Before 1990*. Boston: G. K. Hall, 1985.
Phifer, Mary H. "Southern Personalities: Elizabeth O'Neill Verner, Etcher." *Holland's* Oct. 1929: 14–15, 46.
Phillips, Ted Ashton, Jr. *City of the Silent: The Charlestonians of Magnolia Cemetery*. Columbia: University of South Carolina Press, 2010.
Pollack, Howard. *George Gershwin: His Life and Work*. Berkeley: University of California Press, 2006.
Pollitzer, William S. *The Gullah People and Their African Heritage*. Athens: University of Georgia Press, 1999.
———. "The Relationship of Gullah Speaking of Coastal South Carolina and Georgia to Their African Ancestors." *The Legacy of Ibo Landing: Gullah Roots of African American Culture*. Ed. Marquetta Goodwine and the Clarity Press Gullah Project. Atlanta: Clarity, 1998. 54–68.
Poston, Jonathan. *The Buildings of Charleston: A Guide to the City's Architecture*. Columbia: University of South Carolina Press, 1997.
Powell, Richard J. *Black Art and Culture in the 20th Century*. London: Thames & Hudson, 1997.
Powers, Bernard. *Black Charlestonians: A Social History, 1822–1885*. University of Arkansas Press, 1994.
Pratt, Mary Louise. *Imperial Eyes: Travel Writing and Transculturation*. 1991. London: Routledge, 2017.
Pryse, Marjorie, and Hortense Spillers. *Conjuring: Black Women, Fiction, and Literary Tradition*. Bloomington: Indiana University Press, 1985.
Pujol, Ernesto. "Colonial City Walls and Rice Plantation Paddies: Progress Notes on the Memminger School Courtyard Project for Spoleto 2004." Charleston, S.C.: Spoleto, 2004.
Rabinow, Paul, ed. *The Foucault Reader*. New York: Pantheon, 1984.
Rampersad, Arnold. *The Art and Imagination of W. E. B. Du Bois*. Cambridge, Mass.: Harvard University Press, 1976.
———. "Cosby Criticism of African American Language Skills Sparks Intense Debate, Says the Brokaw Company." *PR Newswire* 28 June 2004.
———. "W. E. B. Du Bois as a Man of Literature." *American Literature* 51.1 (Mar. 1979): 50–68.
Ravenel, Mrs. St. Julien. *Charleston: The Place and the People*. New York: Macmillan, 1929.
Redding, Saunders. *To Make a Poet Black*. Chapel Hill: University of North Carolina Press, 1939.
Reed, Ishmael. "Foreword." Zora Neale Hurston, *Tell My Horse: Voodoo and Life in Haiti and Jamaica*. 1938. New York: Harper & Row, 1990.
Reid, Whitelaw. *After the War: A Tour of the Southern States, 1865–66*. Ed. C. Vann Woodward. New York, 1965.
Reynolds, Gary A., and Beryl Wright. *Against the Odds: African American Artists and the Harmon Foundation*. Newark, N.J.: Newark Museum, 1989.

Rice, James Henry, Jr. *Glories of the Carolina Coast.* Columbia, S.C.: R. L. Bryan, 1925.
Rickford, John, and Russell Rickford. *Spoken Soul: The Story of Black English.* New York: Wiley, 2000.
Riordan, Patrick. "Finding Freedom in Florida: Native Peoples, African Americans, and Colonists, 1670–1816." *Florida Historical Quarterly* 75.1 (Summer 1996): 24–43.
Roach, Joseph. *Cities of the Dead: Circum-Atlantic Performance.* New York: Columbia University Press, 1996.
Roberts, Gene, and Hank Klibanoff. *The Race Beat: The Press, Civil Rights, and the Awakening of a Nation.* New York: Knopf, 2007.
Robeson, Elizabeth. "The Ambiguity of Julia Peterkin." *Journal of Southern History* 61.4 (Nov. 1995): 761–86.
Rodney, Walter. *A History of the Upper Guinea Coast.* Oxford: Oxford University Press, 1970.
Roldán, Cynthia, and John Monk. "Roof Visited Emanuel 8 Times, Fled on Back Roads, GPS Says." *State* [Columbia, S.C.] 13 Dec. 2016 (updated 14 Dec. 2016). https://bit.ly/3ihtv.
Romine, Scott, and Jennifer Rae Greeson, eds. *Keywords for Southern Studies.* Athens: University of Georgia Press, 2016.
Rosaldo, Renato. *Culture and Truth: The Remaking of Social Analysis.* 1989. Boston: Beacon, 1993.
Rosen, Robert. *A Short History of Charleston.* Columbia: University of South Carolina Press, 1997.
Said, Edward. *Culture and Imperialism.* 1993. New York: Vintage, 1994.
Salamone, Frank A. "His Eyes Were Watching Her: Papa Franz Boas, Zora Neale Hurston, and Anthropology." *Anthropos* 109.1 (2014): 217–24.
Santesso, Aaron. *A Careful Longing: The Poetics and Problems of Nostalgia.* Newark: University of Delaware Press, 2005.
Sass, Herbert Ravenel. "The Low Country." *The Carolina Low-Country.* Ed. Augustine T. Smythe et al. New York: Macmillan, 1931. 1–29.
Saunders, Boyd, and Ann McAden. *Alfred Hutty and the Charleston Renaissance.* Orangeburg, S.C.: Sandlapper, 1990.
Savannah Unit, Georgia Writers' Project, Works Progress Administration. *Drums and Shadows: Survival Studies among the Georgia Coastal Negroes.* Athens: University of Georgia Press, 1940.
Schwartz, Charles. *Gershwin: His Life and Music.* Indianapolis: Bobbs-Merrill, 1973.
Scruggs, Charles. "'All Dressed Up but No Place to Go': The Black Writer and His Audience during the Harlem Renaissance." *American Literature* 48.4 (Jan. 1977): 543–63.
Seminole Nation Museum. "The Seminole Wars." www.seminolenationmuseum.org/history-seminole-nation-the-seminole-wars.
Severens, Martha. *Alice Ravenel Huger Smith: An Artist, a Place, and a Time.* Charleston: Carolina Art Association and Gibbes Museum of Art, 1993.
——— . "The Charleston Renaissance." *Carologue* 13.3 (Autumn 1998): 16–21.
——— . *The Charleston Renaissance.* Spartanburg, S.C.: Saraland Press, 1998.
Sexton, Genevieve. "The Last Witness: Testimony and Desire in Zora Neale Hurston's Barracoon." *Discourse* 25.1/2 (Winter/Spring 2003): 189–210.
Shange, Ntozake. *Sassafras, Cypress, and Indigo.* New York: St. Martin's Press, 1982.
Shields, David. *Southern Provisions: The Creation and Revival of a Culture.* Chicago: University of Chicago Press, 2015.

Shuffelton, Frank. "Circumstantial Accounts, Dangerous Art: Recognizing African-American Culture in Travelers' Narratives." *Eighteenth Century Studies* 27.4 (Summer 1994): 589–603.

Schuller, Gunther. *The Swing Era: The Development of Jazz, 1930–1945*. New York: Oxford University Press, 1989.

Simpson, Lewis P. *The Dispossessed Garden: Pastoral and History in Southern Literature*. Athens: University of Georgia Press, 1975.

Singh, Amritjit, and Peter Schmidt. "On the Borders between U.S. Studies and Postcolonial Theory." *Postcolonial Theory and the United States: Race, Ethnicity, and Literature*. Ed. Amritjit Singh and Peter Schmidt. Jackson: University Press of Mississippi, 2000. 3–70.

Singleton, Theresa A. *Conflict and Transcendence: African-American Art in South Carolina*. Columbia, S.C.: Columbia Museum of Art, 1992.

Slotkin, Richard. *The Fatal Environment: The Myth of the Frontier in the Age of Industrialization, 1800–1890*. New York: Atheneum, 1985. Norman: University of Oklahoma Press, 1998.

———. *Gunfighter Nation: The Myth of the Frontier in Twentieth-Century America*. Norman: University of Oklahoma Press, 1992.

———. *Regeneration through Violence: The Mythology of the American Frontier, 1600–1860*. 1973. Norman: University of Oklahoma Press, 2000.

Smart-Grosvenor, Vertamae. *Vibration Cooking, or the Travel Notes of a Geechee Girl*. 1970. New York: Ballantine, 1992.

Smith, Alice Ravenel Huger. *A Carolina Rice Plantation of the Fifties: Thirty Paintings in Water-Color*. New York: Morrow, 1936.

———. "Doorways, Gateways and Stairways of Quaint Old Charleston." *Art in America* 4 (August 1916): 296.

Smith, Alice Ravenel Huger, and Daniel Elliott Huger Smith. *The Dwelling Houses of Charleston, South Carolina*. Philadelphia: Lippincott, 1917.

Smith, Bruce. "S.C.'s ACE Basin Offers Refuge amid Urban Sprawl." *Charlotte Observer* 25 Oct. 2014. https://bit.ly/3j8wWEY.

Smith, Glenn, Jennifer Berry Hawes, and Abigail Darlington. "Roof Says He Chose Charleston, Emanuel AME for Massacre Because They Were Historic, Meaningful." *Post and Courier* [Charleston] 9 Dec. 2015 (updated 14 Sept. 2020). https://bit.ly/2Vg4XeL.

Smith, Mark E. *Stono: Documenting and Interpreting a Southern Slave Revolt*. Columbia: University of South Carolina Press, 2005.

Smythe, Augustine T., Herbert Ravenel Sass, et al. *The Carolina Low-Country*. New York: Macmillan, 1931.

Soltow, James H. *Stella Maris Church: A Sesquicentennial History*. Sullivan's Island, S.C.: Church, 1996.

Southern Accents Press. *Gardens of the South*. New York: Simon & Schuster, 1985.

Spivak, Gayatri Chakravorty. *The Post-colonial Critic: Interviews, Strategies, Dialogues*. New York: Routledge, 1990.

———. "Race before Racism: The Disappearance of the American." *boundary 2* 25.2 (Summer 1998): 35–53.

Steckel, Richard H. "Slave Mortality: Analysis of Evidence from Plantation Records." *Social Science History* 3:3/4 (1979): 86–114.

Stepto, Robert. *From Behind the Veil: A Study of African American Narrative*. 2nd ed. Urbana: University of Illinois Press, 1991.

Stewart, Catherine. "Conjure Queen: Zora Neale Hurston and Black Folk Culture." *Long

Past Slavery: Representing Race in the Federal Writers' Project. Chapel Hill: University of North Carolina Press, 2016. 143–74.

Stewart, Charles, ed. *Creolization: History, Ethnography, Theory.* Walnut Creek, Calif.: Left Coast, 2007.

Stewart, Jessica. "Map Reveals Where Modern Countries Would Be Located if Pangea Still Existed." *MyModernMet* 29 Jan. 2018. https://bit.ly/3fHomfR.

Sundquist, Eric. *To Wake the Nations: Race in the Making of American Literature.* Cambridge, Mass.: Belknap, 1993.

Swain, Joseph. *The Broadway Musical: A Critical and Musical Survey.* Lanham, Md.: Scarecrow, 2002.

Swenson, Charles. "Goldfinch Urging State to Oppose Baruch Claim to Marsh." *Coastal Observer* [Pawley's Island, S.C.] 23 Jan. 2020. https://bit.ly/37eS5b9.

Taussig, Michael T. *Mimesis and Alterity: A Particular History of the Senses.* New York: Routledge, 1993.

Taylor, Douglas. "New Languages for Old in the West Indies." *People and Cultures of the Caribbean: An Anthropological Reader.* Ed. Michael M. Horowitz. Garden City, N.J.: Natural History Press, 1971. 277–88.

Taylor, William Robert. *Cavalier and Yankee: The Old South and American National Character.* New York: Braziller, 1961.

Taylor, William Wesley. "Wrapping the Curtain: Resistance and Identity in the Permeability of Streetspace." Charlottesville: University of Virginia School of Architecture, 26 Mar. 1999.

Thomas, Clarence. *My Grandfather's Son: A Memoir.* New York: HarperCollins, 2007.

Thompson, Robert Farris. *Flash of the Spirit: African & Afro-American Art & Philosophy.* New York: Vintage, 1984.

Threadcraft, Torry. "The Power of Untold Slave Narratives." *Atlantic* 1 Oct. 2018. www.theatlantic.com/entertainment/archive/2018/10/zora-neale-hurston-highlights-unpopular-narratives-barracoon/571789/.

Tidwell, John Edgar, and John S. Wright. "'Steady and Unaccusing': An Interview with Sterling A. Brown." *Callaloo* 21.4 (Autumn 1998): 810–21.

Tindall, George Brown. *South Carolina Negroes, 1877–1900.* 1952. Baton Rouge: Louisiana State University Press, 1966.

Tommasini, Anthony. "Critic's Notebook: All-Black Casts for 'Porgy'? That Ain't Necessarily So." *New York Times* 20 Mar. 2002.

Toomer, Jean. *Cane.* 1923. Ed. Darwin T. Turner. New York: Liveright, 1975.

———. *Cane: An Authoritative Text, Backgrounds, Criticism.* Ed. Darwin T. Turner. New York: Norton, 1988.

———. "The Crock of Problems." *Jean Toomer: Selected Essays and Criticism.* Ed. Robert Jones. Knoxville: University of Tennessee Press, 1996. 55–59.

———. *The Letters of Jean Toomer, 1919–1924.* Ed. Michael Whalen. Knoxville: University of Tennessee Press, 2006.

Trouillot, Michel-Rolph. *Silencing the Past: Power and the Production of History.* Boston: Beacon, 1995.

Turner, Lorenzo Dow. *Africanisms in the Gullah Dialect.* 1949, 1972. Columbia: University of South Carolina Press, 2002.

Turner, Patricia A. *Celluloid Mammies and Ceramic Uncles: Black Images and Their Influence on Culture.* New York: Anchor, 1994.

Twelve Southerners. *I'll Take My Stand: The South and the Agrarian Tradition.* 1930. Baton Rouge: Louisiana State University Press, 1977.

Tzonis, Alexander, and Liane Lefaivre. *Classical Architecture: The Poetics of Order*. Cambridge, Mass.: MIT Press, 1986.
U.S. Census Bureau. "National Population Projections, Table 10." 2017. https://bit.ly/2Ve3sh2.
———. "Population in Colonial and Continental Periods." https://www.census.gov/history/pdf/colonialbostonpops.pdf.
Ustanny, Avia. "Edward Kamau Brathwaite." *Jamaica Gleaner* 6 Jan. 2002. http://www.jamaica-gleaner.com/gleaner/20020106/out/out2.html.
Van Deburg, William L. *Slavery and Race in American Popular Culture*. Madison: University of Wisconsin Press, 1984.
Van Sertima, Ivan. *They Came Before Columbus: The African Presence in Ancient America*. New York: Random House, 1977.
Van Vechten, Carl. "The Negro in Art: How Shall He Be Portrayed?" *Crisis* 31 (Mar. 1926): 219.
Verner, Elizabeth O'Neill. *Mellowed by Time: A Charleston Notebook, Illustrated with Pencil Drawings by the Author*. 1941. Columbia, S.C.: Bostwick & Thornley, 1947.
———. *Prints and Impressions of Charleston. Forty-Eight Etchings with an Introduction by the Artist*. Columbia, S.C.: Bostwick & Thornley, 1939.
Vileisis, Ann. *Discovering the Unknown Landscape: A History of America's Wetlands*. Washington, D.C.: Island, 1997.
Vinovskis, Maris A. "Review: The Demography of the Slave Population in Antebellum America." *Journal of Interdisciplinary History* 5.3 (Winter 1975): 459–67.
Vlach, John Michael. *Back of the Big House: The Architecture of Plantation Slavery*. Chapel Hill: University of North Carolina Press, 1993.
———. *Charleston Blacksmith: The Work of Philip Simmons*. 1981. Columbia: University of South Carolina Press, 1992.
———. *The Planter's Prospect: Privilege and Slavery in Plantation Paintings*. Chapel Hill: University of North Carolina Press, 2002.
Walker, Alice. *In Search of Our Mother's Gardens: Womanist Prose*. New York: Harcourt, 1983.
Wall, Cheryl. "Resounding Souls: Du Bois and the African American Literary Tradition." *Public Cultures* 17.2 (Winter 2005): 217–34.
———. *Women of the Harlem Renaissance*. Bloomington: Indiana University Press, 1995.
———, ed. *Zora Neale Hurston: Folklore, Memoirs, and Other Writings*. New York: Library of America, 1995.
———, ed. *Zora Neale Hurston: Novels and Stories*. New York: Library of America, 1995.
Warren, Robert Penn. *Brother to Dragons: A Tale in Verse and Voices*. New York: Random House, 1953.
Washington, Mary Helen, ed. "Foreword." *Zora Neale Hurston, Their Eyes Were Watching God*. 1937. New York: Harper & Row, 1990. vii–xvi.
Waters, Ethel, with Charles Samuels. *His Eye Is on the Sparrow*. Garden City, N.Y.: Doubleday, 1951.
Webb, Jeff. "Literature and Lynching: Identity in Jean Toomer's *Cane*." *ELH* 67.1 (Spring 2000): 206–26.
Whaley, Emily, as told to William Baldwin. *Mrs. Whaley and Her Charleston Garden*. Chapel Hill: Algonquin, 1997.
White, Graham, and Shane White. *Stylin': African American Expressive Culture from Its Beginnings to the Zoot Suit*. Ithaca, N.Y.: Cornell University Press, 1998.

Wilgus, D. K. "The Negro-White Spiritual." *Anglo-American Folksong Scholarship since 1898*. New Brunswick, N.J.: Rutgers University Press, 1959. 344–64.

Williams, Emily. "Contested S.C. Eco-resort Plan, Flagged as 'Greenwashing,' Up for Key Decision Soon." *Post and Courier* [Charleston, S.C.] 21 July 2020. https://bit.ly/3rNgGgC.

Williams, Raymond. *The Country and the City*. New York: Oxford University Press, 1975.

Williams, Susan Millar. *A Devil and a Good Woman, Too: The Lives of Julia Peterkin*. Athens: University of Georgia Press, 1997.

Williams-Myers, A.J. "Slavery, Rebellion, and Revolution in the Americas: A Historiographical Scenario on the Theses of Genovese and Others." *Journal of Black Studies* 26.4 (Mar. 1996): 381–400.

Wilson, Anthony. *Shadow and Shelter: The Swamp in Southern Culture*. Oxford: University Press of Mississippi, 2006.

Wilson, August. *Ma Rainey's Black Bottom*. New York: Plume, 1985.

Winnubst, Shannon. "Vampires, Anxieties, and Dreams: Race and Sex in the Contemporary United States." *Hypatia* 19.3 (Fall 2003): 1–19.

Witt, Doris. *Black Hunger: Food and the Politics of U.S. Identity*. New York: Oxford University Press, 1999.

Wolfflin, Heinrich. *Principles of Art History: The Problem of the Development of Style in Later Art*. Trans. M. D. Hottinger. 1932. New York: Dover, 1950.

Wood, Marcus. *Blind Memory: Visual Representations of Slavery in England and America, 1780–1865*. Manchester: Manchester University Press, 2000.

Wood, Peter. *Black Majority: Negroes in Colonial South Carolina from 1690 through the Stono Rebellion*. New York: Knopf, 1974.

Woods, Alan. "Porgy and Bess as Propaganda: Preaching to the (Eva Jessye) Choir." *Theatre, War, and Propaganda: 1930–2005*. Ed. M. Scott Phillips. Tuscaloosa: University of Alabama Press, 2006. 25–34.

Woofter, T. J. *Black Yeomanry: Life on St. Helena Island*. New York: Henry Holt, 1930.

Wright, Gavin. *Old South, New South: Revolutions in the Southern Economy since the Civil War*. New York: Basic Books, 1986.

Wright, Richard. "Between Laughter and Tears." *New Masses* 5 Oct. 1937, 22–25.

Wyatt, Robert, and John Andrew Johnson, eds. *The George Gershwin Reader*. Oxford: Oxford University Press, 2010.

Yaeger, Patricia. *Dirt and Desire: Reconstructing Southern Women's Writing, 1930–1990*. Chicago: University of Chicago Press, 2000.

Young, Liz. Interviews with Charlestonians. Ms. 44/30-01. South Carolina Historical Society, Charleston, 1983.

Young, Stark. "Opera Blues: Porgy and Bess." *New Republic* 84.1092 (30 Oct. 1935): 338.

Yuhl, Stephanie E. *A Golden Haze of Memory: The Making of Historic Charleston*. Chapel Hill: University of North Carolina Press, 2005.

———. "High Culture in the Low Country: Arts, Identity, and Tourism in Charleston, South Carolina, 1920–40." Ph.D. dissertation, Duke University, 1998.

Žižek, Slavoj, and Glyn Daly. *Conversations with Žižek*. Cambridge: Polity, 2004.

———. "Holding the Place." *Contingency, Hegemony, Universality: Contemporary Dialogues on the Left*. Ed. Judith Butler, Ernesto Laclau, and Slavoj Žižek. New York: Verso, 2011. 308–31.

———. *How to Read Lacan*. New York: Norton, 2006.

Zweicker, Jason. "Another Brick in the Wall: A Newly Formed Task Force Seeks to Protect a Hidden Part of Charleston's Past." *Charleston Magazine* Jan.–Feb. 2006: 37–38.

INDEX

Abject(ion), 22, 132; and identity, 5, 6, 30; and language, 13
ACE Basin, 18, 52, 209, 224
Adams, E.C.L., 49, 187n, 191n, 200n
Africanisms in the Gullah Dialect, 8, 124
Afro-creole, 42, 112, 114, 122, 128, 135, 196n11, 198n47; and authority, 21–22, 111; and folk consciousness, 111, 127; and environmental mastery, 19; and pioneer generation, 115; and religious practices, 61, 128; and Seminole wars, 117
Afrocentrism, Afrocentrists, 16, 85
Allen, Hervey, 141
Amerindian(s), 22, 27, 28, 46, 115, 189n62. *See also* Indian(s), indigenous, Native American
American Anthropological Association, 122
Amsterdam News, 111
Anthropology, anthropologist(s), 4, 5, 11, 21, 44, 47, 112, 120, 124–25, 128, 187n3, 189n66, 198n49
Antimodernism, 85, 157, 194n23
Appropriation: as "love and theft," 139; and minstrelsy, 166
Architecture: Charleston, x, 50; monumental, x, 89;
Authentic, authenticity, 42, 50, 63,65, 67, 72, 85, 109, 121, 126, 145, 163, 168, 175

Baraka, Amiri 6, 51, 186n7. *See also* changing same
Behar, Ruth, 4, 185n3
Bennett-Coverley, Louise 13, 16
Bennett, John, 88, 157–58, 191n34, 202n44; and Jean Toomer controversy, 160; and miscegenation controversy, 104; and Poetry Society of South Carolina, 49
Bennett, Ralph, 106. *See also* Honey Man
Berry, Wendell, 46, 190n24
Bess, 43, 142, 146, 148, 149–50, 152–56, 166–67, 170, 173, 201n27

Black Atlantic, xix, 18, 23, 112, 188n35
Black Codes, 27, 188n33
Black Indians of Andros Island, 118
Blackface, 142, 144, 164–65; and mask, 72, 92
Blackness, 3, 59, 72, 92, 106, 109, 137, 151
Blues, 197n35; and Ethel Waters, 148; and language, 17; and jazz, 78–79, 85; in poetry, 143; in *Porgy and Bess*, 168, 203n68; as sensibility, 128–29
Boas, Franz, 120, 124–25, 127
Border(s), 14, 23, 29, 32, 64, 112, 116–17, 119, 145, 174, 201n33; the Black, 49, 69, 79, 86, 192n4; crossing or crossers, 26, 64, 120; studies, 34. *See also* frontier
Bragg, Laura, 105, 196n59
Brathwaite, Edward Kamau, 16–17, 186n32
Brown, Anne, 167, 170, 172
Brown, Sterling, 119, 200n11, 201n16; on dialect, "On Dialect Usage," 126; and Zora Neale Hurston, 129, 131
Brown v Board of Education of Topeka, 14
Butler, Pierce, 29

Cabbage Row, 148; *See also* Catfish Row
Calhoun, John C., xv, 40, 51
Cane, 67, 78–80, 158, 192n14, 192n29–31, 196n4; and critical reception, 192n36; and gendered desire, 80, 82, 186n31; and topos, 64, 83–85, 190n12, 192n35, 198n46; and pastoral, 84, 192n33; and John Bennett, 160; 202n49. *See also* Jean Toomer
Canon, 34, 35, 39, 41,78, 88, 138
Carolina Art League, 40
Carolina Low-Country, The, 41, 48, 51, 52, 59–61, 88, 98
Catfish Row, 43–44, 142, 146, 149–151, 153, 155, 169
Changing same, 6, 34, 51, 85, 173; *See also* Amiri Baraka
Charleston Renaissance, ix, xv, 16, 35,39–43, 48–49, 51–52, 60–61, 63, 71, 85, 87–89,

229

93–97, 104–05, 107, 109, 127, 138, 144–45, 147,151, 166, 177, 193n1, 194n28, 195n34
Charleston Renaissance Gallery, 88, 95, 107. *See also* Gibbes Museum of Art
"Charleston, The," 163, 176, 203n68. *See also* James P. Johnson
Charlestonians, Old 41, 109
Chronotope, 43, 53. *See also* Place, as time
City Jail, 147, 154–55
Clothilde, The, 31
Combahee River, 18, 52, 98
Communist Party, 131
Conjure, 122, 132–33. *See also* religion
Cosby, Bill, 14–15, 186n
Creole, 21, 24–26, 39, 42, 48, 183; Afro-creole, 19, 42, 61, 111–12, 115, 117, 122, 127–28, 135, 196n11; Afro-indigenous, 42, 60; as contaminated usage, 18, 26–28; and compromised self, 135; and creolization, 24, 26–27, 32; and language(s), 6, 7, 12–13, 26, 31, 118, 185n1; and lineage(s), xv, 17, 23, 44, 46, 66, 114–15; and pioneer generation, 114–116; and triracial population enclaves, 30
Crèvecoeur, Hector St. Jean de, 24–26, 70, 187n23, 188n31
Crisis, The, 66, 78, 140
Crown, 142, 146, 149–50, 152–53, 155–56
Culture hero, 72, 109, 128, 138

"Darky act," 35, 59–60, 120, 144, 176. *See also* mimicry; minstrel(sy)
Diaspora, 18, 65, 136, 182, 183, 201n14
Double consciousness, 10, 67, 84, 86
Doubleday, Nelson, 40, 90
Dowling, John E., 147
Dowling, Sarah, 147–48, 157, 177, 201n24
Du Bois, W.E.B., xv, 35, 42, 63, 64, 66, 85–86, 104, 124, 162, 182, 190n11, 191n36, 192n5, 196n11, 201n17; and authenticity, 65; on *Cane,* 78–79, 84; and *The Conservation of Races,* 68; and *The Crisis,* 66, 78, 140; on gender, 77, 83, 133; on death of his son, 69; *Dusk of Dawn,* 69–70, 192n5; and folklore, 109; and lynching of Sam Hose, 69–71; and pastoral, 64, 73–76; and *Porgy,* 150; and sociological studies, 64; and sorrow songs," 50, 69; and *The Souls of Black Folk,* 50, 63, 67, 72, 140; and Zora Neale Hurston, 126–127, 201n17. *See also* culture hero
DuBose Heyward Reader, The, 16, 138
Duncan, Todd, 170, 172–74

Eco, Umberto, 83, 151
Education, 5, 8, 13, 41, 66, 73, 76; and class, 129, 143; and Gullah Geechee identity, 147, 153, 177; and Hurston, 111; and race, 100, 128–29, 185n9, 196n53, 199n83
Ellington, Duke, 147, 169, 176, 203n68
Ellison, Ralph, 61, 72, 92–93, 144, 191n49, 192n14, 193n18
Enlightenment, The, 25, 40, 42
Essence(s): racial, 34, 65, 85, 145, 158; as essentialism, 69, 82
Exoticism, 140, 153. *See also* primitivism

Fanon, Franz, 3, 12, 143, 186n23, 187n16
Faulkner, William, 52, 84, 138, 141
Feenda, 115, 187n15, 197n28. *See also* nfinda
FIRE!! Devoted to Younger Negro Artists, 41, 126
First Contact, 6, 24, 113
Fisk Jubilee Singers, 50–51, 68,
Fisk University, 65–66, 103, 127, 135
Florida Writer's Project, 130
Folk, the, 63, 109, 126, 130, 145, 149, 155–56, 166, 169, 175, 182, 198n49; and authenticity, 166; and Black, 64, 66, 68, 111; and community, 42, 83, 84, 151–52; and DuBose Heyward, 144; and identity, 73; as intellectual property, 167; and J.W. Johnson, 125; and modernity, 63, 65, 67, 144–45; and opera, 87, 168, 175; and roots, 129; and speech, 126, 143; and vanishing, 129; and white folk, 151; and Zora Neale Hurston, 120–21, 126, 128, 131
Folklore, 34, 49, 56, 109, 125, 127, 128, 169, 199n70; and collecting 11, 59, 61, 64, 121, 131, 157, 177, 193n37
Folksong, 59, 68
Folktale, 49, 58, 106, 120, 128, 130, 135, 191n54
Follywood, 167
Fort Moosa, 113, 135. *See also* Fort Mose
Fort Mose, 113, 117. *See also* Fort Moosa
Frank North, 161–62
Frank, Waldo, 67, 192n37122
Frazier, E. Franklin, 129, 199n82
Frontier, 14–16, 26, 44, 190n22; *See also* border(s)

Garvey, Marcus, 132
Geechee, 5, 6, 12, 20, 21, 30, 65
General Field Order No. 15, 59
Georgia Writer's Project, 9
Gershwin, George, 163; and Black music, 139,

164, 166; and cast relationships, 172–74; in Charleston, 166–68, 203n71; and critical reception of *Porgy and Bess*, 169, 175; death of Gershwin, 170, 199n2; and Gershwin Centennial, 204n85; and DuBose Heyward collaboration, 149, 157, 164–65, 203n61; and James P. Johnson, 176, 203n68; and musical language of *Porgy and Bess*, 168–69, 174; and social reception, 171
Gibbes Museum of Art, 40, 87, 88, 95, 107, 196n51. *See also* Charleston Renaissance Gallery
Gibbs, Elvira, 177, 204n101
Goat Cart Sam. *See* Samuel Smalls
Golden Age, 43–45, 53, 55, 89, 99, 102, 153, 155, 158
Gone With the Wind, xvi, 1
Gonzales, Ambrose, 11, 13–14, 49, 52, 186n18
Goodwine, Marquetta "Queen Quet," 34, 181, 205n6,
Gordon, Robert Winslow, 52, 59–60, 141, 191n47
Gothic, 153, 154, 155; Southern 55, 144, 190n16, 191n34
Great Awakening, 49
Great Depression, xv, 158
Greene, Harlan, 88, 144
Grimball, Panchita Heyward, 48–51
Grimke, Sarah and Angelina, 29, 188n49
Guardian of Souls, 110
Guggenheim, Solomon, 88, 90, 97, 194n21
"Guilty beauty," 47–48, 56, 63
Gullahbemi, Halim, ix, 181–82, 205n5
Gullah Geechee Cultural Heritage Corridor, ix, xiii, 6, 20, 31, 182
Gullah: and abject status, 5–6, 9, 13–14; and appropriation, 49–50, 58, 60, 109; and "bad Geechee," 30; and carceral identity, 5, 15, 35, 50, 61, 79, 86, 99, 103, 109, 128, 136, 153–55; and creolization, 31–32, 115, 117–20; and displacement/disinheritance, 21, 65; and "good," 30, 152; and literary, 86, 143; and nostalgia, xiii, 48; and purity, 27; and "vanishing," xviii, 10,5, 8, 33–34, 49, 98, 109. *See also* language
Gullah/Geechee People Nation, ix, 34, 182

Hamilton, Anna Hall, 146–48, 156, 178; and grandmother, 3–4, 31
"Harlem: Mecca of the New Negro" issue of *Survey Graphic*, 41

Harlem Renaissance, xv, 35, 41, 51, 57, 67, 71, 103, 106, 111–12, 119–20, 126, 136, 140–41, 143, 145
Harleston, Edwin Augustus, xviii, 42, 103, 105–07, 144; and Charleston's mulatto elite, 104–05; and DuBose Heyward, 160–62; genre paintings, 106; *Mary*, 105–06; *The Old Servant*, 106; political activism, 104–05; and *Portrait of Aaron Douglas, Artist*, 103
Harris, Joel Chandler, 70
Harrison, Birge, 93, 194n34
Harvey, Georgette, 159
Herskovits, Melville, 11, 186n12, 186n19, 189n66
Heterotopia, xv, 113, 120, 122, 135. *See also* place
Heyward, Dorothy, 147, 157, 159, 163–655, 167, 202n54, 202n55, 203n62, 203n72, 204n101
Heyward, DuBose, xix, 35, 40, 138, 144–45, 149, 177; bilingualism, 139, 141–43; and *The Carolina Low-Country*, 57–59; and the color line, 159–63; *The DuBose Heyward Reader*, 16, 88; *Mamba's Daughters*, 105, 137, 161–63; "The New Note in Southern Literature," 140–41; and pastoral, 43–44, 58; and the Poetry Society of South Carolina, 49; *Porgy*, 149–57; *Porgy and Bess*, 164–66. *See also* mimicry
Heyward, Duncan Clinch, 50, 195n38
Heyward, Janie Screven, 50, 178, 200n9
Higginson, Thomas Wentworth, 68–69
Honey Man, 106, 166, 203n70. *See also* Ralph Bennett
Hoodoo, 131–32, 157. *See also* Root(work)
Horse, John, 119
Hose, Sam, 69–71, 83
Huger, Alfred, 41, 52, 57
Hughes, Langston, 124, 126, 32, 135, 143, 150, 190n12, 191n34, 203n68
Hurricane, 17, 44, 99, 150, 195n41
Hurston, Zora Neale, xviii, 4, 35, 42; and Afro-creole authority, 111–12, 119–20, 128, 135; and Franz Boas, 124–25; and feuds, 126, 130, 132; and negative appraisals, 110–111, 122, 129–31; and *Barracoon*, 133–34; and conjure, 122, 132; and folk speech, 125–26, 196n11; and "High John de Conquer," 110; and hoodoo, 131–32; and *Jonah's Gourd Vine*, 121, 125, 129; *and* spirituals, 126–28; and *Their Eyes Were Watching God*, 121–22, 126, 196n11; and voodoo, 132–33

Hutchisson, James, 88, 144, 200n7
Hutty, Alfred, 87–88

Igbo Landing, 58
Imaginary, 34, 93, 97, 139, 145,149, 165, 170, 182
Imperialist nostalgia, 6, 10, 47, 145
Indian(s), 22, 24, 26–27, 29, 32, 57, 113, 180, 188n; and Territory, 119; and war, 46. *See also* Amerindian(s); indigenous; Native American(s)
Indigenous, 19, 22–23, 42, 60, 113–115, 197n20. *See also* Amerindian(s); Indian(s); Native American(s)
Inheritance, 8, 25, 42, 60, 85

Jackson, Bruce, 34, 87. See also *Slave Songs of the Georgia Sea Islands*
Jazz, xv, 78–80, 85, 95, 147–48, 158, 164, 168, 176–77, 208n68; and opera, 164, 175; and poetry, 190n12
Jazz Age, xv, 147, 159, 163
Jefferson, Thomas, xvi, 25, 27, 187n27
Jenkins, Rev. Daniel, 96, 147, 194n26
Jenkins Orphanage Band, The, 147, 177, 194n24
Jenkins Orphanage Band, The, 95–96
Jim Crow, 11, 20, 42, 86, 90, 92–93, 101, 110, 147, 159
Johnson, Charles S., 124, 129
Johnson, James P., 176, 203n58. *See also* "Charleston, The"
Johnson, James Weldon, 35, 42, 129, 192n14; and *Black Manhattan*, 163; *The Book of American Negro Spirituals*, 42; and folk expression, 125–26, 129, 199n71; and *God's Trombones*, 125; and literary friendships, 125–26, 141, 159
Jolson, Al, 157, 164–66
Jones Jr., Charles Colcock, 49
Jones Sr., Charles Colcock, 61, 191n48

Kemble, Fanny, 29
Kikongo, 22
Kongo, 33, 115, 120, 128
Kossula, Oluale, 133–34. *See also* Cudjoe Lewis

Lacan, 55, 71, 143
Landscape(s): cultural x, 18–19, 23, 27, 47, 52, 63, 85, 99, 111, 164, 168, 180, 183; and contested, 42; of correction, 154; and fatality, 48, 55; and gender, 81; and gothic, 155; and hybridization, 24; and memory, 98; and pastoral, 42, 44, 53, 73, 80, 51; and place, xv; and race, 143; and rice, 20, 101; and sanitized, 19, 21; and tragic, 45, 72, 79; and triangular topos, 21, 35, 86, 112; and water, 17, 21–22, 30; and war, 46; and whiteness, 24, 27. *See also* place
Language, xviii, 3, 14–6, 51, 116, 119, 125–26, 141–43, 154, 181, 202n54; and abject(ion), 5–6, 9, 11, 68–69; and appropriation, 49; and "bad English," xviii, 7–8, 11, 86, 185n1, 202n55; and creolization, 5–8, 31–33, 61, 117, 198n47; and dialect, 7, 11–12, 14–17, 50, 86, 108, 118, 125–26, 142–43, 196n11, 198n47, 200n9; and language death, 12, 33–34, 200n13, 205n7; and nation, 13, 17, 186n32; and secret, 3, 8, 115; and three-generation shift, 12; and third space(s), 13, 181; and triangular topos, xviii, 14–16, 26, 35, 86, 183. *See also* Gullah
Lewis, Cudjoe, 133–34. *See also* Oluale Kossula
Lineage: and creole, 24, 44; and Charleston, elite, 163–64, 168, 10, 91; and Charleston, mulatto elite, 161; and contamination, 27, 161; and Gullah Geechee, 31; and Lost Cause, xiv, xvii, 10; and musical, 176, 203n68; and purity, 17; and pastoral, 112; and triangular topos, xviii, 35, 86, 112; and violence, 46
Lissa, 161. See also *Mamba's Daughters*
Locke, Alain, 124, 130, 132, 201n16, 201n17
Lomax, Alan, 135, 203n73
Lost Cause, xv, xvii–xviii, 22, 94, 185n9, 187n3; and Charleston Renaissance, 87; and Cult of, 99; and Gullah Geechee, 103; and imperialist nostalgia, 47; and pastoral, 42, 47; and spirituals, 48, 61; and topos, xviii; and violence, xvii–xviii, 69
"love and theft," 139. *See also* appropriation
Luce, Henry and Clare Booth, 90
Lynch(ing), 70, 74, 80, 152; and mob, 70–71, 7, 75, 83; and narrative, 83; and spectacle, 70, 93, 194n20

MacDowell Colony, 43, 141
Mamba's Daughters, 105, 137–38, 159, 161–63, 196n61, 202n53
Mamoulian, Rouben, 159
Maria, 152–53, 156, 202n46

Maroon(s), 197n20; marronage, 119
Mascogos, 119. *See also* Seminole(s), Black; Seminole(s), Negro Indian Scouts
Mason, Charlotte Osgood, 132, 198n48, 199n93
McKay, Claude, 35, 108, 111, 119, 143, 196n11
McKim, Lucy, 49, 68. See also *Slave Songs of the United States*
Mead, Margaret, 112,
Mellowed by Time: A Charleston Notebook, 90, 193n10, 193n12
Melodrama, 137–38, 144, 190n17
Memory: and African American culture, 51, 68, 77, 105, 134, 144, 174; and American, xvii–xviii, 180; and amnesia, 139; and art, 98, 195n40; and diaspora, Seminole, 118; and Civil War, 30; and false memory, xvii; and history, xvii, 67; and lieux/milieux de memoire, 180, 185n6; and myth, 30, 45, 51, 86–87; and pastoral, 55; and rememory, 18, 54; and the swamp, 23; and slavery, 61; and triangular topos, xviii; and violence, 45, 61, 180
Mencken, H.L., 141. *See also* "The Sahara of the Bozarts"
Mepkin Abbey, 47, 90
Metropolitan Opera, 164, 171, 202n60,
Middle Passage, 28, 32, 58, 76, 110, 180–82
Migration, 5–6, 17, 22, 24, 30, 39, 64, 85, 95, 112, 118, 146, 151, 188n51
Mimicry, 17, 59, 165, 176. *See also* "darky act"; minstrelsy
Minstrel(sy), 42, 65, 68, 106, 126, 166. *See also* "darky act"; mimicry
Miscegenation, 17, 26, 30, 101, 138, 152, 156, 161, 175
Modernity, 16, 35, 40–41, 65, 89, 94–95, 108, 119–20, 145, 198n47, 201n14; also, modernism, 63, 88, 103, 106, 158. *See also* antimodernism
Mosquito Fleet, 44

NAACP, 131, 162, 171, 202n52
Nadir, the, xviii, 69, 92
Nashville Agrarians, 138, 141;
National Park Service, ix, 6
Native American 53, 143
Negro(es), the, xix, 4, 28–29, 34, 49, 64, 66–68, 113, 115, 119, 144; and critical discussion of, 129, 150, 163, 169, 200n2, 201n16; and folk expression, 49, 51, 120, 127–32, 135; and

George Gershwin, 164–67, 203n68; and gifts, 68–69; and DuBose Heyward, 154–56; as intellectual property, 158; and New, 39, 41, 78, 103, 109, 160, 162; and pastoral, 74, 80–81; and "old" or plantation, 42, 52, 55–57, 59–60, 99, 104, 129; and speech, 11, 125–26; and spirituals; and stereotypes, 44, 72, 122–23, 140–41, 143
Negrotarian, 125. *See also* Zora Neale Hurston
New Negro, The, 41
New York Times, 44, 102, 125, 134, 137, 139, 160
Niggerati, 125; *See also* Zora Neale Hurston
Nostalgia: and antimodernism, 194n23; and imperialist, 5–6, 10, 47, 109, 145; and pastoral, 45–46, 54, 75, 77, 150–51, 153, 194n21
Nugent, Richard Bruce, 126
Nullification Crisis, 154

Oglethorpe, James, 117, 197n34
Old Guard, 151–52
Orature, 143. *See also* folk speech
Osceola, 119, 180–81

Parrish, Lydia, 87. See also *Slave Songs of the Georgia Sea Islands*
Pastoral, the, 30, 39, 42–46, 53–59, 71–77, 79–80, 83–85, 99, 102, 112, 136, 137, 139, 150–51, 190n16, 190n17, 190n19
Paternalism, 91, 103, 140
Peterkin, Julia, 35, 142–43, 50, 200n11
Place; and Afro-creole space, 148, 197n28; and chronotope, 43, 53, 87, 90; and folk expression, 126, 128; as heterotopia, xv, 113, 120, 122, 135; and literary, 44, 138, 155; of refuge, 115, 134, 197n28; and social status, 94, 109; and Southern sense of, xv, xviii, 110; and triangular topos, xv, xviii, 23, 35, 86, 112. *See also* Gullah, carceral identity; landscape; swamp; traveling culture; third space
Plantation Echoes, 167
Poetry Society of South Carolina, 40, 49, 88–89, 104, 157, 160
Porgy (character), 146, 147–52, 154–56, 163–66, 169–70, 172, 178; and mother of, 177; *Porgy* (novel), 40, 43–44, 5, 138–139, 141, 144, 149–50, 152, 154–55, 158–59, 163–65
Porgy and Bess (characters), 150, 159; *Porgy and Bess*, 40, 87, 139, 144–45, 149; and art

INDEX 233

Porgy and Bess (*continued*)
world, 87–88, 159, 163–64, 166–67, 169–71, 174–77, 182, 202n43
Port Royal, 29, 57, 68–69
Primitivism, xix, 69, 79, 120, 158
Pringle, Elizabeth Allston, 50, 98–99, 195n38
Pujol, Ernesto, 47–48, 56, 191n28, 201n19
Purity, racial, xviii, 17, 26–27, 30–31, 35, 61, 104, 108–09, 174. *See also* essence(s)

Ragtime, 85, 95
Real, the, 55, 70–71, 97
Reconstruction, xviii, 47,69, 98, 106
Redemption, 42, 47
Religion (and religious practices), 49, 51, 61, 132–34; *God's Trombones*, 125, 199n73; sanctified church(es), 126, 129, 167; and seeking, 128; and sermonic tradition, 125–26, 199n71; and spirit possession, 128. *See also* conjure; hoodoo; root(work); voodoo
Rice, x, xviii, 18–20, 28, 32–33, 52–53, 90, 98, 146, 151; and African technology, 57, 187n3; and Carolina Gold, 18, 99; and coast (of West Africa), 32, 187n14; and identity, 5, 21, 115; and memoirs, 50; and rivers (of South Carolina), 52, 69, 195n38; and Alice R.S. Smith, 98–103, 196n51
Roach, Joseph, 139, 145, 200n12, 201n14
Root(work), 148. *See also* conjure; hoodoo; religion, voodoo
Roots: Afro-creole, 39, 108–09, 112, 120, 126–27, 135, 163, 166; and folk, 65, 129; and linguistic, 112, 117, 166; and routes, 65, 112, 135
Rosaldo, Ronaldo, 6, 47, 122
Rosenwald Foundation, 135
Rutledge, Archibald, 41, 52

"Sahara of the Bozarts, The," 141
Sass, Herbert Ravenel, xix, 41, 52–56, 70, 98, 102, 144, 191n38, 191n39, 191n42
Seminole Nation, 28, 118, 180, 198n44
Seminole: Black, 118; and diaspora, 119; and Negro Indian Scouts 119; and wars, 118–19, 180, 190n23, 197n20, 204n4
Senegambia(n), 18, 32, 58
Serena, 151–52
Sermon, sermonic tradition, 125–26, 199n71. *See also God's Trombones;* religion
Severens, Martha, 88, 91–92, 94–95, 144, 194n29

Sex(uality), 79, 153, 157, 196n11; and stereotype threat related to, 78, 133, 140. *See also* Bess; Zora Neale Hurston
Shadow canon 23, 183
Singing tree, 42, 190n12
Slave Songs of the Georgia Sea Islands, 51, 87. *See also* Bruce Jackson; Lydia Parrish
Slave Songs of the United States, 49. *See also* Lucy McKim
Slavery, African; slavery, Indian, 19
Smalls, Samuel, 146–49, 155
Smith, Alice Ravenel Huger Smith, xix, 91–93, 95, 97–104; 151, 194n21, 195n38, 196n53
Smith, Daniel Elliot Huger, 98, 104, 195n38
Society for the Preservation of Old Dwellings, 40, 89
Society for the Preservation of Spirituals, 40, 48, 59, 61, 89, 98, 127, 142, 151, 167
Sorrow songs, 50, 69, 72; and "The Sorrow Songs," 64, 68. *See also* spirituals
Souls of Black Folk, The, 50, 63–64, 67, 72, 85, 127
Southern Literary Renaissance, 39, 41, 141
Spanish Florida, 113
Spirit possession, 128, 133
Special Resource Study (National Parks Service), 6, 31, 112, 182
Spirituals, 41, 43, 48–52, 56, 59–61, 78, 85, 98, 109, 127–30, 132, 142, 147, 163, 167–68 172, 203n68. *See also* sorrow songs
Spivak, Gayatri, 5, 16
Spoleto Festival USA, ix-x, 137, 184, 204n85
Sporting Life, 148–49, 152–53, 156, 173
Spingarn, Joel, 161, 202n52
St. Augustine, 113–14, 116–17, 197n36
Stereotype, 3, 174; and threat, 25, 42, 129
Stoney, Samuel Gaillard, 50
Stoney, Thomas, 105
Stono Rebellion, 116, 197n36
Sublime, the, 19, 23
Sullivan's Island, xv, 28, 32, 179–80, 204n1
Swamp, 22–24, 27–28, 53–54, 57, 64, 101, 119, 179, 194n20. *See also* place

Talented Tenth, 106, 109, 129, 130–32
Taylor, Anna Heyward, 91, 96, 193n14
Third space, 13, 22, 179–80
Thomas, Clarence, 10–12
Thurman, Wallace, 126
Tillman, George Dionysius, 29–30
Tin Pan Alley, 51, 169
Tommasini, Anthony, 139, 200n2

Toomer, Jean, xviii, 35, 42, 64–67, 78–86, 109, 119–20, 160–61, 191n2, 192n14, 193n37, 202n52. *See also* Cane; W. E. B. Du Bois
Trafficking, human, 46, 115
Traveling (culture), 5, 109–10, 112–13, 120. *See also* place
Triangular topos, xv, xviii, 23, 35, 86, 112. *See also* landscape; language; lineage; place
Turner, Lorenzo Dow, 8, 11, 124. See also *Africanisms in the Gullah Dialect*

Uplift, 4, 66, 69, 106, 130–31, 135, 140

Van Vechten, Carl, 124, 139–41, 164
Verner, Elizabeth O'Neill, xix, 90–91, 93, 96, 147, 177, 193n14, 194n26, 196n53
Vesey, Denmark, xvi, 58, 154
Violence, xiv, xvii, 45–46, 71–72, 77, 79, 82–83, 117, 134, 157, 159, 177, 190n22, 201n14

Voodoo, 130, 132–33
Walker, Alice, 16, 186n31
Walrond, Eric, 119
Wanderer, The, 31
Waring Jr., Thomas R., 189n8, 204n101
Waring Sr., Thomas R., 41, 52
Waters, Ethel, 138, 148, 159, 174
Wells, Ida B., 70, 73
Whiteness, 22, 42, 60, 79, 188n33
Wilkins, Roy, 111
Woodson, Carter G., 124

Young, Liz, 9–10, 34
Young, Stark, 174

Žižek, Slavoj, 55, 71

The New Southern Studies

The Nation's Region: Southern Modernism, Segregation, and U.S. Nationalism
    by Leigh Anne Duck
Black Masculinity and the U.S. South: From Uncle Tom to Gangsta
    by Riché Richardson
Grounded Globalism: How the U.S. South Embraces the World
    by James L. Peacock
*Disturbing Calculations: The Economics of Identity in
Postcolonial Southern Literature, 1912–2002*
    by Melanie Benson Taylor
American Cinema and the Southern Imaginary
    edited by Deborah E. Barker and Kathryn McKee
Southern Civil Religions: Imagining the Good Society in the Post-Reconstruction Era
    by Arthur Remillard
Reconstructing the Native South: American Indian Literature and the Lost Cause
    by Melanie Benson Taylor
Apples and Ashes: Literature, Nationalism, and the Confederate States of America
    by Coleman Hutchison
Reading for the Body: The Recalcitrant Materiality of Southern Fiction, 1893–1985
    by Jay Watson
Latining America: Black-Brown Passages and the Coloring of Latino/a Studies
    by Claudia Milian
Finding Purple America: The South and the Future of American Cultural Studies
    by Jon Smith
The Signifying Eye: Seeing Faulkner's Art
    by Candace Waid
*Sacral Grooves, Limbo Gateways: Travels in Deep Southern
Time, Circum-Caribbean Space, Afro-creole Authority*
    by Keith Cartwright
Jim Crow, Literature, and the Legacy of Sutton E. Griggs
    edited by Tess Chakkalakal and Kenneth W. Warren
Sounding the Color Line: Music and Race in the Southern Imagination
    by Erich Nunn
Borges's Poe: The Influence and Reinvention of Edgar Allan Poe in Spanish America
    by Emron Esplin
Eudora Welty's Fiction and Photography: The Body of the Other Woman
    by Harriet Pollack
Keywords for Southern Studies
    edited by Scott Romine and Jennifer Rae Greeson
The Southern Hospitality Myth: Ethics, Politics, Race, and American Memory
    By Anthony Szczesiul
Navigating Souths: Transdisciplinary Explorations of a U.S. Region
    edited by Michele Grigsby Coffey and Jodi Skipper
Where the New World Is: Literature about the U.S. South at Global Scales
    by Martyn Bone

Red States: Indigeneity, Settler Colonialism, and Southern Studies
    by Gina Caison

The Whole Machinery: The Rural Modern in Cultures of the U.S. South, 1890–1946
    by Benjamin S. Child

Look Abroad, Angel: Thomas Wolfe and the Geographies of Longing
    by Jedidiah Evans

Anne Spencer between Worlds
    by Noelle Morrissette

Romancing the Gullah in the Age of Porgy and Bess
    by Kendra Y. Hamilton

www.ingramcontent.com/pod-product-compliance
Lightning Source LLC
Chambersburg PA
CBHW031725230426
43669CB00007B/248